Business Accounting for Hospitality and Tourism

ONE WEEK LOAN

Series in Tourism and Hospitality Management

Series Editors:

Professor Roy C. Wood
The Scottish Hotel School, University of Strathclyde, UK

Stephen J. Page
Massey University, New Zealand

Series Consultant:

Professor C. L. Jenkins
The Scottish Hotel School, University of Strathclyde, UK

Key textbooks in this series:

Interpersonal Skills for Hospitality Management
M. A. Clark
ISBN 0 412 57330 X, 232 pages.

Hospitality and Tourism Law
M. Poustie, N. Geddes, W. Stewart and J. Ross
ISBN 1 86152 181 2, 320 pages.

Economics for
Hospitality Management
P. Cullen
ISBN 1 86152 179 0, 224 pages.

Tourism in the Pacific
C. Michael Hall and Stephen J. Page
ISBN 0 415 12500 6, 304 pages.

Managing Wine and Wine sales
J. E. Fattorini
ISBN 0 412 72190 2, 200 pages.

Books in this series are available on free inspection for lecturers considering the texts for course adoption. Details of these and any other Thomson Learning titles are available by writing to the publishers (Berkshire House, 168-173 High Holborn, London WC1V 7AA) or by telephoning 020 7497 1422.

Business Accounting for Hospitality and Tourism

H. Atkinson
Department of Service Sector Management
University of Brighton, UK.

A. Berry
Department of Finance and Accounting
University of Brighton, UK.

R. Jarvis
School of Accounting & Finance
Kingston University, UK.

THOMSON
LEARNING

Australia ▪ Canada ▪ Mexico ▪ Singapore ▪ Spain ▪ United Kingdom ▪ United States

THOMSON

LEARNING

For more information, contact Thomson Learning, Berkshire House, 168-173 High Holborn, London, WC1V 7AA or visit us on the World Wide Web at: http://www.thomsonlearning.co.uk

British Library Cataloguing-in-Publication Data
A catalogue record for this book is available from the British Library

ISBN 1-86152-470-6

First published 1995 by Chapman and Hall
Reprinted 1996 by International Thomson Business Press
Reprinted 2001 by Thomson Learning

Printed in Singapore by Seng Lee Press

Contents

Series editors' preface

The Chapman & Hall Series in Tourism and Hospitality Management is dedicated to the publication of high quality textbooks and other volumes that will be of benefit to those engaged in hotel, catering and tourism education, especially at degree and postgraduate level. All the authors in the series are experts in their own fields, actively engaged in teachings research and consultancy in hospitality and tourism. This is a distinctive feature of the series and each book comprises an authoritative blend of subject-relevant theoretical considerations and practical applications and illustrations prepared by experienced writers. Furthermore, a unique quality of the series is that it is student oriented, offering accessible texts that take account of the realities of management and operations in the hospitality and tourism industries, being constructively critical where necessary without losing sight of the overall goal of providing clear accounts of essential concepts, techniques and issues. The tourism and hospitality industries are diverse and dynamic industries and it is the intention of the series to reflect this diversity and dynamism by publishing quality texts that embrace topical subjects without losing sight of enduring themes. In this respect, the Chapman & Hall Series in Tourism and Hospitality Management is an innovative venture committed to quality, accessibility and relevance. The Series Editors are grateful to Chapman & Hall for supporting this philosophy and would particularly like to acknowledge the commitment, expertise and insight of the Commissioning Editor, Steven Reed, whose contribution to the realization of the series has been invaluable.

C.L. Jenkins
R.C. Wood
The Scottish Hotel School
University of Strathclyde.

Preface

This book has been designed and written for the needs of students of Hospitality and Tourism management. It seeks to combine an approach to learning about accountancy that is appropriate to the needs of managers with a focus on two important and growing areas of the service sector.

The guiding philosophy that we used in designing this text was to ensure that the learning was at an appropriate level, was of an appropriate type and was made as easy as possible whilst still retaining academic rigour. Thus, although the book covers an introduction to the areas of financial accounting, financial analysis, management accounting and financial management, it is written with the needs of a manager or potential manager in mind rather than those of a future accountant.

The learning process is facilitated in a number of ways. For example, throughout the text the examples used are related to the industries concerned. These examples are complemented by 'real world' case studies drawn from actual practice. This ensures that accounting is seen in context rather than as a separate and unrelated subject.

The book adopts a step-by-step approach to learning about the use of accounting information. It provides clear definitions and highlights the key concepts in each chapter. At the end of each chapter there are a series of review questions which serve to revise and reinforce the learning contained within the chapters. These are followed by problems for discussion and analysis which allow for the application of the key concepts to real situations and the production of answers based upon the application of those concepts.

This book differs from some other books on this subject through its use of the worksheet as the vehicle to explain the basic relationships with the profit and loss account and cash flow statement. This approach has been successfully applied in many business and accounting courses where other texts adopting this approach are used. Feedback from students and lecturers on these courses have indicated that the approach facilitates their understanding of the way in which transactions and economic events interact as well as providing a sound understanding of the principles of double-entry book-keeping. This has been confirmed by students of Hospitality and Tourism at the University of Brighton who have been the guinea pigs for the application of this approach to services sector studies.

The use of the worksheet also facilitates the transfer of the learning to spreadsheet-based IT packages which the authors believe are an extremely powerful educational tool for more advanced work involving sensitivity analysis etc. However, we have avoided the temptation of combining spreadsheets with the learning process at this stage as our experience has shown that such an approach leads to a concentration on the technical aspects of the problems rather than the overview which is necessary for a complete understanding of the usefulness and limitations of accounting information.

Throughout the text the concept of different users of accounting information is used and the differing needs of these users are identified and explored. The book starts with a simple cash-based business and then by stages introduces more levels of complexity and sophistication. This facilitates a deep and full understanding of accounting statements, their component parts and the relationships between those components. The reader is then introduced to the area of financial analysis where the concern is with the purpose of the analysis as much as with the mechanisms of analysis.

The needs of internal users are addressed in some detail with particular reference to the needs for planning, decision-making and control. Once again the approach adopted is to build upon clear definitions and to reinforce the learning through the use of key concepts, case studies and review questions. The emphasis is upon understanding the usefulness and the limitations of some of the techniques of management accounting and financial management rather than concentrating in detail upon the technical aspects of the construction of budgets or other management reports.

Introduction to accounting | 1

INTRODUCTION

This chapter will introduce you to the role of accounting, its uses and its users. It will also give you an appreciation of the role of accounting within a business organization and of its external impacts. We shall introduce some ideas about the ways in which accounting assists managers in meeting the business objectives through, for example, providing the information necessary to make a decision about buying or renting premises. We shall discuss the impacts of the size and type of organization on accounting. For example, in very small organizations such as a sandwich bar or hot-dog stand the accounting requirements are likely to be less complex than is the case with a larger business such as an international hotel. Another factor that both affects and is affected by accounting is the environment. The effects of the environment on accounting can be through the impact of government legislation as happens every time we adopt a new Companies Act or a new EU directive on accounting is added to the United Kingdom's statute book. Apart from government action, accounting can also be affected at this level by changes in technology. For instance, the introduction of information technology has allowed accounting information to be provided more quickly and efficiently, thus enabling different decisions to be taken than would otherwise have been the case.

In order to understand the role and importance of accounting in the context of business organizations it is first necessary to decide what the word 'accounting' means. If you were to look up the word 'account' in *Roget's Thesaurus* you would be directed to words such as report and narration. Further investigation would reveal that accounting is also referred to as commercial arithmetic, double-entry book-keeping, etc. These alternatives imply totally different things, a report being something that conveys information for a particular purpose, whereas commercial arithmetic implies a mechanical exercise following agreed rules or principles.

In practice, although accounting is normally seen as a series of figures which may give the impression that it is only a form of commercial arithmetic, these are, in fact, merely a convenient way of summarizing and reporting information that would be indigestible in narrative form. For example, if you were asked to provide a report giving details of the value of everything you own it would be simpler to use figures to represent the value rather than words. On the other hand, there are certain things that do not lend themselves to summaries in numerical terms. An example may be the value of good health, the value of lead-free petrol, or even the value of a qualification such as a degree, an HND or whatever.

Apart from problems concerning what can be reported and what should be reported, other problems also need to be considered, for example whether the information can be reported in a numerical format and whether that is the best format. We also need to consider whom the report is for and what it is to be used for. For instance, you may give totally different accounts of your car's capabilities to a prospective buyer and to a mechanic to whom you have taken it for repairs. So we can see that the question of defining accounting has many facets, such as what do you report, how do you report, who do you report to and for what purpose do you report. We shall look at these issues in more detail later in this chapter. Prior to that, in order to get a better idea of what accounting is generally understood to be about, let us examine some definitions contained in the accounting literature.

A definition that is commonly quoted is that produced by the American Institute of Certified and Public Accountants (AICPA) in 1941:

> [Accounting] . . . is the art of recording, classifying, and summarizing, in a significant manner and in terms of money, transactions and events which are in part at least, of a financial character, and interpreting the results thereof.

This definition implies that accounting has a number of components – some technical (such as the recording of data), some more analytical (such as interpreting the results) and some that beg further questions (such as 'in a significant manner': significant to whom and for what?).

Let us consider another definition offered by the same professional accounting body:

> [Accounting] . . . is the collection, measurement, recording, classification and communication of economic data relating to an enterprise, for purposes of reporting, decision making and control.

This gives us a clue to the fact that accounting is closely related to other disciplines (we are recording economic data) and it also gives us some clue as to the uses of accounting information, i.e. for reporting on what has happened and as an aid to decision-making and control of the enterprise.

Another part of the same document sees accounting as:

... a discipline which provides financial and other information essential to the efficient conduct and evaluation of the activities of any organization.

This suggests that the role of accounting information within an organization is at the very core of running it successfully. Thus accounting can be seen as a multi-faceted activity which not only records and classifies information but also provides an input to the decision-making processes of enterprises.

The latter point is brought out more clearly in a later definition provided by the American Accounting Principles Board in 1970 (APB No. 4):

Accounting is a service activity. Its function is to provide quantitative information, primarily financial in nature, about economic entities that is intended to be useful in making economic decisions, in making reasoned choices among alternative courses of action.

Key concept

Accounting

The important points made in these definitions are that:

- accounting is about quantitative information;
- the information is likely to be financial;
- it should be useful for making decisions.

The fact that it was described as a service activity reinforces the point made earlier that in order to understand the usefulness of accounting we need to know who uses it and what they use it for.

FOR WHAT PURPOSE IS ACCOUNTING USED?

This question can be answered at two levels at least: that of the individual and that of the enterprise. If we take the level of the individual first we could say that the individual could use accounting information to help them control the level of their expenditure, to assist in planning future levels of expenditure, to help them raise additional finance (e.g. mortgages, hire-purchase, etc.) and to decide the best way to spend their money. Thus we see that at the level of the individual accounting can have three functions, i.e. planning, controlling, and decision support.

At the level of the enterprise it is used to control the activities of the organization, to plan future activities, to assist in raising finance and to report upon the activities and success of the enterprise to interested parties.

You will note that the major difference between the two is that in the case of an enterprise, apart from its uses in planning, controlling and decision-making which are all internal activities or functions, accounting also has what we could describe as an external function, i.e. that of providing information to people outside the enterprise. The latter function is usually met through the medium of annual accounts or financial reports and is often referred to as financial accounting. The external users may use the information contained in the financial report as part of their decision process or to evaluate what management has done with the money invested in the business. Apart from meeting the needs of external users the system that produces the financial accounting reports also meets some of the needs of internal users. These may be to see the results of the implementation of the plans they put into operation in the last year. This requires information on actual outcomes which can then be evaluated against the projected outcomes. The reasons for differences can then be identified so that appropriate actions can be taken. This is only one of a number of needs that management have, their other needs being met through other reports based upon information provided by the internal accounting system. This internal accounting system, which may be additional to the system which underpins the financial reporting system, is often referred to as the management accounting function. The major difference is that management accounting is primarily directed towards providing information of specific use to managers, whereas financial accounting information, which is often less detailed, has many users apart from managers. This leads us on to the second question which we posed regarding the users of accounting information.

WHO USES ACCOUNTING INFORMATION?

Whether accounting information relates to the activities of an individual or to a business enterprise, its users can be placed in two broad categories:

- those inside the enterprise – the managers, or in the case of a small business the owner (internal users);
- those outside the enterprise – these would include banks, the government, tax authorities, etc. (external users).

Internal users

The major internal user is the management of an enterprise. For a small enterprise this is likely to be the owner, or a small number of individuals in the case of a partnership. However, many businesses are much larger and these may be owned by numerous individuals or groups of individuals as is the case with large enterprises such as Lunn Poly, Grand Metropolitan or British Airways. In many cases the major investors are themselves owned by others as is the case with major financial institutions such as pension funds. In this situation it is extremely unlikely that the actual owners would or could take an active part in the day-to-day running of the enterprise. Consider the chaos if all the people who bought shares in British Telecom tried to take an active part in the day-to-day running of that business. Instead these owners or shareholders delegate the authority to handle the day-to-day running to a group of directors and managers.

These directors and managers are involved in the day-to-day decision-making and are the equivalent of the owners in the small business in terms of their information needs. These needs are normally met through unpublished reports of various kinds which are generally based on information provided through both the financial and management accounting systems. The exact nature of these reports will vary from enterprise to enterprise. For example, an airline may require information about the profitability of each of its routes, whereas for a hotel chain the information required is more likely to be about the profitability of each of the individual hotels, and even about the various functional areas within those hotels.

The form of report will also vary depending on the purpose of the report. For example, if management wish to control what is going on it will need a report on the past transactions and performance, probably measured against some predetermined standard. For planning purposes, however, a forecast of what is likely to happen in the future will be more important. These different forms of reports and ways of grouping information are normally referred to under the generic heading of management accounting and this form of accounting will be the focus of the second half of this book. At this stage, it is worth briefly summarizing the different categories of management accounting reports. To do this we need to make some broad generalizations about the needs of managers, and to categorize those needs in some meaningful way. In practice of course there is a certain amount of overlap between these categories but we need not concern ourselves with that at present. The categories will be discussed in greater detail in Chapters 11 to 19. The broad categories that we have referred in terms of the needs of managers are as follows.

- **Stewardship:** what is often referred to as the stewardship function is in fact simply the need to protect the enterprise's possessions (normally referred to as assets) from theft, fraud, etc.
- **Planning:** the need to plan activities so that finance can be raised, marketing and promotional campaigns can be set up and staffing plans can be made. This is the planning function.
- **Control:** the need to control the activities of the enterprise which may include setting targets, ensuring that there is enough capacity and stock, etc. It will also include identifying where targets have and have not been met so that the reasons for the failure to achieve the targets can be identified. This is referred to as the control function.

- **Decision-making:** the need to make specific decisions (should we provide the service ourselves or buy it in? how much will it cost to provide a particular service? how much money will we need in order to run the enterprise? etc.). This is the decision support function.

A moment's reflection will lead us to the conclusion that the area of management accounting is a vast one in its own right, so rather than getting deeply involved at this stage, let us first look at the other broad area we identified – the needs of the users outside the enterprise, the external users. We will of course be returning to the needs of internal users in more detail in Chapter 12.

External users

We need to establish who the external users are. Fortunately, there have been many reports which have done just that, a good example being *The Corporate Report* published by the Institute of Chartered Accountants in England and Wales (ASC, 1975). The list below, taken from *The Corporate Report*, includes most of the accepted users of external financial reports:

- the owner/s (shareholders in a company);
- those who lend the enterprise money (e.g. bankers);
- those who supply the enterprise with goods or services (suppliers);
- those who buy the enterprise's goods or services (customers);
- the employees of the enterprise;
- the government;
- the general public.

These groups are normally provided with information by means of published annual reports. This is the type of accounting generally referred to as **financial accounting**. In order to decide to what extent these annual reports meet the needs of these external users and to understand more fully the importance of accounting we shall briefly discuss the needs of the external users listed above.

Key concept

Financial accounting

Financial accounting can broadly be thought of as that part of the accounting system that tries to meet the needs of the various external user groups. This it does by means of an **annual report** which usually takes the form of a **balance sheet** and **profit and loss account**.

Owners/shareholders
As we have said, in the case of a small enterprise the owners are likely to be actively engaged in the day-to-day operations of the enterprise.

In these small enterprises therefore the owners' needs will often be met by the management accounting information and reports. As the enterprise grows, however, it is likely that the owners will become divorced from the immediate routine operations of the enterprise and will therefore not have access to the management accounting information, which in any case may be too detailed for their requirements. This is the case in companies quoted on the stock exchange. It is also likely to be the case in a number of other businesses where the functions of management are carried out by people other than the owners.

In all these cases the owner needs to know:

* whether the enterprise has done as well as it should have;
* whether the managers have looked after and made good use of the resources of the enterprise.

In order to evaluate whether the enterprise has done well and whether resources have been adequately used there is a need to be able to compare the results of one enterprise with the results of others. Information of this type is normally based on past results and under certain conditions it could be met by financial accounts.

Owners also need to know:

* how the enterprise is going to fare in the future.

Financial accounting is unlikely to provide this information for a variety of reasons, in particular because it is largely, if not exclusively, based on the past and takes no account of future uncertainties. Past results may be taken into account as one piece of information amongst many when trying to predict the future but in a changing world it is unlikely that these results will be repeated as conditions will have changed.

Although there are limitations on the usefulness of the information contained in annual reports, these are often the only form of report available to an owner who is not involved in the day-to-day activities of the business. Owners therefore have to base their decisions on this information despite its inadequacies. Thus, for example, a shareholder, who is after all a part owner, may use the accounting information contained in the annual report to decide on whether to sell his or her shares in the business by comparing the results of that business with those of another. In practice the involvement of the shareholder in this process of making comparisons is, in the case of a quoted company, likely to be fairly indirect. This is because most of the information contained in the annual reports will already have been looked at by the owners' professional advisers who may be accountants, stockbrokers or financial analysts. The investor and owner are therefore likely to make the decision based on the professional advice they receive rather than by relying upon their own interpretation of the information contained in annual reports. This is not to say that they will rely exclusively on expert information, or that they will not use the information provided in the annual reports for their decision. The reality is likely to be a mixture, the balance of which will depend on the degree of financial sophistication of the shareholder or owner, i.e. the less sophisticated they are in financial terms the more reliance they will have to place on their external advisers.

Lenders

People and organizations only lend money in order to earn a return on that money. They are therefore interested in seeing that an enterprise is making sufficient profit to provide them with their return (usually in the form of interest). This information is normally provided by means of the profit and loss account. They are also interested in ensuring that the enterprise will be able to repay the money it has borrowed; thus they need to ascertain what the enterprise owns and what the enterprise owes. This information is normally provided in the balance sheet.

In practice research (Berry *et al.*, 1987) has shown that UK bankers use a mixture of different approaches to arrive at the lending decision. The choice of approach has been shown to be related to the size of the enterprise. In the case of smaller enterprises the 'gone concern' or security based approach, which emphasizes the availability of assets for repayment in the event of the business going bust, predominates and the emphasis is clearly on the balance sheet. However, with very large businesses the approach adopted is more likely to be the 'going concern' approach where the emphasis is more clearly focused on the present and future profitability of the enterprise. The importance of published accounting information in the form of annual reports for this group cannot be overemphasized; nearly 100% of respondents to a recent survey (Berry *et al.*, 1987) said that these reports were very important and always used in making a lending decision.

Suppliers

Goods and services can either be supplied on the basis that they are paid for when they are supplied or on the basis that they are paid for at some agreed date in the future. In both cases the supplier will be interested to know whether the enterprise is likely to stay in business and whether it is likely to expand or contract. Both of these needs relate to the future and as such can never be adequately met by information in the annual report as this relates to the past.

Suppliers who have not been paid immediately will also be interested in assessing the likelihood of getting paid. This need is partially met by the annual report as the balance sheet shows what is owned and what is owed and also gives an indication of the liquidity of the assets. The reason that we are tentative about the use of the balance sheet in this way is that often the information is many months out of date by the time it is made public as it is normally only published annually.

Customers

Like suppliers, customers are interested in an enterprise's ability to survive and therefore to carry on supplying them with services. For example, if you are a frequent business traveller you need to be sure that the travel agency that does your booking is not likely to go under. The importance of this has increased with the acceptance of the idea of a global market and the recent opening up of Eastern Europe. The customers in this situation will need to see that the enterprise is profitable, that it owns enough to pay what it owes and that it is likely to remain in business and provide a service efficiently and on time. Some of these needs are met at least partially by the profit and loss account and the balance sheet.

The employees

Employees depend on the survival of the enterprise for their wages and as such are interested in whether the enterprise is likely to survive. In the long term, an enterprise needs to make a profit in order to survive. The profit and loss account may assist the employee in making an assessment of the future viability of the company.

The employee may also be interested in comparing how well the enterprise is doing compared to other similar enterprises for the purposes of wage negotiations, although the accounts are only useful for this purpose if certain conditions are met. The accounts can also be used internally for wage negotiations, i.e. without comparisons being made as information about a company's ability to pay and level of profitability can be obtained from the accounts.

The government

The government uses accounting information for a number of purposes the most obvious of which is the levying of taxes. For this purpose it needs to know how much profit has been made. This information is provided in the profit and loss account. The government also uses accounting information to produce industry statistics for the purposes of regulation etc. A recent example has been the requirement for changes in the tenancy arrangements of the major breweries.

It should also be borne in mind that in certain cases the role of the government combines the function of owner (for example, the National Coal Board), customer (the electricity boards) and a public watchdog (environmental protection boards). Equally it can have any one of these and other roles such as regulatory roles etc. For all these purpose the government uses accounting information.

The general public

The general public may require many different types of information about enterprises in both the public and private sector. Much of this information is not supplied directly by financial accounts. For example, the public might be interested in the level of noise pollution resulting from a particular activity such as more frequent flights. This information is not at present provided by accounting reports; however, accounting reports may be useful in informing the public of the ability of an enterprise to absorb the additional costs of providing noise level controls. On the other hand, certain information provided in financial accounts may be of more direct relevance, e.g. the profitability or otherwise of nationalized industries.

From this brief survey of the users of accounting information and the uses to which it can be put it is clear that it has impacts both within the organization and in the wider environment within which enterprises operate and we live. It should also be clear that the government can use accounting as a tool for enterprise control. Before going on to consider in detail its impact upon the environment and the impact of the environment on accounting we should first consider the limitations of accounting information in order that its potential impact is put into context.

LIMITATIONS OF ACCOUNTING INFORMATION

Firstly and perhaps most importantly it has to be stressed that accounting is only one of a number of sources of information available to decision-makers. It may be the case that other sources of information are just as important if not more so than the information contained in the accounts. You will have an opportunity to examine this in more detail in the problems for discussion at the end of this chapter. However, to give you a flavour of what we are talking about, research with bankers (referred to in more detail later) shows that in certain cases a banker's personal interview with a client is as important as financial information. This is probably because accounting generally only reports on financial items, i.e. those that can be expressed in financial (monetary) terms, whereas the information bankers are trying to derive from the interview is more qualitative such as an impression of the ability of the applicant to run a successful business. It could also be the case that the information which accounting provides is only of secondary importance, as might be the case where the business is a cash one such as a fast-food outlet and the information reflected in the published accounts may not be a precise indication of the true turnover of the business.

Even given the role of accounting information in relation to other information we also have to bear in mind that, in general, financial accounting information relates to the past and the decisions that need to be taken relate to the future. Thus, unless the past is a reasonable predictor of the future, the information may have limited value for this purpose. In the real world, because of the impacts of such things as changes in technology, new innovations, changing tastes and inflation, the past is unlikely to be a good predictor of the future.

CASE STUDY 1.1

Grand Metropolitan plc Annual Report 1993

The following are extracts from the Chairman's Report:

COMMUNITY

The GrandMet community strategy detailed in last year's Annual Report continued in 1993. The fundamental aim is to contribute actively to the prosperity of the communities in which GrandMet operates, demonstrating a leadership role in helping others to help themselves. The goals are to develop a better educated and more committed workforce for the future, create thriving communities and develop a more prosperous market for potential consumers.

To achieve this aim, GrandMet concentrates the majority of its projects in carefully defined areas of community focus. Charitable donations benefit communities both through direct financial support and donations in kind. Employee volunteer efforts in community activities are also encouraged.

COMMUNITY FOCUS

GrandMet's community focus is to identify, develop and support programmes which empower individuals, particularly young people, to achieve self-sufficiency. The emphasis is on the education of disadvantaged young people and training them for work.

ENVIRONMENT

Last year's Annual Report described a number of environmental policy guidelines which were to be introduced for all subsidiaries. These included: every GrandMet company having a published policy; a 'beyond compliance' approach to environmental programmes; the promotion of international best practice in developing sound operating procedures and an on-going examination of all existing operations and processes of manufacturing and distribution. Following is a review of progress made during the year.

Environmental policies have now been published which cover all subsidiaries.

The Food sector has evolved its 'beyond compliance' programmes into a new theme of Environmental Excellence focusing on proactive environmental management systems. In the US, chemical releases reported under government programmes continue to decline, assisted by improved control systems at Alpo and Green Giant. The use of gaseous chlorine for water disinfection will have been eliminated at all sites in North America by the end of 1993. European food facilities will have eliminated all gaseous chlorine use in 1994. Solid waste recycling programmes at food manufacturing facilities have resulted in the recycling of 32 per cent of plastics, 81 per cent of cardboard and 94 per cent of metal waste. Overall, waste generation has been reduced 15 per cent year on year.

The Drinks sector also applies excellence to the management of its environmental initiatives. Reviews have been completed at all major production facilities, leading to improved measurement and management of environmental matters. IDV Europe continues its programme of improving effluent treatment systems, with facilities in Scotland and Portugal recently upgraded. Plans are in place to respond to the stringent regulatory programmes being introduced in Europe. In the US, spirits production facilities are continuously improved in advance of developing regulations on the management and control of volatile compounds.

Energy policies now exist in all businesses. Although energy tracking data identifies GrandMet businesses as low energy users, further conservation opportunities are being found and applied. Burger King, for example, has targeted energy reduction of up to 30 per cent in its outlets.

In addition to upgrading production systems, the focus has been on preventative programmes that emphasise sound management and training and the avoidance of pollution and waste.

An environmental Task Force, entirely comprising representatives from the business, has recently been established. With the environmental framework in place, this new structure will place the management and accountability for environmental matters firmly in the control of the business.

Commentary

These extracts show Grand Met's approach to the community and environment in which it operates as well as reporting on other issues likely to be of interest to the general public.

Apart from these problems there is also the question of what is and what is not included in the financial accounts. For instance, some items which, it is generally agreed, should be included in financial reports are often difficult to measure with any accuracy and thus the figures become more subjective. A good example of this problem is a half-finished hotel in Spain or Mauritius. In the latter case the problem is exacerbated by the fact that the main access is by air and the present capacity of the airport is exceeded by currently completed and part-completed hotels. How then do we decide on a figure to represent something that is only half complete? Another example is the problem of deciding how long something is going to last, e.g. a motor vehicle clearly loses value the older it gets. We might decide that a vehicle ceases to be useful to the business after four or five years, but this is to some extent an arbitrary decision as there are many older vehicles that still serve a useful purpose and indeed have been made into tourist attractions in their own right, for example the Orient Express.

CASE STUDY 1.2

British Airways Annual Report and Accounts 1992–93

The following extract provides details of BA's operating statistics.

SCHEDULED SERVICES	1989	1990	1991	1992	**1993**
Traffic and capacity					
Revenue passenger km (RPK) (m)	57,795	61,915	64,734	65,896	**73,996**
Available seat km (ASK) (m)	82,984	86,601	92,399	93,877	**104,507**
Passenger load factor (%)	69.6	71.5	70.1	70.2	**70.8**
Cargo tonne km (CTK) (m)	2,249	2,400	2,463	2,510	**2,691**
Total revenue tonne km (RTK) (m)	7,636	8,290	8,641	8,778	**9,730**
Total available tonne km (ATK) (m)	11,404	12,035	12,929	13,379	**14,695**
Overall load factor (%)	67.0	68.9	66.8	65.6	**66.2**
Passengers carried (000)	22,578	23,671	24,243	23,788	**25,905**
Tonnes of cargo carried (000)	459	498	506	502	**532**
Financial					
Passenger revenue per RPK (p)	5.96	6.37	6.27	6.50	**6.13**
Cargo revenue per CTK (p)	15.25	16.21	15.27	15.78	**14.72**
Average fuel price (US cents/US gallon)	60.22	69.72	89.72	70.94	**69.32**
Operations					
Unduplicated route km (000)	677	685	665	584	**599**
Punctuality (% within 15 minutes)	72	72	73	79	**81**
Regularity (%)	99.0	98.9	98.7	99.2	**99.3**
TOTAL GROUP OPERATIONS					
Total revenue tonne km (RTK) (m)	8,002	8,627	8,979	9,111	**10,313**
Total available tonne km (ATK) (m)	11,868	12,445	13,351	13,818	**15,424**
Passengers carried (000)	24,603	25,238	25,587	25,422	**28,100**
Average number of employees	50,204	52,054	54,427	50,409	**48,960**
RTKs per employee (000)	159.4	165.7	165.0	180.7	**210.6**
ATKs per employee (000)	236.4	239.1	245.3	274.1	**315.0**
Aircraft in service at year end	211	224	230	230	**241**
Aircraft utilisation (average hours per aircraft per annum)	2,886	2,787	2,663	2,708	**2,928**
Revenue aircraft km (m)	364	375	389	390	**431**
Revenue flights (000)	269	274	271	261	**268**
Total traffic revenue per RTK (p)	48.73	51.36	50.54	52.55	**49.28**
Total traffic revenue per ATK (p)	32.85	35.60	33.99	34.65	**32.95**
Net operating expenditure per ATK (p)	30.02	32.52	32.74	32.16	**30.94**
Break-even overall load factor (%)	61.6	63.3	64.8	61.2	**62.8**

Commentary

The relative importance of financial information as a form of reporting will vary from organization to organization. In the case of British Airways the standard financial information is supplemented by detailed operating statistics including load factors and punctuality.

In addition to the problems of deciding how long things will last or what stage of completion they have reached there are certain items which are not only difficult to quantify in terms of their value but about which there are doubts relating to their inclusion in financial reports. For example, the value of a football club is dependent on its ability to attract supporters; this in turn is dependent on its ability to succeed which is dependent on the abilities of the players, etc. However, it is doubtful that a value could be placed on a player as this value will vary with the player's fitness, form, etc. Having said that, Spurs football club included their players in their accounts for 1989 at a figure of £7.8 million.

In addition to the questions raised above there are many environmental factors which need to be taken into account but which cannot be adequately included in accounts although they may be quantifiable in money terms. Examples are the potential market for the product, the impact of European Union (EU) quotas, tariff restrictions and environmental issues. If these were to be included in the annual reports of a business it could lead to a loss of competitive advantage.

Finally we have to deal with the fact that accounting information is expressed in monetary terms and assumes that the monetary unit is stable over time. This is patently not the case, and although there has been much discussion on the problems of accounting in times of changing prices, no agreed solution has yet been found.

We can conclude from the discussion above that whilst it is clear that accounting provides some information that is useful to decision-makers, it has to be borne in mind:

- that the information is only a part of that necessary to make 'effective' decisions;
- that accountancy is as yet an inexact science and depends on a number of judgements, estimates, etc.;
- that the end result of the accounting process can only be as good as the inputs and in times of rising prices some of these inputs are of dubious value;
- that accounting systems can be counterproductive, e.g. the maximization of a division's profit (such as the bars in a hotel) may not always ensure the maximization of enterprise profit.

Nevertheless, it is clear that accounting is vital to the running of a healthy and prosperous enterprise and arguably it is also an essential prerequisite for a prosperous economy. Before leaving this chapter it would be useful therefore to look at accounting in the wider context of the business and its environment. We will examine how the accounting function interacts with and is different from other business functions. We will then examine its contribution to strategic decision-making before placing it within the organizational and wider business environments within which it operates.

ACCOUNTING AS A BUSINESS FUNCTION

The accounting department, like the personnel department, operates, in theory, in an advisory capacity only, providing information for managers to make the decisions. In practice, however, the financial elements controlled by the accounting function and the information it generates are so central to the operation of the enterprise that the influence of accounting is often all-pervasive. Accounting, although essential to the smooth running of the business, does not have as direct an impact as, for example, other service departments, e.g. a hotel's reception service. Its impacts are generally more subtle although they may in certain instances be very obvious. For example, if the accounting information indicates that expenses are running at too high a level this may have dramatic repercussions in other functional areas. Training and recruitment budgets may be instantly frozen having a significant impact on the work of the personnel department and other operating departments, affecting both staffing levels and skills levels. Alternatively it may be that the decision is taken to stop expenditure on a current advertising campaign thus having a direct effect on the work of the marketing department.

Accounting is also unusual in that it can have unintended effects; for example, if targets are set based on occupancy rates this may lead to rooms being discounted or bookings taken from tour operators who have poor or nonexistent credit ratings in order to achieve the sales targets set. It can also be a very dangerous tool if used in the wrong way; for example, targets could be set to achieve cost savings in the food production area with no account being taken of the impacts on quality or employee safety. Similarly if it is used by people who do not understand its limitations it can lead to wrong decisions. If, for example, a person was unaware that accounting as generally used takes no account of rising prices, services could be sold at less than they cost to provide.

The importance of accounting within a business should not be underestimated. It provides the basic information by which managers and owners can judge whether the business is meeting its objectives. Its importance is exemplified by the high salaries which accountants can command and by the prevalence of accountants upon the boards of directors of our major public companies.

Accounting is also different from other business functions in that accounting, as well as being a business function, is itself an industry. The accounting industry or profession sells accounting and other advisory services to other businesses and is a major employer of graduate labour.

FACTORS INFLUENCING THE USE OF ACCOUNTING WITHIN AN ORGANIZATION

Accounting can be and is used within business to evaluate and shape alternative strategies such as providing a laundry service in-house or buying it in from a local specialist concern, thus shaping business plans and activities. At the same time it is itself a function of the type of activity a business engages in and of the strategies a business adopts. In other words the accounting system not only influences business strategies but is itself influenced by the goals, size and structure of the organization. For example, the accounting system that would be appropriate for a small restaurant which provides one distinct product would not be appropriate for a large hospitality operation such as the Hilton Hotel where many other products and services are part of the complete package that customers are purchasing. In the latter case, to be able to identify, for example, the labour associated with a specific functional area would require a much more sophisticated system of accounting. Accounting systems are to a large extent variable depending upon the type of activity or activities in which a business is engaged and upon the levels of activity.

Clearly the organization's goals will have a major impact upon the accounting system used; for example, to develop an accounting system with the primary purpose of measuring profit would be wholly inappropriate for a charitable organization. Similarly the requirements in terms of accounting reports will be very different in the case of a workers' cooperative, the health service and a profit-oriented company. The cooperative members are more likely to be interested in their pay and their share of the surplus generated than in the enterprise's profitability. Shareholders in a company on the other hand are likely to be more interested in judging overall profitability and comparing that with alternative investments. In the case of the health service it may be that the owners, i.e. the general public, are primarily interested in the service received rather than its profitability.

The organizational structure will also have an impact on the type of accounting system that is needed. For example, if a brewery operates all of its pubs by putting managers into them it will need an accounting system that allows for the payment of regular salaries and bonuses based upon achieving pre-set targets. These targets are normally set in terms of barrelage so it will need to know what the normal barrelage for each pub is, it will also need to know the mark up on spirits, soft drinks, etc., and the approximate mix of sales in order to ensure its managers are not pocketing the profits. If, on the other hand, it sets its organization up so that each pub has a landlord who is a tenant of the brewery, the system required will be different as in this case the landlord or landlady is not paid a salary or bonus; his or her wages instead come from the profits made from selling the beers, wines and spirits.

We have already alluded to the effect of the size of the organization in our example concerning the needs of a restaurant and a hotel and the effect of those needs on the accounting system. However, it is worth reiterating the point that the larger and more disparate the organization, the greater is the need for organizational controls through a system of accountability which makes managers responsible for the performance of their divisions or branches and which provides reports that can be used by senior managers to evaluate the performance of their subordinates and of the organization as a whole. As we have already mentioned it is vital that the accounting system is tailored to the needs of the organization otherwise it will not allow management to control the organization and indeed may have dysfunctional effects. In a small business it is often the case that there is little accounting information available on a day-to-day basis. This may be because the operations are sufficiently simple not to warrant much information or, as is more likely, the owner does not have the skills to produce it and the costs of hiring in the necessary expertise are perceived as outweighing the potential benefits. It often happens in these small businesses that the only time accounting reports are produced is at the end of the year to meet the needs of the tax collector or when the bank demands them as a prerequisite to granting a loan or extending an overdraft facility.

Having briefly introduced some factors that influence accounting and accounting systems at a micro level we now consider factors which impact at a macro level. In general the aspects which interact significantly with accounting are the state, technology and labour, although environmental considerations are becoming increasingly important. Accounting is also affected by and affects the economy; for example, a country such as Brazil suffering from hyperinflation has of necessity to use costs other than original costs in its accounting reports because the value of the monetary unit in which accounting information is expressed is changing so fast. Similarly the requirements in the form of accounting information for a socialist country such as Cuba will be quite different from those of western capitalist countries where the measurement of profit is such a dominant force on the form and content of accounting reports. Going back to the impacts of labour, the state, technology, etc., we have already discussed the potential uses of accounting information by employees and employee organizations such as trade unions. We have also mentioned in passing the different forms of organization such as owner-managed businesses, which may be sole proprietorships or partnerships, and companies. In the case of the former there is no requirement for the publication of accounting information whereas for companies not only the form but also the content of their annual reports are laid down by law in the Companies Acts. In addition, for these forms of organization the accounting profession lays down certain rules known as Statements of Standard Accounting Practice (SSAPs) and Financial Reporting Standards (FRSs). A similar situation prevails in most western developed countries although the importance of the legislature *vis-à-vis* professional pronouncements varies from country to country. Finally there are the effects of changes in technology, which have had dramatic impacts within the accounting function as accounting systems have been computerized. This has allowed accountants to free themselves from the more mundane tasks of recording and allowed them to become more involved in decision support and strategic issues. At another level, however, new technology has and is still imposing challenges on accounting thought; systems that were appropriate in a labour-intensive environment are being found lacking in the age of flexible production systems, just-in-time management and computer-controlled environments.

SUMMARY

In this chapter we have tried to give a flavour of what accounting is and of how it pervades both the internal workings of organizations and the external environment. It can be seen to be at one level a functional area of business and at an external level an important determinant of the business's survival through its impacts on shareholders, lenders, employees, etc. We have indicated that there is no perfect accounting report that will meet the needs of all users and that the needs of users vary depending on the purpose to which the report is put. For example, in the case of a small business the owner may wish to show a low profit to reduce the potential tax bill but may need to show a high profit in order to convince the banker to lend the business money. We have tried to indicate that accounting will only be useful if it is used correctly and if its limitations are understood. A failing business will still fail even though it has an excellent accounting system; on the other hand potentially successful businesses have been allowed to go to the wall because the accounting system did not give the warning signs it should have done or gave them too late to allow management to take action to rectify the situation.

Before moving on you should work through the review questions and problems to ensure that you have understood the main points of this chapter.

REFERENCES

ASC (1975) *The Corporate Report*, Institute of Chartered Accountants in England and Wales.

Berry, A., Citron, D. and Jarvis, R. (1987) *The Information Needs of Bankers Dealing with Large and Small Companies*, Certified Accountants Research Report 7, Certified Accountants Publications, London.

FURTHER READING

A fuller discussion of accounting in its wider context can be found in *Financial Accounting*, Chapters 1–3, by J. Arnold, T. Hope and A.J. Southwood (Prentice Hall, 1985).

REVIEW QUESTIONS

1. For what purposes is accounting information used:
   (a) by the individual?
   (b) by the enterprise?
2. Who are the users of accounting information and which accounting reports do they normally use?
3. What are the needs of internal users? Can you identify any other needs of internal users? If so, can you suggest how these would be met?
4. What are the limitations of accounting information?
5. Examples were given for certain of the limitations. Can you give examples of your own?
6. What are the major determinants of a useful accounting system?

PROBLEMS FOR DISCUSSION AND ANALYSIS

1. It was pointed out that accounting information is only a part of the input to the decision-making process. In order to expand your understanding of the role of accounting information, for the situation outlined below:
   (a) identify the accounting information that would be relevant, and
   (b) identify any other information that would be relevant.

   Bed & Co. run a small provincial hotel catering mainly for commercial travellers and other business people. The existing business is reasonably profitable but because of the location there is little chance of expanding the trade. The owners believe there are opportunities to be taken in the home-delivery food market which would utilize the existing surplus capacity for food production. The owners have little knowledge of the market but feel that there is money to be made and that it would be complementary to their existing business.

2. Sloth was left some money in a will and decided that he should give up his job and go into business for himself. Whilst the lawyers were still sorting out the estate he started looking round for a suitable business. After a short while he identified a small bed-and-breakfast business that he felt was worth investing in. He was still uncertain how much he had inherited but thought it was probably between £100 000 and £120 000. The business was for sale for £180 000 so assuming that he could finance the remainder of the purchase price he engaged an accountant to check over the books of the existing business and report back to him. As proof of his good faith he deposited with the business agents the sum of £3000 which he had in savings.

The report from the accountant confirmed his initial impression that the business was worth investing in so he paid the accountant's modest fee of £500. At this stage he discussed his plans more fully with his bank manager who was duly impressed with the professional approach he had taken.

His bank manager pointed out that Sloth had no business experience and as such was a high risk from the bank's point of view. However, in view of their long-standing relationship the bank was prepared to take a chance and the manager indicated that the bank would lend Sloth 40% of the purchase price.

On the basis of this Sloth signed a conditional agreement to buy the business. A short while after this he received a letter from the lawyers stating that his inheritance amounted to only £90 000. He could not raise the additional finance to purchase the business so withdrew from the agreement, recovered his £3000 deposit and purchased the lease on the food concession at a local tourist attraction for £60 000 and employed somebody to run and manage it for him.

You are required to discuss the point at which, in your opinion, the accounting process should begin, giving reasons for your point of view. You should pay particular attention to the dual needs of Sloth as an owner and as a manager.

Wealth and the measurement of profit $\boxed{2}$

INTRODUCTION

In Chapter 1 we established that there are a number of different users
of accounting information, each of whom needs different information
for different purposes. However, there are some items of information
that are required by most users. These relate to what an enterprise
owns, what it owes and some information on how it has performed or
is performing – in other words a measure of performance. The former
information, i.e. that about what an enterprise owns and what it owes,
could be termed the worth of the enterprise or its wealth. This measure
of wealth or worth relates to a point in time. The other information
required is about the way in which the enterprise performed over a
period of time. This performance during a period can be measured as
a change in wealth over time. Thus if you increase your wealth you
have performed better, in financial terms, than someone whose wealth
has decreased over the same period of time. This measurement of
changes in wealth over time is referred to in accounting terminology as
profit measurement. In this chapter we shall consider some of the ways
in which accountants can measure wealth and profit and we shall discuss some of the merits of the alternatives available. We shall also
examine, in some detail, the way in which the choice of a measurement
system affects the resultant profit and wealth measures. To do this we
need to start by defining profit and wealth as these two concepts are
directly linked.

INCOME, WEALTH AND PROFIT

A definition of profit that is widely accepted by accountants is based
around the definition of an individual's income put forward by the
economist Sir John Hicks (1930) who stated:

> Income is that amount which an individual can consume and still be
> as well off at the end of the period as he or she was at the start of
> the period.

This definition offered by Hicks can be illustrated diagrammatically
as:

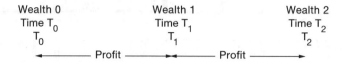

We can see from the diagram that we can arrive at the profit for period 1 by measuring wealth at the start of the period, i.e. at time T_0 and subtracting that figure from our measurement at the end of the period, i.e. T_1. Similarly the profit for the second period can be measured by subtracting the wealth at time T_1 from the wealth at the end of period 2, i.e. at time T_2.

Key concept

Income

A relationship exists between income (or profit) and wealth. The definition above suggests that income can be derived by measuring wealth at two different points in time and the difference between the two figures is the income or profit. An alternative view proposed by other economists suggests that if you first measure income then you can derive wealth. This implies that the relationship is to some extent circular as depicted below. The different views expounded by various economists really relate to how you break into the circle.

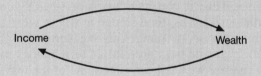

It should also be clear from the diagram of Hicks's definition that **wealth** is **static** and represents a stock at a particular point in time. Thus Wealth 0 is the stock of wealth at time T_0, Wealth 1 is the stock of wealth at time T_1 and Wealth 2 is the stock of wealth at time T_2.

Key concept

Wealth

Wealth is a static measure and represents a stock at a particular point in time. This stock can change over time. Thus the wealth measured at the start of a period will not necessarily be equal to the wealth measured at the end of the period. The difference between the two is the profit or loss for that period of time.

If we look at the way in which profit is depicted in the diagram of Hicks's definition it is also apparent that profit is a flow over time, i.e.

to measure the profit earned over a period of time it is necessary to measure the stock of wealth at the start and end of that period.

> ***Key concept***
>
> *Profit*
>
> Profit represents the difference between the wealth at the start and at the end of the period. Unlike wealth which is essentially a static measure, profit is a measure of flow which summarizes activity over a period.

To summarize, we have shown that we can express the profit for the first period, i.e. from time T_o to time T_1, as:

$$\text{Profit period 1} = \text{Wealth 1} - \text{Wealth 0}$$

Similarly we can express the profit for the second period, i.e. from time T_1 to time T_2, as:

$$\text{Profit period 2} = \text{Wealth 2} - \text{Wealth 1}$$

We have also established that the profit is derived by measuring the wealth of an individual, or an enterprise, at two points in time. This, on the face of it, is reasonably straightforward but let us now look in more detail at what we are trying to measure and how we are to measure it.

We shall start by examining the case of an individual because this will be simpler and more in line with your own experience. The underlying arguments and principles are just the same for an enterprise but the degree of complexity increases in the case of an enterprise, especially a large multinational company. Let us suppose that we asked an individual to measure his wealth, i.e. the sum of his possessions less what he owes.

EXAMPLE 2.1

Alex came up with the following lists of items owned and told us that he owed nothing.

At the start of the year T_0	**At the end of the year T_1**
A new Ford Fiesta 1.0 L	A one-year-old Fiesta 1.0 L
Three new suits	The same three suits
Five shirts	The same five shirts
Four sweatshirts	Five sweatshirts
Four hundred pounds cash	Five hundred pounds cash

Whilst the lists above may accurately reflect what Alex owns and what he owes, we cannot easily see whether he is better or worse off at the end of the year than he was at the start. We could perhaps say with the benefit of our own knowledge of the world that he must be worse off because everything is one year older; this, however, assumes that the value of his possessions decreases with time. In many cases that is a reasonable assumption but clearly there are some cases where the value is increasing; for example, would our attitude change if the car was a 1906 Bentley? Leaving that question aside for a minute, you will have noticed that once we started to discuss the measurement of wealth we also started talking of the more abstract concept of value.

This raises two questions, one of which relates to value which we shall discuss in some more detail later, and the other relates to the way in which we assign value. In the case of the list of possessions above the easiest item to deal with in terms of value is the cash. This is because it has already had a value assigned to it with which we are all familiar, i.e. a monetary value. On the face of it, therefore, it would seem that if we assigned a monetary value to each of the items in the list we would have solved part of our problem at least. In fact it is not as easy as that as we all know the value of money is not stable; we only have to listen to our grandparents or even our parents talking about what money used to buy to realize that the value of money has decreased over time.

If we leave the problem of the changing value of money aside for the present and we use money as a measure of value, then we have no problem with the value of the cash in the bank, but what of the other items? What is the value of the car for example? Is it worth less because it is one year older, and if so how much less? The same line of argument can be applied to the suits and shirts, but in the case of the sweatshirts we do not even know if they are the same sweatshirts – clearly there must be at least one that has been acquired during the year as he has five at the end compared with four at the beginning. We also have yet to establish whether the age is important for the purposes of arriving at a value. In order to be able to decide on that question we need to first look at the possibilities available to us.

Although numerous alternative measures have been proposed many are combinations of those dealt with here. We shall limit our discussion to the most commonly quoted possibilities. For convenience, and in order to help understanding, we shall first deal with those that relate to cost and then discuss those that are based on some concept of value. We start with original cost and then look at historic cost and finally replacement cost.

The definitions of these terms will be explained later in this chapter. The important point to note at this stage is the relationship between wealth and profit and the way in which a change in the measurement of one affects the other. This will be explored in more detail, using the example of Alex.

> **Key concept**
>
> *Original cost*
>
> The cost of the item at the time of the transaction between the buyer and seller.

ORIGINAL COST

The original cost of an item is the cost of the item at the time of the transaction between the buyer and seller. It should be noted that we have made a number of implicit assumptions about there being a willing buyer and willing seller which do not need to concern us at this point. Leaving those aside, on the face of it this seems to be a fairly easy figure to arrive at. It is in fact not so easy. Consider the case of this book. Is the original cost the price you paid in the bookshop? Or is it the price the bookshop paid the publisher? Or do we go back even further to the cost to the publisher? Or further still to the cost to the authors? Each of these is a possible measure of the original cost, but the question is which is the right cost? The answer lies in the idea that the cost is the cost to the individual or enterprise on which you are reporting. This cost is normally referred to as the historic cost.

> **Key concept**
>
> *Historic cost*
>
> The cost incurred by the individual or enterprise in acquiring an item measured at the time of the originating transaction.

HISTORIC COST

Historic cost is the cost incurred by the individual or enterprise in acquiring an item measured at the time the transaction took place. It is extremely important as it underpins most current accounting practice. We can see that the historic cost of the book to you will be different from the historic cost to the bookshop as these are two separate transactions taking place at different points in time. This of course is what keeps the bookshop in business. But let us take our example a stage further – let us assume, for whatever reason, at the end of the year you decide you no longer need this book; you therefore decide to sell it. In this situation you will probably find that the book is no longer worth what you paid for it and therefore the historic cost is no longer a fair representation of the book's worth or of your wealth. In order to tackle this problem, when measuring your wealth at the end of the year you could write the historic cost down to some lower figure to represent the amount of use you have had out of the book. Accounting follows a similar process and the resulting figure is known as the **written-down cost**. This written-down cost can be described as:

The historic cost after an adjustment for usage.

This adjustment for usage is commonly referred to as **depreciation**, and there are a number of alternative ways of arriving at a figure for depreciation which we shall deal with in more detail in Chapter 7.

The problem with historic cost and written-down historic cost is that with the value of money and goods changing over time it is only likely to be a fair representation of value at a particular point in time, i.e. at the point of the original transaction. At any other point it will only be a fair representation of value by chance unless the world is static, i.e. with no innovation etc. Clearly this is not the case and so we should look for alternative measures. One such alternative to the original cost or the historic cost of an item is its replacement cost. This is certainly more up to date and allows for the changes that will take place in a non-static world.

Key concept

Replacement cost

The amount that would have to be paid at today's prices to purchase an item similar to the existing item.

REPLACEMENT COST

The replacement cost of an item is the amount that would have to be paid at today's prices to purchase an item similar to the existing item. It is often very relevant as those of us who have had cars written off will know. In those cases the amount the insurance company pays you often bears no relationship to what it would cost to replace your car, because yours was better than average or had just had a new engine put in. The problem that arises in using replacement cost is firstly that you have to want to replace the item. You may not want to replace a textbook that you used at school as it would no longer be of use to you. Even if we assume that you do want to replace the item, you may find that it is difficult to find the replacement cost, as would be the case with a specialist item such as Buckingham Palace!

It may be the case that even if you could replace an item with an exact replica you may not wish to do so. For example, you may wish to obtain a newer version or one with extra features. The most obvious example of this sort of problem is the replacement of computer equipment, which is constantly expanding in power whilst its size and its price are generally decreasing. This leads us to the same problem as we had with historic cost in that the replacement cost of a computer does not take into account the age of the machine that we actually own. The solution is the same as for historic cost, i.e. estimate the effect of usage and arrive at a written-down replacement cost.

As we can see there are distinct problems in using either historic cost or replacement cost. In a number of situations these are unlikely to be useful measures of value or of wealth. Historic cost is unlikely to be useful when prices change, whatever the reason for that change. Replacement cost, on the other hand, whilst overcoming that problem by using up-to-date costs, is itself irrelevant if there is no intention of replacing the item with an exact replica.

Before reading the next section on alternative measures based on value rather than cost it is worth spending a few minutes thinking of the situations in which historic cost and replacement cost are appropriate and those situations when they are unlikely to be appropriate. This is important because **any measure is only useful if it is the appropriate measure to do the job in hand**. For example, whilst the acceleration of a car may be appropriate in certain circumstances it is irrelevant when doing an emergency stop. Similarly the historic cost or replacement cost of a motor car is unlikely to be useful if we wish to sell that car as the selling price will be governed by other factors. The alternatives to these cost-based measures are measures which are related to value. However, as we shall see, these value based-measures also have their own set of problems.

Key concept

Economic value

Economic value is, or would be, an ideal measure of value and wealth. It is the value of the expected earnings from using the item in question discounted at an appropriate rate to give a present-day value.

ECONOMIC VALUE

The economic value of an item is the value of the expected earnings from using the item in question discounted at an appropriate rate to give a present-day value. The problem is not in defining the measure but in actually estimating the future earnings as this implies a knowledge of what is going to happen in the future. The problems of foreseeing technological change, fashion changes, changes in taste, etc., all make the estimation of future earnings problematic. Even if we assume that this can be done, we are then left with the question of finding an appropriate rate at which to discount the estimated future earnings. The problem here is that every individual may wish to use a different rate depending on his or her circumstances. For example, a millionaire may not worry overmuch if money is available in a year rather than now but if you have no money to buy your next meal the situation is entirely different. We should not totally discount the possibility of using this measure because of these problems since with the use of mathematical techniques relating to probability it is still a useful tool in decision-making. In fact it is the basis underlying techniques such as net present value which are often used in investment appraisal decisions and which we shall discuss in more detail later

---

Key concept

Net realizable value

The net realizable value is an alternative measure of value to economic value. It is the amount that is likely to be obtained by selling an item, less any costs incurred in selling.

NET REALIZABLE VALUE

The net realizable value is the amount that is likely to be obtained by selling an item, after taking off any costs incurred in selling. On the face of it this should be easily obtainable but in practice the amount for which an item can be sold will vary with the circumstances of the sale. The problems of arriving at the net realizable value are very apparent in the second-hand car market where there is a trade price and a range of retail prices. Another good example is the house market where independent valuers can differ as much as £40 000 on a property worth between £110 000 and £150 000. Apart from the problem of arriving at a value other factors will affect the net realizable value. For example, if you are hard up you may be prepared to accept less than the market value in order to get a quick sale. The value in the latter situation is known as the **forced sale value** and this is the most likely value to be obtained where circumstances are unfavourable to the seller. If, on the other hand, the market conditions are neutral as between buyer and seller then the net realizable value is likely to be the **open market value**.

COMPARISON OF MEASURES

It should be clear from the above that plenty of alternative measures are available each of which has its own problems. If you remember, the starting point for this discussion was that we wished to establish whether Alex was better of at the end of the period than he was at the start. Had he made a profit? The problem is not one of finding a concept of profit as there are plenty available within the economics literature apart from the one we have already referred to provided by Hicks (see, for example, Fisher's (1930) income concept and that of Friedman (1957)). The problem is in fact one of measurement as most of these concepts either rely on a measurement of future income streams or on the measurement of wealth.

We have already pointed out that to measure future income streams is extremely difficult in the real world because of the effects of uncertainty. This then leaves us with the alternative of measuring wealth and leads us to the question of finding the most appropriate measure. As we have seen, all the measures put forward so far have inherent problems, and it may be that the solution lies in combining one or more of these measures to obtain the best measure. For the purposes of this introductory text it is probably unnecessary to probe this area in greater depth but some references are given at the end of this chapter which will provide further background for those interested in pursuing the topic. Before leaving this area completely let us reconsider our example based on the wealth of Alex and assign some values to see what effect the choice of measure will have.

Description	Replacement cost £	Year T_0 Historic cost £	Net realizable value £
Ford Fiesta 1.0L	4850	4850	4400
Suits	240	210	30
Shirts	75	75	10
Sweatshirts	50	50	20
Cash	400	400	400

If you study the figures carefully you will notice that the only figure common to all three columns is the cash figure. Apart from the cost of the suits the replacement cost and the historic cost are also identical. In reality this will always be the case at the time the goods are bought, but it is unlikely to be the case at any other time. In this example the fact that the replacement cost of the suits is different from the historic cost would indicate that some or all of these suits were bought when the price of suits was lower than it was at the start of the year in question. In other words the point of time at which we are measuring is different from the date of acquisition and, as we said, in these circumstances the replacement cost is likely to differ from the historic cost.

You should also have noticed that the net realizable value is lower than the historic cost and replacement cost even though some of the items were clearly bought new at the start of the year. Once again this is obviously going to be the case in most situations because personal goods being resold are effectively second-hand goods even though they may not have been used. The situation for a business enterprise is not necessarily the same as in some cases the goods are not bought for use but for resale, e.g. by a retailer or wholesaler. In these cases the net realizable value of the goods bought for resale should be higher than the cost – otherwise the retailer would not stay in business very long.

Let us now look at Alex's situation at the end of the year and assign some values to the items owned at that point in time. We shall then be in a position to measure the profit or increase in wealth and to use this as a basis for discussion of some of the problems of measurement which we referred to earlier.

		Year T$_1$	
Description	Replacement cost	Historic cost	Net realizable value
	£	£	£
Ford Fiesta 1.0 L	3195	4850	3000
Suits	270	210	27
Shirts	80	75	5
Sweatshirts	50	50	15
Cash	500	500	500

You will notice that the figures have changed in all cases except under historic cost where they are the same as at the start of the year except for the cash. This highlights one of the problems with this measure in that it only tells us what an item cost and gives no clue as to what it is worth.

It is also worth looking more closely at the car. As you can see the replacement cost is lower than at the start of the year. This is because the car we are replacing at the end of the year is a one-year-old model rather than a new model. You will also see that the replacement cost is higher than the net realizable value. This is because there would be costs incurred in selling the car so the amount you would get would be reduced by these costs.

Let us now look at what we get in terms of our measures of wealth and profit, starting with historic cost.

Description	Year T$_0$	Year T$_1$
	£	£
Ford Fiesta 1.0L	4850	4850
Suits	210	210
Shirts	75	75
Sweatshirts	50	50
Cash	400	500
	5585	5685

We can now measure the profit under historic cost as we have a figure for wealth at the start and end of the year. Thus using the formula:

$$\text{Wealth 1} - \text{Wealth 0} = \text{Profit}$$

we get:

$$£5685 - £5585 = £100$$

Let us now look at what would happen if we used replacement cost rather than historic cost.

Description	Year T_0	Year T_1
	£	£
Ford Fiesta 1.0 L	4850	3195
Suits	240	270
Shirts	75	85
Sweatshirts	50	50
Cash	400	500
	5615	4100

We can now measure the profit under replacement cost as we have a figure for wealth at the start and end of the year. Thus using the formula:

$$\text{Wealth 1} - \text{Wealth 0} = \text{Profit}$$

we get:

$$£4100 - £5615 = £1515 \text{ loss}$$

In other words according to the replacement cost figures we are £1515 worse off at the end of the year than we were at the start.

Finally let us see what the situation would be if we were using the net realizable value to arrive at our measures of wealth.

Description	Year T_0	Year T_1
	£	£
Ford Fiesta 1.0 L	4400	3000
Suits	30	27
Shirts	10	5
Sweatshirts	20	15
Cash	400	500
	4860	3547

We can now measure the profit under net realizable value as we have a figure for wealth at the start and end of the year. Thus using the formula:

$$\text{Wealth 1} - \text{Wealth 0} = \text{Profit}$$

we get:

$$£3547 - £4860 = £1313 \text{ loss}$$

Once again using net realizable value as the basis of measuring wealth we find Alex is worse off at the end of the year than he was at the start.

You may well be wondering at this point which is the correct answer. The answer to that question takes us back to who is to use the information and for what purpose is it to be used. Clearly this varies from case to case; however, it is more important, at the present time, that you understand that differences arise depending on the valuation method adopted. You may feel that as Alex is clearly worse off at the end of the first year than he was at the start (he no longer has a brand new car) then replacement cost or net realizable value are the better alternatives. However, you must bear in mind that we are trying to measure the amount that can be spent whilst maintaining wealth and that there is therefore a hidden assumption that Alex would want to maintain the wealth he had at the start.

This may not in fact be the case due to changes in circumstances. He may, for example, have been banned from driving which would mean that he does not want to replace his car and this may lead us to the net realizable value model as he would probably want to sell it. However, just because he has lost his driving licence it is likely that he will need to go out even if only to buy food. He is going to need to wear some clothes so to value these on the assumption that they are going to be sold is not a defensible position.

CONCLUSION

We have seen that there are a number of alternative ways of measuring a person's wealth and each has its own problems. One of the most frequently cited problems with both replacement cost and net realizable value is that they are subjective. This is true in many cases. This subjectivity is one reason why accounts are still prepared using historic costs, even though, as we have seen with the simple example of Alex, this can lead to irrelevant information being produced which can in turn lead to wrong decisions being taken. Another reason that is often cited for retaining historic cost in the accounts is that it is a system which is based on what was actually spent and owners of enterprises need to know what their money has been spent on. But to what extent can the latter advantage of historic cost make up for its deficiencies as a measure of wealth and therefore as the basis of the profit measure? This question is and has been the subject of much debate and that debate will continue for many years to come. For our purposes we only need to be aware of the problems associated with using each of the alternatives as they may well lead to different decisions being made.

CASE STUDY 2.1

British Airports Authority Annual Report 1994

The following is an extract from the 1994 accounts of BAA plc:

As at 31 March 1994, the net book value of the Group's tangible fixed assets as reported and on a replacement cost basis, including investment properties at open market value, was as follows:

	1994		1993	
	As reported £m	**Replacement cost £m**	As reported £m	Replacement cost £m
Heathrow	1,576.6	1,835.5	1,159.3	1,438.2
Gatwick	707.0	850.0	633.3	782.4
Stansted	579.9	535.7	575.0	521.6
Southampton	35.7	33.0	29.4	27.0
Glasgow	169.6	175.6	135.7	135.2
Edinburgh	39.0	55.7	34.5	51.4
Aberdeen	48.8	57.0	40.5	50.6
Managed airports	0.2	0.2	0.2	0.2
Total airport subsidiaries	3,156.8	3,542.7	2,607.9	3,006.6
Tangible fixed assets held by other Group companies	410.3	410.3	400.6	400.6
	3,567.1	3,953.0	3,008.5	3,407.2

Commentary

The debate about the most appropriate method of arriving at a figure for the capital of a business has gone on for many years. In the 1980s an alternative valuation base, other than historic cost, was included in published accounts. Although current cost information is no longer required and BAA plc's accounting policies state that, terminal complexes, airfield assets and properties with a significant element of group occupation are included in the accounts at cost less depreciation. BAA plc still see fit to include information highlighting the difference between cost and replacement value of certain fixed assets, and the above extract was included in the notes to the accounts.

From this extract we can see that the difference between the replacement cost and reported, i.e. written-down, historic cost is nearly £386 million. As we have pointed out in this chapter the measurement of wealth and that of profit are directly related. What we can see clearly demonstrated here is the impact such alternative valuations can have on the balance sheet.

SUMMARY

We have looked at a definition of wealth and of profit which is commonly used and indeed underpins current accounting practice, and we have found that there are problems in actually measuring wealth. We have looked at four alternative measures: historic cost, replacement cost, net realizable value and economic value. We have shown by way of a simple example that each of the first three produces a different answer and in the course of our discussion we have pointed to some of the problems and assumptions underlying each alternative. At the present point in time there is no generally accepted right answer, and in fact the most commonly used system is that based on historic cost (although it is worth noting that Philips, the electronics giant, has used replacement costs for a number of years). Finally it should also be pointed out that change is likely to be slow in coming as the present system, based on historic cost, is familiar to all and has, it is argued by some, worked well in the past, although it is unclear what criteria are being used to back up the latter claim.

REFERENCES

Fisher, I. (1930) *The Theory of Interest*, Macmillan, London.
Friedman, M. (1957) *A Theory of the Consumption Function*, Princeton University Press, Princeton, NJ.
Hicks, Sir J. (1946) *Value and Capital*, Clarendon Press, Oxford.

FURTHER READING

For those who wish to examine the economic value approach, a good exposition can be found in *A New Introduction to Financial Accounting* by R.G. May, G.G. Mueller and T.H. Williams (Prentice Hall, 1980).

REVIEW QUESTIONS

1. Profit is normally seen as a flow over time whereas wealth can be described as a stock at a point in time. Explain in your own words the difference between a stock and a flow.
2. There are a number of different ways in which we can measure wealth. List the alternatives discussed in the chapter together with any drawbacks or problems that were identified with their use.
3. In certain situations we said that written-down cost could be used as an alternative. Explain in your own words the difference between cost and written-down cost and suggest when the latter would be more appropriate.

4. What effects, if any, do rapid changes in technology have on the appropriateness of the alternative ways of assigning a cost or value to an item?

PROBLEMS FOR DISCUSSION AND ANALYSIS

1. Under certain circumstances only one of the alternative methods of valuation is the most appropriate. Giving brief reasons for your choice, suggest the most appropriate value to be placed on each item in the following.

   Jean owns a shop which used to sell clothes but she has now decided that given the location she would make more money running a restaurant at the same premises. She has obtained planning permission for the change of use and has bought some of the equipment needed but has not yet started trading. She has made a list of the items the business owns which is reproduced below:
   (a) freehold shop;
   (b) hanging display rail for clothes;
   (c) a two-year-old car which is essential for the business;
   (d) new restaurant tables and chairs;
   (e) cash till;
   (f) quantity of fashion garments that were not sold in the closing down sale.
   You may find that you need more information or have to make some assumptions. This is normal but you should state any assumptions you are making.

2. In the example of Alex in the chapter no allowance was made for the fact that an item had been in use for some time. Whilst it is intuitively obvious that the utility of most things declines over time, it is more difficult to identify the extent of that decline over a given period. In addition even if we could identify the decline in utility and the utility remaining we still have to assign some monetary amount to both parts. We said in the chapter that this was done through the medium of arriving at a written-down cost or value. For each of the following situations suggest, with reasons, the best method for arriving at the written-down cost or value:
   (a) a ticket machine which will produce 10 million tickets and then need to be replaced. Ticket production each year is obviously matched to visitors coming through the gates and estimates are 1 million in year 1, and 1.5 million in year 2. The years after that cannot be forecast with any accuracy;
   (b) a leasehold property on a five-year non-renewable lease;
   (c) a courtesy minibus;
   (d) a microcomputer;
   (e) computer software.

3. Two brothers decided to go into business as suppliers to the catering industry buying and selling ice-making machines. Details of their transactions are set out below.

   They initially bought 100 machines at £200 each and a delivery van for £6000. At the end of six months they had sold 80 of the 100 machines for £300 each. Unfortunately the machine manufacturer had during that time increased the price to £250 each and this was their only source of supply. To make matters worse a competitor had come into the area and was selling the same machines at £280 each. The brothers found that on average over the six months they had incurred costs for advertising, petrol, etc., which amounted to £20 for each machine sold.

   On the basis of the information above, calculate what the brothers' wealth was at the start and end of the six months and what profit had been made.

4. Having calculated the profit for the first six months in problem 3, discuss whether the profit figure is a useful benchmark for measuring the performance of the business, and also whether it is useful as a guide to future profitability.

The measurement of wealth | 3

INTRODUCTION

In Chapter 1 we discussed the objectives of accounting reports, and the influence of users on financial reporting. We also discussed the limitations of accounting information and the role of accounting in business, its effect on business and some of the factors which influence accounting. In Chapter 2 we examined some possible approaches to income measurement from the point of view both of the economist and of the accountant. We will now extend that work to look more specifically at the ways in which accountants actually measure wealth and income.

We suggested that the problem facing accountants is that of finding an appropriate basis for the measurement of wealth. There is also the additional problem that with the complexity involved in the real world a system that only measures wealth and derives income therefrom will not be able to cope with the complexity of present-day enterprises. Consider the problem of a large hospitality group such as Forte plc having to carry out a valuation of all their premises, vehicles, stocks, etc., on one day of the year. The costs of such an operation would make it prohibitively expensive even if it were logistically possible. For companies such as Hanson Trust where operations are carried out on a world-wide basis these logistical problems would be even greater. Such a system would also lead to problems because management or the owners would not be able to make decisions on a day-to-day basis as they would only have information at hand once a year. Because of these problems with annual valuation systems we need to find separate ways of measuring wealth and income.

The measurement of income will be dealt with in detail in Chapter 4. In this chapter we concentrate on the problem of the measurement of wealth and the way in which accounting approaches that problem. We shall look in some detail at the use of the balance sheet as the measure of wealth, at its component parts such as assets and liabilities, and finally at the format in which the balance sheet is presented and the way in which that is influenced by the type of organization, the environment and the needs of the users.

THE MEASUREMENT OF WEALTH

In the case of an individual, we have illustrated that wealth can be found by simply listing the items you own, assuming of course that you don't owe anybody money as this will clearly reduce your wealth. To some extent the same can be said for an enterprise although the level of complexity will of course be greater. The way in which this is done for an enterprise is similar to that for an individual but the resulting statement is called a balance sheet. You should note that the balance sheet relates to a position at one point in time. It is because of this that the analogy to a snapshot is often found in accounting textbooks.

> **Key concept**
>
> *The balance sheet*
>
> The balance sheet is a statement, at one point in time, which shows all the items (assets) owned by the enterprise and all the amounts owed by the enterprise (liabilities).

The definition given in this Key Concept is not intended to be comprehensive – it merely provides us with a basic idea of what we are talking about. Before looking at the balance sheet in more detail it is important to appreciate that, although an enterprise does not exist in the same way as a person, for accounting and for some legal purposes an enterprise is presumed to exist in its own right. It is therefore treated as a separate entity from the person or persons who own or operate it. In broad terms it is possible to account for any unit which has a separate and distinct focus. It may be that this is a hotel or a group of hotels or a more complex organization such as Forte plc. This idea of a separate entity is often referred to in accounting literature as the **business entity principle**. It applies equally to organizations that are not commonly referred to as businesses such as charitable organizations, clubs and societies. The question of whether the entity should be accounted for separately is related to the question of whether it can be seen to have a separate focus as well as the legal situation.

> **Key concept**
>
> *The business entity principle*
>
> The business entity principle states that transactions, assets and liabilities that relate to the enterprise are accounted for separately. It applies to all types of enterprise irrespective of the fact that the enterprise may not be recognized as a separate legal or taxable entity.

Whilst the application of this principle and the reasons for it are fairly self-evident when we are looking at large public companies such as British Airways or Virgin Atlantic, they are less clear with smaller enterprises such as the corner fish and chip shop or a small-scale bed-and-breakfast business. If, for example, you decided to set yourself up letting a few rooms on a bed-and-breakfast basis, for accounting purposes the furniture purchased for those rooms and the money earned as a result of that activity would be treated separately from your own personal furniture and money. This allows the tax authorities to tax you separately on the profits from your business and it also helps you to arrive at the value of your business should you wish at some stage to sell it or take in a partner. The important point to remember is that for each business entity it is possible to account separately and therefore for each entity we can draw up a balance sheet at any point in time. We will now examine balance sheets in more detail.

IMPORTANCE OF BALANCE SHEETS

The purpose of a balance sheet is to communicate information about the financial position of an enterprise at a particular point in time. It summarizes information contained in the accounting records in a clear and intelligible form. If the items contained in it are summarized and classified in an appropriate manner it can give information about the financial strength of the enterprise and indicate the relative liquidity of the assets.

> ### Key concept
>
> *Liquidity*
>
> Liquidity refers to the ease with which assets can be converted to cash in the normal course of business.

It should also give information about the liabilities of the enterprise, i.e. what the enterprise owes, and when these amounts will fall due. The combination of this information can assist the user in evaluating the financial position of the enterprise.

It should be remembered, however, that the financial statements are only one part of the information needed by users and as such the importance of the balance sheet should not be overemphasized.

In the vast majority of cases enterprises draw up a balance sheet at least once a year. It could be done more frequently, of course, or indeed less frequently, although convention dictates that a normal accounting period is a year and tax and other legislation is set up on that basis. It should also be remembered that because the balance sheet represents the position at one point in time its usefulness is limited as the situation may have changed since the last balance sheet was drawn up. For instance, you may draw up a balance sheet every December so if you looked at the balance sheet in October it would be ten months out of date. It may be helpful to extend our earlier analogy and picture a business as a movie and a balance sheet as a still from that movie. Clearly in the case of a movie the still does not give a complete picture and the same can be said for the balance sheet.

We now need to know what balance sheets contain. We have already said that they are similar to an individual's own measurement of wealth. Therefore if you think how you would measure your own wealth you will realize that you need to make a list of what you own (assets) and take away from that what you owe (liabilities). For an enterprise this listing of assets and liabilities at a particular point in time is in fact the enterprise's balance sheet.

Given this information about the contents of a balance sheet, let us look in more detail at what is meant by assets and liabilities. We shall start with assets and consider what constitutes an asset and how assets are classified.

ASSETS

Although we can find many definitions of assets, some of these are less useful than others, and although most contain some of the vital elements of a useful description, a clear working definition is needed. For our purposes we have taken the one provided by R.M. Lall (1968), whose definition is given in the Key Concept below.

Key concept

Definition of an asset

Embodiments of present or future economic benefits or service potentials measurable in terms of monetary units, accruing to the enterprise as a result of economic events, the enjoyment of which by the enterprise is secured by law.

This definition is not dissimilar to that adopted by the accountancy profession and included in international accounting standards. We will now examine its various components in order to make the nature of an asset somewhat clearer.

Future benefits – service potentials

The clear implication in the terms 'future benefits' and 'service potentials' is that, in order to be an asset, there must be some clear expectation that some benefit will be derived by the enterprise either now or in the future. This implies that the item must have some specific useful-ness to the enterprise. An item that has no specific usefulness for the enterprise is therefore not an asset. This is particularly important in times of rapidly changing technology as it suggests that the question of what is and what is not an asset can only be decided on the basis of its usefulness to the enterprise. A good example of the effects of rapidly changing technology has been the impact on office equipment where manual typewriters were superseded by electric and they have in turn been superseded by word processors and desk top publishing.

Similarly, in terms of usefulness, it is fairly obvious that a gold mine full of unmined gold is an asset for a mining business. However, there will come a point where all the gold has been removed and all that is left is a hole in the ground. The hole in the ground is no longer useful to the mining enterprise and as such it ceases to be an asset. However, for a different type of enterprise, e.g. a rubbish disposal business, a hole in the ground is useful. We can therefore conclude that in order to be classified as an asset an item must be useful to the enterprise itself.

Measurable in monetary units

In certain circumstances enterprises may gain future benefits from items which may be impossible or difficult to measure in monetary units. For example, a producer of jams may be able to advertise that they are jam-makers 'By Appointment'. The fact that they have a Royal Appointment may well increase their profits and as such being 'By Appointment' has a benefit to the business. The problem facing accountants is, having decided there is a future benefit, how is that benefit to be measured in monetary terms? In this particular example it would be almost impossible to isolate the effect that the Royal Appointment has in monetary terms and therefore we do not include it in the balance sheet as an asset even though the business is clearly getting a benefit from it. Other examples of items which are clearly of benefit but which are not included for accounting purposes could be a good location, a highly motivated workforce or a reputation for excel-lent service. You will remember from Chapter 1 that we discussed this problem in the context of the limitations of accounting information.

Legal ownership

Many definitions of assets imply that in order to be an asset something must be owned. In reality most assets are owned; however, the asser-tion that ownership is a precondition for the recognition of an asset by an enterprise is not strictly true. For example, a rental agreement for a house entitling you to occupy the house at a rent of £20 a week obviously confers a benefit if the market rental is, say, £90 a week and thus may be seen as an asset. On the other hand, the fact that an individual or enterprise owns an item does not necessarily mean there is any future benefit to be obtained. For example, an old motor car that has failed the MOT test may cease to be an asset, and in fact, unless it can be driven to the breakers yard, it may become a liability.

Accruing to an enterprise

Whilst it may seem patently obvious that the benefits should accrue to the enterprise, i.e. be received by the enterprise at some point in time, it is vital in many cases to be able to separate out the assets of the enterprise from those of the owner for reasons referred to earlier. For example, a factory building is likely to be an enterprise asset as the benefits from its use are likely to accrue to an enterprise. However, if the enterprise is a small restaurant with residential accommodation for the owners above, it is somewhat less clear which part of the building is an asset of the business and which is not. In practice it may well be the case that some of the food and wine stocks are actually physically stored in part of the residential accommodation. There is unfortunately no general rule which can be applied and each case must be considered on its merits. The process of distinguishing between the assets of the owner and those of the business is merely an application of the business entity principle referred to earlier. In simple terms this principle states that the business should be viewed as separate from the owner and therefore accounted for separately.

FIXED AND CURRENT ASSETS

For accounting purposes assets are normally separated as far as possible into sub-categories. The reasoning behind this is that accounting statements should provide information that is useful in making economic decisions. These decisions, it is suggested, can be made more precisely if there is some indication given regarding the nature of the assets of the enterprise. The categories most frequently used are fixed and current assets.

Fixed assets

Although the term fixed assets is used frequently in accounting literature there is no precise definition of what constitutes a fixed asset. One possible definition is:

> An asset that is retained for use in the business and is not for resale in the normal course of business.

This definition suggests that the distinction relates to the usage to which the asset is put. However, the conventional distinction between fixed and current assets requires a further element relating to time and implies some degree of permanency. For example, it is generally accepted that factory buildings are fixed assets as they are retained for use, are not resold and will last for a long period of time. It is this latter element relating to time that is missing from the above definition. If we simply used the definition above hotel stationery would meet the criteria of a fixed asset. It is quite clear, however, that hotel stationery is unlikely to be even semi-permanent and is essentially a different type of asset from the factory building previously discussed. This may lead us to a definition that includes some reference to the life of an asset.

A definition that relates solely to the life of an asset, however, is not on its own sufficient. For example a fixed asset definition could be:

> An asset that will last for a considerable period of time.

This definition is deficient because it says nothing about the use of the asset within the business. Thus, for example, a washing machine would be classified as a fixed asset using this latter definition. However, there are clear differences between the way in which washing machines should be treated in the books of a launderette and in those of an electrical retailer even though the life of the washing machine does not change merely as a result of it being owned by a different business. This leads us to the conclusion that there are two elements involved in deciding what is and what is not a fixed asset, i.e. the **use** to which the asset will be put and the **life** of the asset **within the business**. This provides us with a working definition of a fixed asset.

Key concept

Fixed assets

An asset that is acquired for the purposes of use within the business and is likely to be used by the business for a considerable period of time.

Current assets

As with fixed assets the definition of a current asset is not as clear as might be expected. Some accounting textbooks suggest that current assets are those assets known as circulating assets, i.e. those which are part of the operating cycle. This does not really help as we need to know what an operating cycle is or what circulating assets are.

The operating cycle

It is perhaps easier to understand the term operating cycle if we look at one or two examples. In the case of a shop selling clothes the operating cycle may consist of buying garments and selling them for cash. In the case of a restaurant the operating cycle may involve more processes such as buying a number of ingredients, cooking them, serving them and then collecting the cash. The operating cycle has no fixed time period as this depends on the nature of the business and it may in fact extend over a number of years as would be the case with property development, shipbuilding and other heavy construction industries. In the hospitality business it is unlikely to be this long as the nature of the stocks held will necessarily lead to a short operating cycle. The fact that operating cycles are of different lengths is not vital as in general terms those assets that are part of the operating cycle are similar and these are likely to be items such as stock, cash in the bank, etc.

The realization period

Some accounting texts suggest that what distinguishes current assets from other assets is whether or not they will be realized in the form of cash in the current accounting period. By convention accounting periods are normally one year. If we applied this test strictly we would find that in certain cases such as the shipbuilder referred to above something that is part of the operating cycle will in fact not be realized in the form of cash within a year.

In practice the classification is based on both these principles. For our purposes therefore a useful working definition is that given in the Key Concept below which combines these two properties and therefore overcomes the problems inherent in using either on its own.

Key concept

Current asset

A current asset is one which is either part of the operating cycle of the enterprise or is likely to be realized in the form of cash within one year.

By looking at the definitions of fixed and current assets it should be clear that it is possible to think of some assets that a business might own that do not easily fit within either category. An example of such an asset is a trade name, such as McDonald's, a trade mark or a patent on a product or process which has been developed by the enterprise itself, e.g. Coca-Cola. A number of ways of dealing with this problem have been suggested. However, the American solution of coining the title indeterminate assets and including those assets not easily classified as fixed or current under that heading overcomes most of the main problems and is sufficient for our purposes at this stage.

Having looked at what constitutes an asset and the way in which assets are divided into sub-categories on the balance sheet, we can now turn to the other part of the balance sheet – what is owed, or to use accounting terminology the liabilities.

LIABILITIES

As with the general term assets a useful working definition of liabilities must contain a number of components. A suitable definition is that put forward by Bull (1984) in the Key Concept below.

> *Key concept*
>
> *Liabilities*
>
> The existing obligations of the business to provide money, goods or services to an agent or entity outside the business at some time in the future.

The definition implies that the liability must exist at the present time. It also implies that the date by which that liability must be paid is known. A simpler definition which is adequate for our purposes is:

Liabilities are what the business owes.

An alternative way of looking at them is to view them as claims on the assets of the business.

Current liabilities

Given that we have used a simple definition for liabilities we can also use a simple definition of current liabilities.

> *Key concept*
>
> *Current liabilities*
>
> Those liabilities falling due for payment within one year.

This definition is in fact in line with the heading under which current liabilities are shown in the published accounts of companies. A common example of a current liability is a bank overdraft which, in theory at least, would have to be repaid to the bank on demand. Another example would be where goods or services were bought on credit terms and the supplier had not been paid at the balance sheet date.

Other liabilities

Clearly there are other types of liability which do not have to be repaid in full in one year; an everyday example of this type of liability is a mortgage on a house. In the case of a business, however, this type of liability may take a number of forms such as a bank loan, hire-purchase, a commercial mortgage, etc. These may be repayable in three years, five years or longer. Liabilities of this sort are longer-term liabilities and are normally put under the heading of:

Amounts falling due after more than one year

OWNERS' EQUITY

The owners' equity can be viewed in a number of ways. In a sense it is a liability of the business in so far as it is a claim on the assets. However, it differs from other liabilities in that they have definite dates by which they are to be paid and they are fixed in amount. The owners' equity on the other hand is normally left in the business as long as it is required. Another way of viewing the owners' equity is as a residual claim on the assets of the business after all the other liabilities have been settled. In general, the owners' equity is normally shown under two headings, i.e. that which is put into the business and that which is earned by the business and left in the business. This latter category we will refer to as **retained profits**. In the case of the individual the equity could be seen as analogous with wealth, whereas in the case of a business this owners' equity is often referred to as **capital**. As we showed in Chapter 2, the amount at which this wealth or capital is stated is dependent upon the measure used to arrive at a figure for assets, i.e. historic cost, replacement cost, net realizable value, etc. It is therefore better to view owners' equity as a residual claim rather than as capital or wealth as the latter terms could be taken to imply that an absolute measure is possible.

Key concept

Owners' equity

Owners' equity is in one sense a claim on the assets of the enterprise. It is different from other liabilities in that the amount cannot necessarily be determined accurately. It can be viewed as a residual claim on the assets of the enterprise.

THE BALANCE SHEET EQUATION

As we have already indicated the balance sheet of an enterprise can be viewed as a statement of assets and liabilities at a particular point in time. Because the business is an artificial entity, by definition all its assets belong to someone else. This idea is summed up fairly simply in the balance sheet equation:

$$\text{Assets} = \text{Liabilities}$$

The equation above describes the balance sheet in its simplest form and must always hold true. However, it uses a very loose definition of liabilities and can be further refined to highlight the differences between pure liabilities and owners' equity as follows:

$$\text{Assets} = \text{Liabilities} + \text{Owners' equity}$$

This latter equation can be rewritten to highlight the fact that owners' equity is a residual claim on the assets as follows:

$$\text{Assets} - \text{Liabilities} = \text{Owners' equity}$$

Simple balance sheets

To illustrate the equation above a simple balance sheet may be constructed using the information contained in Example 3.1.

EXAMPLE 3.1

Nosmos – Part 1

Margo has decided that she is tired of working for other people and as she has some money of her own she has decided to open a 'No Smoking' restaurant, hence the name Nosmos. After looking at various alternatives she has decided to buy the lease on a town centre restaurant which has recently gone bust. She is also able to purchase some of the equipment etc. from the liquidators. Her total purchases are as follows.

	£
Lease of premises	7000
Kitchen equipment	1000
Freezer	300
Furniture	800
Glasses, cutlery and tableware	200
Wines and soft drinks	350

She also opens a business bank account and puts £250 into that account to cover day-to-day expenditure.

At this stage we could draw up a list of assets of the business as follows.

Assets	£
Lease of premises	7000
Kitchen equipment	1000
Freezer	300
Furniture	800
Glasses, cutlery and tableware	200
Wines and soft drinks	350
Cash at bank	250
	9900

We could also identify the owners' equity in the business as being £9900, i.e. the amount she put in. Thus the other side of the balance sheet – and indeed the accounting equation – would be:

	£
Owners' equity	9900
	9900

Before moving on it is worth thinking about how we obtained the figure for owners' equity. All we did was to list what Margo's business owned and then as it did not owe anything to anybody but Margo, the owner, we made the balance sheet balance by recording the amount the business owed to Margo, the owners' equity.

Let us take this example a bit further.

EXAMPLE 3.1

Nosmos – Part 2

As the business was just starting Margo decided that until the business got off the ground she would operate partly from home and use her kitchen for some of the food preparation and menu planning. Her house had originally cost her £60 000 in 1985.

This additional information, on the face of it, presents us with a problem as we do not know how much of the £60 000 relates to the kitchen or how much time the kitchen is used for the business. We do know, however, that the business uses some of the house and that the house is an asset; the question is whether it is an asset of Margo herself or of the business and if it is the latter how should we record it and at what amount. To answer this question we need to go back to our definition of an asset (see Key Concept on page 40):

> **Definition of an asset**
> Embodiments of present or future economic benefits or service potentials measurable in terms of monetary units, accruing to the enterprise as a result of economic events, the enjoyment of which by the enterprise is secured by law.

Bearing in mind the business entity principle, we can see from the definition that the kitchen is not an asset of the business as the business is viewed as a separate entity from the owner. It is Margo herself who owns the house and she also retains the legal right to enjoy the benefits from its use. Thus the kitchen is not an asset of the business, as the business has no legal right to enjoy its use. It therefore does not need to be included in the balance sheet of the business.

EXAMPLE 3.1

Nosmos – Part 3

Prior to opening up the restaurant for business Margo realizes that she
needs to buy a microwave if she is to be able to offer a wide choice.
She does not have enough money to finance this and keep enough for
the day-to-day running of the business. She identifies the microwave
she requires which will cost her £400 and approaches her bank which
agrees to make a loan of £500 to the business. She borrows the £500,
puts it in the business bank account and then buys the microwave with
a cheque drawn on that account.

We shall look first of all at this transaction and then draw up a new
balance sheet. The reason we have to draw up a new balance sheet is
that we are now at a different point in time and you will remember that
a balance sheet shows the position at one point in time only.

The actual transaction on its own can be looked at in two stages.

Stage one

The first stage is that she borrows the money from the bank. This has
two effects, i.e. it increases the business assets as the business will get
a future benefit from the use of that money, and it also increases the
business liabilities as the business now owes the bank £500. Thus
viewed on its own this can be depicted as:

Assets	=	**Liabilities**
Cash in bank + £500	=	Loan £500

Stage two

If we now look at the second stage where some of the money in the bank
is used to buy the microwave we can extend stage one and depict this
as:

Assets		=	**Liabilities**
Cash in bank	£500	=	Loan £500
Cash in bank	−£400		
Microwave	+£400		

We can see that all that has happened is that we have exchanged
one asset for another and the totals on either side of the equation have
remained the same.

Before going on to draw up a new balance sheet you should note an
important principle that we have just illustrated. The principle is that
there are two sides to every transaction. At the first stage the two sides
of the transaction were an increase in assets with a corresponding
increase in liabilities. At the second stage there was a decrease in one
asset with a corresponding increase in another asset. This principle is

often referred to as the **principle of duality**, which is essentially a grand sounding title for the principle that all transactions have two sides.

Key concept

The principle of duality

The principle of duality is the basis of the double-entry book-keeping system on which accounting is based. It states that **every transaction has two opposite and equal sides**.

We can now draw up the new balance sheet of Nosmos. Unlike the previous balance sheet this time we will classify the assets into fixed and current assets and group these together to make the balance sheet more meaningful. Another way in which we can make the balance sheet more meaningful is to order the assets in descending order of liquidity, i.e. the more difficult the item is to turn in to cash the less liquid it is. Thus the freezer as a fixed asset is less liquid than the stocks of wines and soft drinks etc. Similarly these are shown as less liquid than the cash at the bank.

You will also note that each of the groups of assets are subtotalled and the subtotal is shown separately. The total of all the assets is then shown, the fact that it is a final total is denoted by being double underlined. It is conventional to use single underlining for subtotals and double underlining to denote final totals.

Having classified and listed the assets of Nosmos we then show the amounts owed by the business subclassified into the amount the business owes to Margo, the owner's equity, and the amount it owes to others.

Balance sheet of Nosmos as at 31 December 1991

Fixed assets	£	£
Lease of premises		7 000
Kitchen equipment		1 000
Freezer		300
Microwave		400
Furniture		800
Glasses, cutlery and tableware		200
		9 700
Current assets		
Wines and soft drinks	350	
Cash at bank	350	700
		10 400
Financed by		
Owner's equity		9 900
Bank loan		500
		10 400

The balance sheet shown has been rearranged to emphasize the differences between the various types of assets and Margo's residual claim on the assets and the other liabilities. It should be noted that the balance sheet is headed up with the name of the business and the date at which the balance sheet is drawn up.

It is worthwhile, before you proceed any further, to re-examine the definitions of fixed and current assets and ensure that you understand why the items above have been classified as they have.

Having done that we can now proceed to examine the determinants of the format of balance sheets and the ways in which they can be used, together with their limitations.

DETERMINANTS OF THE FORMAT OF THE BALANCE SHEET

We shall now examine the purpose of the balance sheet and its limitations. We shall also consider some of the influences affecting the way in which it is presented and the extent to which this is determined by the type of organization, the regulatory framework and the users of the financial statements.

Purpose and limitations

The balance sheet is, in essence, a listing of the assets and liabilities of the enterprise or organization at a point in time. The fact that it represents the position at one point in time is itself a limitation as it is only fully relevant at that point. At any other point in time, as we have seen in the case of Nosmos, a new balance sheet has to be drawn up. This means that in order for the balance sheet to be useful it should be as up to date as possible, and that its utility diminishes the more out of date it becomes. Similarly, in order that it is an accurate measure of the assets and liabilities the values of those assets and liabilities should be as up to date as possible, and herein lies another limitation.

As we saw in Chapter 2 there are a number of ways in which assets can be valued, some of which are more subjective than others. The choice of value is in part related to the purpose for which the balance sheet is to be used. For example, if we want to know how much each item cost then the original, or historic, cost would be appropriate. If on the other hand we wanted to know how much each item could be sold for then the net realizable value may be appropriate. Alternatively if we wanted to know how much the business as a whole was worth it is likely that neither of the aforementioned would be appropriate. Partly because of the difficulties involved in choosing an appropriate valuation and partly because of convention accountants have traditionally used the historic cost as a basis of valuation of assets in the balance sheet.

Clearly in certain cases this has led to assets being stated at a figure which bears little if any relation to the current value of the asset. The most obvious example of this in recent years has been the changes in prices and values of land and buildings. Because of this one often sees land and buildings shown in published accounts at a valuation rather than at cost.

CASE STUDY 3.1

Surrey Group plc Annual Report and Accounts 1994

The following extract provides details of the company balance sheet as at 31 March 1994.

	Note	1994 £'000	1994 £'000	1993 £'000	1993 £'000
Fixed assets					
Tangible assets	12		103		103
Investments	13		5,840		5,604
			5,943		5,707
Current assets					
Debtors	14	321		320	
Creditors					
Amounts falling due within one year	15	24		55	
Net current assets			297		265
Total assets less current liabilities			6,240		5,972
Capital and reserves					
Called up share capital	17		1,813		1,520
Called up deferred share capital	17		5,429		5,429
Share premium account	18		2,513		2,246
Profit and loss account	19		(3,515)		(3,223)

Commentary

You will see the balance sheet classifies the assets between fixed assets and current assets. It then lists the amounts owing currently, to arrive at a figure of net current assets. This is followed by the other liabilities leaving a balance sheet total of net assets, i.e. assets minus liabilities (amounting to £6240 for 1994). This is then balanced on the other side of the balance sheet by the owners' equity, i.e. share capital and reserves.

This balance sheet therefore conforms with our equation on p. 47:

$$\text{Assets} - \text{Liabilities} = \text{Owners' equity}$$

The meaning of the various subheadings and classifications will be discussed in later chapters.

An allied problem to the changes in the prices of specific assets is the fact that the unit of measurement, in our case the pound sterling, does not itself represent a constant value over time. For example, you cannot buy as many goods with a pound today as you could, say, ten years ago. This once again limits the usefulness of the information contained in the balance sheet.

Influences on the format of the balance sheet

There are many influences on the format and content of the balance sheet. At one level there are factors relating to the type of business and the objectives of the preparers of the balance sheet. Then there is the effect of the size and type of organization and who owns it. Finally, and perhaps most obviously, is the effect of the regulatory framework which itself varies from country to country. We will consider each of these in turn and then round off our discussion with a look at the requirements of users and their impact.

The type of business and preparers' objectives

As we have already shown in some of the examples we have used, the activity in which the organization is involved can have dramatic effects on the classification of an asset as in the case of a car belonging to a car dealer where it is in stock compared to one belonging to a manufacturing business where it is a fixed asset. Similarly we have illustrated in the example relating to gold mines that what might not be an asset for one business would be an asset of another business undertaking a different activity. Apart from these cases which are to some extent reasonably clear-cut, the activity can have dramatic effects on the difficulty or otherwise of drawing up a balance sheet. Consider, for example, the problems of a football club when trying to account for star players – Paul Gasgoine may be a good example – or of a high technology business in trying to decide whether the cost of the patent on a new product is going to yield any future benefit when the state of the art is changing so rapidly. Similar problems can be seen in the hospitality industry: for example, how do you value a reputation, a world-class chef, a prime location? How do Disneyworld or McDonald's value their trade names.

Apart from the issues raised by the type of activity in which an organization is involved there are issues relating to the ways in which a business is perceived and the ways in which management would wish the business to be perceived. For example, research by Carsberg *et al.* (1985) has shown that the management of smaller organizations perceive that bankers are interested in the amount of assets available as security for a loan or overdraft. There is therefore a temptation to try to enhance the value of assets perhaps by revaluing the land and building prior to applying for a loan. Similarly in a number of cases where a business is in trouble the assets have been revalued in order to bolster the image of the business and to promote the impression of it having 'a sound asset base'.

The size and type of organization

One of the prime determinants of the content and format of the balance sheet is the type of organizational structure involved. For example, an incorporated business, i.e. a company, is subject to certain rules and regulations imposed by the state whereas a partnership or sole proprietorship has no such restrictions. A company has to produce annual accounts and file a copy of these at Companies House whereas in the case of a partnership there is no such requirement. Similarly a business that is part of a larger organization may well have to comply with the rules and formats of accounts that suit that organization as a whole.

The need to comply with organizational needs may also be affected by who owns the business. For example, a company operating in the UK which is owned by an American company would have to comply with UK regulations but would also report to its owner the US company in a format that complies with US regulations. If we contrast this with a business that is owned by two partners, there are no restrictions or rules imposed on the latter organization and the partners can decide for themselves what format the balance sheet should take and indeed how often it should be drawn up.

Another factor affecting the format of the balance sheet will be the size of the organization. In the example used we have assumed a very small operation and as such all the assets could be individually listed. In the case of a larger, more complex organization there will be a need for assets to be summarized under broad headings as otherwise the level of detail would be such that the user of the statement would find it extremely difficult if not impossible to get an overall picture.

Finally, although they are to some extent interconnected with the type of organization, we should mention the influence of organizational goals. Consider, for example, an organization set up for charitable purposes which may or may not be incorporated: of what relevance to that organization is a classification such as owners' equity? Similarly, if you looked at the accounts of your local authority you would not expect to see a heading for owners' equity or retained profits.

The regulatory framework

Perhaps the most pervasive influence on the form and content of the balance sheet is the state through the medium of legislation. As we have already indicated the format and content of balance sheets as well as the way in which they are drawn up is different in some respects in the UK and in the USA. Even within the UK there are different rules concerning the format and level of sophistication depending on whether the organization is a charity, whether it is a local authority, a company registered under the Companies Acts or a cooperative registered under the Provident and Friendly Societies Act. Even within these categories there can be different rules. For example, a small company may produce abridged accounts for filing with the Registrar of Companies. A public company, on the other hand, also has to comply with the rules and regulations laid down by the Stock Exchange. Additionally there are other rules relating to content laid down for companies by the professional accounting bodies which are known as Statements of Standard Accounting Practice and Financial Reporting Standards. Whilst it is important to appreciate that these differences exist the details of the differences are not relevant for the purposes of this introductory text.

Users of accounts

As we discussed in Chapter 1 there are a number of different users who may have conflicting needs in terms of their information requirements. To some extent the rules and regulations laid down by the state could be said to encompass some of these needs. However, those rules only lay down a minimum requirement. For example, whilst the Companies Acts require that loans and overdrafts should be shown, research shows that bankers would like to see details of the repayment dates of those loans in the accounts. On the other hand, the owners of the company may not wish to have that information made public. A similar conflict arises between the needs of managers who may wish to know what it would cost to replace an asset rather than be presented with a statement which shows them what the asset cost when they bought it, whereas the owners may wish to know what management has spent their money on acquiring and how much each item cost.

CONCLUSION

In this chapter we have defined the nature, purpose and content of balance sheets and highlighted some of the problems in drawing up such a statement. We have also introduced you to the wider context in which accounting reports can be viewed. It is important before proceeding further that you make sure that you understand the definitions involved and can apply them to real problems. As you have seen, the balance sheet can take many forms and clearly in a book of this nature there is no necessity to cover all of them. For the sake of simplicity therefore we will use one format initially and this is given below, together with an explanation for the choice of format. It is important that you understand the reasons for the choice of the suggested format as this will aid you in interpreting accounting information at a later stage.

Suggested balance sheet format

Balance sheet of 'Simple' as at 31 January 1992

Fixed assets	£	£
Land and buildings		200
Equipment		100
Motor vehicles		50
		350
Current assets		
Stocks of wines and spirits	200	
Stocks of perishables	20	
Cash in hand	110	
	330	
Current liabilities		
Bank overdraft	190	
	190	
Net current assets		140
		490
Financed by		
Owners' equity	100	
Retained profits	240	340
Bank loan		150
		490

As numerous formats are available, and these to some extent at least are dependent on the type of organization, we have used a format which we consider to be appropriate to an introductory level text. If you wish to look at other formats you will find them referred to in the further reading at the end of this chapter. Before following a different format, you should ensure that you understand the reasons behind the alternative format and you should consider whether the information given is as clear as in the format suggested above.

Reasons for choosing the format above

The balance sheet is headed with the name of the organization and the date to which the balance sheet relates. As we have already explained, a balance sheet relates to one point in time and that date needs to be clearly stated in the heading.

Within the balance sheet itself we commence with the 'Fixed assets' which are shown in descending order of permanence and liquidity, for example the land and buildings will probably outlast the motor vehicles. They will also take longer to sell if we wished to sell them as we would first have to empty them whereas the motor vehicles could be sold almost immediately.

The 'Current assets' are also shown in descending order of liquidity. For example, in order to turn the wines and spirits into cash we first have to sell them, whereas in the case of the cash no process is required. Note also that all the current assets are added together and a total is given.

A similar rationale applies to the 'Current liabilities' and once again these are totalled. You will find when using other text books that the current liabilities are often headed up 'Creditors: amounts falling due within a year'. This heading is taken from company accounts legislation but given the use later within that legislation of the term 'net current liabilities' it is considered better to stick with the term 'current liabilities' at present.

The next heading is 'Net current assets' and this is arrived at by subtracting the total of the current liabilities from the total of the current assets. If this figure is positive it indicates that, assuming a one-year period, then we should realize enough from selling our current assets to pay the liabilities due within one year. Obviously things in reality are not so clear-cut as we may need to pay large amounts almost immediately, whereas some of our current assets may take a relatively long time to turn into cash. Also there are certain types of business, for example some retailers, where the figure could in fact be negative. If it is negative then the term 'Net current liabilities' is used.

The final figure on the top half of our balance sheet is the total of all the assets less the current liabilities and this is the figure to which the other half of the balance sheet should total. You will see that this total is different from the previous totals in as much as it is double underlined. This is simply a device for differentiating a subtotal from the final total.

The other half of the balance sheet shows the way in which the assets are financed by long-term capital. It is again subdivided in so far as the loans are separated from the amounts due to the owners. Similarly the amounts due to the owners are separately classified between those that the owner contributed to the business and those that the business generated as a result of trading, i.e. the retained profits. As was the case with the other half of the balance sheet the liabilities of the enterprise are in order of liquidity in that the owners' equity is the last amount to be repaid after all the loans and other liabilities are repaid.

SUMMARY

In this chapter we have seen that a balance sheet is an attempt to show the financial position at one point in time. We have also introduced the idea that a business is viewed for accounting purposes as a separate entity from its owner (the business entity principle). From this starting point we have gone on to define assets, liabilities and owners' equity and look at the balance sheet equation. Before moving on to the next chapter you should ensure that you have understood what is contained in this chapter by working through the review questions and the problems given below.

REFERENCES

Bull, R.J. (1984) *Accounting in Business*, 5th edn, Butterworths, London.

Carsberg, B.V., Page, M.J., Sindall, A.J. and Waring, I.D. (1985) *Small Company Financial Reporting*, Prentice Hall International, London.

Lall, R.M. (1968) An enquiry into the nature of assets. *The New York Certified Public Accountant*, November, pp.793–7.

FURTHER READING

Students who wish to examine the regulatory framework in greater depth are referred to *Form and Content of Company Accounts*, Cooper & Lybrand, Financial Training Publications (1986).

Alternatively, looking at the annual accounts of a bank, a manufacturing business and a service sector business would also provide valuable insights.

REVIEW QUESTIONS

1. What are the essential elements of a useful definition of an asset?
2. What are the deficiencies, if any, in the following definition of an asset: 'Assets are the things a business owns'?
3. What are the essential elements of a useful definition of a fixed asset?
4. Explain in your own words the difference between fixed assets and current assets and why it is important to classify assets into subgroups.
5. Explain in your own words what a liability is, and the differences between liabilities and owners' equity.
6. What is the purpose of a balance sheet and what information does it contain?
7. In the chapter we gave examples of situations such as Margo's kitchen where the question was raised about whether the asset was a personal asset or a business asset. Identify similar examples that are likely to occur in the hospitality and tourism industries and state what test you would apply to them to decide whether they were a business asset.

PROBLEMS FOR DISCUSSION AND ANALYSIS

1. In each of the following situations decide whether the item should be classified as a business asset and, if so, suggest how you would arrive at a figure for inclusion in the balance sheet.
   (a) You are running a restaurant and have just been included in a prestigious list of the top ten restaurants of the year.
   (b) You have as one of your employees a world-famous chef who has attracted and continues to attract a high class of clientele. He has been with you for the past ten years and is extremely loyal.
   (c) You own the Savoy hotel in the Strand and are thinking of including the name in the balance sheet as a business asset.
   (d) You have just opened your own theme park and as you have some Disney characters in it you have decided to call it Disneyland and feel that the name should be shown in your balance sheet as it will undoubtedly attract customers.
   (e) You own Compass Airlines which is the largest domestic carrier in your country and you are considering including your routes which you were granted rights to under a government tender as an asset.
   (f) You have just been made the sole agent for a major package holiday company for the next three years with options to renew the contract if both sides are satisfied with the arrangements.

2. Prepare the balance sheet of Smallstays from the following information and comment on the position of the business as shown by that balance sheet.

	£
Freehold land and building	240 000
Mortgage on land and building	168 000
Cash in tills	500
Furniture, fixtures and fittings	43 600
Office furniture	2 300
Bank overdraft	20 700
Courtesy car	3 200
Bank loan	23 000
Owners' equity	?

3. In each of the following situations identify whether the item should be included in the balance sheet of Transport of Delight at 31 December 1991, and if so at what amount and under which heading. Transport of Delight is a tour operator specializing in Safari Holidays. In all cases reasons for your decision must be given.
   (a) A freehold shop bought in July 1991 for £88 000.
   (b) A mortgage of £50 000 taken out to buy the shop in July 1991.

    (c)   Brochures and publicity material which cost £8000 and office supplies which cost £200.

    (d)   Three jeeps each costing £16 000, which Transport of Delight ordered on 20 December 1991 but which were finally delivered and paid for on 2 January 1992.

    (e)   Shop fittings which were worth £3000 and had been bought at an auction by Transport of Delight for only £1500 prior to opening the shop in July 1991.

    (f)   A VW Golf costing £3500 which the owners of Transport of Delight had bought in November 1991 for their son to use.

    (g)   One photocopier which was rented from Office Equipment Supplies at an annual rental of £200.

    (h)   One fax machine which Transport of Delight had bought in November 1991 for £600.

    (i)   A bank overdraft which amounted to £6500 on 31 December 1991.

    (j)   Three large frame tents which Transport of Delight had bought for £1200 in October. One of these had unfortunately been badly damaged when there was a small fire in the storage area and is no longer usable.

4. Using the information in question 3 calculate the owners' equity and draw up the balance sheet of Transport of Delight as at 31 December 1991.

5. Jane owns a free house and has tried to get everything together ready for the business accounts to be drawn up. She has drawn up the list of items below. You are required to identify with reasons the balance sheet heading under which each item should be classified, and the amount at which it should be included.

    (a)   A motor car bought from a hard-up customer at a cost of £3500, the retail price of which was £5000.

    (b)   Pub furnishing which cost £4000.

    (c)   Optics and bar equipment which cost £1000.

    (d)   Freehold premises which had cost £280 000.

    (e)   The cost of refurbishing and redecorating the pub £2000.

    (f)   Stock of beers etc. which had cost £790.

    (g)   Toasted sandwich maker bought from the previous owner when the pub was bought. At that time the value was agreed at £200 but it was subsequently discovered that it was faulty and Jane has had to pay out £40 to get it repaired.

    (h)   A new washing machine and tumble drier which cost £600. These Jane tells you are used to wash tea-towels as well as doing the family washing.

    (i)   A television which is sited in the public bar and is rented from Radio Rentals at an annual cost of £96.

(j) Jane's own car which cost £4000. This is used mainly for business but Jane also uses it for the family when she can get time off.

(k) Customer goodwill which Jane reckons she has built up. She thinks that this would be worth at least £20 000 if she sold the pub tomorrow.

(l) A bank loan for £3500 repayable within three months.

(m) A twenty-year mortgage taken out on the property amounting to £184 000 has not been fully repaid. The amount still outstanding is £120 000.

(n) Takings awaiting banking and cash floats of £1300.

The profit and loss account 4

INTRODUCTION

We have already seen that we can measure profit by measuring wealth at two points in time. We have also shown that the way in which wealth is measured in accounting terms can be roughly equated with balance sheets, and we have looked at some of the issues arising from the alternative choices in respect of assigning monetary values to wealth measurement.

In this chapter we will be concerned with an alternative way of measuring profit: using a profit and loss account. Our starting point and approach is very similar to that taken in the previous chapter. We look at what a profit and loss account is, why it is important, why it is produced and what it contains. We then consider some determinants of the content of a profit and loss account and some of the issues that have to be dealt with when drawing up such an account.

IMPORTANCE OF PROFIT AND LOSS ACCOUNTS

Unlike a balance sheet which communicates information about a point in time, the profit and loss account relates to a period of time. It summarizes certain transactions taking place over that period. In terms of published reports the period is normally one year although most businesses of any size produce profit and loss accounts more regularly – usually quarterly and often monthly. These monthly or quarterly accounts are normally for internal consumption only. However, banks often request copies or make the production of such accounts a condition of lending money. The reason the banks require these accounts on a regular basis is that they need to monitor the health of the business they are lending to. They want to be confident that the managers of the business are aware of what is happening and taking action to rectify the situation if the business is making losses.

As far as owners and managers are concerned, if they want the business to flourish, there is little point in finding out at the end of the year that the price at which goods or services were sold did not cover what it cost to buy those goods or provide those services. By that stage it is too late to do anything about it. If the problem is identified at the end of the first month it can be dealt with immediately by putting up prices, reducing the level of services, buying at a lower price or whatever is appropriate to the particular business.

Clearly the profit and loss account is a very important statement as it tells you whether a business is profitable or not. We have all heard the expression 'what is the bottom line?' The bottom line referred to is the amount of profit made by a project, or business. By comparing that profit with how much wealth is needed to produce it, you can decide whether to invest in a business or undertake a project. Other factors which also need to be taken into account when making such a decision are the risks involved and your own judgement of future prospects. These will help you decide whether the return as measured by the profit and loss account is adequate. Therefore, it can be argued that the profit and loss account provides some of the basic financial information for a rational decision to be made. We should remember, however, that although most of us think of business as being primarily motivated by profits, this is not always the case. Many small businesses make profits which are unsatisfactory from the point of view of a rational economic assessment, but the owners' motivation may not be profit orientated, they may simply hate working for any boss, or they may value leisure more than additional profits. This is a clear example of the dangers of looking at accounting results out of context.

Having talked about why a profit and loss account is important let us now look at what it is and what it contains. We have said that it is a statement covering a period of time, normally one year, and that its purpose is to measure profit, i.e. the increase in wealth. It does this by summarizing the revenue for that period and deducting from that the expenses incurred in earning that revenue. The process is therefore simple but to be able to do it we need to look at the definitions of revenue and expenses.

REVENUE

Let us take a fairly standard definition of revenue and look at it in some detail so that we understand what it means.

Key concept

Revenue

Revenue is the gross inflow of cash, receivables or other consideration arising in the course of the ordinary activities of the enterprise from the sale of goods, from the rendering of services and from the use by others of enterprise resources, yielding interest, royalties and dividends.

As is usual with definitions, the one above seems on the face of it fairly complex. This is because it is trying to cover all eventualities. In most cases revenue is so obvious that it hits you between the eyes. For example, we would all agree that in a restaurant the revenue is going to be the amount that the meals are sold for, and in most cases that amount will all be in cash, or its equivalent, in the till. However, if we complicate it a bit more and we find our restaurateur supplies hospitality for the directors' dining-rooms of a couple of local businesses who settle their bills every month, then we find that in order to define revenue we have to not only include cash sales but also the other sales for which the restaurateur has not yet been paid. These latter amounts are referred to as 'receivables' by American textbooks or as 'debtors' in the UK. These debtors of course are shown in our balance sheet as assets because we will get a future benefit from them. We shall discuss the treatment of debtors in more detail in Chapter 6.

Let us develop our example of the restaurateur a bit further to illustrate other parts of the definition. Let us assume that, as well as supplying the local businesses who pay monthly, he also supplies his accountant with a regular hospitality service, but instead of the accountant paying cash the arrangement is that the accountant does the accounts for nothing instead of charging the normal fee of £520 per year. The restaurant's services are effectively being sold to the accountant; all that has happened is that instead of the accountant paying the restaurateur £10 per week and then the restaurateur paying the accountant £520 at the end of the year, they have simply agreed to exchange one service for another service. These services from the restaurateur to the accountant are an example of what is referred to in the definition as 'other consideration'.

At this stage we should have a fair idea of what revenue is and the essence is that it relates to goods and services sold. However, we need to be careful to ensure that we only include in revenue sales that are part of our normal business activity. To illustrate let us assume that the restaurateur sells one of his two restaurants. Should this be seen as revenue or is it different from selling meals? Clearly the answer is that it is different because without an outlet that part of the business will cease to exist, whereas one meal more or less does not threaten its existence. Thus we need to differentiate normal sales of goods and services from the amounts arising from the sale of what is essentially the fabric of the business. These latter amounts will be dealt with separately and we will explore their treatment in more detail in Chapters 8 and 9.

Finally, before leaving our restaurateur illustration, let us assume that having sold one of the restaurants, the restaurateur decides to invest the money in some shares or in the building society until such time as new premises can be found. In this situation the money invested, which is effectively surplus to immediate requirements, will generate additional revenue in the form of interest or dividends. This is a form of revenue which is different from our main source of revenue. It would, in this case, be shown separately but included in the total revenue for the period. In certain cases, however, the interest may be the major source of revenue, if, for example, the main activity of a business is lending money. Similarly, dividends may be the main source of revenue for an investment trust. This is once again dependent upon the nature of the business in the same way as we found that what was an asset for a rubbish disposal business was not necessarily an asset for a gold mine.

So we can see that, although broadly speaking revenue is synonymous in many cases with sales, the actual revenue of a business is dependent upon the type of business and the particular activity giving rise to the revenue. In the example we have used we have seen that in its simplest form revenue was equal to cash sales. However, for some business activities the distinctions are not so clear and this leads to problems in deciding what revenue relates to a particular period. This of course would not be a problem if accounting periods were the same as the period of a business cycle. For example, if a housebuilder takes 18 months to build and sell a house there is no problem in finding the revenue for the 18 months. Unfortunately, the normal accounting period is 12 months and, as we have pointed out earlier, management and others need information on a more regular basis than that. What then is the revenue of our housebuilder for the first six months, or for the first year? This leads us to the question of when revenue arises and when should it be recognized. To help in answering this we adopt a principle known as the **realization principle**.

THE REALIZATION PRINCIPLE

This principle is defined in the Key Concept below.

Key concept

The realization principle

The realization principle states that revenue should only be recognized:

- when the earning process is substantially complete; and
- when the receipt of payment for the goods and services is reasonably certain.

You may have noticed that, unlike our definitions which tend to be fairly precise and all inclusive, this principle is carefully worded to avoid too much precision. It is meant to provide some basic criteria which can then be applied to the particular circumstances. The final decision on whether revenue is recognized is in practice often a matter of judgement rather than fact. Before looking at an example, let us look at the wording used in the realization principle. Firstly you will see that it talks of 'process', which implies a period rather than a point in time; it also talks of 'substantially complete' which leaves the question of what is substantial: is it two-thirds or 90% or what? The principle also talks of payment being 'reasonably certain' – once again this leaves room for the exercise of judgement and raises the question of what is 'reasonable certainty' in an uncertain world.

Obviously if we sell services or goods to a reputable customer of long standing we are going to be reasonably certain that we will be paid. If, on the other hand, we sell services to a shady character then we may be a lot less confident that we will be paid. Rather than looking at numerous examples of this type let us start by looking in general terms at a production and selling process such as our restaurant, irrespective of the goods or services being provided, and examine the possible points at which we could recognize revenue in accordance with the realization principle.

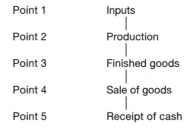

Point 1	Inputs
Point 2	Production
Point 3	Finished goods
Point 4	Sale of goods
Point 5	Receipt of cash

Clearly it is unlikely that revenue would ever be recognized at Point 1 but as we will see all the others could be appropriate in different circumstances. If we start at the end of the process, i.e. point 5, on the face of it, this seems to be a safe place to recognize revenue as the earnings process is likely to be complete and payment is certain because the cash has been received. In many cases point 5 is the appropriate point – as for example in the case of a restaurateur dealing only with cash customers. However, the restaurateur also had some other sales which were paid for monthly in arrears, so those may have to be recognized at point 4 as at that point the earning process is complete and payment is reasonably certain. On the other hand, if we take our housebuilder and used either of these points we would get a situation where there was no revenue for the first 17 months but a lot in the eighteenth month. Of course in practice, even in the case of our housebuilder, if there was a contract to build the house for someone then cash would have been paid on account. The point we are making here is that point 4 and point 5 are not necessarily appropriate in all cases.

One could argue that for a shipbuilder points 4 and 5 are inappropriate as cash is received throughout a contract and the point of sale is in fact before the production process starts. In this case, as a ship takes a number of years to build, it is also inappropriate to choose point 3 as this would lead to all the revenue arising in one year. Therefore it may in fact be that point 2 is appropriate if the earning process is 'substantially' complete and it is likely that payments on account will have been received. A similar argument applies to the cases of a property developer or building subcontractor.

From the discussion above it should be obvious that each case needs to be judged on its merits. You may, for example, like to think about when the appropriate time for revenue recognition would be for the following businesses.

- a local Wimpy Bar;
- a hotel with a fixed-term contract to provide rooms for aircrew from a major airline at a fixed price;
- a goldmine where all output is bought by the government at a fixed price;
- an aircraft manufacturer.

If you have applied the realization principle you should have had little problem with the first example but the others are more problematic and are discussed more fully at the end of the chapter. If you feel unsure of your own solutions you may wish to refer to that discussion before proceeding any further.

THE MATCHING PRINCIPLE

The problem of when to recognize revenue is very important because the profit and loss account is based upon the revenue for a period and the expenses for that period. Before going on to discuss expenses we should first discuss how we establish which expenses to include. This is done by means of the matching principle.

Key concept

The matching principle

We must match the revenue earned during a period with the expenses incurred in earning that revenue.

If we consider the matching principle we can see that expenses must be matched with revenue. Therefore, it is clear that the realization principle is of prime importance as it defines the revenue with which the expenses have to be matched. Thus if we include additional revenue then we must also include expenses incurred in earning that additional revenue. On the face of it this matching is fairly straightforward. However, there are a number of areas where problems may arise. These may be to do with timing (as we shall discuss later in this chapter) or a combination of timing and uncertainty as the facts in Case Study 4.1 illustrate.

EXPENSES

Key concept

Expense

An expense is an expired cost, that is a cost from which all benefit has been extracted during an accounting period.

Whilst the definition given in the Key Concept above is fairly straight-forward, it leads us on to having to define what a cost is. As you have seen in Chapter 2, there are numerous ways of arriving at a cost. However, for our present purposes we can say that a cost means a money

---

CASE STUDY 4.1

British Airports Authority plc Annual Report 1994

The following extract from the notes to the accounts provides information on airport projects:

> Airport assets include £7.62 m in respect of Terminal 5 Heathrow Airport where a planning application has been submitted. If consent is not forthcoming, the cost relating to this project will be charged to the profit and loss account in the year in which the decision not to proceed is taken.

Commentary

This extract from the accounts of BAA illustrates the problems of matching in conditions of uncertainty. In this case BAA have to decide how to treat development expenses associated with projects where the outcome is uncertain. Many organizations make speculative investments in the hope that these projects will provide future benefit. The problem is really whether an asset exists, i.e. is there future benefit to be obtained, and is that benefit reasonably certain? BAA will exercise prudence and write off the expense if it appears that the benefits will not materialize. The concept of prudence is explored in more detail later in this book (Chapter 5). At this stage the reader should be aware that accounting does not always involve hard and fast rules and thus judgement must be exercised as in the case of the realization principle.

sacrifice or the incurring of a liability in pursuit of the business objectives.

Some examples of costs are

- wages, which normally involve a money sacrifice;
- use of electricity, which normally involves incurring a liability to pay at the end of a quarter;
- purchase of equipment, which will normally incur a money sacrifice or a liability;
- purchase of goods for resale, which will normally incur a money sacrifice or a liability.

Although all of the examples can clearly be seen to fit our definition of costs they are not necessarily expenses of the period. For example, the equipment is likely to last more than one period so it cannot be seen as an expired cost. Similarly the goods bought for resale may not, in the case of a furniture retailer for example, be sold during the period and they therefore cannot be seen as an expense of the period for two reasons. Firstly, the benefit has not expired as we will be able to sell those goods at some time in the future. Secondly, they cannot be matched against the revenue earned during the period. There are other situations where the point at which a cost is incurred and the point at which the benefit arises do not coincide. These we will discuss in more detail shortly.

Before we do that it is worth emphasizing once again that we are dealing with a separate business entity and only costs relating to the business objectives can ever become expenses. This is very important as in many cases, especially with small businesses, the owner and the business are to all intents and purposes the same, but we are only drawing up accounts for the business. Thus if we find that a bill has been paid to buy a new double bed for a newsagent's business this cost is not an expense of the business because it relates to the owner personally not the business; obviously, if the business was a hotel, then it is likely that it would relate to the business. Personal items, such as the newsagent's purchase of a double bed, often go through a business bank account but need to be separated out and shown as withdrawals of the owner's capital rather than business expenses.

These withdrawals are often referred to in the accounting literature as drawings. We could provide numerous examples of these some of which are less obvious than others. For example, is the tax and insurance of the car a business expense if the car is also used for family transportation? The guiding principle, however, in making a judgement is whether or not the cost has been incurred in pursuit of the objectives of the business.

We shall return to the discussion of drawings later, but let us now consider some possible situations in which we have to decide whether a cost which is clearly a business cost is an expense of the period. There are three possible situations that we need to discuss. These are where:

- costs of this year are expenses of this year;
- costs of earlier years are expenses of this year;
- costs of this year are expenses of subsequent years.

Costs of this year are expenses of this year

This is the most normal situation and is also the simplest to deal with. It occurs when an item or service is acquired during a year and consumed during that same year.

Note that no reference is made to whether the item acquired has been paid for. It may be that it has still not been paid for even though it has been acquired and used. A common example is telephone calls which are only paid for at the end of the quarter. The question of the timing of payment is not relevant to the process of matching expenses and revenues.

Costs of earlier years are expenses of this year

These can be divided into those that are wholly used up in the current period and those that are partly used up in the current period.

Wholly expenses of this year

The most obvious example of this is the stock of drink in a bar at the end of the year. The cost of buying those goods has been incurred in the year just ended but at the year end the benefit has not expired; they are therefore assets at the year end. However, in the next year they will be sold and thus will become expenses of the next year. The process that has occurred can be illustrated with an example.

EXAMPLE 4.1

If we buy additional stock for our bar in November 19X1 but do not sell those stocks until January 19X2 and we have a year end on 31 December 19X1, then that stock of drinks is an asset at that date, i.e. 31 December 19X1 as the benefit is not used up. The cost has, however, been incurred in that year (the year to 31 December 19X1). In 19X2 the goods are sold and therefore the benefit is used up and there is an expense for the year ended 31 December 19X2 although the cost was incurred in the previous year. This can be seen diagrammatically as follows.

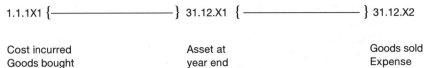

A similar situation arises when services are paid for in advance and are not fully used up at the end of the accounting period. For example, if the rent is payable quarterly in advance on 31 March, 30 June, 30 September and 31 December and the enterprise has a year end on 31 December, then the cost will be incurred in Year 1 for the quarter to 31 March Year 2. However, the benefit will be used up in the first quarter of Year 2 and thus the expense belongs to Year 2. The rent for the first quarter of Year 1 would, of course, have been paid in the December preceding the commencement of Year 1.

These expenses are normally referred to as 'prepaid expenses' and frequently arise in respect of rent and water rates. For an individual the most obvious example of this type of expense is annual subscriptions to clubs and societies, car insurance, road fund licence, etc.

All of these examples refer to costs incurred in the past which are expenses of the current year. Another category that needs to be considered is where costs have been incurred in the past and only part of the benefit is used up in the current year.

Partly expenses of current year

An everyday example of this is any consumer durable, e.g. a car, washing machine, television, etc. In all these cases the costs are incurred at a point in time but the benefits are expected to accrue over a number of years. In a business enterprise the equivalent of our consumer durable is a fixed asset such as equipment, fixtures and fittings, etc. The allocation of the cost of these items to subsequent accounting periods is called depreciation and this will be dealt with in more detail in Chapter 7.

Other situations for a business where a cost may relate to more than one period arise frequently. For example, if we assume that the car insurance on the business cars was payable on 1 July 19X2 then half of that cost would be used up and become an expense for 19X2 and half would be used up and be an expense of 19X3. The crucial test is whether the benefit has been used up at the year end. If not there is a future benefit and we therefore have an asset.

Costs incurred this year which are expenses of later years

In the last two paragraphs we have given examples where although the cost was incurred this year only part of the expense relates to the current year. In these cases some, or all, of the costs incurred in the current period may be expenses of future periods. Examples which we have already mentioned are car tax, insurance, business rates, etc. The due date for payment of these is unlikely to coincide with the end of the accounting period, nor would we want them to as this would lead to an uneven cash flow. Other examples are goods held in stock at the year end and fixed assets bought during the year. In the case of goods held in stock the whole of the costs are incurred this year but the expense relates to next year. In the case of fixed assets some of the expense may relate to the current period, if the assets have been used in the current period to generate revenue, and the remainder will relate to one or more future periods. A similar situation can arise when a cost is incurred this period which partly relates to the next period.

If we take as an example annual car tax we can see that if we pay for that in the current year 19X2 on 1 July then part of that cost will relate to next year 19X3 and will be accounted for as an expense of that period.

$$1.1.1X2 \ \{ \underline{\qquad\qquad\qquad} \} \ 31.12.X2 \ \{ \underline{\qquad\qquad\qquad} \} \ 31.12.X3$$
$$\text{Tax paid} \qquad\qquad\qquad \text{Tax paid}$$

$$\{ \underline{\qquad} \ \text{Expense period} \ \underline{\qquad} \}$$

Having looked at revenues and expenses we now need to recap on how these fit together in the profit and loss account before looking at a simple numerical example.

THE PROFIT AND LOSS ACCOUNT

The purpose of this statement is to measure the profit or loss for the period. It does this by summarizing the revenues for the period, matching the expenses incurred in earning those revenues and subtracting the expenses from the revenues to arrive at the profit or loss. This could be depicted as:

$$\text{Revenue} - \text{Expenses} = \text{Profit}$$

or:

$$R - E = P$$

Before going on to examine what the profit figure could be used for let us see how this fits with the measurement of wealth described in Chapter 3.

In Chapter 3 we said that profit is the difference between wealth at the start and end of the year, i.e.

$$\text{Wealth } 1 - \text{Wealth } 0 = \text{Profit } P_1$$

or:

$$W_1 - W_0 = P_1$$

The alternative way of measuring profit was to take expenses from revenue. We also said in Chapter 3 that wealth in accounting terms was measured by assets minus liabilities. The resultant figure, i.e. the residual, was referred to as the owners' equity. Thus we said that at a point in time T_0 the owners' equity is:

$$\text{Assets } T_0 - \text{Liabilities } T_0 = \text{Owners' equity } T_0$$

If we add to the owners' equity at T_0 the profit for the period T_0 to T_1 then the resultant figure will be our wealth at T_1 which will equal our assets minus liabilities at T_1, i.e.

$$\text{Assets at } T_1 - \text{Liabilities at } T_1 = \text{Owners' equity at } T_0 \pm \text{Profit}$$

or:

$$A\,T_1 - L\,T_1 = OE\,T_0 \pm (R - E)$$

This shows us that there is a relationship between the profit and loss account and balance sheet. The nature of that relationship will become clearer in Chapter 5. However, let us now look at an example of a profit and loss account and then consider what it is used for, its format and its limitations. In Example 4.2 we use the following transactions of Bradies, a local cafe, and see what should go into the profit and loss account for the year to 31 December 1990.

EXAMPLE 4.2

Bradies

Bradies is a small cafe situated near the main wholesale market and catering for the early morning and breakfast trade. It was set up at the start of the year. Its transactions for 1990 its first year are summarized below.

Dates	Description	Amount
		£
1 January	Purchase of freehold premises	80 000
1 January	Insurance of premises for year	2 000
1 March	Estate car purchased	8 000
1 March	Car – tax and insurance for a year	300
1 July	Purchase of sewing machine	300
Various	Wages to general help for the year	9 000
	Provisions used during the year	12 000
	Provisions held at the year end	200
	Cash takings	30 000
	Motor expenses and petrol	1 200
	Money withdrawn by Brady	6 000

Let us first consider each of these transactions in detail.

- **Purchase of freehold**. The benefit arising from this cost has clearly not expired during the period although some part of the benefit may have been used up. At this stage we will not try to measure the part used up but we should bear in mind that at a later stage we will need to make such allocations.
- **Insurance of premises**. This is clearly a cost and an expense of the year in question and should be included in the profit and loss account.

- **Purchase of estate car**. As with the freehold shop the benefit is likely to be available over many periods and we should theoretically allocate to the profit and loss account for the year the amount of the benefit used up. This allocation is done by means of a depreciation charge which we will deal with later in this book. At this stage therefore we will merely note the idea that an allocation should be made. This of course assumes that the estate car is being used for business rather than private use.
- **Car – tax and insurance**. This was paid for in advance on 1 March for a full year. At the end of our accounting period, i.e. 31 December, we will have used ten months' insurance and tax, i.e. 10/12 of the total. The expense for the period therefore is 10/12 of £300, i.e. £250. The remaining £50 relates to the next year and is an asset at the end of the year as the business will receive some future benefit. This and similar items are discussed in more detail in Chapter 6.
- **Purchase of sewing machine**. We know that Bradies is a cafe; it is therefore highly unlikely that the sewing machine was bought for use by the business although it has been paid for out of the business bank account. This is not therefore an expense of the business nor is it an asset of the business as the business will not get any future benefit. It is, in effect, a withdrawal of capital by the owner and should be treated as drawings.
- **Wages for year**. This is clearly a business expense as the wages are paid to the general assistant and the benefit has been used up. From the information we have, the whole £9000 relates to the accounting period and therefore the expense charged to the profit and loss should be £9000.
- **Provisions used during the year**. These provisions, we assume, have been consumed by customers; we therefore no longer have them and will not get any future benefit from them. Thus the whole of the £12 000 is an expired benefit and as such should be charged as an expense in the current year's profit and loss account.
- **Provisions held at the year end**. These provisions are still held by the business at the end of the year. The benefit from these is still to come in the form of cash when they are sold. These provisions held in stock are therefore an asset rather than an expense of the period we are dealing with. Note that the test being applied is whether there is a future benefit or whether the benefit is past. If the former is the case there is an asset; if it is the latter situation then there is an expense.
- **Cash takings**. This is the revenue of the business for the year and as far as we can tell it is the only revenue. The full amount of £30 000 should be shown as sales revenue in the profit and loss account.
- **Motor expenses and petrol**. Once again as the benefit from these has expired the whole of the £1200 should therefore be charged as an expense to the current year's profit and loss account.
- **Money withdrawn by Brady**. Given the present information we cannot categorically say whether this is a business expense or not. If it

is in effect wages for Brady's work it could be argued that it is a genuine business expense. If, on the other hand, it has simply been withdrawn because Brady has decided to buy a new boat for personal use then it is clearly drawings. For the present we will classify it as drawings.

We can now draw up the profit and loss account of Bradies for the year ended 31 December 1990.

Profit and loss account of Bradies for the year ended 31 December 1990

	£	£
Sales revenue		30 000
Cost of provisions used		12 000
Gross profit		18 000
Premises insurance	2000	
Car tax and insurance	250	
Wages	9000	
Motor expenses	1200	12 450
Net profit		5 550

You will notice that we have shown a gross profit and a net profit. Gross profit can be defined as:

Sales less cost of goods sold.

Net profit can be defined as:

Gross profit less operating costs, administrative costs and other charges.

The reason for showing a gross profit is to enable Brady to see that the business is doing as well as it should. Most retail businesses know what percentage of the selling price is profit and what is cost. Brady, for example, has costs of 40% of the selling price and would expect a gross profit margin of 60% of the selling price. If next year the gross profit margin was only 50% Brady would want to know why. The answer must lie with either the sales figure, i.e. the price of meals etc. has been reduced, or all sales have not been included. This latter is very difficult to control in a cash business. Another explanation could be that the cost of provisions used has increased because the price from the suppliers has risen or there are provisions for private use included. In many businesses it could also be that the end of year stock has been incorrectly calculated thus allocating more of the total purchases to the year than should be the case. In the particular example we have chosen, this is unlikely to be the case due to the perishable nature of most of the stock held.

The net profit figure, as can be seen from the definition above, can be affected by numerous expenses. It is the figure often referred to as the bottom line. You may see sets of accounts in which the owners' drawings are deducted from this figure to arrive at a figure of profit retained in the business. The reason for not taking drawings off the net profit figure is similar to the argument for the use of the gross profit. A business will normally incur similar expenses year to year, i.e. Brady will probably need an assistant next year, will have to pay insurance, etc. These amounts will be reasonably constant and the net profit as a percentage of sales should therefore be reasonably constant. The owners' drawings on the other hand may fluctuate widely from year to year and therefore to include these in the calculation of net profit would mean that the net profit would fluctuate widely as well. This would make any analysis of the performance of the business more difficult than if the drawings are taken after the net profit has been determined.

DETERMINANTS OF THE FORMAT OF THE PROFIT AND LOSS ACCOUNT AND ITS USES

Unlike the balance sheet which represents the position at a point in time the profit and loss account tries to represent a series of transactions over a period of time. Let us look at what determines the format of the profit and loss as this, to some extent, determines its usefulness and its limitations. For this we will follow a similar format to Chapter 3 in that we will look at the type of business and the preparers' objectives, the size and type of organization, the regulatory framework and the influence of users of accounts.

The type of business and the preparers' objectives

To a limited extent the type of business activity will determine the presentation and context of the profit and loss account. For example, in the case of a small cafe type business such as Bradies, arriving at a gross profit figure may be useful but in a service business such as, for example, a hotel which is highly labour intensive, the revenue earned may bear little if any relationship to inputs of physical goods. Thus the type of activity has an effect on what is being reported and how it should be reported. Similarly the objectives of the preparers of information often has an effect on the profit and loss account. If, for example, the accounts are being prepared for tax purposes the owner may wish to reduce profit, or defer it to the next year if at all possible. On the other hand, if the accounts are to be used to borrow money then a healthy profit may be what is required to be portrayed.

Whilst we should not give the impression that the profit can be manipulated at will, it is clear from our discussion that there are a number of areas of judgement which allow slightly different results to be obtained from the same basic data. The extent to which manipulation is practised is often limited by the fact that there are a number of conflicting requirements which mean that manipulation of the profit one way for one purpose is detrimental for another purpose. It should also be borne in mind that the accuracy of the profit and loss account can only be as good as the information on which it is based. Thus if Brady only records every second meal served through the till the accounts will only record those takings that go through the till as they will be drawn up from till records and money banked.

The size and type of organization

As with the balance sheet a prime determinant of the content and format of the profit and loss account is the type of organizational structure involved. The content and format of the profit and loss account for a company is determined by the relevant Companies Acts as well as being subject to regulations imposed by the professional accounting bodies. These latter regulations are contained in Statements of Standard Accounting Practice (SSAPs) and Financial Reporting Standards (FRSs). Another important determinant is ownership in so far as a company may have to produce accounts that comply with both UK and US regulations, for example.

For other types of organizations such as sole proprietorships and partnerships there are virtually no regulations covering format. Because the profit and loss is being prepared for owners, who are also managers, it is normally the case that for these organizations the level of detail in the profit and loss account is greater than you would find in the published accounts of a public company. The reason for this is that the annual report as well as being a report on performance, also acts as a basis for management decisions about the organization. In a large organization the accounts for external consumption are only one form of accounts as regular profit and loss accounts are normally prepared for internal use by the managers and these internal reports will generally be more detailed than the reports produced for external users.

Finally it is important to remind ourselves that the type of organization and the organizational goals may make a profit and loss account less relevant and in some cases irrelevant. Should charitable organizations make profits, from providing nursing care for example, or is the prime interest in how any surplus monies have been used to further the aims of the charity? In many cases a different statement is more appropriate to the needs and aims of the particular organization.

The regulatory framework

As we said in Chapter 3 there are a number of influences on the format and content of the published accounts including the profit and loss account. In some countries a particular influence that is more relevant to the profit and loss account than the balance sheet is the taxation legislation. This is not the case in the UK but in some other European countries such as Germany unless an amount is in the profit and loss account it may not be allowable for tax purposes. This can lead to what, in effect, are not expenses in that there is still a future benefit to be obtained being charged as expenses in the current year in order to maximize the tax advantage and minimize the tax bill for the year.

Users of accounts

The users of accounts often have different requirements from each other. As we have said owner managers would normally require more detailed information. The tax authorities often require specific information to decide whether a particular expense is allowable for tax purposes. They may, for example in the case of Bradies, require details of the mileage done on business and the private mileage done in the estate car. Apart from these influences there is also the whole issue of confidentiality, whereby each business does not necessarily want its competitors, or indeed its customers, to know how much profit it is making.

SUMMARY

In this chapter we have identified what revenue is and explained two important principles, i.e. the realization principle and the matching principle. We have also looked at the question of what constitutes a business expense and seen that:

- expenses are not necessarily the same as costs;
- all costs must relate to the business before they can even be considered as expenses.

We have also pointed out that both the definition of assets and of expenses relate to benefits to the business. The important difference is that assets give future benefits whereas expenses relate to benefits used up in the accounting period. This leads us to a series of questions relating to assets and expenses which may assist in the correct classification of items. These questions may be summarized in the form of a decision tree as in Figure 4.1.

Discussion of recognition of revenue for examples in the chapter

- **A local Wimpy Bar.** The business is likely to be mainly cash based so point 5 is probably most appropriate.
- **A hotel with a fixed-term contract to provide rooms for aircrew from a major airline at a fixed price.** Clearly point 5 is too late as prior to this the earnings process is complete and payment is reasonably certain. However, in this case the sale of the services has taken place before the services are provided, i.e. when the contract was negotiated. Thus at this point the earnings process is not substantially

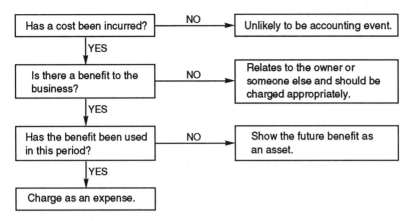

Figure 4.1 Classification of assets and expenses.

complete. The logical point to recognize revenue is therefore immediately after the service has been provided, i.e. after the rooms have
been occupied. If, however, the hotel has a fixed contract in terms of
the number of rooms and the duration of the stay irrespective of
occupancy, an earlier point may be appropriate. In this case the
revenue could be recognized when the rooms are due to be used
irrespective of whether the service is in fact used. This is the point at
which the service is provided which would not normally be appropriate for the casual guest.
- **A gold mine**. A similar argument could be applied here as the earnings process is substantially complete at the point of production and
payment is certain as the government buys all output.
- **An aircraft manufacturer**. Your answer here will depend on the
assumptions you have made. If, for example, you have assumed that
the aircraft manufacturer is making to order then your judgement of
certainty of payment would be different than if you assumed that it
produced aircraft and then tried to sell them. Similarly if you
thought of an aircraft producer as producing Boeing 747s you may
have thought of the production process as spreading over a number
of years in which case point 2 may have been your judgement. If, on
the other hand, you thought of the manufacture of light aircraft such
as Piper Cubs you may have assumed a shorter production cycle in
which case point 2 would not be appropriate.

FURTHER READING

Readers interested in pursuing the question of when revenue should be
recognized may refer to an interesting discussion in J.H. Myers (1959)
The critical event and the recognition of net profit. *The Accounting
Review*, October, pp.528–32.

REVIEW QUESTIONS

1. In your own words define revenue.
2. At what point should revenue be recognized?
3. In your own words define an expense.
4. How does an expense differ from a cost?
5. 'Expenses are always the same as costs for a period.' Discuss the truth of the above statement using examples to illustrate your argument.
6. What is the purpose of a profit and loss account and who would use it?
7. Describe the difference between an expense and an asset.
8. In what circumstances would it be inappropriate to recognize a cost as either an expense or an asset?

PROBLEMS FOR DISCUSSION AND ANALYSIS

1. Early in the chapter we produced a generalized five-stage model of the production process. Whilst that model clearly fits with a manu-facturing business it may be less appropriate to service industries. In each of the following situations provide a possible model of the process and the points at which revenue could be recognized:
   (a) the provision of hotel rooms;
   (b) a tourist attraction charging a flat, all-inclusive entrance fee such as a theme park;
   (c) a restaurant;
   (d) a travel agent selling package holidays;
   (e) a package tour operator selling directly to the public.

2. Flights of Fancy is a travel agency which deals with flights, package holidays and holiday insurance. When a customer requires a flight booking, a £50 deposit is required with the balance due one month before the flight. For package holidays a deposit of £100 per person is required with the balance due when the holiday is confirmed. In both cases the tickets are issued 14 days before the start of the holiday or flight and at that point Flights of Fancy becomes liable to pay the tour operator or airline. In the case of travel insurance no deposit is required but the whole premium has to accompany the final payment for the flight or holiday package.
   Discuss the point at which Flights of Fancy should recognize the revenue for each of its three services.

3. There are two partners in The Roadside Rendezvous, a restaurant and night club. They each have withdrawn £5000 from the business in cash during the year. A has also taken drinks and food which cost £600, and which had a selling price of £1000, from the business for

personal use. A has been paid wages of £18 000 and B has been paid £12 000 in wages.

Discuss how each of the above should be dealt with in the accounts, giving reasons for your decisions.

4. In each of the following situations, discuss whether the item would be included in the profit and loss account for the year to 31 October 19x1 and at what amount. The business is that of a 50-roomed hotel which also runs a restaurant and bar. It was opened a year ago.

(a) Receipts from room bookings paid for when the rooms were used amounted to £300 000 of which all but £2000 had been received in cash by 31 October 19x1 and the remainder was received in November 19x1.

(b) Money due from conference organizers for rooms provided during September and October on a block booking at a discounted price. This amounted to £22 000 and it was received in full by 31 December 19x1.

(c) Bar and restaurant takings amounting to £200 000 of which £1500 had not been banked at 31 October. This was banked the following day.

(d) The costs of the food bought during the year amounted to £40 000 and there was £1000 worth of food in the deep freeze etc. at the end of 31 October. All of this had been paid for by 31 October 19x1.

(e) The bar stock at 31 October was valued at £2000 and the costs of the liquor sold during the year amounted to £65 000.

(f) Wages paid in respect of the bar and restaurant amounted to £94 000 for the year.

(g) As regards the hotel the related wage costs were £96 000 which included the reception staff, porters and housekeeping staff.

(h) The manageress's salary was £30 000 and she was also entitled to a bonus of 1% of the takings from any room bookings over £200 000 a year.

(i) The owner who worked full time in the business paid himself a salary of £20 000 and also withdrew £5000 in cash from the business to pay a pressing personal debt.

(j) The motor expenses paid in the year were broken down as follows:

Annual road tax on car and minibus paid 1 January	£300
Annual insurance on above paid 1 January	£480
Repairs and petrol for vehicles	£600
Annual road tax on owner's car paid 1 June	£100*
Annual road tax on owner's wife's car paid 1 June	£100*
Annual insurance on owner's car paid 1 June	£120*
Annual insurance on owner's wife's car paid 1 June	£120*
Repairs and petrol for the owner's cars	£800

*The charge for road tax had gone up by £20 per vehicle on the previous year and insurance premiums had risen by 20%. All these charges are paid annually in advance. The owner used his car virtually solely for the business and had done so from when the hotel opened.

(k) The following bills were also paid relating to the year:

Electricity (payable at end of each quarter)	1 February	£540
	1 May	£450
	1 August	£450
	1 November	£600
TV licences	1 November 19x0 to 31 October 19x1	£500

(l) The TVs were on a rental contract which was paid monthly in arrears. Up to 31 October 19x1 there had been eleven payments of £800 made.

5. Based upon your decisions, draw up a profit and loss account for 19x1 using the information above.

Introduction to the worksheet 5

INTRODUCTION

In Chapter 3 we discussed the question of how we measure what a business is worth at a particular point in time by using the balance sheet, whilst in Chapter 4 we discussed the measurement of the profit for a period of time through the use of the profit and loss account. We also indicated that the profit could be measured either using the profit and loss account or by taking the increase in wealth over a period of time. Because of the complexity of most business organizations and the number of transactions involved we need to have a system from which the details for inclusion in the balance sheet and profit and loss account can be drawn. This system also needs to have some built-in checks and balances to ensure as far as possible that transactions are not omitted and to allow us to trace back to the original source any errors that are identified. To cope with these and other demands a form of recording known as double-entry book-keeping was developed. This system of double-entry book-keeping is based on a rule known as **the principle of duality** (see Key Concept on p.50). This was discussed in some detail in Chapter 3, and it was further exemplified in our discussion of the balance sheet equation which we defined as:

$$\text{Assets} = \text{Liabilities} + \text{Owners' equity}$$

We also showed that the owners' equity was increased by the profits made by the business, and we defined profit as:

$$\text{Profit} = \text{Revenue (R)} - \text{Expenses (E)}$$

We can therefore see that if the balance sheet at the start of the period is stated as:

$$\text{Assets (A) at } T_0 = \text{Liabilities (L) at } T_0 + \text{Owners' equity (OE) at } T_0$$

then the balance sheet at the end of the period can be depicted as:

$$\text{Assets } T_1 = \text{Liabilities } T_1 + \text{OE } T_0 \pm (R - E)$$

DOUBLE-ENTRY BOOK-KEEPING

From the above equations it should be clear that there is a relationship between assets, liabilities, owners' equity, revenue and expenses, and that with every transaction recorded we must ensure that there are two sides in order that the equation remains true. This may seem complicated but it will become much clearer when you see how the double-entry system of recording works.

Key concept

Application of the principle of duality

Applying the duality principle to our equation we find that, if we increase our assets, we must have:

either:	increased our liabilities;
or:	made a profit;
or:	increased our owners' equity.

In other words the principle of duality when applied to the balance sheet equation holds that both sides of the equation must always be equal.

We shall deal with fairly simple examples to illustrate the principles, which are the same no matter how complex the business. It is normally the number of transactions that is the problem rather than the complexity, and most large businesses – and indeed some fairly small businesses – have to have very sophisticated recording systems to deal with the thousands of transactions that take place during a year. This is of course one of the major uses, if not the major use, of computers in business today. Computers not only provide a vehicle for recording the accounting transactions but the more sophisticated systems will also analyse the data and produce reports such as balance sheets, profit and loss accounts and other reports tailormade to the particular needs of the users or managers of that business. For our purposes, however, we do not need to introduce a high level of sophistication to understand the principles involved and we can in fact set up a perfectly adequate double-entry book-keeping system using a spreadsheet approach in the same way as computer packages such as Lotus 1–2–3 use a spreadsheet. We will refer to our manually produced spreadsheet as a worksheet and we will use the worksheet to illustrate the basics of double-entry book-keeping.

The worksheet is set out in the form of the balance sheet equation with columns being headed up as appropriate to the situation. We will use the following simple data to illustrate the worksheet.

EXAMPLE 5.1

Peter started up a small business specializing in home-delivered pizzas. The first transactions that took place were:

1. To open a business bank account and deposit £3000 of Peter's own money.
2. To buy a motorbike for £800 cash.
3. To buy some ingredients for £300 cash.
4. To get a bank loan of £1000.
5. To have a pizza oven built for £2000 cash.

Each of these transactions have been entered on the worksheet (version 1) below and you should look at that whilst reading the description of what has been done.

Before looking at the transactions in detail let us briefly talk about the way in which the worksheet has been set up. You will notice that there is a column in which the transaction is identified and described. This identification and description in our case has been done via the item number. You could include a fuller description, however: the date, the invoice number, the name of the suppliers involved or whatever is appropriate.

After the column containing the description there are columns for each asset purchased and these are separated from the liabilities and owner's equity by a double space. Thus we have in effect across the top of our worksheet the balance sheet equation:

$$\text{Assets} = \text{Owners' equity} + \text{Liabilities}$$

Having made that very important point let us now examine each of the transactions in turn and see how they have been entered into our double-entry worksheet.

To make things easier the transactions are repeated and are followed by the worksheet and then by descriptions of how they are entered on the worksheet.

1. To open a business bank account and deposit £3000 of Peter's own money.
2. To buy a motorbike for £800 cash.
3. To buy some ingredients for £300 cash.
4. To get a bank loan of £1000.
5. To have a pizza oven built for £2000 cash.

Peter's worksheet: Version 1

	Assets				= Equity + Liabilities	
	Cash	Bike	Stock	Oven	Owner's equity	Loans
	£	£	£	£	£	£
Item 1	3000				3000	
Item 2	−800	800				
Item 3	−300		300			
Item 4	1000					1000
Item 5	−2000			2000		
Balance	900	800	300	2000	3000	1000

- **Item 1.** In the case of this transaction Peter expects to get a future benefit, therefore we have an asset. So we have opened a column for cash and entered the amount paid into the bank account. On the other side of our worksheet we have opened a column entitled
  owner's equity and have entered in that column the amount the owner, Peter, has put into the business – in effect the amount the business owes the owner. Before moving on to the next item it is worth noting that if we were to total up our worksheet we would have the figures for the balance sheet at that point in time. This holds true at every stage as long as all transactions up to the balance sheet date have been recorded.
- **Item 2.** For this transaction we have opened another column in which we have recorded the bike as an asset as it will give a future benefit, and we have also deducted the amount we paid for the bike from the cash column. The worksheet if totalled now would still balance and would correctly record that the business owns a bike which cost £800 and has £2200 in the bank.
- **Item 3.** Next we used some of our cash to purchase a stock of ingredients for the pizzas. We therefore need to record that our asset cash is reduced by £300 and that we have a new asset stock which cost us £300. You should remember that we have classified the stock as an asset because we assume that we will get a future benefit from it when it is made into pizzas and sold.
- **Item 4.** In this transaction we borrowed some money and put it in our bank. The amount in the bank is therefore increased by the amount of the loan £1000 and on the other side of the worksheet we open a column in which we record the fact that the business has a liability, i.e. it owes somebody money, in this case £1000. Once again if we were to total up our worksheet at this point in time we would find that it balanced.
- **Item 5.** This transaction involves using one asset, our cash, to purchase another, the pizza oven. Once again the pizza oven can be

viewed as an asset of the business as the business is going to get some future benefit. So all that is needed is to open a column for our new asset and show that it cost £2000 and reduce the amount we have in our bank by the same amount.

From an examination of the worksheet it should be obvious that every transaction involves two entries. For example, when the owner pays in the money an entry is made in the cash column and one is made in the owner's equity column. It should also be apparent that if all the columns are totalled the worksheet will always balance. If either of these points is not clear to you it is important that you look again at what has been done so that you understand both before moving on.

You may have noticed that in the worksheet all the transactions are ones that only affect the balance sheet. In order to provide a clearer understanding of the way in which the worksheet is used and how profit and loss account transactions are recorded we will extend our example by a few more transactions.

EXAMPLE 5.1

Further information

6. Peter hired someone to make the pizzas which Peter then delivered. The pizza cook was paid £250 for the month.
7. Peter sold pizzas for £900 in the month using up all the ingredients.

- **Item 6.** We can assume that when Peter paid the wages there was an expectation that there would be a future benefit because the cost of the ingredients held has increased by the amount spent on changing them from their original form to their final form. We could record these wages either as an asset in their own right or add them to the cost of the goods bought and call that finished stock. We will take the latter course in this example. Thus the entry we need to make is to open a column for finished goods, reduce the cash by £250, and record the £250 spent in the finished goods column.

  However, we have said that the cost of the finished goods is the cost of the raw materials plus the wages and at present we have only dealt with the wages. To deal with the raw materials we need to reduce the stock column by £300 and add that amount to the finished goods column.
- **Item 7.** Clearly we have some sales revenue here so we can open a new column which we will title 'profit and loss account' and in this we will enter sales of £900. We also need to enter the increase in cash of £900 in the cash column.

If at this stage we were to draw up a balance sheet it would balance and show us that a profit of £900 had been made. However, that would be incorrect because we have not applied the matching principle, that is we have not shown any expenses incurred in producing the sales of £900. We can try to identify these expenses directly as we know they consist of the cost of the ingredients and the wages, in other words the amount in the finished goods column. An alternative would be to look at each of our assets and ask ourselves the question: is there a future benefit to be obtained or has the benefit expired? If there is a future benefit then we have an asset; if the benefit has already passed then we have an expense. If we did this, in this case, we would have to come to the conclusion that as we had sold the pizzas represented by the figure of £550 in the finished goods column and had received the benefit from selling them in the form of £900 in cash, then these are clearly not an asset any longer and should be charged as an expense of the period. We thus have to make a further adjustment to our worksheet which we will call item 7(a). Our new worksheet will now be as follows.

Peter's worksheet: Version 2

	Cash	**Bike**	**Stock**	**Oven**	**Assets** **Finished goods**	**= Owner's equity**	**Equity + Liabilities** **Loans**	**Profit & Loss**
	£	£	£	£	£	£	£	£
1	3000					3000		
2	−800	800						
3	−300		300					
4	1000						1000	
5	−2000			2000				
	900	800	300	2000		3000	1000	
6	−250				250			
6			−300		300			
7	900							900
7(a)					−550			−550
	1550	800	0	2000	0	3000	1000	350

Before leaving this simple example let us extract from the worksheet a balance sheet at the end of the period in question and a profit and loss account for the period.

Balance sheet of Peter at the end of the period

Fixed assets	£
Bike	800
Pizza oven	2000
	2800

Current assets
Cash   <u>1550</u>
                        <u>4350</u>

Financed by
                          £
Owner's equity   3000
Profit   <u>350</u>
                        3350
Loans   <u>1000</u>
                        <u>4350</u>

A careful study of the figures in the balance sheet and a comparison with the last line of the worksheet will make it clear that the balance sheet is in fact the bottom line of the worksheet after appropriate classifications have been made.

Profit and loss account of Peter for the period

                          £
Sales revenue   900
Cost of goods sold   <u>550</u>
Profit for the period   <u>350</u>

You will notice that the profit and loss account is simply a summary of the profit and loss column in the worksheet.

If we consider what we have done in the example we can see that the system of double-entry is merely a convenient way of recording transactions in a logical manner. The system is not complex – all it requires is an understanding of addition and subtraction together with the knowledge that the equation must always balance. It also requires the application of our definitions to classify a particular transaction correctly so if you have had problems in understanding why a transaction is dealt with in a particular way you should return to Chapters 3 and 4 and reread the definitions.

ERRORS

Before going on to try an example yourselves it is worth spending some time reflecting on what we have just said by reference to the last example. If we look at any of the columns we can see that there is simply addition and subtraction taking place; a good example is the cash column where we make additions as money comes into the business and make deductions as money is spent. Another feature of the system that is not so obvious is that if we make mistakes there is an automatic check because in the end the worksheet will not balance. If this turns out to be the case we have two ways of finding the error: we can either do a line by line check to ensure that each of our lines balanced or we can total the columns at various stages to see where the error is likely to be. For example, if we had an error in the worksheet we have just done we could look at the totals after entering item 4 or item 5 or whatever. Quite often the error is reasonably obvious as the amount involved gives us a clue. The easy way to illustrate this is to put some deliberate errors into the context of the worksheet we have just completed.

Single entry error

Let us assume that we forgot the basic rule that each transaction has two sides and when we paid the wages we simply deducted the £250 from the cash column. Our worksheet would appear as follows.

Peter's worksheet: version 3

	Cash	Bike	Stock	Oven	Finished goods	Owner's equity	Loans	Profit & Loss
	Assets					**= Equity + Liabilities**		
	£	£	£	£	£	£	£	£
	900	800	300	2000		3000	1000	
6	−250							
6			−300		300			
7	900							900
7a					−300			-300
	1550	800	0	2000	0	3000	1000	600

You will notice that because we did not record the other side of the wages transaction the amount charged to the profit and loss account in respect of the goods we sold is only £300 and the profit is increased to £250. If we now add up the two sides of our worksheet we find that the assets side totals £4350, i.e. £1550 + £800 + £2000, whereas the other side totals £4600, i.e. £3000 + £1000 + £600. The difference between the two is £250 which, of course, should direct us to the wages as the likely cause of the problem.

Incorrect double-entry

Another common cause of errors is incorrect double-entry. In this case two sides are recorded but they do not leave the equation in balance. Let us assume, for example, that we had got the entry for the wages correct but that we had incorrectly classified the £900 Peter obtained from selling the goods as an increase in cash and an increase in finished goods rather than as sales revenue. The resultant worksheet would then be as follows.

Peter's worksheet: Version 4

	Cash	Bike	Stock	Oven	Assets Finished goods	=	Equity Owner's equity	+ Liabilities Loans	Profit & Loss
	£	£	£	£	£		£	£	£
	900	800	300	2000			3000	1000	
6	−250				250				
6			−300		300				
7	900				900				
	1550	800	0	2000	1450		3000	1000	0

You will notice that we no longer have a cost of goods sold which is of course logically consistent because due to our error we no longer have any goods sold. What we have instead is a worksheet that has assets that total £5800 while the other side totals £4000. The difference in this case is £1800, which is twice the amount involved in the error.

Addition, subtraction and transposition errors

Another common cause of errors is that we have simply failed to add or subtract correctly. The only way round this problem is to recheck all our totals and all our addition and subtraction. We can reduce the size of that task by balancing our worksheet on a regular basis so that we know where the error is likely to be. A similar problem is a transposition error where, for example, we recorded the total of our cash column as £5150 instead of £1550 – in other words we transposed the order of the 1 and the 5. This is a common error and happens to all of us. In this case we can identify that it may be a transposition error because the difference of £3600 is divisible by 9. This will always be the case if we simply transpose two figures, for example 45 as 54, 97 as 79, etc. Notice that although the difference is divisible by 9 it does not necessarily have the number 9 in the difference.

Before moving on we suggest that you draw up your own worksheet for the following set of transactions and compare them with the answer given at the end of the chapter. If your answer varies from the one given try to identify what you have done, e.g. misclassified an item as the purchase of an asset. When you have this you can then compare your explanation with our explanation of that item. Your entries do not necessarily have to be identical to ours as there are many different ways of setting up the worksheet and of arriving at the correct answer to show the position at the end of the month. We can illustrate this by reference to the example based on Mary's business which is set out below.

EXAMPLE 5.2

Mary decided to start a business doing the catering for company functions. She had saved up some money of her own but this was not enough to start so she had obtained an interest free loan from her parents. The transactions of the business, which were all cash, for the first month were as follows.

Day 1 Opened a business bank account and paid in £500 of her own money.

Day 2 Paid into the bank £2000 which she had borrowed from her parents for use by the business.

Day 3 Found suitable premises and paid four weeks' rent of £200 a week.

Day 4 Went to an auction and bought the following equipment: 50 complete place settings £300, table linen £500

Day 5 Bought an old VW Kombi for £900.

Day 6 Had publicity material printed costing £300 which included sending it out as a mail shot.

Day 8 Placed adverts in the local paper for three days at a cost of £240.

Day 9 Received her first order worth £800 for a function taking place in two days' time.

Day 10 Bought food for the function for £200 and spent the day preparing the food.

Day 11 Hired a couple of friends to help with serving and paid them each £20 for the session. The function was a success and she got paid her £800.

Day 12 Had the table linen laundered at a cost of £30.

Day 15 Received another booking for the next week. This time the price she quoted was £2000 as it was larger function.

Day 19 Purchased food and drinks for the function at a cost of £450.

Day 20 Employed a friend to help with the preparation for the whole day at a cost of £40.

Day 21 Employed three friends to help with the session for £20 each.

Day 22 Collected her payment of £2000 for the function.

Day 23 Had the table linen laundered at a cost of £60.

Day 24 Bought £50 of replacement place settings as some had been broken when loading the van after the function.

Day 25 Paid £100 for repairs to the Kombi.

Day 26 Placed a block advert in the local paper costing £180.

Day 27 Received bookings for five more functions next month at a price of £900 each.

Day 28 Decided that as things were going so well she would repay her parents £200.

Day 31 Paid the electricity up to date of £200.

To illustrate the different treatments possible let us consider the transaction on day 3 where Mary paid four weeks' rent in advance. The question arises: is this an expense or an asset? Let us consider the alternatives.

On day 3 it is reasonably clear that we have an asset in that we will get a future benefit in the form of the use of the premises for four weeks. On the other hand, if we are recording the transaction for the first time at the end of the month we can then argue that the transaction is an expense because at that point in time the benefit has expired. Thus we could record on day 3 the payment and an asset and then re-evaluate all our assets at the end of the month as we have done on our worksheet, or conversely we could wait till the end of the month and just record an expense. We would recommend at this stage that you adopt the former treatment for two reasons: firstly that it ensures that you re-evaluate all your assets at the end of the month, and secondly that shortcuts often cause more problems than they are worth if you are unfamiliar with the area.

Another transaction that is worthy of mention is the printing on day 6 and the advertising on day 8 and other days. In these cases a similar dilemma to that already identified with the rent exists. However, there is another problem in that, whereas with the rent we knew that there was going to be a future benefit, in these cases it is far from certain that there will be a future benefit. In other words we do not know when we place the advert whether anyone will reply to it and even if they do whether they will book a function. In these cases we apply a principle known as 'prudence' which basically argues that unless you are reasonably certain of the future benefit then you should not recognize an asset. This is similar to the rule for the recognition of revenue which we discussed in Chapter 4. Prudence, however, goes somewhat further as it encourages us to state assets at low values rather than recognizing an uncertain increase in value, and it suggests that if we think that there is a reasonable chance of a loss we should recognize that loss immediately rather than waiting until it arises.

Key concept

Prudence

The prudence principle can be summed up as: anticipate no profits and provide for all possible losses.

As you are probably beginning to recognize, accounting is not just about recording; it is also about exercising judgement within a framework of broad and often very general principles. The important factor to remember as you work through the example above is that you are making judgements and applying the definitions set out in the previous two chapters and you need to be aware of what you are doing and why you are doing it. You should now attempt to produce your own worksheet and extract a profit and loss account and balance sheet.

If your worksheet is correct the balances on the bottom line of your worksheet should be those in the balance sheet set out below. The profit and loss account follows the balance sheet and is merely a summary of the profit and loss column on the worksheet.

Even if you find your answer is correct, before proceeding to the next chapter, you should read the explanations for the treatment of the transactions on days 3, 6, 9, 11, 20, 24, 25 and 31 as these are of particular interest and will assist you in the future. If your answer disagrees with ours the full worksheet and explanations are given in the appendix at the end of the chapter.

CASE STUDY 5.1

The Zoological Society of London Annual Report 1994

The following extract is from Note 8 to the accounts and provides details of curtailment costs in anticipation of closure in 1992:

	1993 £'000s	1992 £'000s
A provision was made at 31 March 1992 for the estimated costs that would have arisen on the closure of London Zoo. The amount included provision for statutory redundancy payments, and liabilities for the early termination of contracts. Following the subsequent decision to rescind the closure announced on 17 June 1992, this provision has been reversed.	(1,110)	1,110
Provision for permanent diminution in value of fixed assets at London Zoo written back	(3,897)	3,897
Release of Grants for purchasing fixed assets written back	3,753	(3,753)
Net (Credit)/Charge	(1,254)	1,254

Commentary

London Zoo was facing closure in 1992 so a provision for closure costs was included in the accounts for 1992. This is another demonstration of the prudence concept being exercised. However, the Zoo managed to avoid closure so in 1993 the amendments to the accounts had to be reversed.

Balance sheet of Mary's business at the end of the month

	£
Fixed assets	
Equipment	800
Van	900
Current assets	
Cash	650
	2350
Financed by	
	£
Owner's equity	500
Profit for the month	50
	550
Loan	1800
	2350

Profit and loss of Mary's business for month one

	£	£
Sales revenue		2800
Cost of food etc.		650
Gross profit		2150
Expenses		
Rent	800	
Wages	140	
Advertising and publicity	720	
Repairs to van	100	
Breakages	50	
Laundry	90	
Electricity	200	2100
Net profit		50

SUMMARY

This chapter has introduced you to the worksheet and the concept of duality which states that for accounting purposes there are two sides to every transaction. We have also shown the importance of asking ourselves some basic questions regarding what exactly is an asset, an expense, etc. Hopefully we have also illustrated that simply by referring back to the definitions contained in Chapters 3 and 4 most if not all the problems you are likely to encounter can be solved.

We have also provided, by means of the worksheet, a simple vehicle for recording, checking and extracting a balance sheet and profit and loss account. We have shown that the basis of accounting is very simple as long as you follow the basic principles and for those times when you do lapse the system used on the worksheet should provide you with a simple and effective check. Finally we have introduced you to the idea that accounting is not a science, that it involves elements of judgement, and we have provided you with the 'prudence' concept as a useful tool to assist in arriving at your judgement.

REVIEW QUESTIONS

1. Describe in your own words what is meant by the concept of duality.
2. In each of the following cases describe the two entries required on the worksheet.
   (a) The owner pays £500 into the business bank account.
   (b) A cash till is bought for the business for £100 paid for from the bank account.
   (c) The business buys wine for stock for £200 paid in cash.
   (d) The rent of the premises for the first week of £100 is paid at the end of the week.
   (e) A customer makes a reservation for a party of 30 people for an evening at an all-inclusive price of £30 per head.
   (f) The wages of the employee amounting to £60 are paid.
   (g) The customer and his party have their party and pay the bill of £900 in cash.
3. In situations where doubt exists as to whether a transaction has resulted in an asset or expense, what questions should be posed?
4. If some doubt still remains how should a choice be made? Explain any principles involved.

PROBLEMS FOR DISCUSSION AND ANALYSIS

1. In each of the following situations discuss the potential effect on the business and suggest possible ways in which those effects could be reflected on the worksheet.
   (a) The owner starts up a new business and pays into the business bank account £1000. In addition it is decided that the owner's car will be used exclusively for the business. The car was purchased last year at a cost of £5000 but a similar one-year-old car could be bought for £4500 now.
   (b) A reservation was made for a suite of rooms for two nights at an agreed price of £800. However, prior to taking up the reservation the customer changed his mind and decided that he did not want the suite after all.
   (c) A customer who ate at your restaurant the previous night comes in claiming that he had food poisoning as a result of the meal. He had been with his partner the previous night and their bill had come to £48. The options available to you are:

(i) give the customer a rebate on the meal of £24 as his partner had no ill effects;

(ii) refund the full amount of the bill to the customer;

(iii) offer the customer and his partner a free meal of their choice.

(d) A guest staying at your hotel had booked for two weeks on your holiday special and paid the cost of £700 in advance. At the end of the first week she has to leave as her parents are seriously ill. The day after she leaves you are able to relet the room for the remaining six nights at the normal daily rate of £70 per night.

Your stated policy on cancellation is that if the room can be relet up to 80% of the moneys paid in respect of the cancelled booking can be refunded.

2. Seal has recently gone into business running a small guest house providing bed and breakfast. Details of the first month's transactions are given below.

Day 1 Opened a bank account and paid in £50 000 of her own money.

Transferred the ownership of her car to the business at an agreed price of £2000.

Obtained a mortgage from the bank for £140 000 and paid £180 000 to the vendor, the balance of £40 000 coming from the business bank account.

Day 2 Contracted with a firm of decorators to paint and paper all the guest rooms at a price of £1000 payable in cash immediately.

Day 3 Bought furniture for all the guest bedrooms for £2400.

Day 5 Placed advert in local paper saying that the guest house would be re-opening in one week's time under new management. The advert cost £200 and was paid for immediately.

Day 8 Bought furniture for the dining room and guest lounge for £2800 and paid in cash.

Day 9 Bought tableware, linen, cutlery, etc., for £800.

Day 12 Bought in stocks of food £80 ready for opening the following week.

Day 14 Opened the guest house for business and was able to let all eight rooms for the week at £30 per night per room. All the guests paid in advance.

Day 15 Banked the £1680 received from the guests.

Day 20 Replenished the food stocks at a cost of £80.

Day 21 Paid laundry bill of £40.

Day 22 Let all the rooms for the next seven days on the same terms as previously and banked the £1680.

Day 25 Replenished the food stocks at a cost of £80.

Day 26 Received reservations for two rooms for the following week.

Day 27 Paid laundry bill of £40.

Day 28 Drew £300 from the bank for her own wages.

Day 29 Let five rooms for three nights at £30 per night and banked the money.

Only one of the guests who had made a reservation arrived and they paid for three days as they had decided that they were only going to stay until the end of the month. As they arrived in the evening the money was not banked until the following day.

Bought enough food to last until the end of the month for £60.

Day 31 Paid the telephone bill £30 and the electricity bill £60.

Required:

(a) In each situation where there are two possible treatments discuss the arguments in favour of and against each alternative.

(b) Based upon the outcome of your discussions draw up a worksheet and enter the above transactions.

(c) Extract a balance sheet at the end of the month and a profit and loss account for the month.

(d) Discuss the performance of the business for the period as revealed by the accounts you have prepared paying particular attention to its cash position and its profitability.

APPENDIX: ANSWER TO EXAMPLE 5.2

Worksheet of Mary's business

	Cash	Rent	Equipment	Assets Van	Stock	= Equity	Equity + Liabilities Loans	Profit & loss
	£	£	£	£	£	£	£	£
Day 1	500					500		
Day 2	2000						2000	
Day 3	−800	800						
Day 4	−300		300					
	−500		500					
Day 5	−900			900				
Day 6	−300							−300
Day 8	−240							−240
Day 10	−200				200			
Day 11	−40							−40
	800							800
*					−200			−200
Day 12	−30							−30
Day 19	−450				450			
Day 20	−40				40			

	Cash	Rent	Equipment	Assets Van	Stock	= Equity	Equity + Liabilities Loans	Profit & loss
	£	£	£	£	£	£	£	£
Day 21	–60							–60
Day 21*					–490			–490
Day 22	2000							200
Day 23	–60							–60
Day 24	–50		50					
Day 24			–50					–50
Day 25	–100							–100
Day 26	–180							–180
Day 28	–200						–200	
Day 31	–200							–200
Balance	650	800	800	900	0	500	1800	850
Day 31**		–800						–800
Balance	650	0	800	900	0	500	1800	50

* You will notice that every time we finished a function we immediately transferred the cost of the food from our stock column to the profit and loss as an expense. This transfer was carried out because we no longer expected a future benefit and therefore we no longer had an asset. An alternative treatment would be to do this exercise at the end of the month.

** When we complete our worksheet it is important to review our assets and ask ourselves the question: are these still assets? If, as in this case, the answer is no then we need to transfer their cost to the profit and loss account as an expense of the period.

Transaction summary

We have set out below the transactions that took place together with the treatment of those transactions on the worksheet and, where appropriate, explanations of that treatment and acceptable alternatives. If there are any items that you still do not understand you should try to examine them in terms of the basic definitions referred to in Chapters 3 and 4.

Day 1 Opened a business bank account and paid in £500 of her own money.

Here we have created a business asset in the form of cash at the bank and have also opened an account to show the owner's stake in the business under the heading of owner's equity.

Day 2 Paid into the bank £2000 she had borrowed from her parents for use by the business.

Once again the business has acquired an asset as it will get a future benefit from the cash at the bank. It has also acquired an obligation to pay somebody some money and as such has a liability for the amount borrowed.

Day 3 Found suitable premises and paid four weeks' rent of £200 a week.

We have already discussed this transaction in the main body of the chapter. Our treatment has been to reduce our asset cash in the bank and to record an asset of the prepaid rent from which we will derive a benefit in the future.

Day 4 Went to an auction and bought the following equipment:
50 complete place settings £300
table linen £500

Clearly by paying out £800 we have reduced our cash at the bank, so that is one side of the entry. The other side is to record the equipment as an asset as we will get a future benefit from it. We have classified it as a fixed asset as there is no intention to resell and it is to be used in the business to generate future benefits.

Day 5 Bought an old VW Kombi for £900.

This is exactly the same as the previous transaction – we have merely exchanged one asset, cash at the bank, for another, a van.

Day 6 Had publicity material printed costing £300 which included sending it out as a mail shot.

You should refer back to the text for a detailed discussion of the reasons for our treatment of this item. What we have done is to apply the prudence principle and treat the item as an expense, charging the item to the profit and loss at the same time as reducing our cash at the bank by £300.

Day 8 Placed adverts in the local paper for three days at a cost of £240.

This is the same as the previous transaction and should be treated in the same way. We reduce the cash at the bank by £240 and charge that amount to the profit and loss account.

Day 9 Received her first order worth £800 for a function taking place in two days' time.

There is no need to record this as the earnings process has not started and therefore could not be described as substantially complete so we should not recognize revenue. If you have shown a sale at this stage reread the definition of revenue given in the previous chapter.

Day 10 Bought food for the function for £200 and spent the day preparing the food.

Clearly by paying out £200 we have reduced our cash at the bank, so that is one side of the entry. The other side is to record the food as an asset as we will get a future benefit from it. In this case it falls within the definition of a current asset.

Day 11 Hired a couple of friends to help with serving and paid them each £20 for the session. The function was a success and she got paid her £800.

In the case of the payments to the friends one side of the transaction is clear inasmuch as the cash at the bank has clearly been reduced by £40. The question that then arises is whether there is an asset or an expense. We have shown the cost of the wages as an expense because at the end of the day no future benefit will arise from this particular expenditure. Thus the £40 is charged to the profit and loss as an expense.

As far as the £800 is concerned this will increase the cash at the bank and we can recognize this as revenue as it conforms with the realization principle. We will therefore include that in our profit and loss column.

Finally we need to charge the cost of the food as an expense as there is no longer any future benefit to be obtained. Thus applying the matching principle we reduce the stock and charge £200 to the profit and loss account.

Day 12 Had the table linen laundered at a cost of £30.

This is a similar situation to the wages, although in this case it could be argued that there will be some future benefit from the expenditure. In reality what is happening is that the linen is merely being restored to its original condition and no additional benefit will accrue as a result of the expenditure. We therefore reduce the cash at the bank by £30 and charge it to the profit and loss as an expense.

Day 15 Received another booking for the next week. This time the price she quoted was £2000 as it was larger function.

The answer here is the same as for day 9 – the earnings process has not started so we do not recognize revenue yet.

Day 19 Purchased food and drinks for the function at a cost of £450.

This is the same as the previous purchase of food – we will get a future benefit so we reduce our cash at the bank asset and increase our asset stock by £450.

Day 20 Employed a friend to help with the preparation for the whole day at a cost of £40.

In this case it could be argued that there is a future benefit as the friend's work has hopefully enhanced the value of the food. Thus we decrease the cash at the bank by £40 and increase the stock by £40.

Day 21 Employed three friends to help with the session for £20 each.

This is the same as the transaction on day 11. The cash at the bank is reduced by £40 and the wages are charged to the profit and loss as an expense.

Day 22 Collected her payment of £2000 for the function.

Clearly at this stage we can recognize the £2000 as revenue as the earnings process is complete and payment is certain. The entries are to increase cash at the bank by £2000 and include it as revenue in the profit and loss account. In fact given that the payment was reasonably certain we could have recognized the revenue on day 21.

Day 23 Had the table linen laundered at a cost of £60.

This is the same as day 12 and the same argument applies, so we reduce the cash at the bank by £60 and charge it as an expense to the profit and loss account.

Day 24 Bought £50 of replacement place settings as some had been broken when loading the van after the function.

In this case there will be a future benefit from the replacement settings so we decrease cash at the bank by £50 and increase the asset by £50. If we now look at the asset we find that we have £350 included for table settings some of which no longer exist. So we have to reduce the asset by £50, representing the broken place settings, and charge that amount as an expense as the benefit has been used up in earning the £2000 from the function on day 21.

Day 25 Paid £100 for repairs to the Kombi.

We need to decide whether this expenditure is going to provide a future benefit or whether it is an expense. To do this we need to ask ourselves the question: has the expenditure added to the asset? If it has then there is no problem in recognizing the transaction as one which creates an asset. If, however, the expenditure merely restores the asset to the state it was in previously then it is doubtful that it relates to an asset and applying the prudence principle we would be safer to charge it to the profit and loss account as an expense, which is what we have done. In essence this is a shorthand way of recording two events. The first is that the engine blew up so reducing the future benefit we could expect from the asset; if we knew the extent of this reduction we could have charged that as a past benefit. If we had done that then the repairs could legitimately be viewed as enhancing the future benefit to be obtained in respect of the reduced asset. This whole process is in fact circumvented because we do not know what the loss in value of future benefits was. We therefore are in effect using the cost of repairs as a surrogate for that loss in value.

Day 26 Placed a block advert in the local paper costing £180.

This is the same as the transaction on day 8. The future benefit is uncertain and therefore applying the prudence principle we reduce the cash at the bank by £180 and charge that amount as an expense to the profit and loss account.

Day 27 Received bookings for five more functions next month at a price of £900 each.

This is the same as the previous order on day 9. The earnings process has not started and therefore no revenue should be recognized.

Day 28 Decided that as things were going so well she would repay her parents £200.

This is a different transaction from any of the ones we have dealt with so far – those have dealt with expenditure of cash either for a past or future benefit. In this case we have reduced our cash at the bank in order to pay back an amount the business owes – in other words we have used some cash to reduce our liability. Thus we reduce the amount shown as owing in the loan column by the £200 and we reduce the amount of cash at the bank we have by £200.

Day 31 Paid the electricity up to date of £200.

Here we have a reduction of the cash at the bank in respect of the use of electricity over the past month. The benefit here has clearly expired and we therefore have an expense.

Stock, debtors and creditors $\boxed{6}$

INTRODUCTION

In the examples we have used so far in the book we have ensured that they have been kept as simple as possible in order to illustrate the concepts which we have introduced. However, in reality not all businesses buy and sell goods or services for cash. They do not all conveniently sell all the goods or services they have purchased in one period by the end of that period, nor are they all in their first year of trading. In this chapter we shall relax these simplifying assumptions and in so doing we will move from cash-based accounting – which is what we have dealt with so far – to accrual-based accounting.

We shall start with a discussion of the nature of stock and the issues of valuation. We shall then move our discussion on to the question of how stock is dealt with in the accounts of a business and the effect that changes in stock values may have on the balance sheet and profit and loss account. We will then move on to discuss how to deal with sales made on credit terms, that is where the customer is allowed time to pay after the goods or service have been provided. A part of this discussion will involve a consideration of how to deal with the amounts owing, commonly referred to as debtors. We shall then consider how to deal with the situation where a business pays in advance for services, as is commonly the case with insurance where premiums tend to be payable in advance. Finally, in relation to debtors we shall look at how we account for the situation where the customer does not pay.

After looking at what happens when we provide goods or services on credit we shall move on to a consideration of how we deal with supplies of goods and services that we receive on credit terms. We shall also look at the situation where, although we know that we owe money for services provided such as electricity, we do not know the exact amount that we owe. Finally under this heading we shall consider some transactions that are more prevalent in the tourism and hospitality industries than elsewhere. These are concerned with deposits and payments in advance. This type of transaction occurs frequently when, for example, a flight or a holiday is booked.

STOCK

Most businesses in the hospitality industry will carry stocks of food and beverages so that they can supply the needs of their customers. In the tourism industry generally stock will be less important as travel agents or tour operators provide services rather than goods and as such do not hold stocks. However, many tourist attractions also incorporate restaurants, souvenir shops, etc., and these operations will need to hold a stock of goods. In the case of the restaurant it will be food for conversion into meals and in the case of the souvenir shop it will be goods for resale. All businesses will in addition keep some stocks of notepaper and general office supplies. In effect what we have just done is to provide a definition of stock which is set out as the Key concept below.

> ### Key concept
>
> *Stocks*
>
> Stock comprises goods purchased for resale, or goods purchased for conversion into goods for resale, or consumable stores. The distinguishing feature of stock is the intention to resell the item or to use it in a relatively short period of time.

If you study this definition of stock you will notice that it states that the distinguishing feature is the intention to resell or to use the goods in a short period of time. Although this also applies to the hospitality industry it is easier to illustrate its importance by thinking of other industries. For example, if a business owns a car it will normally be classified as a fixed asset as the intention is to use it in the business for a considerable period of time. On the other hand, if the business is that of a car dealer then the cars are held with the intention to resell them in the short term and as such in the books of the car dealer they would be classified as stock.

In fact if we look at other industries we find that the whole question of stock and how we arrive at the cost of that stock can be much more complicated. For example, a car manufacturer is likely to hold a stock of raw materials such as steel for body parts and stocks of components such as headlamps, carburettors, etc. In addition it will have some cars that are part way through the production process. These part finished products are normally referred to as work in progress. It will also have some finished cars ready for delivery to retailers which will be referred to as finished goods. In such an industry it may be relatively easy to arrive at the cost of the raw materials and the finished goods but it is much more difficult to arrive at the cost of the work in progress. In order to do this we have to identify how near it is to completion and

decide which costs to include. Should the cost include all the component costs and all the labour costs, and if not, which ones should be
included and which should be excluded? Luckily in the industries with
which we are concerned the issues concerning stock are generally
simpler and more clear cut.

Valuing stock

In most cases in the hospitality and tourism industry to arrive at the
figure for stocks held at the end of the accounting period is a fairly
straightforward process. All that is required is that the stock is counted
at the end of the period and the number of items is then multiplied by
their cost to arrive at the figure for inclusion in the accounts. There are
of course complications, for example arriving at a figure for how much
beer is left in barrels or how much spirit is left in bottles, but in general
the process is fairly simple. Even problems that are common in other
industries such as the identification of slow-moving and obsolete stock
tend to be self-evident.

CASE STUDY 6.1

Guinness plc Annual Accounts 1993

The following extract is from the notes to the accounts providing
information on stocks held:

16. STOCKS	1993 £m	1992 £m
Raw materials and consumables	164	172
Work in progress	18	15
Stocks of maturing whisky and other spirits	1,470	1,426
Finished goods and goods for resale	170	197
	1,822	**1,810**

Stocks of maturing whisky and other spirits include financing costs amounting to £546m (1992 – £528m). A net adjustment to stocks of £17m (1992
– £17m) has been credited to the profit and loss account within net trading
costs comprising £121m (1992 – £125m) of interest incurred during the
year less £104m (1992 – £108m) in respect of sales during the year.

Commentary

Here is a classic example of the different types of stocks held, ranging from raw materials through to finished goods. However, because
of the nature of the industry there is a special type of stock, e.g.
maturing whisky, which is treated in a slightly different way, as
explained in the note: financing costs, i.e. interest, are included in
the cost of that stock.

Having ascertained the quantities of the goods the business holds the next stage is to put a value to them. In doing this it is necessary to comply with a general rule for stock valuation which states that stock should be valued at the lower of cost and its net realizable value.

> ### *Key concept*
>
> *The valuation rule*
>
> Stock should be valued at the lower of cost and net realizable value.

The application of this rule is in line with a more general accounting principle known as the prudence concept which states that profits and increases in value should not be anticipated but losses and decreases in value should be recognized as soon as they are foreseeable. In most cases in the industries with which we are concerned the application of the stock valuation rule will not cause any problems as the net realizable value is likely to be more than the cost. However, examples where it might apply are in souvenir shops where goods were purchased which for some reason did not sell and which have to be sold at less than cost in order to get rid of them.

> ### *Key concept*
>
> *The prudence concept*
>
> Profits should not be anticipated and revenue should not be recognized until its realization is reasonably certain.
> Provision should be made for all potential losses.

Stock and the cost of goods sold

We said in the introduction that we had made some simplifying assumptions in our examples so far about businesses buying and selling everything within one accounting period. In fact it would be exceptional if this happened. In reality most businesses will have some goods in stock at the start of the year, will purchase more goods during the year and will still have some left at the end of the year. In some industries the mechanism for identifying what has been sold is very sophisticated. For example, many major supermarket chains have an EPOS system which is an electronic point-of-sale stock ordering and stock record updating system. This means that every time the cashier rings up a sale of a tin of baked beans the stock records for that store are updated. In general sophisticated systems of that sort are not widespread and in many cases the way in which a business arrives at what the goods that it has sold actually cost is by adding the purchases during the year to the cost of the goods held at the start of the year and deducting what is still held at the end of the year. This can be written as an equation as follows:

$$\text{Opening stock} + \text{Purchases} - \text{Closing stock} = \text{Cost of goods sold}$$

The information for use in this equation can be derived as follows:

Opening stock   from the balance sheet at the start of the year;
Purchases   from suppliers' invoices;
Closing stock   from a physical stock count at the end of the year.

Returning to the equation, it is clear that if we get any of the figures wrong it will make the cost of sales wrong. This in turn will, as we shall see, make the profit figure wrong. Let us take a simple example to illustrate this.

EXAMPLE 6.1

The Skopelos Taverna

The Skopelos Taverna had at the start of the year £40 000 of fixed assets, £11 000 cash in the bank and £3000 of stock. Thus the owners' equity was £54 000. During the year they made sales of £60 000, paid wages and other expenses of £36 000 and bought food and beverages amounting to £10 000.

We can start by putting the opening position on a worksheet which will look as follows:

The Skopelos Taverna worksheet: version 1

		Assets	=	Equity +	Liabilities
	Cash	**Stock**	**Fixed assets**	**Equity**	**Profit & loss**
	£	£	£	£	£
Balances	11 000	3 000	40 000	54 000	

The worksheet should be fairly familiar to you so we can now enter the transactions for the year as follows:

The Skopelos Taverna worksheet: version 2

		Assets	=	Equity +	Liabilities
	Cash	**Stock**	**Fixed assets**	**Equity**	**Profit & loss**
	£	£	£	£	£
Balances	11 000	3 000	40 000	54 000	
Sales	60 000				60 000
Purchases	−10 000	10 000			
Expenses	−36 000				−36 000
Subtotal	25 000	13 000	40 000	54 000	24 000

We now need to establish how much stock we had at the end of the period and use our equation to establish the cost of goods sold. If we assume that the closing stock figure is £2000 then our equation would be:

Opening stock + Purchases − Closing stock = Cost of goods sold

£3000   + £10 000   − £2000   = £11 000

The worksheet would now look like the one below:

The Skopelos Taverna worksheet: version 3

Assets = Equity + Liabilities

	Cash	Stock	Fixed assets	Equity	Profit & loss
	£	£	£	£	£
Balances	11 000	3 000	40 000	54 000	
Sales	60 000				60 000
Purchases	−10 000	10 000			
Expenses	−36 000				−36 000
Subtotal	25 000	13 000	40 000	54 000	24 000
Cost of sales		−11 000			−11 000
Balance	25 000	2 000	40 000	54 000	13 000

The stock column in fact contains all the elements of the equation and we can see that the cost of sales is £11 000 and the profit for the year is £13 000. If we look at the last line of the worksheet we can also see that Skopelos has total assets of £67 000 at the end of the year, i.e. cash £25 000 plus stock £2000 plus fixed assets £40 000.

If we now assume that there was a miscalculation when arriving at the closing stock figure and the actual stock held was only £1500 the effect on the worksheet would be as shown below:

The Skopelos Taverna worksheet: version 4

Assets = Equity + Liabilities

	Cash	Stock	Fixed assets	Equity	Profit & loss
	£	£	£	£	£
Balances	11 000	3 000	40 000	54 000	
Sales	60 000				60 000
Purchases	−10 000	10 000			
Expenses	−36 000				−36 000
Subtotal	25 000	13 000	40 000	54 000	24 000
Cost of sales		−11 500			−11 500
Balance	25 000	1 500	40 000	54 000	12 500

You can see that the total assets have gone down from £67 000 to

£66 500 and that profit has been reduced from £13 000 to £12 500. Thus it is clear that it is important to get the stock figures right as it not only affects the asset value but it also has a direct effect on the profit for the year.

This effect on the profits can be more dramatic than the effect on the balance sheet. For example, in the case of The Savoy Hotel, in its accounts for 1991 it had stocks amounting to £7 million out of total assets of £114 million, so even if the stock figure was out by £1 million it would have little effect on the total assets. However, given that in that year the profits before taxation amounted to only £2.2 million a £1 million error in the closing stock figure would have had a dramatic impact on the profit for the year.

DEBTORS AND PREPAYMENTS

In America debtors, that is amounts owed to the business, are frequently referred to as amounts receivable and you may find initially that this is easier to remember and is more meaningful than the term debtors. As we say in the Key concept below debtors arise as a result of sales of goods or services being made on credit terms, that is where the payment is received some time after the service has been provided. In the hospitality and tourism industry this is likely to be sales of services to other business customers and large institutions.

Key concept

Debtors

Debtors arise when a business sells goods or services to a third party on credit terms, i.e. when the goods or services are supplied on the understanding that payment will be received at a later date.

The problem with sales on credit is that we should recognize the revenue in line with the realization principle as the earnings process is substantially complete and payment is reasonably certain. However, as we have no cash coming into the business we cannot record anything in that account. If we simply record the sales revenue we will have a one-sided entry and our worksheet will not balance. The way we deal with this is to open another column which we call debtors and enter the amount owed to the business in that column. This is clearly an asset as the business will get a future benefit when the money is received, and given that debts are normally paid within a year this conforms with the definition of a current asset which we discussed earlier in the book.

Prepayments

Items which are treated in a similar way to debtors are prepayments. These, as the name implies, are payments made in advance. They may be for rent, insurance, vehicle tax or could in fact be deposits lodged for hotel reservations etc. In the case of prepayments we need to look at the proportion that has been used up which is an expired benefit and therefore should be charged to the profit and loss account, and at the proportion which will give a future benefit and therefore should be included in the balance sheet. These prepayments, although classified as current assets in the same way as debtors, are somewhat different in so far as they are payments made by the business and the future benefit will be in a form other than cash.

EXAMPLE 6.2

The Kings Hotel

The Kings Hotel has the following transactions during the period from 1 January to 31 March:

Sales for cash	£20 000
Sales on credit	£60 000
Cash received from debtors	£44 000
Annual insurance premium	£ 8 200
Wages	£28 000

If we enter these transactions on a worksheet it will look as follows:

Kings Hotel worksheet: version 1

	Assets			=	Equity + Liabilities	
					Owners'	
	Cash	**Debtors**	**Prepaids**		**equity**	**Profit & loss**
	£	£	£		£	£
Cash sales	20 000					20 000
Credit sales		60 000				60 000
Cash from sales	44 000	–44 000				
Insurance	–8 200		6150			–2 050
Wages	–28 000					–28 000
Balance	27 800	16 000	6150		0	49 950

As you can see, when we make the credit sales they are recorded as revenue in the profit and loss account and also recorded as a debtor. When we receive any money from our debtors this is entered in the cash column and the asset debtors is reduced by the amounts received. For the insurance premium we split the £8200 into two components.

One of these is the expense of £2050, i.e. the insurance in relation to the three months that have just gone. The other is the prepayment of £6150 which is the amount that relates to the nine months still to come.

An alternative approach would be to enter the whole of the insurance premium as payment in advance and then review the assets at the end of the period and write off any expired benefits as expenses at that time. If we did this the worksheet would be as shown in version 2:

Kings Hotel worksheet: version 2

		Assets	=	Equity +	Liabilities
	Cash £	**Debtors** £	**Prepaids** £	**Owners' equity** £	**Profit & loss** £
Cash sales	20 000				20 000
Credit sales		60 000			60 000
Cash from sales	44 000	−44 000			
Insurance	−8 200		8200		
Wages	−28 000				−28 000
Balance	27 800	16 000	8200	0	−52 000
Insurance expense			−2050		−2 050
Final balance	27 800	16 000	6150	0	49 950

As you can see, the end result is the same. The advantage is that this presentation clearly shows what we have done. This is extremely useful in cases where an error is made. The choice of which presentation to use is a personal one but we would recommend that you use the latter and that you get into the habit of reviewing all the balances, in terms of whether they are still assets or liabilities, before finally extracting a balance sheet and profit and loss account. The advantages of this approach will become more obvious as we proceed.

Bad debts

As we have pointed out, in the hotel and catering industry debtors are often a major asset and need to be carefully controlled. The ways in which this can be done are considered in some detail in Chapter 17 when we deal with working capital management. If the debtors are not carefully controlled then, given that there is always a number of businesses that fail every year, the chances of debts being uncollectable or bad will increase. Before leaving the question of debtors and prepayments let us consider how we would deal with a situation where when we come to the end of the quarter and review the balances we find that some of the amounts owed by customers are uncollectable.

EXAMPLE 6.2

The Kings Hotel – further information

Of the £16 000 Kings Hotel is showing as debtors it is only likely to receive £10 000 because a major customer who owed £6000 has gone into liquidation and the liquidator has responded to the demand for payment with a letter stating that there is no money left to pay the bill.

In this situation the £6000 is not an asset as any future benefit expired when our customer's business failed.

The first question that arises is, was it a genuine sale? In other words, were we at the time of making the sale reasonably certain that we would receive payment? If the answer is yes, then we have correctly recognized the revenue and the debtor. What needs to be done now is to deal with the situation that has arisen subsequently as a result of later events. This is done by reducing the amount shown as debtors by £6000 and charging the £6000 as an expense of the period. The worksheet would now appear as follows:

Kings Hotel worksheet: version 3

	Assets	=	Equity +	Liabilities
	Cash £	Debtors £	Prepaids £	Owners' equity £	Profit & loss £
Cash sales	20 000				20 000
Credit sales		60 000			60 000
Cash from sales	44 000	–44 000			
Insurance	–8 200		8 200		
Wages	–28 000				–28 000
Balance	27 800	16 000	8200	0	52 000
Insurance expense			–2050		–2 050
Bad debt		–6 000			–6 000
Final balance	27 800	10 000	6150	0	43 950

It is worth noting that the bottom line now represents assets which have a future benefit at least equal to the amount shown.

Having looked at how debtors and prepayments are dealt with we can now consider how to deal with the situation where we receive goods or services before paying for them.

CREDITORS, ACCRUALS AND DEFERRED INCOME

Just as customers expect credit terms when dealing with your business you as an established business would expect to be offered such terms by your suppliers. It is normally only when a business is just starting or in exceptional cases that trade credit is not given. The amounts you owe in respect of this trade credit is now shown on a company's balance sheet under the heading 'amounts payable within one year'. The question we have to address is how a business would deal with goods or services supplied on credit as it may have used them before it has to pay the supplier. However, before we deal with that question we need to explain the difference between creditors and accruals.

Creditors

Creditors arise as a result of goods or services being supplied to an enterprise for which an invoice is subsequently received and for which no payment has been made at the date of receipt of the goods or services. As we have already said most established businesses will work on the basis of payment being due some time after the goods or services have been supplied. At the date at which we draw up a balance sheet therefore we need to acknowledge that there are amounts owing (liabilities) in respect of these supplies. These are normally referred to as creditors in the UK or as amounts payable in the US.

Accruals

Accruals are in some ways similar to creditors in that they relate to amounts due for goods or services already supplied to the enterprise. They differ not because of the nature of the transaction but because at the time of drawing up the balance sheet the amounts involved are not known with certainty. This is usually due to the fact that the invoice for the goods has not been received. A common example of a situation where this arises is telephone bills which are always issued in arrears; other examples are electricity and gas bills. These are also generally received after the end of the quarter to which they relate. In these situations therefore all we can do is to estimate what we think is owed for the service the business has used during the period. This estimate may be based on the last quarter or the previous year or on some other basis which the business considers more accurate.

Deferred income

In the tourism industry in particular, apart from trade creditors you will often find under the heading of amounts payable within one year monies received in advance. This could be for tickets in the case of an airline, or as holiday deposits or payments in advance on holidays in the case of tour operators and travel agents. These amounts can be very significant and are commonly described under the heading deferred income. This clearly acknowledges the fact that these monies are related to services that are still due to customers at the year end. The fact that the income is deferred is in line with the realization principle as the earning process cannot be described as substantially complete.

CASE STUDY 6.2

Airtours plc Annual Report and Accounts 1993

The following is an extract from Note 12 to the accounts on creditors:

	The Group 1993 £000	The Group 1992 £000	The Company 1993 £000	The Company 1992 £000
Amounts falling due within one year:				
Unsecured loan stock	20,142	–	20,142	–
Trade creditors	118,999	85,828	34,968	29,117
Current taxation	16,904	18,057	7,413	12,421
Social security and other taxes	4,958	1,235	649	237
Other creditors	10,306	7,112	6,374	3,831
Proposed dividends	8,997	6,164	8,997	6,164
Accruals	35,480	12,474	8,194	4,899
Amounts due under finance leases	333	367	90	367
Revenue received in advance	59,151	34,578	47,424	31,994
	275,270	165,815	134,251	89,030

Commentary

Airtours shows deferred income as 'revenues received in advance'. It is a significant amount, accounting for approximately one-fifth of all creditors due within one year.

Key concept

Creditors, accruals and deferred income

- Creditors are amounts owing at a point in time, the amounts of which are known.
- Accruals are amounts owing at a point in time, the amounts of which are not known with any certainty.
- Deferred income relates to amounts received from customers where the earnings process is not substantially complete.

An example may help to clarify the treatment of creditors, accruals and deferred income and the differences between them.

EXAMPLE 6.3

Panorama Air Tours

For the year to 31 December 19X1 Panorama Air Tours had the following transactions.

1. Paid £20 000 of owners' own money into a business bank account together with £10 000 borrowed from the bank.
2. Leased an aircraft for the year at a cost of £25 000.
3. Purchased £20 000 of aircraft fuel from a supplier on credit of which £1000 worth was left at the end of the year.
4. Paid the electricity bills for lighting and heating for three quarters amounting to £1500.
5. Paid advertising costs of £10 000 and owed £2000 in respect of advertising at the end of the year.
6. Paid the fuel supplier £18 000 for fuel purchased.

If we enter the above transactions on a worksheet and explain how they are dealt with, we can then deal with the other transactions of Panorama Air Tours. Our worksheet for the first transactions will look like this:

Panorama Air Tours worksheet: version 1

	Bank £	Fuel stocks £	Owners' equity £	Profit & loss £	Loan £	Creditors £
Item 1	20 000		20 000			
	10 000				10 000	
Item 2	–25 000			–25 000		
Item 3		20 000				20 000
		–19 000		–19 000		
Item 4	–1 500			–1 500		
Item 5	–10 000			–10 000		
				–2 000		2 000
Item 6	–18 000					–18 000
Balance	–24 500	1 000	20 000	–57 500	10 000	4 000

Let us examine each of the transactions in turn.

- **Item 1**. We are by now all familiar with transactions of this type which create an asset and a corresponding liability either in the form of money owing to the owner or to some other party.
- **Item 2**. Here we exchange one asset for another, in this case cash for the use of a plane for the year. At the end of the year the benefit is used up so we have an expense.
- **Item 3**. This is slightly different from the previous examples which have dealt with the purchase of goods. Up to now we have assumed that the stock was paid for when we received it. In this case, however, we are only told that during the year we bought fuel for £20 000. We have no idea, at present, how much we have actually paid out in respect of these items or how much is still owing. Therefore we show that we are owing money for all the items and open up a column for our creditors and show £20 000 in that column.

  We do, however, know that of the £20 000 of fuel only £1000 was left at the end of the year. Therefore the other £19 000 must have been used during the year and as such we should show it as an expense so we reduce the asset 'stock of fuel' by £19 000 and charge that amount to the profit and loss account.

- **Item 4**. This also looks familiar as we receive a bill for electricity which is paid for in cash and the service has been used up and is therefore an expense of the period. However, it should be borne in mind that we have in fact only paid for three quarters whereas we have consumed a year's supply of electricity. We therefore need to make some provision for the other quarter. A safe estimate could be that the fourth quarter's bill would be the same as the other quarters, i.e. approximately £500. It may of course turn out to be more or less. We are not, however, attempting one hundred per cent accuracy, rather we need to give a reasonable picture of the situation.
- **Item 5**. This is similar to the previous transaction as we know that we have used up £10 000 in advertising and have paid for that. But we also know that the actual expense should be £12 000, i.e. the £10 000 of advertising we have bought and paid for plus the £2000 which we still owe money for and which we need to include in creditors. There is of course the question of whether there is a future benefit to be gained from the advertising but we have invoked the prudence principle and assumed no tangible benefit will arise in the future.
- **Item 6**. We now know that of the £20 000 we owe to the fuel supplier £18 000 was paid in the year. We therefore need to reduce our cash by that amount and reduce the creditors by the same amount.

Let us now return to the question of the electricity bill. We said we need to make an accrual which we estimated to be £500. Let us see how this affects our worksheet using the balances from the version 1 above.

Panorama Air Tours worksheet: version 2

	Bank £	Fuel stocks £	Owners' equity £	Profit & loss £	Loan £	Creditors £	Accrual £
Item 1	20 000		20 000				
	10 000				10 000		
Item 2	–25 000			–25 000			
Item 3		20 000				20 000	
		–19 000		–19 000			
Item 4	–1 500			–1 500			
Item 5	–10 000			–10 000			
				–2 000		2 000	
Item 6	–18 000					–18 000	
Balance	–24 500	1 000	20 000	–57 500	10 000	4 000	
Accrual				– 500			500
	–24 500	1 000	20 000	–58 000	10 000	4 000	500

As we can see the balance sheet still balances and it now gives a truer picture of the goods we own and the amounts we owe. If we look at the example so far it is obvious that what is missing is any income.

EXAMPLE 6.3

Panorama Air Tours – Further information

The details of the income of Panorama Air Tours and other transactions in 19X1 are given below.

7. Panorama sold £50 000 worth of tours during the year of which £40 000 were for cash and £10 000 were on credit.
8. Panorama received £9000 from debtors during the year.
9. Panorama also received £5000 in respect of air tours for 19X2.
10. Paid interest on the loan of £500 in respect of the half year to 30 June 19X1.
11. Paid rent of £7500 of which £1500 was in respect of 19X2.

The revised worksheet for 19X1 would be as shown below.

Panorama Air Tours worksheet: version 3

	Bank £	Fuel stocks £	Debtors & prepaid £	Owners' equity £	Profit & loss £	Loan £	Creditors & accruals £
Item 1	20 000			20 000			
	10 000					10 000	
Item 2	–25 000				–25 000		
Item 3		20 000					20 000
	–19 000				–19 000		
Item 4	–1 500				–1 500		
Item 5	–10 000				–10 000		
					–2 000		2 000
Item 6	–18 000						–18 000
Balance	–24 500	1 000		20 000	–57 500	10 000	4 000
Accrual					–500		500
	–24 500	1 000		20 000	–58 000	10 000	4 500
Item 7	40 000		10 000		50 000		
Item 8	9 000		– 9 000				
Item 9	5 000						5 000
Item 10	–500				–500		
Item 11	–7 500		7 500				
	21 500	1 000	8 500	20 000	–8 500	10 000	9 500

You will see that we have combined the creditors and accruals in one column and introduced a new column for debtors and prepaids. The sales, cash received and debtors have been dealt with in the same way as they were in Example 6.2 on the Kings Hotel. The money received in advance for next year has been treated as deferred income and included under creditors and accruals, although as you will see later it is separately identified in the balance sheet and in fact we would have been more correct if we had opened a separate column for this item. The interest on the loan has been treated as an expense but at present we have treated the rent as all being prepaid. If we now review the position we can see that of the rent £6000 has been used up during the year and we can also see that we owe interest for the second half of the year. Taking these into account will lead us to the worksheet below.

Panorama Air Tours worksheet: version 4

	Bank £	Fuel stocks £	Debtors & prepaid £	Owners' equity £	Profit & loss £	Loan £	Creditors & accruals £
Item 1	20 000			20 000			
	10 000					10 000	
Item 2	−25 000				−25 000		
Item 3		20 000					20 000
		−19 000			−19 000		
Item 4	−1 500				−1 500		
Item 5	−10 000				−10 000		
					−2 000		2 000
Item 6	−18 000						−18 000
Balance	−24 500	1 000		20 000	−57 500	10 000	4 000
Accrual					−500		500
	−24 500	1 000		20 000	−58 000	10 000	4 500
Item 7	40 000		10 000		50 000		
Item 8	9 000		−9 000				
Item 9	5 000						5 000
Item 10	−500				−500		
Item 11	−7 500		−7 500				
	21 500	1 000	8 500	20 000	−8 500	10 000	9 500
Interest					−500		500
Rent			−6 000		−6 000		
	21 500	1 000	2 500	20 000	−15 000	10 000	10 000

We can now extract a profit and loss account and balance sheet for 19X1. These are shown below.

Profit and loss account for Panorama Air Tours for the year ended 31 December 19X1

	£	£
Sales		50 000
Lease charges	25 000	
Fuel used	19 000	
Advertising	12 000	

Electricity	2 000	
Loan interest	1 000	
Rent	6 000	65 000
Loss for the year		15 000

Balance sheet of Panorama Air Tours at 31 December 19X1

Current assets	£	£
Fuel stocks	1 000	
Debtors	1 000	
Prepayments	1 500	
Cash at bank	21 500	
	25 000	
Amounts due in under one year		
Trade creditors	4 000	
Accruals	500	
Loan interest payable	500	
Deferred income	5 000	
	10 000	
Net current assets		15 000
		15 000
Financed by		
Owners' equity		20 000
Loss for year		15 000
		5 000
Loan		10 000
		15 000

Having now established how to deal with debtors, creditors accruals and prepayments, let us now examine what happens in the second year to Panorama Air Tours.

EXAMPLE 6.3

Panorama Air Tours – further information

For the year to 31 December 19X2 Panorama Air Tours had the following transactions.

1. Leased the aircraft for the year at a cost of £25 000.
2. Purchased £25 000 of aircraft fuel from a supplier on credit of which £2000 worth was left at the end of the year.
3. Paid the electricity bills for lighting and heating for four quarters amounting to £2300 of which £500 related to 19X1.
4. Paid £8000 for advertising and owed £1000 in respect of advertising at the end of the year.
5. Paid the fuel supplier £24 000 for fuel purchased.
6. Sold £80 000 worth of tours during the year of which £20 000 were on credit.

7. Received £16 000 from debtors during the year.
8. Panorama also received £8000 in respect of air tours for 19X3.
9. Paid interest on the loan of £1000.
10. Paid rent of £6000.

It is worth briefly considering some of these items before we enter them on a worksheet. We can start with the fuel used. Here we have to apply the formula set out earlier in this chapter to find what we have used during the year:

| Opening stock | + | Purchases | – | Closing stock | = | Cost of fuel used |

Thus we have:

| £1000 | + | £25 000 | – | £2000 | = | £24 000 |

Moving on from how much fuel was used we can now look at how much is owed to the supplier and we can apply a similar logic to that used for stock. In the case of payments for fuel we find that Panorama has bought £25 000 of fuel during the year and has paid the supplier £24 000. However, we must bear in mind that part of the £24 000 payment is to pay off the £2000 still owing at the end of 19X1. To find out how much is owing at the end of year two we can use the formula:

| Opening creditor | + | Purchases | – | Payments | = | Closing creditor |

Thus we have:

| £2000 | + | £25 000 | – | £24 000 | = | £3000 |

With advertising we are aware that £2000 of the £8000 paid in respect of advertising costs is a payment of the amount owed and included in creditors at the end of 19X1, and we also know that £1000 was owed at the end of 19X2. So we can rearrange the formula to reflect the information we have and that which is missing as follows.

| Payments | + | Closing creditor | – | Opening creditor | = | Purchases |

Thus we have:

| £8000 | + | £1000 | – | £2000 | = | £7000 |

In the case of electricity we know that we owed £500 at the start of the year and paid £2300 during the year. Therefore £1800 must relate to the three quarters of 19X2 and we will need to make an accrual for the fourth quarter in the same way as last year. A similar logic applies to the loan interest paid.

Moving now to the sales and debtors we can apply the same logic. If we had debtors of £1000 at the start of the year and sold tours on credit amounting to £20 000 during the year then the total we were owed was

£21 000. Of this we have received £16 000 and therefore at the end of 19X2 we are owed £5000.

In the case of sales we know that £80 000 of tours were sold during 19X2 and we also know that we had already sold and received money in advance for £5000 of tours which we showed as deferred income at the end of 19X1. So our total income from tours carried out during 19X2 is £85 000.

We have to deal with the deferred income at the end of 19X2 in the same way as in 19X1. The final item to deal with is the rent where we had a prepayment of £1500 at the start of the year and have paid £6000 during 19X2. The amount due in respect of 19X2 must be £4500, i.e. £6000 annual rent less the amount prepaid £1500. Therefore of the £6000 paid in 19X2 £1500 must be a prepayment for the first quarter of 19X3.

If you now enter the transactions on a worksheet it should look something like the one below.

Panorama Air Tours worksheet year 19X2

	Bank £	Fuel stocks £	Debtors & prepaid £	Owners' equity £	Profit & loss £	Loan £	Creditors & accruals £
Balances	21 500	1 000	2 500	20 000	−15 000	10 000	10 000
Item 1	−25 000				−25 000		
Item 2		25 000					25 000
		−24 000			−24 000		
Item 3	−2 300				−1 800		− 500
Item 4	−8 000				−6 000		−2 000
					−1 000		1 000
Item 5	−24 000						−24 000
Item 6	60 000		20 000		80 000		
Item 7	16 000		−16 000				
Item 8	8 000						8 000
Item 9	−1 000				− 500		− 500
Item 10	−6 000		6 000				
	39 200	2 000	12 500	20 000	6 700	10 000	17 000
Electric					− 600		600
Deferred income					5 000		−5 000
Interest					− 500		500
Rent			−6 000		−6 000		
	39 200	2 000	6 500	20 000	4 600	10 000	13 100

We can now extract a profit and loss account and balance sheet for 19X2 as follows:

Profit and loss account for Panorama Air Tours for the year ended 31 December 19X2

	£	£
Sales		85 000
Lease charges	25 000	
Fuel used	24 000	
Advertising	7 000	
Electricity	2 400	
Loan interest	1 000	
Rent	6 000	65 400
Profit for the year		19 600

Balance sheet of Panorama Air Tours at 31 December 19X1

	£	£
Current assets		
Fuel stocks	2 000	
Debtors	5 000	
Prepayments	1 500	
Cash at bank	39 200	
	47 700	
Amounts due in under one year		
Trade creditors	4 000	
Accruals	600	
Loan interest payable	500	
Deferred income	8 000	
	13 100	
Net current assets		34 600
		34 600
Financed by		
Owners' equity		20 000
Profit and loss at start of year	(15 000)	
Profit for 19X2	19 600	4 600
		24 600
Loan		10 000
		34 600

SUMMARY

In this chapter we have dealt with stock and the rule for stock valuation. We have also looked at how stock is dealt with in the accounts and its effect on the balance sheet and profit and loss account. From there we moved on to how accrual accounting deals with cases where the timing of cash flows is such that if accounts were prepared on the basis of cash flows the matching principle would be contravened. We have shown how sales on credit are included as revenue and how the amounts not received at the end of the year are dealt with as debtors and shown as current assets as they will provide the business with a future benefit. We have also examined the way in which payments in advance can be dealt with in order that expenses are matched against revenue. In addition we have shown how accrual accounting allows bad debts, where the future benefit has expired, to be dealt with. From the point of view of services and goods supplied to the business we have seen how creditors are dealt with and how accruals arise. Of particular interest in the case of the tourism industry is the way in which deposits and payments in advance are dealt with and we saw how accrual accounting can easily cope with these problems. The principle that is common to all these items is that the accounts should comply with the matching principle and the balance sheet should record the rights to future benefits and what the business owes at a particular point in time.

REVIEW QUESTIONS

1. What type of stock is likely to be held by a restaurant?
2. What would be the effect on the profit if goods costing £6000 were excluded from the opening stock figure?
3. What are the effects of omitting goods costing £500 from the year-end stock figure?
4. Why is it necessary to value stock at the lower of cost and net realizable value?
5. In your own words describe what a creditor is and when it arises.
6. Explain the difference between creditors, accruals and deferred income.
7. Why are debtors and prepayments classified as current assets?
8. When do prepayments arise and how do they differ from accruals?
9. Explain the matching principle.
10. Why is it necessary to identify debtors and creditors?
11. How do debtors affect the profit and loss account?

PROBLEMS FOR DISCUSSION AND ANALYSIS

1. You are the auditor of Inflight Caterers and have attended the stock count on the last day of the company's accounting year. Inflight Caterers' accountant has calculated from their own stock sheets that the stock at the end of the year is worth £43 000 at cost. They have worked out that, given that stock at the start of the year was £38 000, their cost of sales is £212 000.

   While checking on the stock you find the following discrepancies.
   (i) The accountant had not included two pages of stock in the calculation of the closing stock as these had been left in the

stores by the stock counters. The cost of the stock contained on these sheets you calculate was £2000.

(ii) You also find that some of the stock in one of the freezers has totally defrosted as the stock counter had unplugged the freezer to plug in a heater to keep the room warm while the count was underway. The stock contained in the freezer had cost £280.

(iii) You also find that when calculating the cost of sales figure an invoice for £15 000 from a supplier for goods received and used during the year had been excluded from the calculations.

Required:

(a) Calculate the purchases for the year from the information provided by the accountant.

(b) Identify what effect each of the discrepancies unearthed would have on the closing stock, and the cost of sales.

2. In each of the following situations describe the way the transaction would be dealt with in the accounts of Thrift Hotels and identify, where appropriate, the effect on the balance sheet and profit and loss account.

  (a) Purchase of wines and spirits on credit terms.
  (b) Receipts from corporate customers in respect of balances outstanding on credit sales.
  (c) Payment of interest on a loan.
  (d) Repayment of a loan.
  (e) Provision of rooms and meals on credit.
  (f) Payment to supplier in respect of foodstuffs already delivered and used.
  (g) Payment of wages to housekeeping staff.
  (h) Payment of salaries to the management team.
  (i) Payment of an electricity bill from last year.
  (j) Payment of rent quarterly in advance.
  (k) Withdrawal of cash from the business by the owner.
  (l) Receipt of cash from the owner.
  (m) A customer going into liquidation owing money.

3. On 1 March 19X1 Barbara paid £50 000 into a business bank account as capital for her new business which was going to provide guided bicycle tours of Holland.

March 2 Bought eleven bicycles for £250 each.

        6 Paid an agency £20 000 to design a brochure and £2000 to print 5000 copies.

        9 Organized a series of ten weekly adverts in a quality national newspaper advertising the tours at a cost of £400 per entry and obtained credit terms whereby she paid one month after the adverts appeared.

     10 Took an office in a local business centre at a monthly rental of £400 a month payable monthly in advance.

12 Had an additional telephone line installed to cope with a fax machine.

13 Purchased a fax machine for her office at a cost of £240 and paid for this in cash.

17 Received some initial enquiries and sent out copies of the brochure.

24 Received deposits of £50 each from twenty people each booking a two-week holiday.

25 Made bookings for accommodation with a hotel group in Holland and sent them a deposit of 10% of the cost which amounted to £560.

30 Received deposits of £50 each from a further thirty people each booking a two-week holiday.

At the end of the month she still had 4400 brochures left.

Required:

(a) Discuss how each transaction should be treated.

(b) Discuss what, if any, accruals and prepayments are or should be involved.

(c) Using only the information contained in the question draw up a worksheet, balance sheet and profit and loss account.

(d) What other information would you require in order to get a more accurate profit and loss account and balance sheet?

Fixed assets and depreciation $\boxed{7}$

INTRODUCTION

The definitions of assets and of fixed and current assets were discussed in Chapter 3. In that chapter we adopted the definition of an asset which had been suggested by R.M. Lall. This definition is reproduced below.

Key concept

Definition of an asset

Embodiments of present or future economic benefits or service potentials measurable in monetary units, accruing to an enterprise as a result of economic events, the enjoyment of which by the enterprise is secured by law.

The distinction that we have made between assets and expenses is that an asset relates to present or future benefits whereas an expense relates to past or expired benefits. Thus if a restaurant has food and beverage stocks at the year end these are shown as an asset as there will be a future benefit from them. The cost of the food and beverages sold during the year on the other hand would be charged as an expense as any benefit has been received. Some of the assets that a business holds will change form during a period or from one period to the next. For example, debtors become cash, or they become expenses as is the case when a debt becomes uncollectable. This applies to all assets but in the case of fixed assets it takes longer to use up the future benefits than it does with current assets. We have already defined fixed assets and that definition is reproduced below.

Key concept

Definition of a fixed asset

An asset that is acquired for the purposes of use within the business and is likely to be used by the business for a considerable period of time.

The fact that these assets neither change form nor get used up in a short period poses some problems for accountants. The problems can be viewed from the perspective of the balance sheet or from the perspective of the impact on the profit and loss account. From the point of view of the balance sheet, which tells us what we own at a particular point in time, we have to try to identify the amount of the future benefit left in a fixed asset at the end of each year. On the other hand, from the perspective of the profit and loss account, we need to measure the amount of the future benefit used up during the year in order that we can match this expense with the revenue earned during the year. Whichever way we choose to look at the problem, we are still left with the issue of how to measure the future benefit to be derived from the use of the asset. This can be illustrated by returning to the definition of profit adopted by accountants. This, we said in Chapter 2, could be seen as being derived from the definition of income provided by Sir John Hicks. This definition is reproduced below together with the diagram which we used to illustrate it.

Key concept

Income – Hicks's definition

Income is that amount which an individual can consume and still be as well off at the end of the period as he or she was at the start of the period.

We can see from the diagram that wealth at T_0 plus the profit for the period will give us wealth at T_1. Thus we can either measure the wealth in the form of future benefits at the end of each period which brings with it the problems of valuation (discussed in Chapter 2), or we can try to measure the profit by matching the revenue with the benefits used up during the period.

We shall first consider the approach based upon the idea of measuring the future benefits to be derived from our fixed assets which is theoretically possible. We could, for example, measure the benefits to be derived from selling the services which our fixed assets help us to provide. In a world in which there is uncertainty, however, this process is far from straightforward. For example, what is the effect of competition on our market share? What is the effect of a change in taste or fashion? It may be that the opening of a new hotel, instead of increasing the total market, merely segments the existing market and thereby reduces the customer base available to the existing hotels.

It is, in fact, extremely difficult to measure the future benefit in the long term as we do not know what changes the future will bring, therefore we cannot estimate their effects. This leaves us with the alternative approach, i.e. measuring expired benefits and matching those with revenues. The problem with this approach is that if you were able to tell how much benefit had expired you would then be able to work out what the unexpired or future benefit was. This, we have just argued, is extremely difficult to do in reality because of the problems of uncertainty.

Traditionally accounting has solved this conundrum by the simple expedient of valuing assets at cost unless there is reasonable certainty that this value is incorrect, either because it is lower or because it is clearly higher. In the 1970s and for most of the 1980s, land and buildings have had a higher value than their cost. However, a building bought in the mid 1980s was likely to have a lower value in 1992 than its cost due to the slump in the property market and the effects of the recession. This illustrates the difficulties associated with measures other than cost. Therefore the problem of identifying future benefits is generally avoided by simply recording fixed assets at cost. Accounting does, however, try to take some cognizance of the fall in value of the fixed assets and the need to match revenue with expenses. This is done by means of a depreciation charge, which is a way of spreading the original cost of a fixed asset over its useful life and thereby charging the profit and loss account with some amount relating to the use of the asset.

This approach does not, in itself, solve the problem of how to deal with uncertainty as the useful life of a fixed asset is itself uncertain. Other issues also arise with this approach. For example, how does a fixed asset differ from a current asset? What is the cost of a fixed asset? How should we spread the cost over the useful life? We need to examine each of these issues if we are to understand what the profit and loss and balance sheet figures mean.

DIFFERENCE BETWEEN FIXED AND CURRENT ASSETS

We have already defined fixed and current assets in Chapter 3 and if you look at the definitions you will see that the difference is, in the main, related to the intention regarding the use of the asset and to the nature of the business. In simple terms a bed is not a fixed asset in the case of a retailer of beds because it is not the intention of the dealer to use it within the business for a considerable period of time. However, it will be a fixed asset in the case of a hotelier. The problem with a definition that relies on the intentions of the business is that these may change if the nature of the business changes. This may mean that an asset that was classified as a fixed asset may be reclassified with corresponding effects on whether the asset is subject to depreciation. As these problems rarely arise, for our purposes we can safely ignore them.

THE COST OF A FIXED ASSET

On the face of it the question of what an asset costs should present few if any difficulties. This is true in some cases, but in a great many cases the answer is less clear. To illustrate the point let us look at the situation where a business buys its premises. If we were to read the legal contract between the seller and the buyer we would find within that contract an agreed price. We could therefore argue that the cost is that agreed price, but were you to talk to someone who has recently purchased premises you would find that there were other costs associated with the transaction such as solicitors' fees, surveyors' fees, etc. The question is should these be treated as part of the cost of the asset or are they expenses? In this particular situation the way in which accounting might answer the question is to argue that the amounts involved would not be material when compared to the cost of the premises. This is not really a very satisfactory solution as it merely avoids the question rather than answering it. Accounting does not, in fact, provide an answer to this problem. There are some broad guidelines which accountants use which we will illustrate by examining some possible examples and identifying the basis of the decision.

Before doing that, however, we need to explain the idea of materiality. This is a concept often used in the accounting literature and like a number of other concepts such as prudence it provides a rule-of-thumb approach to assist in making judgements.

Key concept

Materiality

Broadly, an item can be said to be material if its non-disclosure would lead to the accounts being misleading in some way.

For example, the cost of a dishwasher is likely to be material in the case of a small restaurant but in the case of Forte the effect on the fixed assets would be negligible as they are measured in millions. Thus materiality is a relative measure and all aspects of the situation need to be looked at before a decision is made. Having introduced the idea of materiality we can now move on to try to establish the guidelines we referred to above through a series of examples.

EXAMPLE 7.1

Purchase of a courtesy minibus by a hotel for £12 600. The price includes number plates, sign-writing the hotel's name and logo on the minibus and one year's road fund licence.

It is clear that in this example we have a fixed asset. The question is only how much did the fixed asset cost. Included in the £12 600 is the cost of number plates, the sign-writing and one year's road fund licence. The road fund licence could hardly be described as a fixed asset as it only lasts for one year, whereas the number plates, name and logo are clearly part of the cost of the fixed asset in that they will remain with the van over its useful life.

EXAMPLE 7.2

Let us now assume that as the hotel did not have the cash to buy the minibus outright, it was purchased on hire-purchase. The hire-purchase contract allowed the hotel to put down a deposit of £6400 and then make 24 monthly payments of £300. Thus the total cost of buying the same minibus would be £13 600 as compared to the cash price of £12 600.

The fact that the hotel has decided to finance the purchase in a different way has, on the face of it, added to the cost of purchasing the minibus. However, this is somewhat misleading as the cost of the minibus is in fact the same. What has happened in this case is that the hotel has incurred an additional cost which does not relate to the minibus itself. This additional cost relates to the cost of borrowing money, which is effectively what hire-purchase is. If the hotel had borrowed money through a bank loan and then paid cash for the minibus the cost of the minibus would have been the cash price and the interest on the loan would be dealt with separately. Thus in the case of hire-purchase all that needs to be done is to identify the part of the payments that are interest charges and deal with those in the same way as we would interest on loans. In this particular example the interest is £1000, i.e. the full HP price of £13 600 less the cash price of £12 600. The £1000 interest would of course be charged to the profit and loss account as an expense over the 24 months it takes to pay the hire-purchase company.

EXAMPLE 7.3

A hotelier bought an existing hotel, which had originally cost £8000 to build and which was somewhat run down, for £300 000. It was decided that the hotel would have to be completely refurbished before opening. The cost of the refurbishment amounted to £80 000 and the refurbishment took three months to complete for which period business rates of £10 000 were due.

The starting point is the basic cost of the hotel which was £300 000. The fact that it had cost £80 000 to build is not relevant; what we need to bring into the accounts of our hotelier is the cost to that business, not the original cost. With the other costs, though, the decisions are less clear-cut. For example, should the cost of refurbishment be included? One answer would be to argue that in order to obtain the future benefits from the asset we needed to incur this cost so this is in fact a payment for those future benefits. If we followed that line of argument we could then include these costs as part of the cost of the fixed asset. This would seem a reasonable line of argument as long as we are happy that the future benefits are likely to exceed the costs incurred to date. This is clearly a question of judgement because of the uncertainty surrounding the estimation of future benefits.

You will have noticed that we referred specifically to the refurbishment, but what of the rates for the period of refurbishment? Here, the argument is less clear. On the one hand it is possible to argue that, whereas the refurbishment has enhanced the value of the hotel as it has made it more attractive to stay there, the payment of rates has had no such effect. An alternative argument could be that it is as much part of the cost of the refurbishment as the paint or the labour involved as the refurbishment takes time to carry out.

In fact, the latter argument is the one adopted by Friendly Hotels Plc as the extract in Case study 7.1 from their accounting policies statement illustrates.

We can see from these examples and the case study that there is no nice easy solution to the problem of what should and should not be included in the cost of fixed assets. Each case is judged upon its merits and a decision is made about whether the cost should be included in the expenses for the year or added to the cost of the asset. The broad rule of thumb that can be used to assist in these decisions is, has there

---

CASE STUDY 7.1

Friendly Hotels plc Annual Accounts 1992

The following extract is from the Notes to the financial statements on expenditure on properties:

> Rent, rates and other premises expenses, including interest charges, incurred in the period from acquisition, construction and refurbishment of a property up to three months after it is first available for letting or sale of accommodation, are capitalized and included in the cost of the property.

been an enhancement of the potential future benefits? If there has, then the cost should be added to the asset. If, on the other hand, the effect is simply to restore the status quo, as is the case with car repairs, then it is more reasonable to treat those costs as expenses of the period in which they arise. This approach conforms to the prudence concept which we have referred to earlier.

THE USEFUL LIFE OF FIXED ASSETS

In our introduction we mentioned the useful life of the asset and how we spread the cost over the useful life. This raises a number of issues. How do we judge the useful life? What cost do we spread over the useful life? How do we spread it? The latter point will be dealt with below in our discussion of depreciation, but it is worth examining the other two before we move on to that discussion. The first question posed was how do we judge the useful life? The answer is that all we can hope for is a reasonable approximation. The reason we can only approximate comes back to the question of uncertainty in respect of the future. Similarly if we try to arrive at the cost that we wish to spread over the useful life we could argue that we should take into account anything that we will be able to sell our asset for when it is no longer viable to use it in our business. This amount, the residual value, is only a guess because of the uncertainty involved. In reality it is quite likely that such issues are sidestepped and that assets are classified into broad groups which are then assumed to have a useful life based upon either past practice or the norm for the industry. These norms are only fixed in the short term. Clearly, with improvements in materials and technology, it is likely that the useful life of a computer, for example, is different now to what it was twenty years ago.

It should be clear from our discussion that there is no magic formula for arriving at either the cost or the useful life. Bearing this in mind we can now examine the way in which we spread the cost over the useful life. As we have already mentioned, this is done by means of depreciation.

DEPRECIATION

We have suggested some reasons for charging depreciation which we will discuss more fully shortly. What we have not done is to define depreciation precisely; instead we have tried to give a flavour of what depreciation is. However, no discussion of depreciation would be complete without at least looking at the definition provided in Statement of Standard Accounting Practice (SSAP 12) Accounting for Depreciation (see Key concept below).

> ### *Key concept*
>
> *Depreciation*
>
> '... the measure of the wearing out, consumption or other loss of value of a fixed asset whether arising from use, effluxion of time or obsolescence through technology or market changes.'

This definition is, in fact, difficult to comply with because, as we have already pointed out, the fixed asset is normally included at cost not at value, therefore to measure the loss in value would be inconsistent. It also assumes that we will be able to take into account changes in technology and the market. This might be possible in the short-term but it is much more difficult in the long term. As fixed assets are essentially long term assets the requirement to take into account these changes in technology and the market is, in practice, difficult to comply with. Whilst we could spend considerable time analysing the definition it is more important that we consider the question of why we depreciate assets and what depreciation can and cannot be expected to achieve.

Why depreciate?

One reason already mentioned is that of matching the revenue earned in a period with the expense connected with earning that revenue. In essence the argument for matching the cost of goods sold with the sales or of matching expenses with sales is the one being applied here. The major difference is that some of these other items are ascertainable with a reasonable degree of accuracy, whereas depreciation as we have pointed out is only an estimate and subject to all sorts of inaccuracies.

A second and more contentious reason for providing for depreciation is in order to maintain the capacity of a business to continue to provide a service, i.e. to maintain operating capacity. Clearly if, in the case of our hotel, the beds come to the end of their useful life the hotel will need more beds if it is to carry on business. This of course assumes that it would wish to replace the beds. This assumes that the same service is to be provided in the same way as previously which is probably reasonable with the example chosen. However, in the case of a travel operator such as P&O new technology may have made the current equipment on their ships obsolete or major changes such as the opening of the Channel Tunnel may mean that they do not wish to replace all their cross Channel ferries. This question is directly related to our original problem in Chapter 3 of measuring one's wealth or how well-off one is. Such a measure depends on how you define wealth and whether that changes over time. For example, a car may be seen as an asset until such time as the world runs out of petrol reserves. At that stage we probably will not want to include a car in our measurement of wealth. Therefore, in such a set of circumstances to have retained profits in order to ensure we always had a car would not have been appropriate.

Maintenance of operating or service capacity is also contentious because in fact all accounting depreciation does is to spread the original cost and maintain the original money capital. This means that in fact capacity is not maintained through depreciation as no account is taken of changes whether they be in prices, in technology or in consumer demand. All of this means that we cannot guarantee that we will have enough money left in the business as a result of our depreciation charges to replace an existing machine with one of equal capacity should we so wish.

Having made the point that there is no guarantee that the depreciation charges will equal the requirements for replacement because of changes in those requirements and in the environment, let us look at how depreciation would maintain capital if the value of money, technology, the requirements of the business in question and the environment did not change. We will start by looking at an example to see what happens if we ignore depreciation and then how it is dealt with in terms of the accounts.

EXAMPLE 7.4

Terri's hot-dog stand

Terri buys a hot-dog stand for £4000 and sets up in business. In addition to the hot-dog stand £1000 cash is put into the business which is subsequently used to buy stocks for making hot dogs.

At the end of the first year the sales have been £6000 and the total expenses including the cost of the hot dogs, repairs to the hot-dog stand and running costs were £3000; all the stock has been sold so all the money is in cash. Thus the business has £4000 in cash, the original £1000 plus the money from sales of £6000 less the expenses paid of £3000.

Terri therefore withdraws £3000 on the assumption that the business is still as well off as it was at the start. That is the business had at the start of the year a hot-dog stand plus £1000 in cash: it still has the hot-dog stand so there only needs to be £1000 left in for the status quo to be maintained.

Let us also assume for convenience that the situation is repeated for the next three years.

Under these assumptions the profit and loss accounts and balance sheets of the business would be as follows:

Profit and loss accounts of Terri's business

	Year 1 £	Year 2 £	Year 3 £	Year 4 £
Sales revenue	6000	6000	6000	6000
Cost of sales	3000	3000	3000	3000
Profit	3000	3000	3000	3000
Withdrawal	3000	3000	3000	3000
Retained profit	0	0	0	0

Balance sheets of Terri's business

	Year 1 £	Year 2 £	Year 3 £	Year 4 £
Fixed assets				
Hot-dog stand	4000	4000	4000	4000
Current assets				
Cash	1000	1000	1000	1000
	5000	5000	5000	5000
Financed by	£	£	£	£
Owners' equity	5000	5000	5000	5000
	5000	5000	5000	5000

If we assume the hot-dog stand would last four years we can see that in fact the balance sheet at the end of year 4 is wrong as the hot-dog stand has come to the end of its useful life and there is no future benefit to be derived from keeping it. If we want the balance sheet to include as assets only items that reflect future benefits the balance sheet at the end of year 4 should be:

	£
Fixed assets	
Hot-dog stand	Nil
Current assets	
Cash	1000
	1000
Financed by	£
Owner's equity	1000
	1000

As we can see, there is not enough money left in the business to replace the hot-dog stand and in this situation the business cannot continue. If we compare our results with our definition of profit, introduced in Chapter 2 and reproduced above in the Key concept on p.128, it is clear that our profit measure must have been wrong as Terri is not as well off at the end of year 4 as at the beginning of year 1.

The problem has been that the profit has been overstated because no allowance has been made for the fact that the hot-dog stand has a finite useful life which is being eroded each year. If we assume that the cost should be spread evenly over the four years and call this expense depreciation then our profit and loss accounts would appear as follows.

Revised profit and loss accounts of Terri's business

	Year 1	Year 2	Year 3	Year 4
	£	£	£	£
Sales revenue	6000	6000	6000	6000
Cost of sales	3000	3000	3000	3000
Gross profit	3000	3000	3000	3000
Depreciation	1000	1000	1000	1000
Net profit	2000	2000	2000	2000
Withdrawal	2000	2000	2000	2000
Retained profit	0	0	0	0

As can be seen the net profit has been reduced by £1000 for the depreciation each year and Terri has withdrawn only £2000 each year. The balance sheets would now be:

Revised balance sheets of Terri's business

	Year 1	Year 2	Year 3	Year 4
	£	£	£	£
Fixed assets				
Hot-dog stand	4000	4000	4000	4000
Depreciation	1000	2000	3000	4000
Net book value	3000	2000	1000	0
Current assets				
Cash	2000	3000	4000	5000
	5000	5000	5000	5000
Financed by				
	£	£	£	£
Owner's equity	5000	5000	5000	5000
	5000	5000	5000	5000

The effect of charging depreciation in the profit and loss account was to reduce the net profit which in turn led to a reduction in the amount withdrawn each year. The reduced withdrawal has led to the cash balance increasing each year by £1000 until at the end of year 4 there is £5000 in the bank and Terri is in a position to replace the hot-dog stand, assuming of course that the price has not changed. If you compare the two sets of balance sheets there is another change: this is that the fixed asset reduces each year by the amount of the depreciation charge. These two effects should not be mixed up; the increase in cash is as a result of withdrawing less and **not** as a result of providing for depreciation. The latter does not in itself affect the cash balance as is obvious if we work through year 1 of this example on a worksheet.

Worksheet showing year 1 of Terri's business

	Cash £	Hot-dog stand £	Owner's equity £	Profit & loss £	Depreciation £
Depreciation	1000	4000	5000		
Sales	6000			6000	
Expenses	–3000			–3000	
Depreciation				–1000	1000
Withdrawal	–2000			–2000	
Balance	2000	4000	5000	0	1000

As you can see the depreciation charge does not affect the cash column in any way.

An alternative way of dealing with depreciation on a worksheet is to reduce the asset column by the depreciation. If we did this our worksheet would appear as shown below. We would, however, recommend that wherever possible the worksheet should include a separate column for depreciation as this adds to the clarity and allows one to identify roughly how far through its useful life the asset is at the end of the year. In our example we can see that it cost £4000 and £1000 depreciation has been charged so we know we are a quarter of the way through its estimated useful life. This of course assumes that we know either the useful life or the rate of depreciation being used.

Alternative worksheet of Terri's business for year 1

	Cash £	Hot-dog stand £	Owner's equity £	Profit & loss £
Start	1000	4000	5000	
Sales	6000			6000
Expenses	–3000			–3000
Depreciation		–1000		–1000
Withdrawal	–2000			–2000
Balance	2000	3000	5000	0

In the example of Terri's business we have assumed that the cost should be spread evenly over the life of the asset. This is known as straight line depreciation and is one of a number of alternative methods that can be used as the basis for providing depreciation. Each of these alternatives will give a different figure for the deprecation charge for the year and as a result the 'written down value', often also referred to as the 'net book value', will change. This is illustrated in more detail in Example 7.5 after our discussion of methods of depreciation. Before going on to that discussion it is worth refreshing your memories on what 'written down value' is.

> **Key concept**
>
> *Written down value*
>
> This is the cost of the fixed asset less the total depreciation to date. In certain cases, such as buildings, where the asset has been revalued, the written down value is the valuation less the total depreciation to date.

METHODS OF DEPRECIATION

There are a number of alternative methods of depreciation. The choice of the appropriate method, at least theoretically, would depend upon the nature of the asset being depreciated. In practice, however, the only methods in common usage are the straight line method and the reducing balance method, and the former is used by the vast majority of businesses. As we shall see a case can be made for using different methods for different assets or classes of assets. It would be useful for you to look at the accounting policies statements in published accounts to try to identify the reasons underlying the choice of depreciation method.

The straight line method

We have already seen that this is a very simple method which probably explains why so many companies use it. The assumption, with regard to asset life that underlies the choice of this method is that the asset usage is equal for all periods of its useful life. The way in which the depreciation charge is calculated is to take the cost of the asset less the estimate of any residual value at the end of the asset life and divide it by the useful life of the asset. Thus an asset which cost £1300 and which has an estimated life of four years and an estimated scrap value of £100 would be depreciated by £300 per year. This was arrived at by using the formula given below:

$$\frac{\text{Cost} - \text{Residual value}}{\text{Useful life}} = \text{Depreciation charge}$$

In our case this works out as follows:

$$\frac{£1300 - £100}{4} = £300 \text{ per annum}$$

Reducing balance method

This method assumes that the asset declines more in the earlier years of its life than in the later years. In fact it is likely that in most cases the cost of repairs would rise as the asset gets older so this method when combined with the cost of repairs is likely to produce a more even cost of using an asset over its full life. It is less frequently used than the straight line method probably because it is slightly more difficult to calculate, although with the increasing use of computers this should not really cause any problems. The method applies a pre-calculated percentage to the written down value, or net book value, to ascertain the charge for the year. In order to arrive at the percentage we use the following formula:

$$\text{rate of depreciation} = 1 - \sqrt[\text{Useful life}]{\frac{\text{Scrap Value}}{\text{Cost of asset}}}$$

Comparison of the two methods

EXAMPLE 7.5

Let us take the situation where a business has an asset which has an estimated useful life of three years, cost £20 000 and has an estimated scrap, or residual, value of £4000:

For the straight line method we need to depreciate at £5333 a year, i.e.

$$\frac{20\,000 - 4000}{3} = £5333 \text{ per annum}$$

For the reducing balance method we first need to find the rate of depreciation to apply. In this case it will be 41.5% which we arrive at by using the formula above:

$$\text{Rate of depreciation} = 1 - \sqrt[3]{\frac{£4000}{£20\,000}}$$

$$0.415 \text{ or } 41.5\%$$

This rate is now applied to the net book value, i.e. the cost less depreciation to date.

Year	Straight line method			Reducing balance method		
	Balance sheet		**Profit & loss**	**Balance sheet**		**Profit & loss**
		£	£		£	£
	Cost	20 000		Cost	20 000	
1	Depreciation	5 333	5333	Depreciation	8 300	8300
	Net book value	14 667		Net book value	11 700	
	Cost	20 000		Cost	20 000	
2	Depreciation	10 666	5333	Depreciation	13 160	4860
	Net book value	9 334		Net book value	6 840	

Year	Straight line method Balance sheet		Profit & loss	Reducing balance method Balance sheet		Profit & loss
		£	£		£	£	
	Cost	20 000		Cost	20 000	
3	Depreciation	16 000	5334	Depreciation	16 000	2840
	Net book value	4 000		Net book value	4 000	

As can be seen from the example the charge to the profit and loss account in each year and the accumulated depreciation in the balance sheet is quite different under the two methods, although both methods charge, in total, the same amount and come to the same residual value. Under the straight line method the charge to the profit and loss is £5333 each year so the accumulated depreciation rises at £5333 a year. Under the reducing balance method the charge to the profit and loss is based on 41.5% of the balance at the end of the previous year. Thus in year 1 it is 41.5% of £20 000, in year 2 it is 41.5% of £11 700 and in year 3 41.5% of £6840.

As we have said, both methods achieve the same result in the end as under both methods the asset is written down to its residual value at the end of year 3. It is the incidence of the charge to the profit and loss account which varies, not the total charged. Whilst in theory the choice of depreciation should be governed by the nature of the asset and the way in which the benefit is used up, in practice, little, if any, attention is paid to this. However, it is worth spending some time discussing when each method would be appropriate.

We have said that the straight line method implies that the benefit is used up in an even pattern over the asset's useful life. This suggests that it is time that is the governing factor rather than use. Only in a situation where there is no change in the amount of use would an asset be used evenly throughout its useful life. In the case of a cross Channel ferry therefore it would seem that the straight line method would not be appropriate as the engines, for example, will wear out faster if more journeys are done. On the other hand, if we think of a building the fabric of the building is likely to erode as a result of the passage of time rather than use and for this asset the straight line method would seem more appropriate. In fact, although the Accounting Standard (SSAP 12) on depreciation requires that buildings are depreciated some hotel groups do not depreciate certain buildings for what they consider to be good reasons. Examples are given in Case study 7.2.

For assets where the reduction in the useful life relates to usage, the question that arises is what method should we use? There is, in fact, no generally accepted method that relates depreciation directly to use. However, it could be argued that the reducing balance method is more appropriate in these situations as it charges more in the earlier years when the equipment or vehicle is likely to give the most benefit in terms of trouble-free use. In most cases the cost of establishing precisely how long a piece of equipment or a vehicle will last is likely to be greater than the benefit to be gained from having a more accurate depreciation charge.

REVALUATION OF FIXED ASSETS

Up until the last few years of the 1980s the price of land and buildings have risen virtually every year. Given the fact that these assets have a long life, their inclusion in the balance sheet at historic cost is likely to seriously understate their value. Thus it is common practice to show land and buildings at valuation rather than cost. The reluctance to show land and buildings in the balance sheet at a figure that seriously understates their value is understandable given the profits made in the 1960s by asset strippers who bought up businesses that were still trading at a cheap price solely to realize the value of the property through selling the land and buildings. For our purposes we do not need to understand the detailed accounting treatment of revaluations. We do, however, need to be aware that if we increase the value of one

---

CASE STUDY 7.2

The Greenhalls Group plc Annual Accounts 1993

The statement of accounting policies relating to tangible fixed assets and depreciation provides the following information:

> Depreciation is not provided on non-industrial freehold and long leasehold properties as it is the Group's policy to maintain them out of expenditure charged to revenue, to a standard which ensures their estimated residual values, based on prices at the time of acquisition or revaluation, exceed net book values.

Buckingham International plc Annual Report 1992

The statement of accounting policies on fixed assets and depreciation provides the following information:

> In the opinion of the directors, the continuing policy of renovation and improvement makes the estimated residual value of the freehold and long lease property such that any depreciation charge would be immaterial.

Commentary

In the first example the reason is related to the maintenance, through upkeep, of the value of the assets making depreciation unnecessary. By contrast, in the second example there is the additional argument that the depreciation charge will not be material.

side of our balance sheet by including land and buildings at a value higher than their cost, there will be a corresponding increase in the other side of the balance sheet. This increase should be shown as a revaluation reserve and will be included as part of the total equity.

SALE OF FIXED ASSETS

Before leaving the discussion of fixed assets and depreciation we should examine the situation that arises when we sell a fixed asset. It should be obvious from our discussion above that the net book value of the asset, i.e. the cost less depreciation to date, is unlikely to bear any resemblance to the market price of that asset. This means that when an asset is sold the selling price will either be less than or exceed the net book value and a paper loss or profit will arise. If, for example, we sold the asset in Example 7.5 at the end of year 2 for £8000 then under the straight line method there would be a paper loss of £1334, i.e. the net book value of £9334 compared with the proceeds £8000. On the other hand, if we had been using the reducing balance method we would show a paper profit of £1160, i.e. the net book value of £6840 compared to the sale proceeds of £8000. We have referred to these as paper profits and losses because what they really are is a combination of factors. These could include changes in the market for the asset or the goods or services it produces, changes in technology or more simply the difference between our estimate of the future benefit being used up and the actual benefit used up. In other words, they are a measure of the error in our estimates. We shall now look at the way in which the disposal of a fixed asset is treated using the worksheet to illustrate the effect on the profit and loss account and the balance sheet.

EXAMPLE 7.6

A business bought an asset for £15 000. It estimated the useful life as three years and the scrap or residual value as £3000. The business uses straight line depreciation. For the purposes of illustration we shall assume that its sales are £14 000 a year and the total expenses are £9000 each year for years 1 and 2. We shall also assume that at the end of year 2 it sold the fixed asset for £6000.

The depreciation charge calculated using the formula given earlier is £4000 a year.

Worksheet

Year 1	Cash	Asset	Disposal	Owners' equity	Profit & loss	Depreciation
	£	£	£	£	£	£
Asset	−15 000	15 000				
Sales	14 000				14 000	
Expenses	−9 000				−9 000	
Depreciation					−4 000	4000
Balance	−10 000	15 000		0	1 000	4000
Year 2						
Sales	14 000				14 000	
Expenses	−9 000				−9 000	
Depreciation					−4 000	4000
Balance	−5 000	15 000		0	2 000	8000
Asset		−15 000	15 000			
Depreciation			−8 000			−8000
Sale proceeds	6 000		−6 000			
Balance	1 000	0	1 000	0	2 000	0
Loss on sale			−1 000		−1 000	
Final balance	1 000	0	0	0	1 000	0

You will notice when you look at the worksheet that the full depreciation is charged both in year 1 and in year 2. The reason for this is that the asset was used for the full year in both years; if it had been used for less than a full year then to be correct we would have needed to time apportion the charge. At the end of year 2, having used the asset for the full year, we decide to sell the asset. As you can see this involves a number of entries on our worksheet which we will examine in turn.

For clarity we have opened a separate account in our worksheet which we have called a 'Disposal' account. An alternative way would have been to deal with all the entries in the fixed asset column but that is more difficult to follow. First, as we have sold the asset we need to transfer the cost and any depreciation associated with that asset to a disposal column. We receive some cash in exchange for the asset so we show the cash in our cash column and in our disposal column. This leaves us with a balance on our disposal column of £1000 which is the amount of the paper loss we have made. This paper loss is transferred to the profit and loss account.

Our worksheet once again shows the correct position as we have no asset and no depreciation associated with an asset. The profit to date is reduced by £1000 because of the underestimate or paper loss in respect of the use of the asset for the two years.

The alternative way of dealing with the disposal on a worksheet is as follows. (**Note**: The worksheet given below starts from the balances at the end of year 2 after the depreciation for the year has been charged but before the disposal of the asset has been dealt with. The major difference is that instead of opening a new account to deal with the disposal all the entries are put through the existing accounts.)

Some find this latter format easier to follow and work with. The choice of which way the entries are put on the worksheet is in fact irrelevant – it is the principle involved that is important.

Worksheet alternative presentation

	Cash £	Asset £	Owners' equity £	Profit & loss £	Depreciation £
Balance	–5000	15 000	0	2000	8000
Depreciation		–8 000			–8000
Sale proceeds	6000	–6 000			0
	1000	1 000	0	2000	0
Loss on sale		–1 000		–1000	0
Final balance	1000	0	0	1000	0

In published accounts of companies there is a requirement to show the fixed assets, additions and disposals, and movements in respect of depreciation in full. An example of such disclosure is given in Case study 7.3.

SUMMARY

In this chapter we have re-introduced the definitions of assets and of fixed assets and examined some of the problems associated with arriving at the cost of a fixed asset and estimating its useful life and residual value. We have also considered the nature of depreciation and why it is charged to the profit and loss account together with the way in which it is treated in a balance sheet. We have seen that there are two methods of depreciation in common usage and examined the differences between these and the effects on the profit and loss account and the balance sheet. Some examples of the different rates of depreciation being applied to different assets are provided in Case study 7.4 below. Finally we have discussed and illustrated the way in which a revaluation and a sale of a fixed asset is dealt with via the worksheet and how a revaluation is reflected in the balance sheet.

REFERENCES

Statement of Standard Accounting Practice No.12 (1987) *Accounting for Depreciation*, Accounting Standards Committee.

CASE STUDY 7.3

Chessington World of Adventure Ltd Annual Report 1992

The following extract from the Notes to the accounts provides information on the tangible assets of the company:

	Freehold land and buildings £000	Long-term leasehold properties £000	Fixtures and equipment £000	Animals £000	Assets in the course of construction £000	Total £000
Cost						
At 1 January 1992	10 078	366	20 110	75	32	30 661
Transfers	32	–	–	–	(32)	–
Additions	516	–	902	9	117	1 544
Intercompany additions	–	–	24	–	–	24
Disposals	–	–	(53)	(10)	–	(63)
At 31 December 1992	10 626	366	20 983	74	117	32 166
Depreciation						
At 1 January 1992	1 734	33	4 769	–	–	6 536
Intercompany additions	–	–	12	–	–	12
Charge for the year	435	7	1 459	–	–	1 901
Eliminated in respect of disposals	–	–	(39)	–	–	(39)
At 31 December 1992	2 169	40	6 201	–	–	8 410
Net book value						
At 31 December 1992	8 457	326	14 782	74	117	23 756
Net book value						
At 31 December 1991	8 344	333	15 341	75	32	24 125

Commentary

The fixed asset note shown above is slightly unusual. It includes the normal requirements in respect of showing the assets split amongst the various types of fixed assets and the additions and disposals of the assets as well as the movements on depreciation. Interestingly one class of fixed assets shown is animals, and you can see in Case study 7.4 how these are treated in respect of depreciation. Another point to note here is that there is a transfer during 1990 from 'Assets in the course of construction' to 'Freehold land and buildings'. This obviously represents an asset that was completed and brought into use during the year.

FURTHER READING

A fuller treatment of alternative methods of depreciation can be found in *Accounting and Finance: A Firm Foundation*, by Alan Pizzey

(Cassell, 1990) or in *Modern Financial Accounting*, by G.A. Lee (Van Nostrand Reinhold, 1986).

A full discussion on depreciation can be found in *Depreciating Assets: An Introduction* by W.T. Baxter (Gee, 1980).

A fuller discussion of the treatment of revaluations in accounts can be found in *Financial Accounting – An Introduction* by Aidan Berry (Chapman & Hall, 1993).

CASE STUDY 7.4

Chessington World of Adventure Ltd Annual Report 1992

The following is an extract from the accounting policy on depreciation:

> No depreciation is provided on freehold land, assets in the course of construction and animals. Other fixed assets are depreciated on a straight line basis over the estimated useful lives of the assets concerned. The principal expected economic lives are:

Freehold buildings	10 years to 50 years
Fixtures and equipment	3 years to 50 years
Long term leasehold properties	50 years

The Rank Organisation Annual Accounts 1993

The following is an extract from the Notes to the accounts providing information on tangible assets:

Company	Leasehold land and buildings £m	Fixtures fittings tools and equipment £m	Total £m
Cost at 31 October 1992	1.4	2.9	4.3
Additions	–	0.6	0.6
Disposals	–	(0.4)	(0.4)
Cost at 31 October 1993	1.4	3.1	4.5
Depreciation at 31 October 1992	0.4	1.6	2.0
Depreciation for year	0.2	0.4	0.6
Disposals	–	(0.3)	(0.3)
Depreciation at 31 October 1993	0.6	1.7	2.3
Net book amount at 31 October 1993	**0.8**	**1.4**	**2.2**
Net book amount at 31 October 1992	1.0	1.3	2.3

The net book amount of leasehold land and buildings at 31 October 1993 includes £0.8m (1992 £1.0m) in respect of leases with less than 50 years to run.

Commentary

Disposals clearly show that depreciation associated with fixed assets that are sold is written back in. You will see the impact on accumulated depreciation for fixtures, fittings, tools and equipment. The charge for this year is nearly wiped out by the writing back of the depreciation associated with the items sold.

Tottenham Hotspur plc Annual Accounts 1993

The notes to the accounts provide the following information on depreciation:

Depreciation:
Freehold land is not depreciated.

Leasehold property is amortised over the term of the lease.

Other fixed assets are depreciated on a straight line basis at annual rates appropriate to their estimated useful lives as follows:

Freehold properties	2%
Motor vehicles	20%
General plant and equipment	10%–33%

Luton Town Football and Athletic Co. Ltd Annual Accounts 1992

The notes to the accounts provide the following information on depreciation:

Depreciation
Depreciation is provided on all fixed assets, other than freehold land, at rates calculated to write off the cost or valuation of each asset over its expected useful life, as follows:

Freehold buildings	– 2% per annum on cost
Leasehold buildings	– over the remaining lease term
Office furniture, fixtures, fittings, and equipment	– 10%–20% per annum on the reducing balance
Motor vehicles	– 25% per annum on cost
Leased gymnasium equipment	– 33 $\frac{1}{3}$% per annum on cost

Commentary

We can see here that companies in the same or similar sectors often have different methods of depreciation. For example, Luton Town uses the reducing balance method whereas Tottenham Hotspur uses the straight line method for their fixtures and equipment. They also use different rates of depreciation – Luton depreciates motor vehicles over four years whereas Tottenham depreciates the same assets over five years. In this case the value and number of vehicles is unlikely to result in a material difference, but it is easy to see how for companies with large fleets of vehicles such differences could affect the ease of comparability between them.

REVIEW QUESTIONS

1. What is the purpose of depreciation?
2. Why is it unlikely that depreciation will provide for replacement of the fixed asset?
3. What factors need to be taken into account in determining the useful life of an asset?
4. On what basis do we decide what should and should not be included in the cost of a fixed asset?
5. Describe what is meant by the net book value and the written down value of an asset?
6. What are the assumptions underlying the two main methods of depreciation?
7. An expense has been defined as a past or expired benefit. In what way does depreciation differ from other expenses?
8. In the chapter we described the profit or loss arising on the disposal of a fixed asset as a paper profit or loss. Explain how this profit differs from that arising from the sale of meals in a restaurant.

PROBLEMS FOR DISCUSSION AND ANALYSIS

1. In each of the following situations discuss the most appropriate method of depreciation and the period for depreciation, giving reasons for your choice.

   - **Land and Buildings.** The land was purchased for £300 000 and £400 000 was spent on the erection of the factory and office accommodation.
   - **Motor vehicles.** The hotel owns a number of vehicles all of which were bought from new. The owners have decided to trade in the vehicles for new models after four years or 60 000 miles, whichever is sooner. The anticipated mileage figures are 12 000 miles per annum for the company cars and 20 000 miles per annum for the minibus.
   - **Machinery, equipment and furniture.** The machinery etc. owned by the business can be broadly classified into three types as follows.
     – **Type 1.** Machinery which is integral to the buildings such as lifts. Some of the buildings are owned, some are on 40-year leases and some are on 10-year leases. This machinery, being integral to the buildings, has no residual value and has a normal life of approximately 15 years before it requires major overhaul or renewal.
     – **Type 2.** Kitchen equipment which is expected to last for 10 years and have a residual value of 5% of its original cost.
     – **Type 3.** Bedroom and other furniture which has an estimated useful life of 10 years before it wears out. However, based upon the need to project an image appropriate to its market niche it is

likely that much of the furniture will need to be replaced after four or five years.

2. Stayawhile's draft balance sheet at 31 March 1992 is given below. During the year to 31 March 1992 the business made a profit of £20 000 before depreciation had been charged and before dealing with items 1 and 2 below.

Item 1 On 30 September 1991 a new car had been acquired at a cost of £6000. The amount has been included under the fixed asset total but no depreciation has been charged.

Item 2 On 31 March 1992 a new computer booking system was installed and the old one was sold for £1000. The cheque from the purchaser was banked on that day but is not reflected in the bank balance as no accounting entries have been made in respect of this sale. At 31 March 1991 the old computer was recorded at cost of £20 000 and had accumulated depreciation of £12 000.

Stayawhile follows the following accounting policies in respect of depreciation.

Land   – not depreciated;
Buildings   – 2% per annum straight line;
Equipment – 20% per annum straight line;
Cars   – 25% per annum straight line.

In the year of acquisition or disposal assets are depreciated on a time apportionment basis.

Draft balance sheet of Stayawhile at 31 March 1992

	Cost £	Depreciation £	Net book value £
Fixed assets			
Land	80 000		80 000
Buildings	230 000	46 000	184 000
Equipment	80 000	48 000	32 000
Vehicles	30 000	12 000	18 000
	420 000	106 000	314 000
Current assets			
Bank		38 000	
		38 000	
Net current assets			38 000
			352 000

Financed by	£
Owners' equity	100 000
Retained profits	232 000
Profit for year	20 000
	352 000

Required:

(a) Discuss, with reference to appropriate accounting principles and standards, the way in which each of the items above should be treated.
(b) Make appropriate accounting entries on a worksheet, calculate the revised profit for the year ended 31 March 1992 and extract a revised balance sheet at that date.

3. The transactions in respect of Barry's business are set out below:

Month 1 Barry bought the lease of an existing restaurant for £90 000 using his own money and paid another £20 000 into the business bank account. He also contracted with a firm of decorators to refurbish the dining area by the end of the month at a price of £6000 which he paid at the end of the month from the business bank account.

Borrowed £40 000 from the bank repayable in equal instalments over five years.

Month 2 Re-equipped the kitchen with new equipment at a cost of £22 000.

Bought furniture, fittings, etc., for the dining area for £14 000 and paid for this immediately.

Month 3 Bought china, cutlery, glassware, etc., for £2000 and paid for this immediately.

Bought stocks of food and beverages for £4000 on one month's credit.

Month 4 Hired staff and opened for business.

Cash receipts from diners for the month amounted to £6000.

Staff wages and on-costs were paid amounting to £2500.

Bought further stocks of food and beverages for £2000 on one month's credit.

Paid his suppliers £4000.

Month 5 Cash receipts from diners for the month amounted to £8000.

Staff wages and on-costs were paid amounting to £2500.

Bought further stocks of food and beverages for £3000 on one month's credit.

Paid his suppliers £2000.

Month 6 Cash receipts from diners for the month amounted to £10 000.

Staff wages and on-costs were paid amounting to £2500.

Bought further stocks of food and beverages for £3500 on one month's credit.

Paid his suppliers £3000.

At the end of the six months his food and beverage stocks amounted to £3500.

The lease on the property had fifteen years to run when he took over the restaurant.

(a) Which assets would you classify as fixed assets and at what figure would you capitalize them?

(b) What, if any, alternatives are there to your suggestions in answer to part (a) and why do you consider your suggestions better?

(c) What advice would you give Barry concerning depreciation of his fixed assets?

(d) Would your advice change if the lease had 30 years unexpired at the date of acquisition, and if so, why would it change?

(e) Produce a worksheet of Barry's business using the following additional information:

- interest due, but not yet paid, on the bank loan for the six month period amounts to £2000;
- Barry has decided that the costs of refurbishment should be included as part of the cost of the property;
- depreciation is to be provided using the straight line method over the following periods of time:

Lease	15 years
Equipment	10 years
Furniture, fittings, etc.	8 years
China, cutlery, glassware, etc.	4 years

(f) Produce a balance sheet and profit and loss account for Barry's restaurant for the six months.

(g) Barry decided to treat his china and glassware as a fixed asset and depreciate it over four years. How would you suggest he accounts for breakages and replacements?

Financing and business structures 8

INTRODUCTION

So far, we have largely been concerned with the assets of the organization. Although we have introduced you to some forms of finance as we have worked through the book, we have not looked specifically at the way an organization finances it assets and its operations. In this chapter, we shall be considering the different forms of finance a business uses and the effects of the organizational structure upon the sources of finance available. We shall also consider the financing structure of an organization and its effect on financial risk. For our purposes, we differentiate between business risk, which applies equally to all firms in an industry with some variations relating to size and diversity, and financial risk. Financial risk is related to the capital structure of a business, i.e. the way in which it finances its assets, and by adjusting the the type of finance or the mix of equity finance to debt finance the financial risk can be altered.

In terms of the types of finance available, any attempt to classify different types of finance is problematic. However, for our purposes it is useful to look at sources of finance in some broad categories. The sources we have chosen relate to the period for which the finance is intended. We shall consider different sources of finance under the headings of short-term finance, medium-term finance and long-term finance. Before commencing our discussion of the different types of finance it is important to appreciate that the choice of appropriate finance can be vital to the long-term success of a business. The finance ideally should match the purpose for which it is to be used. For example, using what is essentially short-term finance for the purchase of a building merely creates problems when the financier has to be repaid. The building is still needed and therefore replacement finance has to be found. Similarly, taking out a loan repayable over 20 years to buy an asset that is only going to be needed for a few years would leave the business in the position of having to pay interest on money it does not need. These are, of course, extreme examples but they do serve to illustrate the point that the finance must be matched with the purpose for which it is to be used. In this regard, when choosing between various sources of finance, a business needs to bear in mind the use of the finance, the limitations of the source of finance, the costs, the repayment terms and timing, and the availability of alternatives, In considering the various forms of finance we shall endeavour to follow a pattern of providing a general description of the source of finance and then, discussing its uses, limitations, costs and availability.

SHORT-TERM FINANCE

Although there is no generally accepted definition for short-term finance, convention suggests that it is finance for a period less than a year. Short-term finance, in general, should be used to finance short-term capital requirements such as working capital, i.e. financing stock and debtors. There are a number of sources of finance that are available. The most common are trade credit, bank overdraft and factoring which we shall consider below.

Trade credit

We have already come across trade credit in Chapter 6 which dealt with accrual accounting including debtors and creditors. As we pointed out there, it is normal for a supplier to allow its business customers a period of time after the goods have been delivered before payment is required. The period of time and the amount of credit a business gets from its suppliers is dependent upon a number of factors. These include the 'normal' terms of trade of that industry, the supplier's view of the business's creditworthiness and how much it values the custom of that business customer. Thus, for example, a new hotel group is likely to get less favourable terms than Grand Metropolitan.

Trade credit is widely used as a source of finance by businesses. This is done by buying goods and paying for them some period after they are delivered. In general, trade credit provides short-term finance that can be used to finance, or partially finance, debtors and stock. As such its importance varies from industry to industry and to some extent within an industry depending, in part, on the size of the firm involved. In general, hotels and restaurants do not rely heavily on trade credit as a source of finance. This is because of the nature of their assets which are generally dominated by the costs of their buildings and other fixed assets and their relatively low stockholding requirements. In the licensed trade, however, many small businesses, i.e. publicans, do rely quite heavily on trade credit and this reliance makes them vulnerable if that credit is not managed effectively. In this regard, the objective is to take as much time to pay as is reasonable without affecting the supplier's judgement of your creditworthiness. If too long a period is taken, the supplier is likely to be reluctant to allow the same favourable terms next time. Where a business is experiencing problems, the temptation to extend the repayment date has often led to the withdrawal of any period of credit. This leaves the business in the position that all supplies have either to be paid for in advance or on a cash on delivery basis. Businesses that rely too much on trade credit run the risk of losing their line of credit and ultimately of bankruptcy or liquidation. Although suppliers are generally reluctant to take such steps, if they believe that they are more likely to recover their money by such a course of action that is what they will do.

Trade credit is often thought of as cost-free credit. However, this is not strictly true as quite often suppliers allow a small discount for early payment. Therefore taking the full period to pay has an opportunity cost in the form of the discount forgone. This opportunity cost has to be weighed against the availability of funds within the business or the cost of raising additional funds.

Factoring

If a business makes sales on credit, it will have to collect payment from its debtors at some stage. Up until that point, it will have to finance those debtors, either through trade credit, an overdraft or its own capital. The costs of this finance can be very high and many small businesses will be hard up against their limits in terms of their overdraft and the amount and period of trade credit taken. In order to release the money tied up in debtors the business can approach a factoring company, which is a finance company which specializes in providing a service for the collection of payments from debtors.

Essentially, the way the system works is that the factoring organization assesses the firm's debtors in terms of risk and collectability. It then agrees to collect the money due on behalf of the business concerned. Once an agreement is reached the factoring company pays the business in respect of the invoices for the month virtually straightaway. It is then the factoring organization's responsibility to collect from the debtors as soon as possible. The factoring company charges for this in the form of a fee or by 'buying' the debtors at a discount. This form of finance is therefore more expensive than trade credit but can be useful as it allows the business to concentrate on production and sales and improves the cash flow. Because of the nature of the customer base in the hospitality industry which may be dominated by individuals rather than other business customers, the usefulness of factoring as a source of finance is likely to be very restricted.

Bank overdrafts

Banks provide business with short-term finance for working capital, either in the form of short-term loans or, more commonly, in the form of an overdraft. The difference is that a loan is for a fixed period of time and interest is charged on the full amount of the loan, less any agreed repayments, for the period. An overdraft by contrast is a facility that can be used as and when required and interest is only charged when it is used. Thus, if a business knows that it needs money for a fixed period of time then a bank loan may be appropriate; on the other hand, if the finance is only required to meet occasional short-term cash flow needs then an overdraft would be more suitable. We shall discuss loans in more detail under the heading of medium-term finance.

Although many businesses use overdrafts as a semi-permanent source of finance this is not how the banks would like to see this form of finance used. Bank managers like to see a business bank account, on which an overdraft facility has been provided, swinging between having money in the bank account and using the overdraft. They do not see an overdraft as a form of permanent working capital.

A bank overdraft carries with it a charge in the form of interest and often a fee for setting up the facility. The latter, which is a one-off charge, has become more common in recent years. As far as the interest is concerned, the rate of interest charged is related to the risk involved and the market rates of interest for that size of business. In general, the more risk involved the higher the rate of interest. Due to the fact that they operate in a volatile market small firms tend to be charged higher rates of interest than large firms.

In addition, banks will normally require security which can take various forms. In the case of a small business, whether it is a company or not, the security could be a charge on the assets of the business. In many cases, however, the property is already subject to a charge as it is mortgaged. In these situations the bank may take a second charge on the property or on the owner's home or homes if more than one person is involved. Alternatively, or in addition, the bank may require personal guarantees from the owner or, in the case of a limited company, the directors.

For larger companies, the security may be a fixed charge on certain assets, or a floating charge on all the assets. In the case of very large companies the risk involved is lower and the competition between the providers of finance is greater, therefore overdrafts are not only cheaper but they are also more easily accessible and security is less of a factor.

MEDIUM-TERM FINANCE

There are a number of sources of medium-term finance that can be used by a business. We shall limit our discussion to medium-term loans, leases and hire-purchase.

Loans

As we pointed out, an alternative to overdraft finance for short-term finance requirements is bank loans. In general loans should only be used when finance is required for a known period of time. Ideally that period should relate to the life of the asset or the purpose for which the finance is to be used. Loans can be obtained for short-term, medium-term or long-term finance.

Compared to an overdraft facility which can be used as and when needed, a loan is more permanent. Repayment of the loan is negotiated at the time the loan is taken out and is generally at fixed intervals. They are often secured in the same way as overdrafts and if the repayment conditions are not met then the lender will take action to recover the outstanding amount.

Bank loans are often granted for a specified purpose and limitations may be imposed regarding the use of the loan and the raising of other finance while the loan is outstanding. Unlike an overdraft, the cost of this form of finance is known in advance as interest accrues from the time the business borrows the money irrespective of the fact that it may not use it straightaway. In common with other forms of finance discussed so far, the rate of interest charged and the availability of this source of finance is dependent upon the size of the business and the lender's assessment of the risk involved. Thus, in general, the larger and more diversified a business is the easier will be their access to this form of finance.

Hire-purchase

An alternative way of financing the acquisition of an asset is through the use of hire-purchase. Under a hire-purchase agreement a finance company buys the asset and hires it to the business. Thus a business can acquire the asset and use it even though it has not yet paid for it in full. During the period of the hire-purchase agreement the finance company owns the asset. The hirer has the right to use the asset and carries all the risks associated with using that asset. Thus, for example, if a car is purchased on hire-purchase, the hirer would be responsible for all the repairs and costs associated with the use of that car in the same way as if they had bought the car directly. At the end of the period of the hire-purchase agreement the ownership of the asset is transferred to the hirer. A normal hire-purchase agreement consists of a deposit and a set number of payments over a number of years.

This type of finance can only be used when a specific asset is purchased, i.e. the finance is for a specified asset purchase. It cannot be used for financing working capital requirements or any other purpose. The hire-purchase company actually pays the supplier of the asset directly and the asset belongs to the hire-purchase company. If repayments are not made in accordance with the hire-purchase agreement the hire-purchase company has the right to repossess its property.

The monthly repayments consist of an amount which includes both a repayment of the capital borrowed and a charge for interest. The rate of interest charged will be dependent upon the market rate of interest but is likely to be higher than the interest on a bank loan.

Hire-purchase is available to all businesses and individuals subject, of course, to the hire-purchase company being satisfied with the creditworthiness of the person or business using the hire-purchase. The amount of money that can be raised via hire-purchase is limited to the price of the asset.

Leasing

A lease is an agreement between a lessor, the person who owns the asset, and a lessee, the person who uses the asset. It conveys the right to use that asset for a stated period of time in exchange for payment but does not necessarily transfer ownership at the end of the lease period. The period can vary from a very short period to 10 or more years. In common with hire-purchase, this form of finance is tied to a specific asset. Thus its use as a source of finance is limited to the purchase of capital items. Leasing companies will often provide leases tailored to the needs of an industry. For example, in hotels it is possible to obtain lease finance for the internal telephone system or even the complete furnishing of a hotel.

In general the cost of leasing is similar to that of hire-purchase. The major difference between the two sorts of finance is that, in general, leases tend to be for a longer period of time and are frequently used as a source of finance for specialized assets. In essence there are two distinct types of leases – operating leases and finance leases. An operating lease is the same in reality as renting the equipment and usually applies to items such as photocopiers etc. This is reflected in the definition given in the Key concept below.

Key concept

An operating lease

A lease where the underlying substance of the transaction is a rental arrangement.

The underlying economic substance of a finance lease, on the other hand, is equivalent to borrowing money from a finance company and then using that money to buy an asset. This is reflected in the definition given the Key concept below.

Key concept

A finance lease

A lease where the underlying substance of the transaction is a financing arrangement.

Sale and lease back

The sale and lease back of property is a popular source of finance for hotel companies and some shipping companies. A company that owns freehold properties or long leasehold properties can release money for use elsewhere in the business or for expansion by selling the property to a finance or insurance company for the full market value and then renting the property back from that company. Such rental agreements tend to be very long term, frequently 99 years or more and have regular rent reviews built into the agreement. The vendor is normally still responsible for maintenance and insurance of the building.

The advantages of such an arrangement from the point of view of the vendor is that the money released can be used for other purposes. As such the question of whether such an arrangement would be advantageous is largely dependent upon the use of the funds and the benefits obtained from their use. If this exceeds the cost of the rentals plus the loss of any increase in the value of the property then there will be an advantage in entering into such an arrangement. However, the fact that the business no longer owns the property and its effect on its total borrowing capability needs to be carefully considered before going ahead with a sale and lease back arrangement.

An example of some of the disclosures required in respect of leases is provided in Case study 8.1 below.

LONG-TERM FINANCE

The number of alternative sources of long-term finance available are, to some extent, dependent upon the type of organization involved. We shall start our discussion with debt finance, such as long-term loans, which are more generally available, and then move on to discuss equity finance. The latter discussion will be subdivided in terms of organization types, i.e. sole proprietorships, partnerships and limited companies, as these affect the type of equity finance available. In respect of limited companies, we shall limit our discussion to private limited companies.

Debt finance

This is the term given to any source of long-term finance that is not equity finance. Often, debt finance is seen exclusively as long-term interest bearing finance. This is, in fact, a misconception as all the finance we have discussed so far has been debt finance. We shall look at two broad categories of long-term debt finance, i.e. long-term loans which are available to all organizations, and debentures and loan stock which tend to be used by incorporated businesses.

CASE STUDY 8.1

British Airways Annual Report and Accounts 1993

The following extract from the Notes to the accounts shows that tangible fixed assets for the group amounted to £4230 million. The extract breaks this figure down by class of asset and shows whether they are owned, under finance lease or hire-purchase agreement.

10 TANGIBLE ASSETS

£ million	Fleet	Property	Equipment	**1993**	Total 1992
GROUP					
COST OR VALUATION					
Balance 1 April	4,496	592	554	**5,642**	5,183
Exchange adjustments	129			**129**	13
Additions	942	63	70	**1,075**	947
Disposals	(151)		(11)	**(162)**	(334)
Reclassification of capitalised interest					(9)
Refund of progress payments	(32)			**(32)**	(158)
Balance at 31 March	5,384	655	613	**6,652**	5,642
DEPRECIATION					
Balance 1 April	1,667	172	331	**2,170**	2,049
Exchange adjustments	7			**7**	4
Charge for the year	231	19	62	**312**	295
Provision against aircraft not in current use	4			**4**	8
Disposals	(62)		(9)	**(71)**	(185)
Reclassification of capitalised interest					(1)
Balance at 31 March	1,847	191	384	**2,422**	2,170
NET BOOK AMOUNTS					
31 March 1993	3,537	464	229	**4,230**	
31 March 1992	2,829	420	223		3,472
UTILISATION AT 31 MARCH					
Assets in current use					
Owned	1,787	347	176	**2,310**	2,057
Finance leased	590		6	**596**	347
Hire purchase arrangements	875			**875**	695
Progress payments	224	117	47	**388**	313
Assets not in current use	61			**61**	60
	3,537	464	229	**4,230**	3,472

Commentary

You can see that a high proportion of the fleet of aircraft (approx. 41%) are either under finance lease or high-purchase agreement. You will find that for many other airlines this percentage is even higher.

Long-term loans

As we have said, a loan can be used for short-term, medium-term or long-term finance. Long-term loans have the same characteristics as short- and medium-term loans as regards the purpose of the loan and the repayment of the loan. Interest rates are likely to be different as these will need to be adjusted to take into account the higher risk associated with lending money for a longer period of time. Long-term loans are often for a specific purpose, e.g. the purchase of property, and the time period is affected by the life of the asset, the repayments required and the willingness of the lender to lend money. For many small businesses these loans often take the form of a commercial mortgage on property.

Apart from loans related to property, which are effectively commercial mortgages, the period of these loans is less in the UK than in Germany and Japan where long loan periods are more common. This may reflect a reluctance on the part of banks and other financial institutions to lend money for long periods of time. This was starting to change in the late 1980s and early 1990s when building societies were beginning to take advantage of the deregulation of financial services to enter this market. Unfortunately, but perhaps understandably, a number of them got their fingers badly burned. This was probably due to a number of factors, including a lack of expertise which was in residential lending to individuals against income rather than to companies against a set of accounting numbers. In addition the recession was starting and interest rates were still rising. This meant that a number of organizations which had been operating on tight margins went out of business with consequential effects on the demand for, and price of, commercial property. Therefore, there are still limitations on the availability of long-term loans especially for the purchase of assets other than property. As is the case with all the other types of finance we have discussed, the availability of this source of finance is also heavily dependent upon the lender's assessment of the creditworthiness of the prospective borrower.

In the case of large companies, especially those such as international hotel groups, there is also the opportunity to raise funds from the European market and other markets around the world as is evident from Case study 8.2 below.

Debentures and loan stock

These are terms used for particular types of long-term loans to limited companies. They basically mean the same thing and are essentially long-term loan finance. The main difference between these and the long-term loans which are also available to other types of organization is that interest tends to be fixed and repayment tends to be at a fixed point in time rather than over the period of the loan as would be the case for a commercial mortgage or other long-term loan. Debentures and loan stock are issued by the company raising the finance and can usually be traded on what are known as secondary markets. The price at which these debentures etc. can be sold and bought on the secondary market will not be the same as the price at which they were issued. This variation is related to changes in interest rates over time. In virtually all debenture deeds there is a right to repayment or appointment of a receiver if interest is not paid when due. The cost of this type of finance is similar to that for long-term loans and is affected by the market rate of interest when the debenture loan stock is issued, the security available and the risk involved. For this reason, they are more commonly seen in the accounts of larger companies.

EQUITY FINANCE

The other major source of long-term finance is equity finance, and here we need to look at organizational types as this can have a major effect on the type and amount of finance available.

Sole proprietorships

In the case of a sole proprietorship, as we have seen, the only sources of equity finance are those supplied by the owner and the retained profits. In many small businesses, the amount of funds that the owner has available to put into the business is limited. This means that the only source of equity finance is retained profits. In a fast-growing business it is unlikely that there will be sufficient retained profits to finance expansion. As such, sole proprietorships, in common with many small businesses, become very reliant on debt finance and, as we shall see, this exposes them to more risk as a downturn in the market, or an increase in interest rates, could have a dramatic impact on their ability to service the debt. Unlike debt finance equity finance has no limitations in terms of the use to which it is put.

Partnerships

Partnerships, as the name implies, are organizations that are owned, and often managed, by a number of individuals. They are most common among professionals; thus we see doctors, dentists, lawyers, architects and, of course, accountants working in partnerships. In essence, the sources of equity finance for partnerships are the same as for sole proprietorships, i.e. money contributed by the owners and retained profits. There are, of course, more people involved so more equity can be raised through contributions by the owners. Partnerships are governed by the legislation contained in the 1890 Partnership Act and by case law. In general the main difference between partnerships and sole proprietorships is that, whereas the sole proprietor is the only person responsible for the debts, in a partnership the partners are 'jointly and severally' liable. This means that if a partner cannot pay their share of the debts the other partners must pay. The other important difference is related to the division of profits, which must be

---

CASE STUDY 8.2

Forte plc Annual Accounts 1994

The following extract from the Notes to the accounts provides information on bank and other borrowings:

	Group		Company	
	1994 £ million	1993 £ million	1994 £ million	1993 £ million
Secured loans				
10% First Mortgage Debenture Stock 2018	200	–	200	–
*Other secured loans (average interest rate 10.0%)	37	59	–	13
Total secured loans	237	59	200	13
Unsecured loan				
6.75% Sterling Subordinated Convertible Bonds 2008	90	–	90	–
9.375% Sterling Eurobond 2003	100	–	100	–
*Floating Rate Sterling Notes 1998 (6.1875%)	50	–	50	–
8.375% Sterling Eurobond 1997	100	100	100	100
7.75% US$175m Eurobond 1996	117	118	117	118
*Floating Rate Sterling Notes 1996 (6.2875%)	100	–	100	–
5.375% US$200m Eurobond 1994	140	135	140	135
Sterling Commercial Paper	–	39	–	39
US Dollar Domestic Commercial Paper	–	7	–	7
*Other unsecured loans (average rate 9.2%)	228	733	155	594
Total unsecured loans	925	1,132	852	993
Total loans	1,162	1,191	1,052	1,006
Bills of exchange	10	100	10	100
Bank overdrafts	63	37	48	17
Total bank and other borrowings	1,235	1,328	1,110	1,123
Due within one year	248	534	211	438
Due after one year	987	794	899	685
Total bank and other borrowings	**1,235**	**1,328**	**1,110**	**1,123**

Commentary

As can be seen, an international hotel group, in common with other international companies, has access to a number of different financial markets to raise finance. The study of the forms of finance available in the international marketplace is a subject in its own right and is outside the scope of this book.

divided amongst the partners in accordance with the partnership agreement.

We shall be looking at the subject of partnerships in more detail in Chapter 9 where the accounting problems of partnerships will be discussed. For our purposes here, we can look at partnerships as having the same sources of equity finance as sole proprietorships. The only difference is that they are likely to have access to a greater supply of funds. In addition there may be differences in relation to the availability of retained profits as some partners may leave more profits in the business than others. This will of course depend upon the individual partners' requirements for funds.

Limited companies

Limited companies have the advantage, from an investor's point of view, that the liability of the owners is limited to the amount they have invested in the company. As with partnerships and sole proprietorships, the major source of equity comes from the owners through the issue of ordinary shares.

Ordinary shares

In the case of companies, the equity is divided into ordinary shares which represent contributed capital, and reserves which represent profits made by the company. Each share has a nominal or par value, e.g. 10p or £1. This value has little significance in terms of the price at which the shares are bought and sold on the stock market. It is, however, the figure at which the shares are shown in the accounts. In the case of an existing company any new shares issued after the company has been trading are likely to be issued at a price in excess of the nominal value. The difference between the nominal value and the price at which the share is issued is put to a special account known as the share premium account. This is often referred to as a 'capital reserve account'. Essentially it is non-distributable except under specific circumstances laid down in the Companies Acts.

As with any other form of organization, the other main source of equity capital is retained profits. Unlike a sole proprietorship or partnership, a company distributes its profits by way of dividends. The directors decide on the amount of dividend to be paid and the timing of the dividends, and until a dividend is declared by the directors the shareholders have no prima facie right to a dividend. Dividends can be paid during the year and/or at the end of the year. If they are paid during the year they are referred to as interim dividends and the dividend at the end of the year is referred to as the final dividend. Dividends are treated differently from drawings which, as we have seen, are normally deducted from the owner's equity. They are not deducted from capital and are shown as an appropriation of profit, i.e.

they are deducted from the profit after tax. There are also differences relating to tax which we shall not concern ourselves with here.

A company has the advantage over a sole proprietorship or a partnership in that it can issue shares to whoever it wishes in whatever proportions it wishes. The shareholders do not have to take part in the management of the company, and in most large companies the vast majority of shareholders play virtually no part in the management of the company. They merely invest their money and take the risk that they will get better returns, in the form of their share of the profits, than they would by investing in safer fixed interest investments. Ultimately, all the profits belong to the shareholders, so if they do not get their share of the profits in the form of dividends, i.e. the profits are retained in the company, their share of the profits and future profits is reflected in the price at which they could sell their shares.

Issue of shares

Companies when they are formed are set up with a specified authorized share capital. This is the maximum amount of share capital that can be raised through the issue of shares. It can be increased subsequently by the members of the company but until that happens it forms an effective ceiling on the amount of equity finance that can be raised from shareholders directly. Ordinary shares can be issued either as a full price issue, as a rights issue, or as a bonus issue.

Full price issues

In the case of a full price issue, as the name suggests, the share is issued at the market price. In the case of a company quoted on the stock exchange or the unlisted securities market this price is already known. In the case of a private company a value would have to be put on the company and then divided by the total number of shares to arrive at a market price. As we have said, it is likely that this price will exceed the nominal or par value, and the excess over the par value will be shown in an account known as the share premium account.

Rights issues

An alternative to a full price issue is to offer the additional shares to the existing shareholders only, on the basis that they have a right to buy shares in proportion to their existing holding. This type of share issue has the advantage of retaining the existing spread of share holdings and the existing status quo in terms of relative voting power. Rights issues are normally offered at a price slightly below market price. The reasons for this are that this form of share issue is cheaper to administer than an open to all full price issue, and a lower price also encourages shareholders to exercise their rights and buy the shares.

Bonus issues

The other alternative we mentioned was a bonus issue. These are also referred to as capitalization issues and sometimes scrip issues. In this case no money is raised; the purpose of the bonus issue is to increase the number of shares in issue. This has the effect of reducing the price per share and making the shares more marketable. A bonus issue may have as its objective a reduction in the share price or it may be used for other reasons such as boosting shareholder confidence. In effect, what happens is that a transfer is made from one of the reserves to the share capital account.

Preference shares

Apart from ordinary shares, a company can also issue preference shares. Unlike ordinary shares a preference share normally has a fixed dividend and even if more profits are made the preference dividend remains the same. In addition they normally carry a right to preference in the order of payment in the event of the company going into liquidation. They are therefore less risky than ordinary shares and appeal to a different sort of investor. Whether these shares should be classified as equity or debt would depend on the particular type of preference shares in question and the rights attaching to them. Preference shares may be redeemable or non-redeemable. They may carry a right to dividends on a cumulative basis, i.e. if the directors do not pay any dividends in a year the preference shareholders will have a right to be paid that year's dividend and any others that have not been paid before the ordinary shareholders can be paid any dividend. Some preference shares are participating preference shares, whereby they get a share of profits if the profit is over a certain figure.

From an accounting point of view they are shown as a separate class of shares. Any premiums on the issue of preference shares go to the share premium account in the same way as premiums on ordinary shares and are not separated in any way. If the preference shares are redeemed the company is obliged by the Companies Act to transfer an amount equivalent to the par value of the shares redeemed into a non-distributable reserve known as the capital redemption reserve. This in effect means that in a legal sense preference shares are seen as more akin to equity than debt as no such legal requirement exists for the redemption of loans or debentures.

FINANCING STRUCTURES AND FINANCIAL RISK

The mix of debt finance and equity finance is known as gearing and it affects the financial risk of an enterprise. Basically the more reliant a business is on debt finance, i.e. the more highly geared, the greater the risk. The risk we are referring to here is that if interest rates go up or the profit margin comes down the enterprise would not be able to pay the interest or repayments due on its debt finance. There are, of course, advantages to being highly geared as well as disadvantages as Example 8.1 illustrates.

EXAMPLE 8.1

Highrisk has equity capital consisting of 20 000 ordinary shares of £1 each. It has retained profits of £10 000 and has £40 000 in loans on which interest at 3% above the base rate, which currently stands at 12%, is due.

Lowrisk has equity capital consisting of 40 000 ordinary shares of £1 each. It has retained profits of £10 000 and has £20 000 in loans on which interest at 3% above the base rate, i.e. 15%, is due.

Situation 1

Both companies make sales of £100 000 and their net profit before interest is 10% on sales.

The profit and loss accounts for the two companies would be as shown below:

	Highrisk £	**Lowrisk** £
Sales	100 000	100 000
Cost	90 000	90 000
Net profit	10 000	10 000
Interest	6 000	3 000
Available for equity shares	4 000	7 000
Profit per share	0.20	0.17

As you can see, the ordinary shareholders of Highrisk are getting a better return than the shareholders of Lowrisk. They are getting 20p per share return as compared to 17p per share in Lowrisk, even though both companies have the same sales, costs and net profit before interest charges.

EXAMPLE 8.1

Situation 2 – increased costs

In this situation, instead of making a net profit before interest of 10% of sales, the companies find that they can only make 8%.

In this case the profit and loss accounts of the two companies would be as follows:

	Highrisk £	Lowrisk £
Sales	100 000	100 000
Cost	92 000	92 000
Net profit	8 000	8 000
Interest	6 000	3 000
Available for equity shares	2 000	5 000
Profit per share	0.10	0.13

In this case the profit margin of both businesses has fallen by the same amount. As a result, the profit available for the equity shares has dropped in both cases. However, the effect on the profit per share is more dramatic in the case of Highrisk than it is in the case of Lowrisk.

EXAMPLE 8.1

Situation 3 – increased interest rates

In this situation the facts are the same as in Situation 2 above, i.e. the net profit before interest is 8% on the sales. However, in addition, the base rate of interest moves to 13% and therefore the interest on the loans moves up to 16%.

In this case the profit and loss accounts of the two companies would be as follows:

	Highrisk £	Lowrisk £
Sales	100 000	100 000
Cost	92 000	92 000
Net profit	8 000	8 000
Interest	6 400	3 200
Available for equity shares	1 600	4 800
Profit per share	0.08	0.12

These examples illustrate the effects of high gearing which are to increase the returns to shareholders but at the same time make them more vulnerable to decreases in the profit margin. These can be caused by a reduction of sales or an increase in costs. In addition, their returns are also affected more by increases in interest rates than those of a low geared company.

It is worth mentioning that the lower the share of the business that is financed by equity, the more difficult it is to raise debt finance. Banks in the UK like to see a ratio of one to one, i.e. they will lend money, all other things being equal, so that the debt finance is equal to the equity share. There is often a clause to that effect included in the loan agreement. If the clause limits the amount of borrowing to the equity total then decisions on how much profit to retain, whether to revalue land and buildings, etc., can have a dramatic effect on the company's ability to raise finance.

SUMMARY

In this chapter we have considered the main types of short-term, medium-term and long-term finance that are available to all organizations. We have also looked at equity finance in the form of contributed capital and retained profits. The effects of different organizational forms on the sources of equity finance have been discussed and the effects of the mix of debt to equity finance on the returns to equity shareholders have been discussed and illustrated. It is important to remember that one vital point raised in this chapter was that the type of finance used should relate to the purpose for which that finance will be used.

FURTHER READING

J. Arnold, T. Hope and A.J. Southwood (1985) *Financial Accounting*, Chapter 11, Prentice Hall.
Λ. Pizzey (1990) *Accounting and Finance: A Firm Foundation*, 3rd cdn, Chapter 21, Cassell.

REVIEW QUESTIONS

1. Why is it important to match the type of finance with the purpose of raising that finance?
2. What are the forms of short-term finance discussed in the chapter?
3. What are the main differences between equity finance and debt finance?
4. What are the differences between drawings and dividends?
5. What does the term highly geared refer to?
6. What are the advantages and disadvantages of being highly geared?
7. What do the following terms mean and what are their basic characteristics?
   (a) Nominal or par value
   (b) Share premium
   (c) Capital redemption reserve
   (d) Rights issue
   (e) Bonus issue
   (f) Preference shares

PROBLEMS FOR DISCUSSION AND ANALYSIS

1. A friend who has her own pizza home delivery company has been to see the bank manager about borrowing some money to finance the acquisition of a new van and a new pizza oven. The bank manager has said that, in view of the current financial structure of the company, the bank would not be prepared to provide funds unsecured. The latest balance sheet of the company is given below.

Balance sheet

	Cost £	Depreciation £	£
Fixed assets			
Equipment	20 000	5 000	15 000
Vehicles	12 000	4 000	8 000
	32 000	9 000	23 000
Current assets			
Stock		1 200	
Cash		500	
		1 700	
Creditors: falling due within one year			
Trade creditors		2 500	
Taxation		3 600	
Bank overdraft		4 300	
		10 400	
Net current liabilities			(8 700)
Creditors: falling due after one year			(5 000)
			9 300
Financed by			£
Ordinary shares			5 000
Retained profits			4 300
			9 300

Required:
(a) Advise your friend what alternative sources of finance are available and which would be appropriate for the purpose of buying a van and buying a new machine.
(b) Explain why, in your opinion, the bank manager was not prepared to lend unsecured.

2. Ben was planning to open a fish and chip shop. He has produced the following projections for the first year based on his experience of the area and some careful research.

	£
Sales	36 000
Cost of 10-year lease	30 000
Refurbishment	3 000
Equipment	20 000
Stock of fish, etc.	1 000
Rent	2 000
Electricity	900
Wages	8 000
Personal drawings	5 000

Ben estimates that the costs of fish etc. required to make the sales target of £36 000 will be £12 000.

He says that the equipment will last for five years and has no residual value. He has £40 000 in savings but is reluctant to invest the whole of that. He has been offered a loan of £20 000 to help buy the lease at an interest rate of 10% per annum for the first year with no repayments required during that year. After the first year the rate will be 4% above base rate. Base rate currently stands at 12%.

Alternatively he can borrow money using a bank overdraft at a rate of 17% per annum.

Required:
(a) Calculate what Ben's profit would be if he put in all his own money and borrowed anything else he needs. (**Hints**: The receipts and payments have to be looked at in terms of their regularity and their timing.)
(b) Calculate what Ben's profit would be in the first year assuming he takes the loan.
(c) Calculate what Ben's profit would be in the second year assuming he does not take the loan and sales and costs are the same as the first year.
(d) Calculate what Ben's profit would be in the second year assuming he takes the loan.
(e) Ben has asked you to advise him on the choice between the two alternatives. How would you advise him and what reasons would you give?

Final accounts and organizational structures 9

INTRODUCTION

In this chapter we shall consider how the final accounts of an organization are extracted from the worksheet. We shall also discuss alternative formats of final accounts, and how these relate to different forms of organization, for example a partnership as compared to a limited company. This will expand the discussion in the previous chapter and look more specifically at the ways in which the types of organizational structure impacts on its financial reporting. We shall also consider as part of that discussion the advantages and disadvantages of the different organizational forms available.

OBTAINING THE FINAL ACCOUNTS

Prior to our discussion of final accounts we shall first illustrate where the figures that are included in the final accounts are derived from. For this purpose we shall work through a simple example which will bring together the ideas covered in Chapters 5, 6 and 7.

EXAMPLE 9.1

Graham opened a new business selling specialist hiking holidays. During the first year the following transactions took place.

1. Opened a business bank account and paid in £30 000 of his own money.
2. Bought a minibus for £15 000 and paid for it in cash.
3. Placed advertisements in the weekend supplements of the quality newspapers costing £4000 and paid for these during the year.
4. Sold complete holidays for a total of 120 people who each paid £200 for a week's hiking holiday.

5. Paid for petrol and other expenses relating to the minibus amounting to £1700.
6. Paid for hire of camp sites and other overnight accommodation amounting to £3600 and still owed £900 at the year end.
7. Paid telephone bills and other miscellaneous bills amounting to £970.
8. Withdrew £7000 for his own use.

Let us first see what the worksheet would look like for Graham's business. This is given below:

Graham's worksheet: version 1

	Assets		=	Equity		+ Liabilities
	Cash	**Minibus**		**Owner's equity**	**Profit & loss**	**Creditors**
	£	£		£	£	£
Item 1	−30 000			30 000		
Item 2	−15 000	15 000				
Item 3	−4 000				−4 000	
Item 4	24 000				24 000	
Item 5	−1 700				−1 700	
Item 6	−3 600				−4 500	900
Item 7	−970				−970	
Item 8	−7 000			−7 000		
Balance	21 730	15 000		23 000	12 830	900

You should make sure that you understand the entries on the worksheet above before moving on. If you have problems refer back to the appropriate chapters.

Before we move on to the next stage of preparation of the final accounts we need to check that we have not made an error in our double-entry. This we do by ensuring that the final line balances. We can now move on to the next stage where final adjustments are made for accruals, depreciation, etc. These adjustments are often referred to in the literature as end of period or end of year adjustments.

End of period adjustments

End of period adjustments, i.e. those adjustments which have to be made at the end of an accounting period, refer to items such as providing for the depreciation charge for the period, identifying any bad debts, accruals or prepayments, etc. These have all been covered in Chapters 6 and 7 and you should be familiar with the way in which they are dealt with.

EXAMPLE 9.1

Further information

At the end of the year Graham decides that the minibus will have a scrap value of £3000 and should be depreciated over five years. He also tells you that he still owes £8400 to a hotel group for meals. The amount has been in dispute as there was some confusion over the discounts offered but the dispute has now been settled and Graham intends to pay the full amount.

Entering these adjustments would result in the worksheet shown below. You will notice that we have had to open a new account (column) to deal with the changes and then arrive at a new balance. The adjustments which we have labelled meals and depreciation are sometimes also labelled 'end of period' or 'final' adjustments.

Graham's worksheet: version 2

	Assets		=	Equity		+ Liabilities	
	Cash	Minibus	Owner's equity	Profit & loss	Creditors	Depreciation
	£	£	£	£	£	£
Item 1	30 000		30 000			
Item 2	–15 000	15 000				
Item 3	–4 000			–4 000		
Item 4	24 000			24 000		
Item 5	–1 700			–1 700		
Item 6	–3 600			–4 500	900	
Item 7	–970			–970		
Item 8	–7 000		– 7 000			
Balance	21 730	15 000	23 000	12 830	900	
Meals				–8 400	8400	
Depreciation				–2 400		2400
Balance	21 730	15 000	23 000	2 030	9300	2400

We shall now consider the way in which final accounts are produced and the rules and regulations governing their format.

Final accounts

Before we look at the regulations and the effects of different organizational forms we should remind ourselves of the way in which the final accounts, i.e. the balance sheet and the profit and loss account, are derived from the worksheet. This may be more readily understood if we consider the example of Graham's business. We shall therefore extract the final accounts from the worksheet above.

Profit and loss account of Graham's business for the year ended on 30 June 19X9

	£	£
Sales		24 000
Cost of holidays sold		12 900
Gross profit		11 100
Advertising	4000	
Minibus expenses	1700	
Telephone	970	
Minibus depreciation	2400	9 070
Net profit		2 030

You will remember that the profit and loss account merely summarizes what is contained in that column of the worksheet. It is titled the profit and loss account for the period ended on a certain date. This emphasizes that the profit and loss account is a period statement and here we can contrast it with the heading of the balance sheet below. This you will remember is at a particular point in time – a snapshot.

Balance sheet of Graham's business as at 30 June 19X9

	£	£
Fixed assets		
Minibus at cost	15 000	
Depreciation	2 400	12 600
Current assets		
Cash	21 730	
	21 730	
Current liabilities		
Creditors	9 300	
	9 300	
Net current assets		12 430
		25 030
Financed by		£
Owner's equity		30 000
Less: Drawings		7 000
		23 000
Profit and loss		2 030
		25 030

You will have noticed that the balance sheet merely takes the final line of the worksheet, with the exception of the drawings, and classifies it under appropriate headings to enable the reader to interpret the information more readily. As far as drawings are concerned these are deducted from the owner's equity as they do not represent a business expense. We will be dealing with the subject of interpretation in more detail in Chapter 10. Prior to that, however, we need to consider the effect of different forms of organizational structure on the final accounting reports.

FORMS OF ORGANIZATION

There are many forms of organization – a sole proprietorship, a partnership, a company, a group of companies as well as multinational conglomerates. In addition there are other less common forms such as cooperatives, trusts, friendly societies, provident societies, etc. Each of these organizational forms requires slightly different accounts. This may be due to the needs of the users being slightly different or to other factors such as the impact of legislation – for example, companies are governed by the Companies Acts – or other regulations, for example those imposed by the stock exchange. Rather than attempting to deal with all the different forms of organizations we will concentrate our discussion on the more common forms: the sole proprietorship, the partnership and the limited company.

We shall commence our discussion with the smallest and perhaps the most common form of business organization, the sole proprietorship.

THE SOLE PROPRIETORSHIP

The balance sheet and profit and loss account in this case are fairly straightforward as the business is set up as a simple form of organization in accounting terms. As the term sole proprietorship implies this is a business with a single owner who is also normally the manager and in many cases the only person involved in the business. As a form of business organization it is very easy to set up as all that is really required is a business bank account. There is little recognition in law and there are no formal guidelines for the format of the accounts.

However, the fact that the business and the owner are not seen as separate legal entities could be a problem if the business gets into difficulties as the owner is liable for all the debts of the business and may have to sell personal possessions such as the family home to meet those debts. In addition this form of organization relies heavily on the owner for finance and this can lead to problems if and when the business wants to expand. This is due to the fact that small business owners often have fairly limited funds at their disposal as they have already invested their surplus funds in the business when it was started. These problems can be alleviated if not solved by, for example, introducing a partner to the business. A partner may bring additional funds, skills or contacts. Alternatively the owner may set up a company. Although this limits the liability of the owners, unless additional investors are found it does not necessarily solve any of the problems of a lack of finance, skills, etc.

An illustration of a set of accounts of a sole proprietorship type of business is provided by the example we have just looked at.

PARTNERSHIPS

A partnership exists where two or more people enter into an agreement to run a business together. This can have a number of advantages in that the additional person may bring new finance to the business, and/or they may bring new skills or contacts etc. In essence, partnerships are similar to a sole proprietorship in that the partners are not limited in terms of their liabilities. They are jointly and severally liable for the debts of the partnership, i.e. they are liable on an individual as well as a collective basis. The total risk is the same; all that happens is that the risk is spread among a greater number of people. Partnerships are also similar to sole proprietorships in that there are no rules governing the format of accounts so these can be tailored to meet the needs of the users of those accounts. However, as you can imagine, there is more potential for conflict when there is more than one owner and as such there is considerable case law surrounding partnerships as an organizational form.

For our purposes, we only need to consider some of the more common issues arising in accounting for partnerships. We shall start by considering the most basic situation where two people enter into an equal partnership, each putting in the same amount to the business and sharing profits equally. For accounting purposes all we need to do is to open a separate owner's equity account for each owner; these are generally referred to as 'partner's capital' accounts. We also need to open another account for each owner, or partner, to record other less permanent transactions; these are commonly referred to as 'partner's current' accounts. They record such things as the individual partner's entitlement to profit, their drawings, etc.

It is important in law that the capital transactions and other transactions are separated as different legal treatments may be applied to each of these amounts if the partnership were to cease to exist. For our purposes we can work on the basis that the capital account relates only to deposits and withdrawals of capital from the business and all other items are recorded via the current accounts. Let us use a simple example to illustrate how straightforward partnership accounting should be.

EXAMPLE 9.2

Sarah and Sally – Part 1

Sarah and Sally go into business together, sharing profits equally. Sarah put in £2000 to the business whilst Sally put in £8000. They buy some fixed assets for £6000, some stocks of beverages for £900 and put the rest into a business bank account.

Before going on to the transactions of the period let us first examine how we would record the information to date on our worksheet.

Worksheet of Sarah and Sally in partnership: version 1

	Assets		=	Equity + Liabilities	
	Cash	**Fixed assets**	**Stock**	**Sarah's equity**	**Sally's equity**
Item 1	10 000			2000	8000
Item 2	–6 000	6000			
Item 3	–900		900		

As you can see, all that we have had to do is to open a separate account for each partner which we have called Sarah's equity and Sally's equity. More correctly these should be referred to as capital rather than equity so from now on we will adopt that title.

EXAMPLE 9.2

Sarah and Sally – Part 2

During the first year they sold meals for cash amounting to £30 000 and bought food and beverages amounting to £9000; other expenses amounted to £4000 and they had goods in stock at the end of the year amounting to £1300. The fixed assets are to be depreciated over 10 years straight line with no residual value.

Recording the above on the worksheet we find that at the end of the year there is a profit of £16 800 to be divided between the two partners. You will see that on the worksheet reproduced below we have opened partners' current accounts and have put their shares of the profits in their current accounts.

Worksheet for Sarah and Sally in partnership: version 2

	Cash	Fixed assets	Stock	Sarah's capital	Sally's capital	Profit & loss	Sarah's current	Sally's current
	£	£	£	£	£	£	£	£
Cash in hand	10 000			2000	8000			
Fixed assets	–6 000	6000						
Stock	–900		900					
Sales	30 000					30 000		
Stock	–9 000		9000					
Expenses	–4 000					–4 000		
Depreciation		–600				–600		
Cost of sales			–8600			–8 600		
Balance	20 100	5400	1300	2000	8000	16 800		
Distribution						–16 800	8400	8400
	20 100	5400	1300	2000	8000	0	8400	8400

You should also have noticed that because the profit has been distributed to the partners via their current accounts the final balance on the profit and loss column is nil.

As you can see, the principles involved are very simple. It is really only a question of separating the various transactions. What often makes it more complex is that the partnership agreement itself may be complicated. For example, a partnership agreement may require that interest is paid on the balances on the partners' accounts, or just the balances on the capital accounts. It might require that certain partners get paid salaries or a bonus, and each of these may happen before or after profits are split. Finally a partnership agreement may require that profits are split according to some other formula than equal shares. Each of these situations can be easily handled if the partnership agreement is well drafted as all one does is follow the instructions contained within it.

Before we look at an example to illustrate how this is done let us examine some of the reasons why these requirements are included in partnership agreements.

Interest on capital

This is usually included in a situation where the partners contribute uneven amounts of money to the partnership. For instance, as Sarah had put in £2000 to Sally's £8000 they may decide to compensate Sally for the fact she has more money at risk by paying interest on the capital before dividing the profit. This is illustrated in Part 3 of our example.

EXAMPLE 9.2

Sarah and Sally – Part 3

Sarah and Sally decided that, as their capital invested was not equal, interest at 10% would be paid on the balances on their capital accounts before the profit was divided.

The new version of the worksheet would be as shown below.

Worksheet for Sarah and Sally in partnership: version 3 after charging interest at 10%

	Cash	Fixed assets	Stock	Sarah's capital	Sally's capital	Profit & loss	Sarah's current	Sally's current
	£	£	£	£	£	£	£	£
Cash in hand	10 000			2000	8000			
Fixed assets	−6 000	6000						
Stock	−900		900					
Sales	30 000					30 000		
Stock	−9 000		9000					
Expenses	−4 000					−4 000		
Depreciation		−600				−600		
Cost of sales			−8600			−8 600		
Balance	20 100	5400	1300	2000	8000	16 800		
Interest						−1 000	200	800
Balance	20 100	5400	1300	2000	8000	15 800	200	800
Distribution						−15 800	7900	7900
	20 100	5400	1300	2000	8000	0	8100	8700

By comparing this with the previous worksheet, you can see that the only effects are on the amounts in each partner's current account. Under the previous set of assumptions Sarah and Sally were both entitled to £8400 whilst now Sarah is entitled to £8100 and Sally to £8700. This is because the interest is charged to the profit and loss first and this affects the resultant distribution.

Payment of salaries or bonus

A payment of a salary or a bonus is often a way of rewarding a particular partner for getting new business or for putting in more work in the business than the other partners. If, for example, Sarah worked in the business every day of the week whereas Sally was rarely involved in the day-to-day running of it they may decide that Sarah should receive a salary.

EXAMPLE 9.2

Sarah and Sally – Part 4

Sarah and Sally decided that Sarah should receive a salary of £6000 a year before interest was paid and before the profit was divided up.

The resultant worksheet would be as shown below. Once again it is important to notice that the amount of the profit has not changed but that the partner's shares of the profit have been altered to reflect their various inputs to the business. As before the final balance on the profit and loss account after the distributions is nil.

Worksheet for Sarah and Sally in partnership: version 4 after charging salary and interest at 10%

	Cash	Fixed assets	Stock	Sarah's capital	Sally's capital	Profit & loss	Sarah's current	Sally's current
	£	£	£	£	£	£	£	£
Cash in hand	10 000			2000	8000			
Fixed assets	–6 000	6000						
Stock	–900		900					
Sales	30 000					30 000		
Stock	–9 000		9000					
Expenses	–4 000					–4 000		
Depreciation		–600				–600		
Cost of sales			–8600			–8 600		
Balance	20 100	5400	1300	2000	8000	16 800		
Salary						–6 000	6 000	
Interest						–1 000	200	800
Balance	20 100	5400	1300	2000	8000	9 800	6 200	800
Distribution						–9 800	4 900	4900
	20 100	5400	1300	2000	8000	0	11 100	5700

In this case the fact that Sarah is paid a salary has a major effect on the profit that is finally distributed. You should note, however, that it has no effect on the interest as this is based on the capital invested which is not affected.

Uneven shares of profit

Because partners bring different skills, expertise and connections to a business venture it is not uncommon for the partners to decide to share profits in some other ratio than equally.

EXAMPLE 9.2

Sarah and Sally – Part 5

Sarah and Sally decided that because Sally had a number of contracts which were the backbone of the business that she should take 60% of the profit and Sarah would have the other 40%.

The worksheet would now be as follows.

Worksheet for Sarah and Sally in partnership: version 5 after charging salary and interest at 10% profits split 40:60

	Cash	Fixed assets	Stock	Sarah's capital	Sally's capital	Profit & loss	Sarah's current	Sally's current
	£	£	£	£	£	£	£	£
Cash in hand	10 000			2000	8000			
Fixed assets	−6 000	6000						
Stock	−900		900					
Sales	30 000					30 000		
Stock	−9 000		9000					
Expenses	−4 000					−4 000		
Depreciation		−600				−600		
Cost of sales			−8600			−8 600		
Balance	20 100	5400	1300	2000	8000	16 800		
Salary						−6 000	6 000	
Interest						1 000	200	800
Balance	20 100	5400	1300	2000	8000	9 800	6 200	800
Distribution 60:40						−9 800	3 920	5880
	20 100	5400	1300	2000	8000	0	10 120	6680

As before the only alteration is to the distribution of the profit; the calculation of the profit itself is unaffected. This change in profit sharing arrangements, like the previous ones, affects the balance on the individual partner's current accounts. It is worth noting whilst we are on the subject of current accounts that these accounts are used not only to record distributions of profits etc. at the end of the year, but they are also used to record withdrawals from the business as these occur through the year.

Partnership final accounts

Before leaving this introduction to the subject of accounting for partnerships we shall look at the format of the partnership final accounts and compare it with those of a sole proprietorship. The important aspects of partnership accounts which are reflected in the final accounts are

- each partner's equity should be separately identified;
- a split should be made between capital and other amounts due to the partners.

The majority of the non-capital transactions will be reflected in the balances on the current accounts. It may be that a partner makes a loan to the partnership, in which case this would be dealt with separately in the same way as any other loan rather than being included in the partner's current account.

Profit and loss account of Sarah and Sally's partnership for the year ended on 30 June 19X9

		£	£
Sales			30 000
Cost of sales			8 600
Gross profit			21 400
Expenses		4000	
Depreciation		600	4 600
Net profit			16 800
Distributions			
Salary	Sarah		6 000
			10 800
Interest	Sarah	200	
	Sally	800	1 000
			9 800
Profit share	Sarah	3920	
	Sally	5880	9 800
			Nil

If you compare the format of this profit and loss account with the one for Graham's sole proprietorship which we completed earlier in this chapter you will see that the only difference is that the partnership profit and loss account has a 'distribution statement' added on. Although this is often shown as part of the profit and loss account there are no hard and fast rules and it would be equally acceptable for it to be a separate report. The way in which the accounts are presented is largely up to the partners involved. This is also true for the balance sheet of the partnership. For our example the balance sheet is as follows.

Balance sheet of Sarah and Sally's partnership as at 30 June 19X9

	£	£
Fixed assets		
Fixed assets	6 000	
Depreciation	600	5 400

Current assets

Stock	1 300	
Cash	20 100	
	21 400	

Current liabilities

Creditors	Nil	
	Nil	

Net current assets		21 400
		26 800

Financed by £

Partners' capital accounts

	Sarah	2 000	
	Sally	8 000	10 000

Partners' current accounts

	Sarah	10 120	
	Sally	6 680	16 800
			26 800

We can see that the major difference in terms of the balance sheet is in the section relating to how the business is financed. Where the owners' equity is divided between the owners and subdivided according to its permanency. The more permanent investment is in the capital accounts, and the less permanent in the partners' current accounts.

As we have seen the fact that a business is set up as a partnership provides us with more accounting problems than if it were a sole proprietorship but also potentially can provide the business with greater access to skills and finance. However, the owners are still liable for the whole of the debts of the business should it go bankrupt. It is mainly for this reason that many small businesses are set up as limited companies, and it is this popular form of business organization which we shall now consider.

LIMITED COMPANIES

Unlike the partnership and the sole proprietorship, a limited company is recognized as a separate legal entity which is quite distinct from its owners. As such the debts incurred in the normal course of business are those of the company. In the case of a default in payment it is the company which has to be sued rather than the owner. The fact that the owners may also be the managers and the only employees is irrelevant in the eyes of the law.

Generally, companies are set up in a particular form to meet the requirements of the business concerned. For non-commercial organizations, i.e. those whose main aim is not to make a profit but which require the legal status of a company, it is likely that the company to be set up will be a company limited by guarantee. In this type of company, the members promise to contribute a guaranteed amount should the company fail. The amount of such a guarantee is normally limited to £1 per member but may be any other amount. The advantage of a company limited by guarantee is that no one individual can gain control by buying out others as would be the case if shares were issued.

For commercial organizations, the more common form of company is used. This is one where shares are issued to the owners, the shareholders. In this case their liability is limited to the nominal value of the shares. These companies can be either private companies or public companies, and the latter category can be listed or unlisted. 'Listed' is a term referring to the fact that the company's shares are traded on a recognized stock exchange. We need not dwell on the detailed differences between the various types of company. However, we can broadly say that private companies are generally easier to form but their shares cannot be freely traded on a stock exchange, whereas public companies (plcs) have shares which are freely transferable and must have a share capital in excess of £50 000. Public companies are also subject to more restrictions and regulation than private companies and may well be subject to other forms of regulation such as the stock exchange requirements which would not apply to private companies.

We shall limit our discussion to private companies and discuss the advantages of this type of organization over those already dealt with. The main advantage has already been mentioned – the limitation on the liability of the owners of the business in the event of the business being insolvent. Other advantages come from the ability to arrange distribution of profits and indeed of control by means of the share ownership of the various investors or classes of investors. For example, in the case of Sarah and Sally, although they put unequal amounts into the business under partnership law they both would have an equal say in any decisions being made as would any new partner they took on in the future. If, however, they set up their organization as a company they could arrange the voting rights as they wished as each share issued normally carries the right to one vote although non-voting shares can also be issued. Therefore, through the issue of different types of shares they could adjust the amount of power and control each shareholder could exercise.

There are disadvantages to the limited company as an organizational form mainly to do with the fact that they are subject to various pieces of regulatory legislation. For example, they are required to produce accounts annually and to have these audited by a recognized firm of auditors which can be expensive. A copy of the audited accounts have to be lodged at Companies House where they are available for inspection. The form of these accounts is also subject to the requirements of company law which requires that a company's accounts should comprise of:

- the company's balance sheet;
- the company's profit and loss account;
- the directors' report;
- the auditors' report.

In addition to these general requirements there are detailed requirements covering the format and content of the actual accounts. Many of these requirements have already been discussed and illustrated in the earlier chapters, but to discuss these requirements in greater detail is outside the scope of an introductory text such as this. Instead we have included an illustrative set of accounts for a private company which will be discussed to highlight the areas of difference between the accounts of the limited company and the other forms of organization dealt with in this chapter. We shall commence our discussion with a look at the profit and loss account.

Profit and loss account of Trails Ltd for the year to 31 July 19X3

	Notes	£	19X3 £	19X2 £
Sales	1		60 000	45 000
Cost of sales			10 000	9 000
Gross profit			50 000	36 000
Distribution costs		4 000		2 500
Administration costs		41 000	45 000	30 000
Profit on ordinary activities	2		5 000	3 500
Taxation	3		1 600	1 400
Profit after taxation			3 400	2 100
Dividends – interim	4	1 000		
– final	4	1 600	2 600	1 100
Transfer to reserves			800	1 000

The first difference is contained in the title of the profit and loss account where the fact that Trails is a limited company is stated. In addition the profit and loss contains comparative figures for the previous year, as well as references to a number of notes. These notes normally contain greater detail than can be shown on the face of the accounts and as such are an integral part of the analysis of the accounts of a company. The detailed disclosure contained in these notes is laid down in the Companies Act legislation and the accounting standards. The use of the notes to the accounts in financial analysis will be discussed in more detail in Chapter 11.

We can see that, apart from the notes, the format as far as the gross profit is familiar. However, we then find expenses being classified into broad categories which are laid down in the legislation. This is one of the two alternative formats allowed in that legislation. Those who wish to read about the alternative format and the detailed legislation will find more information in the books included in the further reading at the end of this chapter. It is worth noting that compliance with the

Companies Acts means that the level of detail disclosed is generally less than one would expect for an equivalent small business.

As far as the notes to the accounts are concerned, there are detailed requirements regarding disclosure of turnover contained in the Companies Act and in some accounting standards, but the latter generally only apply to larger and more complex organizations than we are discussing here. In respect of the profit on the ordinary activities the note would, in most cases, include details of depreciation and amortization charges, directors' emoluments, auditors' remuneration, and hire of plant and equipment. Other items may also be disclosed here depending on the circumstances of the company concerned.

You will remember that we said earlier that companies are recognized as separate entities for taxation purposes and are subject to corporation tax. In contrast the sole proprietorship and partnership are not separate legal or taxable entities and the profit is only taxable as income of the owners so is only subject to income tax rather than corporation tax. The detailed breakdown of the taxation charge is normally provided by way of a note.

Moving on through the profit and loss account we find that note 4 relates to the distribution of the available profit. This gives details of the dividends per share. This part of the profit and loss account can be seen as analogous with the distribution statement in the partnership accounts which we have just considered.

The dividends themselves are in fact a form of distribution to the owners (the shareholders) and are pro rata to the number of shares held. The fact that there is an interim and final dividend in one year and not in the other is not unusual as the declaration of any dividend and the timing of the dividend depends upon the needs of the business, the availability of both profits and liquid funds to pay them and other factors which are outside the scope of this introductory text.

The final line of the profit and loss relates to the transfer to reserves which is the residual balance being transferred to the profit and loss or other reserves. The breakdown of the transfers to each reserve would be given as part of the requirements for disclosure in relation to the balance sheet which we will now consider.

Balance sheet of Trails Ltd as at 31 July 19X3

	Notes	£	19X3 £	19X2 £
Fixed assets				
Intangible assets	5		10 000	11 000
Tangible assets	6		50 000	56 000
			60 000	67 000

Current assets			
Stocks	7	1 000	1 000
Cash at bank and in hand		22 500	12 000
		23 500	13 000
Creditors: amounts falling			
due in less than one year			
Creditors		4 000	3 000
Taxation	3	2 600	1 400
Dividends	4	1 600	1 100
		8 200	5 500
Net current assets		15 300	7 500
Creditors: amounts falling			
due after more than one			
year	8	10 000	10 000
Total net assets		65 300	64 500
Capital and reserves		£	£
Share capital	9	60 000	60 000
Retained profits	10	5 300	4 500
		65 300	64 500

As you can see the top half of the balance sheet is very similar to those we have encountered before, apart from the inclusion of dividends and taxation and the fact that a lot of the detail is left to the notes to the accounts. For example, notes 5 and 6 would contain details of the various classes of the fixed assets, the fixed assets bought and sold during the year as well as the depreciation or amortization to date, and the charges for the year. The detailed disclosure requirements in respect of the intangible fixed assets are contained in the Companies Acts and the various accounting standards, for example SSAP 13, *Accounting for Research and Development*, and SSAP 22, *Accounting for Goodwill*.

Similarly the note on stock would provide the detail necessary to comply with the legislation and SSAP 9, *Stocks and Long Term Contracts*, and the note on 'Creditors: amounts falling due after more than one year' would give the details of loans and debentures, repayment dates and interest rates in accordance with the requirements of the legislation.

You will note that the balance sheet shows the 'Total net assets'. This reflects a proprietary view of the business whereby the accounts are being prepared from the owners' perspective rather than being a report from an entity viewpoint where the distinction between the various forms of long-term finance may be less relevant. As a result of taking this proprietary view the other half of the balance sheet is somewhat different. It consists of the owners' equity split between the share capital and the reserves. As we discussed in Chapter 8 the share capital may consist of different types, details of which need to be provided in the notes. Similarly there may be a number of different types of reserves such as revaluation reserves, and once again details of the reserves and the movements on these need to be given in the notes. In our illustration the only reserve is the retained profits which is similar to the account for that purpose in the case of a sole proprietorship.

SUMMARY

In this chapter we have introduced the idea that different organizational forms require accounts in different formats and that there are reasons for the different organizational forms which impact upon the

---

CASE STUDY 9.1

Merrydown plc Annual Report and Accounts 1993

The extracts below from the financial statements show the profit and loss account and balance sheets for 1993:

Group Profit and Loss Account

for the year ended 31st March 1993

	31 MARCH 1993 £	31 MARCH 1992 £
TURNOVER	19,162,695	17,308,782
Cost of sales (including excise duty)	9,879,404	8,715,094
GROSS PROFIT	9,283,291	8,593,688
Other operating expenses	6,956,209	6,242,618
PROFIT ON ORDINARY ACTIVITIES BEFORE INTEREST PAYABLE	2,327,082	2,351,070
Interest payable	621,480	424,970
PROFIT ON ORDINARY ACTIVITIES BEFORE TAXATION	1,705,602	1,926,100
Taxation	580,827	678,179
PROFIT ON ORDINARY ACTIVITIES AFTER TAXATION	1,124,775	1,247,921
Dividends	737,060	509,242
RETAINED PROFIT FOR YEAR	£387,715	£738,679
EARNINGS PER ORDINARY SHARE	13.03p	15.24p

Balance Sheets

at 31st March 1993

	GROUP 1993 £	1992 £	COMPANY 1993 £	1992 £
FIXED ASSETS				
Intangible assets	7,350,000	–	7,350,000	–
Tangible assets	8,570,458	8,239,294	6,057,333	5,761,436
Investments	–	–	1,655,442	1,655,442
	15,920,458	8,239,294	15,062,775	7,416,878
CURRENT ASSETS				
Stocks	7,953,184	6,078,309	7,631,876	5,537,178
Debtors	5,666,399	4,414,865	7,809,719	6,654,277
Cash at bank and in hand	–	21,617	–	10,526
	13,619,583	10,514,791	15,441,595	12,201,981
CURRENT LIABILITIES				
CREDITORS: amounts falling due within one year	8,472,436	7,576,136	8,301,492	7,183,531
NET CURRENT ASSETS	5,147,147	2,938,655	7,140,103	5,018,450
TOTAL ASSETS LESS CURRENT LIABILITIES	21,067,605	11,177,949	22,202,878	12,435,328
CREDITORS: amounts falling due after more than one year	6,476,757	–	6,476,757	–
PROVISIONS FOR LIABILITIES AND CHARGES	666,988	625,986	588,303	578,094
ACCRUALS AND DEFERRED INCOME	84,434	100,304	84,434	100,304
	7,228,179	726,290	7,149,494	678,398
NET ASSETS	£13,839,426	£10,451,659	£15,053,384	£11,756,930
CAPITAL AND RESERVES				
Called up share capital	2,729,845	1,819,229	2,729,845	1,819,229
Share premium account	5,245,266	881,570	5,245,266	881,570
Revaluation reserve	2,144,066	2,051,830	1,268,258	1,268,258
Profit and loss account	3,720,249	5,699,030	5,810,015	7,787,873
SHAREHOLDERS' FUNDS	£13,839,426	£10,451,659	£15,053,384	£11,756,930

Commentary

Most of the items contained in the accounts of Merrydown you are already familiar with. However, in the balance sheet you will not have seen the heading 'deferred taxation' before. This is simply an amount of taxation that will fall due in future years beyond the next 12 months. It arises as a result of differences in the rules for arriving at taxable profit compared with the accounting profit.

In the profit and loss account we have come across all the items with the exception of 'earnings per share'. This figure is calculated applying rules laid down in Accounting Standard SSAP 3, but broadly it is the profit after tax divided by the number of shares. Those readers interested in the exact method of calculation and definitions should refer to SSAP 3 and any relevant Financial Reporting Standard.

accounting formats. For example, in the case of a partnership there is a need to differentiate between the amounts belonging to each partner and to distinguish between those amounts that are more permanent in nature and those that are temporary. It should be apparent that the requirements are in the main logically derived and that the differences that do exist are relatively minor in accounting terms. This is as it should be: the most appropriate form of organization should be governed by sound business considerations rather than by accounting requirements or burdens imposed by legislation.

REFERENCES

Statement of Standard Accounting Practice No.9 (1975) *Stocks and Long-term Contracts*, Accounting Standards Committee.
Statement of Standard Accounting Practice No.13 (1987) *Accounting for Research and Development*, Accounting Standards Committee.
Statement of Standard Accounting Practice No.22 (1984) *Accounting for Goodwill*, Accounting Standards Committee.

FURTHER READING

J. Blake (1981) *Accounting Standards*, 3rd edn, Pitman, London.
Coopers & Lybrand (1986) *Form and Content of Company Accounts*, Financial Training Publications.

REVIEW QUESTIONS

1. Explain the meaning of the term 'final adjustments'.
2. Explain the difference between a sole proprietorship and a partnership.
3. Explain the reasons why partnership agreements often contain clauses relating to interest, bonuses, salaries and division of profits.
4. Why is it advantageous to set a business up as a limited company?

5. What are the differences between a sole proprietorship and a limited liability company?
6. Describe how the choice of organizational form determines the format of the final accounts.

PROBLEMS FOR DISCUSSION AND ANALYSIS

The information below forms the basis for the questions which follow.

Kate sets up a business on her own as a sole proprietorship and has the following balance sheet at the end of year 1.

Balance sheet of Kate's business at the end of year 1

	Cost £	Depreciation £	Net book value £
Fixed assets			
Equipment	24 000	4 800	19 200
Vehicle	6 000	1 500	4 500
	30 000	6 300	23 700
Current assets			
Stock		1 000	
Cash in hand		1 500	
		2 500	
Current liabilities			
Creditors		6 000	
Bank overdraft		4 500	
		10 500	
Net current liabilities			−8 000
			15 700
Financed by			£
Owner's equity			10 000
Profit for year		22 000	
Less: Drawings		16 300	5 700
			15 700

At the end of the first year Kate realized that although the business was profitable she could hardly take out enough money to live on because she was heavily reliant on her bank and creditors already. She also found that a lot of her time which could have been used to produce more goods was being taken up selling goods, collecting debts and generally doing administrative work.

She therefore decided at the start of the second year to take in a partner who would put in an additional £5000 into the business and would be able to do some of the selling and other tasks after Kate had trained him. The agreement was a verbal agreement only on the first day of the new year and the two of them agreed to share profits equally.

In the second year the summarized transactions of the business were as follows:

- Sales: cash £60 000, on account £10 000.
- Moneys received from debtors £8000.
- Purchases, all on credit £12 000.
- Moneys paid to creditors £9000.
- Moneys introduced by new partner, Jamie, £5000.
- Other expenses incurred and paid, mainly wages £37 000.
- Drawings by Kate £7000 and by Jamie £5000.
- Goods in stock at the end of the year £1400.

1. The current partnership agreement between Kate and Jamie has the advantage of being simple. If you were advising Kate would you suggest any alternatives to the present agreement and, if so, why?
2. What, if any, additional accounts need to be opened in the second year to cope with the fact that the business is now a partnership and for what reason are they needed?
3. How do you propose to deal with the following:
   (a) the balance of £5700 from year 1, i.e. the profit after drawings;
   (b) the drawings from the business by Kate and Jamie in year 2;
   (c) the money introduced by Jamie in year 2.
4. Produce the final accounts of the partnership for year 2 in a form suitable for a partnership.
5. Discuss what changes would need to be made if Kate and Jamie decided to form a company to take over the business to protect both partners' interests as they stand under the current partnership agreement.

Cash flow statements 10

INTRODUCTION

In this chapter we shall consider cash flow statements, the information they provide and their uses. At present cash flow statements are supplementary statements for all companies and any reporting entity whose accounts purport to give a true and fair view. They provide additional information to that contained in the balance sheet and profit and loss account. In this chapter we shall discuss the need for cash flow information and then move on to look at the contents of the cash flow statement. Finally we shall demonstrate how such statements are constructed. In Chapter 11 we shall look at how the information contained in this statement is interpreted.

THE NEED FOR CASH FLOW INFORMATION

In Chapter 1 we identified the users of accounts based on the discussion provided in *The Corporate Report* (1975). Apart from identifying the potential users of accounting information that report also identified the type of information they would need. Amongst other types of information, it clearly identified the need for information on the liquidity of the enterprise. The initial action taken by the accounting profession was to require virtually all companies to provide a statement of source and application of funds. However, from 1992 the statement of source and application of funds has been replaced by a cash flow statement. It is worth considering what information such a statement provides, and why that information is important. We have already said that users need information about the liquidity of a business, but we need to understand what this means in order to understand why they need it.

At its most basic this information is about where money comes from and how it is used. To be useful such information needs to differentiate between regular cash flows which are likely to be repeated, e.g. those arising from selling services, paying wages, etc., and other cash flows, e.g. new capital being introduced to the business or new fixed assets being purchased or sold. By separating out these two categories of cash flows the user should be better equipped to arrive at a judgement about what may happen in the future.

So we now know what type of cash flow information should be provided but the questions that arise are: why do we need an additional statement? and why, at a general level, is cash flow information important? Taking the latter question first it is important to appreciate that in order for a business to be successful it needs two things. The first of these is that it be profitable in the long run. The profit and loss account helps the user to arrive at a judgement in relation to the profitability of a business. The second requirement is that it be able to pay its debts as they fall due. As we explained in Chapter 8 if suppliers and lenders are not paid they will take action to call in a receiver and have the business wound up. The problem is that the profit and loss account and balance sheet provide very limited information on this aspect of the financial performance of a business.

Such information can be very revealing. For example, in the case of Polly Peck which went into receivership in 1991, despite a trading profit of £139 m Polly Peck had a net cash outflow from operations of £129 m. In other words although it was making a profit it was paying out more than it was getting in. This example underlines the fact that in order to survive a company needs to be both profitable and solvent. In the case of Polly Peck the company was profitable but was not solvent even in the short term.

WHAT DOES A CASH FLOW STATEMENT SHOW?

Having established the need for a statement of cash flow we need to look in more detail at what the statement shows. In broad terms, as we have pointed out, it tells us where we got money from, and how it was used. The money coming in is referred to as cash inflows whilst money going out is referred to as cash outflows. The difference between the cash inflows and the cash outflows is known as the net cash flow which can be either a net cash inflow or a net cash outflow depending on the magnitude of the two components. Typical cash inflows would be monies generated from trading, commonly referred to as cash flows from operations, monies from new share issues or other forms of long-term finance, and any monies received from the sale of fixed assets. Typical outflows would be monies used to buy new fixed assets, to pay tax and dividends and to repay debenture holders or other providers of long-term capital. As we shall see the cash flow statement separates these cash flows into various categories. The format we shall follow is that recommended in the accounting standard known as Financial Reporting Standard No. 1 (FRS 1) issued in 1991. We shall use the example of a cash flow statement shown as Example 10.1 as the vehicle for explaining what a cash flow statement contains. We shall then look at an example of how such a statement is constructed.

EXAMPLE 10.1

Sample cash flow statement

	£	£
Net cash inflow from operating activities		2500
Returns on investments and servicing of finance		
Interest received	(100)	
Dividends paid	(1250)	
Net cash flow from returns on investment and servicing activities		(1350)
Taxation		
Corporation tax paid	(1500)	
Net cash outflow from taxation		(1500)
Investing activities		
Payment to acquire tangible fixed assets	(450)	
Receipts from sales of tangible fixed assets	50	
Net cash outflow from investing activity		(400)
Net cash outflow before financing		(750)
Financing		
Issue of ordinary share capital	150	
Repayment of loan	(75)	
Net cash inflow from financing		75
Increase in cash or cash equivalents		(675)

As you can see the cash flow statement shows cash flows under five separate headings. The first of these relates to cash flow from operating activities, broadly trading activities. This figure is arrived at by adjusting the profit figure by items that do not involve cash flows, e.g. depreciation, and by movements in creditors, debtors, stock, etc. It tells us what the cash flow from the normal activities of the business is. Clearly in most cases this should be a positive cash flow, i.e. a cash inflow. The note below provides an illustration of how this figure is reconciled to the other figures in the balance sheet and the profit and loss account.

Reconciliation of operating profit to net cash flow from operating activities

	£
Operating profit	2070
Depreciation charges	440
Loss on sale of tangible fixed assets	6
Increase in stocks	(22)
Increase in debtors	(111)
Increase in creditors	117
	2500

You will note that an increase in stocks is shown in brackets indicating that money has been used to pay for that increase. Similarly some money has been used to provide more credit to customers. This is shown as a cash outflow in respect of debtors. We can also see that some of these cash outflows have been financed by taking more time to pay our suppliers resulting in an increase in creditors.

The second heading in the cash flow statement relates to money earned from investments. This may be in the form of interest on surplus money invested or dividends from investments in other businesses. Also included under this heading are monies paid to those people who provide finance. These may be in the form of dividends or interest. Each type is shown separately allowing the user to identify from the rest of the information in the accounts whether these are discretionary, as is the case with dividends on ordinary shares, or compulsory as is likely to be the case with interest. This separation is important as although a business can delay the declaration and payment of dividends it will need to cover its non-discretionary outgoings by its cash flow from operations if it is to survive in the short term.

The third heading relates to cash flows in respect of taxation, specifically money paid out and recovered in respect of corporation tax. We pointed out in Chapter 9 that, unlike unincorporated businesses such as sole proprietorships and partnerships, companies are liable to corporation tax on their profits. The calculation of the tax liability and the timing of the payment of this tax is subject to complex regulations which you do not need to understand. It is important, however, to recognize that tax is normally payable in the year following the year in which the profit is made so this is a recurrent cash flow rather than a one-off. The amount of tax payable and therefore the amount of the cash flow will, however, differ from year to year.

The next heading is concerned with investing activities. This would include amounts received from the sale of fixed assets and cash outflows in respect of the purchase of fixed assets. Clearly such cash flows are different from those we have discussed so far. They tend to be non-recurrent as an individual fixed asset can only be sold or replaced once.

The final heading is the cash flows relating to the financing of the business. This would include amounts received from share issues, new loans or debentures, in other words from long-term financing. It would also show amounts paid out in respect of loans or debentures that have been repaid during the year and in respect of any shares redeemed.

The final figure shown on the cash flow statement is the increase or decrease in cash or cash equivalents. This can be reconciled fairly easily with the information in the balance sheet. However, in order to do that we need to know what is included under this heading. The definition of cash equivalents included in FRS 1 is given in the Key concept below.

> **Key concept**
>
> *Cash equivalents*
>
> Short-term, highly liquid investments which are readily convertible into known amounts of cash without notice and which were within three months of maturity when acquired, less advances from banks repayable within three months from the date of the advance.

Before moving on to work through an example of how these statements are constructed it is worth reflecting on what the cash flow statement used in Example 10.1 tells us about the business in question. The first item to note is that, unlike Polly Peck, the business has a positive cash inflow from operations. However, if we look at the cash outflows that are recurrent we find that the cash outflows in respect of dividends and tax exceed the net cash inflow from operations. This may or may not be a cause for concern depending upon two factors. The first is whether the tax due for next year is as much as that paid this year. The second factor is whether the dividends are likely to be the same next year. We can find out the answers to these questions from the balance sheet and the profit and loss account as the tax and dividends will be included there.

The cash flow statement also highlights the fact that the business is investing in fixed assets and by looking at the information contained elsewhere in the accounts you could arrive at a judgement about whether this is additional capacity or replacement of existing capacity. It is also worth noting that it is raising new long-term capital, this may indicate future expansion. Finally the fact that there is a decrease in cash and cash equivalents needs further investigation. This can be done either via the notes to the cash flow statement or directly from the movements on the balance sheet from one year to the next.

PREPARING A CASH FLOW STATEMENT

Having examined the end product in some detail we shall now work through a simple example and use that as a vehicle for explaining the ideas involved. We shall start with a new business and see how the cash flow statement is prepared from the basic transaction information.

EXAMPLE 10.2

Carrots Cafe

On 1 April 19X1 Rob opened a vegetarian restaurant which he set up as a company called Carrots Cafe. He arranged an overdraft facility of £10 000 if he needed it.

The transactions for the first twelve months are summarized below.

- April: Rob bought 10 000 ordinary shares of £1 nominal value. He purchased catering equipment for £8000 on one month's credit and paid for this at the end of the month. He purchased tables and chairs etc. for £10 000 and paid cash.
- The takings for the first year amounted to £57 000.
- The purchases from suppliers amounted to £10 000 in total and of this an amount of £600 was still owing to the wine merchant at the end of the year.
- Rob did a quick stocktake at the end of the year and reckoned that the wines and consumables in stock had cost £1600.
- Wages were paid on a daily basis and amounted to £14 000 for the year.
- The annual rent was £6000 and this was fully paid at the end of the year.
- Electricity, gas and telephone bills of £1400 had been paid and it was estimated that another £600 was owed at the end of the year.
- It was decided to depreciate the equipment over four years and the fittings over five years using the straight line method. Neither the equipment nor the fitting were expected to have any scrap value.
- The accountant calculated that he would owe corporation tax of £3000 and the director decided to declare a dividend of £5000 for the year, none of which was paid in the year.

Stage 1

The first stage is to record the transactions on a worksheet. This would appear as shown below.

Worksheet of Carrots Cafe for the year ended 31 March 19X2

Description	Bank	Equipment	Fittings	Stock	Shares	Profit & loss	Creditors & accruals	Tax	Dividend
	£	£	£	£	£	£	£	£	£
Capital	10 000				10 000				
Equipment		8000					8000		
Fittings	–10 000		10 000						
Equipment	–8 000						–8000		
Sales	57 000					57 000			
Supplies	–9 400			10 000			600		
Wages	–14 000					–14 000			
Rent	–6 000					–6 000			
Electricity	–1 400					–2 000	600		
Cost of sales				–8 400		–8 400			
Depreciation		–2000	–2 000			–4 000			
Balance	18 200	6000	8 000	1 600	10 000	22 600	1200		
Tax						–3 000		3000	
Dividends						–5 000			5000
Final balance	18 200	6000	8 000	1 600	10 000	14 600	1200	3000	5000

From the worksheet we can now produce the cash flow statement. The first figure we need to arrive at is the net cash inflow from operating activities. We shall initially concentrate on using the information from the worksheet. However, in order to facilitate your understanding we shall also look later in this chapter at how the cash flow statement can be produced from the final accounts for Carrots Cafe.

Stage 2

Using the information contained in the worksheet, we first need to calculate the net cash flow from operating activities. We shall do this using the information contained in the profit and loss column and the cash column. We shall start by identifying those items in the profit and loss column that are associated with cash coming into the business (the cash inflows) and cash being paid out of the business (cash outflows).

In terms of the cash inflows, we can see from the cash column that the money received in respect of sales amounted to £57 000. In terms of the cash outflows relating to operations, we find that £9400 was paid to creditors in respect of stock purchased during the year. In addition, Carrots Cafe paid £6000 for rent, £14 000 for wages and £1400 for electricity etc. If you look at all the other figures in the profit and loss column you will see that they do not affect the bank column and there is therefore no cash inflow or outflow. From this we can calculate our 'Net cash inflow from operating activities' as follows.

	£	£
Cash from cash sales and debtors		57 000
Less:		
Cash paid for purchases	9 400	
Rent	6 000	
Wages	14 000	
Electricity etc.	1 400	30 800
Net cash inflow from operating activities		26 200

We now need to look for the other cash flows. These are easily identified on the worksheet by looking at the bank column. There is a cash inflow of £10 000 when the shares were issued, and a cash outflow in respect of the purchase of the equipment of £8000 and for the fittings amounting to £10 000. As regards the tax liability and the dividend neither of these amounts have been paid out during the year so they do not affect the cash flow statement for this year. Thus we have all the information required to prepare our cash flow statement which would appear as follows.

Cash flow statement of Carrots Cafe

	£	£
Net cash inflow from operating activities		26 200
Returns on investments and servicing of finance		
Dividends paid	—	
Net cash flow from returns on investment and servicing activities		—
Taxation		
Corporation tax paid	—	
Net cash outflow from taxation		—
Investing activities		
Payment to acquire tangible fixed assets	(18 000)	
Net cash outflow from investing activity		(18 000)
Net cash inflow before financing		8 200
Financing		
Issue of ordinary share capital	10 000	
Net cash inflow from financing		10 000
Increase in cash or cash equivalents		18 200

PREPARING THE CASH FLOW STATEMENT FROM FINAL ACCOUNTS

At the start of Example 10.2 we said that there were two ways of arriving at a cash flow statement. The easiest is working from a work-sheet or other prime records which is what we have just done. An alternative is to work from the information in the final accounts which, although applying the same principles, uses some different techniques. We shall now look at these techniques in respect of Carrots Cafe. For this purpose we need to reproduce the final accounts of Carrots Cafe which are given below. You should note that as it is the first year there is no opening balance sheet. However, in order to illustrate the technique we have included a comparative balance sheet with nil balances.

Profit and loss account of Carrots Cafe for the year ended 31 March 19X2

	£
Sales	57 000
Cost of sales	8 400
Gross profit	48 600
Administration expenses	26 000

	£
Operating profit	22 600
Taxation	3 000
Profit after tax	19 600
Dividend	5 000
Retained profit	14 600

Note

Depreciation on the equipment and fittings amounting to £4000 is included in the Administration expenses.

Balance sheet of Carrots Cafe as at 31 March 19X2

	Cost £	Depreciation £	£	19X1 £
Fixed assets				
Equipment	8 000	2 000	6 000	0
Fittings	10 000	2 000	8 000	0
	18 000	4 000	14 000	0
Current assets				
Stock		1 600		0
Bank		18 200		0
		19 800		0
Creditors: falling due within one year				
Creditors		1 200		0
Tax		3 000		0
Dividend		5 000		0
		9 200		0
Net current assets			10 600	0
			24 600	0
Financed by			£	£
Ordinary shares			10 000	0
Retained profit			14 600	0
			24 600	0

The first figure we need to identify is the cash flow from operations. This we can do by extracting the figures from the profit and loss account and balance sheet. From the profit and loss we need the operating profit and all those items not involving cash flows, in this case depreciation. These non-cash flow items need to be added back to the profit to get to a figure representing the cash flows. We then need to identify any amounts included in the figure used in arriving at the profit for which a cash flow has not yet taken place. These are sales on credit where the cash has not yet been received, i.e. the increase in debtors, and increases in stocks. Similarly we need to identify any purchases for which no payment has been made, the increase in creditors. This can be done from the balance sheet. A useful technique is to add an extra column to the balance sheets to show these changes as shown below.

Balance sheet changes of Carrots Cafe

	Cost £	Depreciation £	19X2 £	19X1 £	Changes £
Fixed assets					
Equipment	8 000	2 000	6 000	0	6 000
Fittings	10 000	2 000	8 000	0	8 000
	18 000	4 000	14 000	0	14 000
Current assets					
Stock		1 600		0	1 600
Bank		18 200		0	18 200
		19 800		0	19 800
Creditors: falling due within one year					
Creditors		1 200		0	1 200
Tax		3 000		0	3 000
Dividend		5 000		0	5 000
		9 200		0	9 200
Net current assets			10 600	0	10 600
			24 600	0	24 600
Financed by			£	£	£
Ordinary shares			10 000	0	10 000
Retained profit			14 600	0	14 600
			24 600	0	24 600

We can now derive the figure for the net cash flow from operating activities, as shown below.

	£
Operating profit	22 600
Depreciation charges	4 000
Increase in stocks	(1 600)
Increase in creditors	1 200
	26 200

If we now look at the balance sheet changes column this will provide us with the basis to complete the rest of the statement. We can see that we have invested in fixed assets as there is an increase in fixed assets of £14 000 shown in our changes column. However, we know from the 19X2 balance sheet that this figure is arrived at after taking off depreciation. We also know from Chapter 8 that depreciation does not involve any cash flows so we need to add this back to find what we spent on the fixed assets as follows.

	£
Net change in fixed assets	14 000
Add: Depreciation charge for the year	4 000
Actual change in fixed assets	18 000

In reality, with fixed assets there are likely to have been many movements. However, the purchases for the year can normally be found in the note to the accounts relating to fixed assets.

Working down the balance sheet changes column we have already dealt with the changes in stock, debtors and creditors in arriving at the cash flow from operations. This takes us to the tax and the dividends, which are still owing in this case so have not involved any cash flow. Once again in reality there is usually an opening balance and a closing balance which when combined with information from the profit and loss account will enable us to identify the cash flows. For example, if we calculated that what we owed in tax for the year was £30, we would show this as the tax charge in the profit and loss account. If at the start of the year we owed £10 in tax and we owed £25 at the end of the year we could then calculate what had been paid during the year as follows.

	£
Tax owing at the start of the year	10
Tax charge for the year	30
	40
Tax owing at the end of the year	25
Therefore the tax paid is	15

A similar calculation could be done in respect of dividends. These calculations can be fairly complex in reality; however, you only need to concern yourselves with the principle in order to facilitate your understanding.

Returning to the changes column on our balance sheet we find that there has been a change in share capital, which in this case represents monies paid in to the business. We need to bring this into our cash flow statement under the appropriate heading. The only other change is to retained profit and we have already dealt with profits in arriving at our cash flow from operations so this has already been covered. We are now able to draw up the cash flow statement which would of course be the same as the one already completed.

Before leaving the discussion of Carrots Cafe it is worth returning to the cash flow statement and commenting on what information it gives us. We can see that the business is not only profitable but it also has a net cash inflow during the year.

CASE STUDY 10.1

Stakis plc Annual Accounts 1993

The following extract from the financial statements shows the group cash flow statement:

	1993 £000	1992 £000
Net Cash Inflow from Operating Activities	29,480	47,176
Returns on Investments and Servicing of Finance:		
Income from investments (excluding losses on sale)	438	576
Interest received	2,905	3,056
Interest paid	(187,761)	(29,190)
Dividends paid	(2,941)	(1,225)
Net Cash Outflow from Returns on Investments and Servicing of Finance	(18,359)	(26,783)
Taxation		
Corporation tax repaid	5,062	1,412
Investing Activities:		
Purchase of fixed assets and expenses of revaluation	(13,919)	(18,211)
Sale of business	49,984	11,203
Sale of fixed assets	2,676	2,489
Acquisition of subsidiary	(7,022)	–
(Purchase)/sale of investments	(2,258)	1,000
Net Cash Inflow (Outflow) from Investing Activities	29,461	(3,519)
Net Cash Inflow Before Financing	45,644	18,286
Financing:		
Issue of ordinary share capital	38,735	–
New short term bank loan	6,802	–
Expenses relating to share issues	(1,220)	–
Net Cash Inflow from Financing	44,317	–
Increase in Cash and Cash Equivalents	89,961	18,286
Analysis of movements in total borrowings:		
Increase in cash and cash equivalents (shown above)	89,961	18,286
New bank loan repayable after three months	(6,802)	–
Loan notes issued in connection with acquisition of subsidiary	(3,405)	–
Net reduction in borrowings	79,754	18,286

Commentary

As you can see from the statement above there was a large increase in cash amounting to nearly £90 million. The majority of this came from the sale of part of the business (nearly £50 million) and the issue of new shares which raised nearly £39 million. Although these major movements will be reflected elsewhere in the accounts the cash flow statement does serve to highlight these quite major changes.

SUMMARY

In this chapter we have introduced the cash flow statement and looked at the ways in which it can be produced. More importantly we have tried to give an indication of what information can be obtained from such a statement and why that information is important. Perhaps the major message that the reader should take from this chapter is that a business cannot survive merely by being profitable. It also needs to stay solvent and this aspect of the business also has to be properly managed. We shall be discussing how cash flows can be managed later in this book. Before leaving cash flow statements it is worth looking at an example from a set of published accounts one of which is shown above as Case study 10.1.

REFERENCES

Accounting Standards Steering Committee (1975) *The Corporate Report*, ASC, London.

FURTHER READING

A. Berry (1993) *Financial Accounting – An Introduction*, Chapter 13, Chapman & Hall, London.

REVIEW QUESTIONS

1. What is the main aim of a cash flow statement?
2. What are the claimed advantages of the cash flow statement?
3. How does 'net cash flow from operating activities' differ from operating profit?
4. How does an increase in the depreciation charge affect the operating profit and the 'net cash flow from operating activities'?
5. What is meant by cash and cash equivalents?

PROBLEMS FOR DISCUSSION AND ANALYSIS

1. Discuss the impact of each of the items below on the balance sheet, profit and loss account and cash flow statement, giving reasons for your answer where appropriate.
   (a) During the year the company sold a company car with a net book value of £5000 for £3000.
   (b) The company also revalued its land from its original cost of £130 000 to £200 000.
   (c) The building which had cost £200 000 and on which depreciation of £60 000 had been provided was revalued to £300 000.

(d) The company had also made an issue of 100 000 8% £1 preference shares at a price of £1.20 per share.

(e) The company had paid back a long-term loan to the bank of £80 000.

(f) The company declared dividends at the end of the year of £40 000 and paid the £30 000 dividend declared at the end of the previous year.

2. Information on the transactions of Themed Rides in its first year of trading are given below.

April 19X5
- Issued 100 000 £1 ordinary shares for £100 000.
- Purchased two rides for £30 000 each and paid immediately.
- Bought a truck for £10 000 and paid immediately.
- Paid tax and insurance on the truck of £400.
- Purchased advertising space costing £3000 on one month's credit.

May 19X5 – March 19X6
- Took gate receipts of £90 000.
- Purchased further advertising space costing £20 000, all on credit.
- Paid creditors £18 000.
- Paid wages of £45 000.

At the end of the year the directors decided to depreciate the truck over five years and the rides over three years using straight line depreciation and assuming no residual value. The accountant had calculated that no corporation tax liability would arise and the directors had decided to declare a dividend of £10 000.

Required:

(a) Produce a worksheet for Themed Rides.

(b) Produce a balance sheet and profit and loss account for Themed Rides.

(c) Produce a cash flow statement for Themed Rides.

(d) Identify any additional information about Themed Rides that the user can get from the cash flow statement that would not have been apparent in the profit and loss account and balance sheet.

Financial statement analysis 11

INTRODUCTION

In the chapters so far we have concentrated on building an understanding of what financial statements are and what they contain. We shall now consider the ways financial statements can be analysed. This chapter is not intended to be comprehensive; instead it offers some guidelines on how to approach financial analysis and some basic tools of analysis. The approach adopted considers the needs of the person for whom the analysis is being undertaken, in other words the 'user group'. Using this approach it is possible to establish the form of analysis most appropriate to these needs. As a potential manager you may be in a position of potential investor, customer or supplier. Conversely you may want to raise money for your business and an understanding of what potential financiers are looking for will be helpful in this situation. We shall limit our discussion to some of the 'user groups' identified in Chapter 1 and we shall start our discussion with the needs of providers of finance, i.e. investors, lenders and creditors. We shall then move on to look briefly at the needs of those user groups more directly involved in the business, i.e. managers and employees.

USERS OF FINANCIAL INFORMATION

Investors

'Investors' is a generic term for those who invest in a business but within it there are a number of different types of people with different needs. In Chapter 9 we introduced you to the term equity investor which covered owners in the case of sole traders and partnerships and ordinary shareholders in the case of companies. We need to establish what this group have in common, and what distinguishes the equity investor in a large company from the equivalent in a sole proprietorship. In general, equity investors take on all the risks associated with ownership and are entitled to any rewards after other prior claims have been met. In the case of a sole trader the equity investor, i.e. the owner, is also likely to be heavily involved in the management and day-to-day running of the business. If this is the case the needs of the owners will be the same as those of managers (discussed below). In the case of larger organizations such as large private companies and all public companies, it is likely that there will be a separation of ownership and management. For large businesses this leads to greater emphasis being placed on the accounts as a means of meeting the information needs of the equity investors who can be characterized by the term 'absentee owners'. However, since the information required to meet the needs of equity investors is broadly the same we would suggest that their basic needs can be met by providing information about:

* profitability, especially future profitability;
* management efficiency (for example, are assets being utilized efficiently?);
* return on their investment:
  – within the firm;
  – compared with alternatives;

* risk being taken:
  – financial risk;
  – business risk;

* returns to owners:
  – dividends;
  – drawings etc;
  – capital growth.

Preference shareholders

These were discussed in Chapter 8 where we said that there are many types of preference share. However, these shareholders will normally be entitled to a fixed rate of dividend and to repayment of capital prior to the ordinary shareholders in the event of the business being 'wound up'. Therefore, these shareholders are likely to be interested in:

* profitability, mainly future profitability;
* the net realizable value of the assets;
* the extent to which their dividends are covered by profit.

If we compare these needs with those of equity investors we can see that preference shareholders are more interested in the extent to which income is at risk rather than the growth of the business. In this way their needs are similar to providers of long-term loans. However, although both long-term lenders and preference shareholders get a return on their investment at a fixed rate, there are important differences between them. In the case of a long-term loan the interest has to be paid whether or not profits are made. By contrast preference dividends are not due to be paid until they are declared by the directors of the company. This is one of the reasons why the interest on loans is treated as an expense in arriving at the profit before taxation whereas the preference dividend is shown as an appropriation of profit after tax. The difference in the way in which they are dealt with in the accounts also reflects the different treatments in tax legislation. Interest on a loan is allowed for tax purposes as an expense in arriving at the taxable profit whereas preference dividends are not. A further difference between loans and preference shares is that loans are repayable at some specified point in time whereas, unless specifically stated (as in the case of redeemable preference shares) preference shares are 'permanent capital'. In this way they are more similar to ordinary shares: the capital is only repaid if the business ceases to exist. We can now move on to consider other providers of capital, i.e. short-term, medium-term and long-term lenders.

Lenders

This group can be conveniently subdivided into three sub-groups: short-term creditors and lenders, medium-term lenders and long-term lenders.

Short-term creditors are normally trade creditors, i.e. those who supply the business with goods on credit. Their areas of interest are similar to those of short-term lenders. These would be:

- liquidity/solvency – short term;
- net realizable value of the assets;
- profitability – future growth;
- risk (financial and business).

Medium-term lenders may well be bankers and other financial institutions. Their areas of interest would be:

- profitability (future profits provide cash for repayment of loans);
- security and the nature of the security;
- financial stability.

Long-term lenders will have the same needs as medium-term lenders unless they are secured lenders. In the case of secured lenders their areas of interest are likely to be:

- profitability;
- risk, especially financial risk;
- security (net realizable value of specific assets);
- interest cover (how well their interest is covered by the profits being made).

As can be seen these different types of lender have broadly the same needs in terms of their total information requirements. It is the emphasis that changes depending on whether one is looking from a short-term, medium-term or long-term perspective. We shall now consider the needs of internal users and we will concentrate on those of management and employees.

Management

It is very difficult to describe the needs of managers as they will vary greatly from situation to situation. They will, however, be interested in all the information referred to above as they are likely to be judged on their performance by outside investors or lenders. They may also need to access that information in their role as a supplier of services to other businesses where they are in fact trade creditors. Similarly as customers of other businesses they are interested in the ability of that business to go on supplying their needs and therefore in the ability of that business to survive. In addition, they require information to help them with planning, e.g. cash forecasts and profit forecasts. They will also require detailed information on the performance of the business and the parts of the business to enable them to manage the business on a day-to-day basis. This information could include such things as profitability by major product, costs per product, impact of changes in sales or component mix, etc. These needs and the ways in which they can be satisfied are dealt with in detail in Chapters 12 to 19.

Employees

Employees are interested in judging job security and in assessing their wages in terms of relative fairness. Their areas of interest are likely to be:

- profitability – average profits per employee for the purposes of productivity bargaining;
- future trends in profits;
- liquidity.

There has been considerable debate over the extent to which these needs are met by conventional accounts and whether an alternative statement such as a statement of value added – would meet their needs better.

COMMON USER NEEDS

The list of users covered in the preceding sections is not intended to be comprehensive. We have tried to provide a flavour of the different needs of the various groups and to indicate that some of these will not be provided from the annual accounts. At this stage we need to establish what, if any, needs are common. Some common needs which can be readily identified are profitability, liquidity and risk. The problem is how these are measured and how to judge good or bad performance. Before going on to discuss those issues in detail, let us first examine the common needs in more detail.

Information about profitability is the most obvious common need. This information is of two types, that relating to the past and that relating to future profitability. Other clear common needs are requirements for information about financial risk and about 'liquidity' (or 'solvency' as it is often called). Another theme that emerges concerns the return on the investment in the business. This has other measures associated with it such as the riskiness of that return (dividend cover or interest cover). There are also a number of needs that are more specific to particular user groups. A good example of these is the security measures used by lenders. Before we examine how these common needs can be analysed we need to discuss the context in which the analysis should take place.

Key concept

Financial analysis

Good financial analysis requires that the **person** for whom the analysis is being done is clearly identified together with the **purpose** of the analysis. It is unlikely to be useful if it does not take into account as many **relevant factors** as possible.

CONTEXT FOR FINANCIAL STATEMENT ANALYSIS

Before doing any analysis it is important to remember that it must be seen in a wider context rather than merely being viewed as a mechanical exercise using various techniques. Some of the factors that are directly relevant to any analysis of business performance are discussed in the following sections.

The size of the business

The fact that a business is the size of, say, Forte makes it less vulnerable to the decisions of others outside the organization. A banker is likely to ask for security from the small business whereas with Forte the name itself may well be enough security. Similarly, to compensate for the higher risk, a banker might only lend money to a small business at a rate of 3% or 4% above base rate whereas for a well-known quoted company the rate would be much lower. Another area of difference apart from those relating to security and risk is in the analysis of performance. In a small business there is little point in expecting too much consistency when doing trend analysis as, because these businesses tend to operate at the margin and have few products, there are often odd years. For a larger more diversified business these odd years in one area of the business are often balanced by performance in other areas.

The riskiness of the business

Apart from size, the nature of the business needs to be taken into account. For example, a new theme park, e.g. EuroDisney, will have a different level of risk and return than an established airline such as British Airways. Other factors which affect the risk, known as business risk, are the reliance on a small number of services, a small customer base, and of course vulnerability to competition.

The economic, social and political environment

Examples of the way in which the economic, social and political environment affects industry can be found in virtually any daily paper. If the pound goes down relative to the dollar, this will affect tourism and firms selling holiday packages abroad will suffer whilst those selling accommodation in the UK are likely to gain. Similarly, changes in interest rates often have fairly dramatic effects on firms if they are financed by a large amount of borrowing in the form of loans or overdrafts. The effects of the social environment tend to be more subtle, but a study of recent history would show a movement towards acceptance of profit as the prime motivation for business whereas in some other countries this is balanced with regard for the environment or for ensuring full employment. These social changes frequently coincide with political changes although the environmental issue is a good example of a social effect which is likely to transcend political changes.

Industry trends and the effects of changes in technology

In order to make any judgements about performance and more especially about the future it is vital to understand the pressures affecting the industry. For example, in the late 1970s and early 1980s most of the major British toy manufacturers were wound up. This was in part due to changes in the nature of the industry and the product. The industry was being affected by cheap imports, the impact of large buyers and the high rates of inflation and interest. The product required in the marketplace was also changing to more electronic toys rather than the traditional die-cast model cars such as those made by Dinky. In recent years we have seen within the tourism and hospitality industry vast changes as a result of technological innovation, especially in the area of booking systems.

Effect of price changes

We have just mentioned high rates of inflation, but the effects of price changes may also be more specific. For example, the price of property in recent years has been rising faster than the general increase in prices. Over the last 20 or more years, a number of proposals for taking account of price changes in corporate reports have been put forward, some of which will be discussed in the following chapters. None of these have gained general acceptance to date. However, the fact that the perfect solution has not been found does not mean that the problem can be ignored as even low rates of inflation of 5% can mean that what appears to be gentle growth is in fact a decline. It should be pointed out that although we normally think of price changes in terms of price rises there are many examples where the effect of new technology, competition and economies of scale have led to reductions in price. The most obvious examples are in the electronics industries and the computer industry. For example, a calculator cost approximately £15 for the most basic model at the start of the 1970s; an equivalent today would be less than £5.

PROJECTIONS AND PREDICTIONS OF THE FUTURE

While we can all take a guess at the future, clearly there is a case for taking into account the opinion of those more closely involved with the business and also those who have expertise in the industry or in analysing likely economic trends. Financial analysis must, after all, provide some clue to the future as the decision that the user needs to make relates more closely to what is going to happen rather than what has happened.

Having looked at some of the factors which need to be taken into account it should be clear that although a set of accounts may contain some of the information a lot of other information will have to be obtained from other sources. These other sources of information can be conveniently subdivided into information from sources external to the business and those internal to the business. Some examples of these other sources are discussed below.

Sources external to the business

- **Government statistics**. Examples of these are the monthly *Digest of Statistics*, Department of Trade and Industry statistics and HMSO publications.
- **Trade journals**. These may be specific to the trade or more general professional or business journals such as *Management Today* or Marketing Weekly.
- **Financial press**. A lot of information can be gleaned from the financial pages of quality newspapers, from *The Financial Times* and from specialist publications such as the *Investors' Chronicle*.
- **Databases**. There are now a number of on-line databases, such as *Datastream, Excel*, etc., which can be accessed for information. These contain information about other companies, industry statistics and economic indicators.

- **Specialist agencies**. These agencies will provide an industry-wide analysis, a specific analysis of a firm, general financial reports, credit scoring services and many other services.

The first three of these sources are likely to be fairly readily accessible in good libraries. The others are more specialist and access is likely to be more limited and much more expensive.

Sources internal to the business

Chairman's statement or review of the year's activities

In the case of public companies a chairman's statement is normally included with the annual accounts. It contains summarized information on the year as well as some predictions for the future. The information contained should not be taken at face value as it is likely to reflect one point of view which itself may be biased. It may be that the statement highlights only the positive side rather than giving the whole picture. As a senior lending banker commented: 'It is as important to ascertain what is left out as it is to ascertain what has been included.'

Directors' report

This is a statutory requirement for all companies and the information contained therein is laid down in the Companies Acts. The statutes, however, lay down a minimum and that is therefore normally all the information that is given.

The balance sheet

This gives information about the position at a point in time and it is therefore really only valid at that point in time. Given that the median time for publication by large companies is over three months after the balance sheet date and for small companies it is thought to be at least ten months, the information may have very little bearing on the current position. This question of how timely the information is has a major bearing on what can be achieved from an analysis of the accounting information contained in the published accounts.

The profit and loss account

In common with the balance sheet the information contained is probably fairly old by the time it is published. Another problem is that the information tends to be summarized which may mean that the performance of the weaker parts of a business are not necessarily readily apparent as they are offset by the performance of the stronger parts.

The accounting policies statement

As we have seen there are a number of different ways of dealing with such items as depreciation – is the reducing balance or straight line method being used? Many other items contained in a set of accounts can be treated in a number of ways, all of which are acceptable. It is therefore vital to understand the basis which has been adopted and this should be stated in the statement of accounting policies. Unfortunately, all too often in reality these statements are of such generality that they are fairly meaningless. For example, it is not uncommon to find a statement on depreciation which says 'depreciation is charged on the straight line method over the useful life of the assets'. The problem with such a statement is that different assets have different lives and different residual values – in fact it is quite likely that different businesses will come to different estimates of both of these for the same asset. This leads to problems of comparability between different companies as the basis adopted will affect the profits, balance sheet values, etc. Within the same business the problems are to some extent alleviated by the requirement to follow the basic accounting concept of consistency.

Key concept

Consistency

The consistency concept states that once an accounting policy is adopted it should not be changed from year to year. This is applied fairly rigorously to limited companies as their financial reports are covered by legislation and are subject to an audit report. For unincorporated businesses such as partnerships and sole proprietorships it is likely to be less rigorously applied.

Notes to the accounts

These are vital to any financial analysis as they contain the detailed information. Without that information the level of analysis available is likely to be very superficial especially in complex business organizations. The problem that users often find with the notes is that the level of detail and the complexity and technical language used are not helpful to their general understanding of the treatment of various items in the accounts.

Cash flow statement

This is a statement contained in the accounts of medium and large-size limited companies. The purpose of the statement is to provide some information about the origin of the cash coming into the business and how that cash was spent. It broadly distinguishes between the cash flows arising out of the normal operations of the business and other cash flows. The latter group are then further subdivided into those relating to returns on investments and servicing of debt, those to do with taxation, those arising from the purchase or sale of fixed assets and those from changes in the long-term financing of the business. Finally the statement reconciles the above with the movements in cash and cash equivalents.

Auditors' report

Every company is subject to an annual audit of its accounts and included in the accounts is a report from the auditors stating whether in the opinion of the auditors the accounts show a 'true and fair' view. As far as financial analysis is concerned this report is best treated as an exception report – in other words, unless it is qualified in some way no account needs to be taken of it. It is worth mentioning that for most bankers it does add credibility to the figures. It does not, however, mean that the accounts are correct in all their details and quite often the report contains a number of disclaimers in respect of certain figures.

THE COMMON USER NEEDS EXPLAINED

We have identified common needs such as profitability, liquidity, financial risk, etc., but before we can carry out any analysis we need to know what is meant by these terms. We shall therefore discuss what each term means and identify what we are trying to highlight with our analysis. For this purpose we shall use the example of Leek Hotels Ltd to illustrate the issues being discussed.

EXAMPLE 11.1

Leek Hotels Ltd

Profit and loss account of Leek Hotels Ltd for the year to 31 July 19x4

	Notes	19X4 £000	19X3 £000
Sales	2	26 558	20 921
Cost of sales		11 513	9 287
Gross profit		15 045	11 634
Administration costs		9 824	8 030
Operating profit		5 221	3 604
Other operating income	3	627	271
		5 848	3 875

Interest payable	5	813	704
Pre-tax profit		5 035	3 171
Taxation	8	755	662
Profit after tax		4 280	2 509
Dividends	11	1 615	827
Retained profit		2 665	1 682

Profitability

Looking at the first of our needs relating to profitability, it is intuitively obvious that the starting point for this information should be the profit and loss account. Before looking at the information contained in the profit and loss we need to establish what information is needed.

We need some sort of relative comparison. Is the business more profitable than it was last year? Is it more profitable than a similar business, or even a dissimilar business? Each of these require us to measure the profit relative to something else. The last question cannot be answered by simply looking at one set of accounts. We need to compare a number of different businesses and to do this we have to make sure that the accounts are comparable. For example, are they depreciating the assets over the same time period. Remember the shorter the time period the greater the charge therefore the smaller the final profit figure. It is for these comparisons that the accounting policies statement is required. To start with we shall concentrate on comparisons over time within our own business.

If we look at Leek Hotels Ltd we find that the business made more profits this year, when it earned £5 035 000 profit before taxation, than last year when the figure was only £3 171 000. The question that now arises is whether it is more profitable because it is selling more, i.e. £26 558 000 this year as compared to £20 921 000 last year, or whether it is more efficient, or is it a combination of the two?

We can go some way to answering that by simply working out what the increase in sales was and what the increase in profit was. In this case the sales increased by approximately 27%, i.e.

$$£26\,558 - £20\,921 = \frac{£5\,637}{£20\,921} \times 100 = 27\%$$

The profit, however, increased by nearly 60%, i.e.

$$£5035 - £3171 = \frac{£1864}{£3171} \times 100 = 59\%$$

Thus we have discovered that not only is Leek Hotels making more profit by selling more but it is also making a greater profit on each sale. However, we do not know whether this seemingly favourable change is because this year was a good year or whether last year was a bad year, nor do we know whether we have had to invest a lot of money in order to increase the profitability. The former question can only really be satisfactorily answered by comparisons over a longer period of time than two years and by then comparing Leek Hotels Ltd with a similar business in the same industry. The second question can perhaps be answered in the case of a small company by looking at what return the profit represents relative to the amount invested. This then begs the question: what is the amount invested? Often in the case of a small business the major investment made by the owner is the time spent in the business and this is not reflected in the balance sheet. In the case of a public company, on the other hand, there is normally very little relationship between the amount shown in the accounts and the amount you would have to pay to buy the company.

For the present we can look at the balance sheet, reproduced below, as a rough guide in the absence of anything better. We can see that in this case the investment in the form of capital and reserves has changed dramatically – £42 105 000 last year to £62 842 000 this year. Therefore we would have expected profits to have risen as a result of the increased investment in the business and this partly explains the profit increase.

EXAMPLE 11.1

Leek Hotels Ltd – further information

Balance sheet of Leek Hotels as at 31 July 19X4

	Notes	19X4		19X3	
		£000		£000	
Fixed assets					
Tangible assets	13	73 425		58 606	
Investments	14	4 327		81	
		77 752		58 687	
Current assets					
Stocks	15	335		297	
Debtors	16	5 481		4 946	
Cash at bank and in hand		303		734	
		6 119		5 977	
Creditors: Amounts falling due in one year	17	15 880		12 168	
Net current liabilities			(9 761)		(6 191)
Total assets less current liabilities			67 991		52 496
Creditors: amounts falling due after one year	18		5 149		10 391
			62 842		42 105

Capital and reserves		£000	£000
Share capital	20	23 514	12 627
Share premium	21	8 856	5 647
Revaluation reserve	22	25 504	21 528
Profit and loss acount	23	4 936	2 271
Other reserves	24	32	32
		62 842	42 105

Before leaving the question of profitability we need to discuss the question of the future profitability of the business as this was identified as a common need for many users. The fact that a company has been profitable is comforting but if you want to make a decision about whether to buy into a business or sell up you need information about the future not the past. This information is not contained in the profit and loss account, although it could be argued that information on the past is the best guide to the future. In practical terms the only way you can form an opinion about the future is by using a combination of information including past profits, knowledge of the industry, predictions about the economy and many other factors.

Profitability – summary

- Profitability requires comparisons:
  - over time;
  - with other businesses.

- Profitability relates to:
  - the past for evaluation;
  - the future for prediction.

Liquidity and financial risk

We shall deal with these two together as they are both related to the financing of the business. The area of financial risk or long-term solvency is of vital importance as there are many cases where a business has gone under because of cash flow problems even though it was profitable. The introduction of the cash flow statement should go some way to alerting users of this problem. There are also cases where two companies in the same line of business produce dramatically different results purely because of the way they are financed. The effects of this financial risk, often referred to as gearing, were illustrated in Chapter 8.

In the UK, in general, debt finance does not normally exceed the equity finance although the extent to which this generalization holds true is to some extent dependent upon the size of the business and the industry sector. In large businesses the debt finance is probably likely to be around 30% of the total financing. On the other hand, because of a shortage of equity finance many small businesses rely very heavily on debt as the major source of finance. The fact that in general the debt does not exceed the equity is largely a result of the banks' policies of lending on a pound for pound basis, i.e. for each pound of your money you put in the business the bank will lend a pound. Whilst this is not a hard and fast rule it is effectively used as the benchmark by bank managers in the clearing banks in the UK. It is interesting that different countries seem to adopt different benchmarks. For example, banks in Germany and Japan tend to lend well above the one for one norm.

In the case of Leek Hotels Ltd there is £5 149 000 of long-term borrowing. However, there is also a bank overdraft of £5 542 000 included in the creditors figure. The fact that the long-term borrowing is so low compared to the equity investment of nearly £63 000 000 may be a good thing as the company is only making £5 035 000 on the capital invested. This is less than 10% and at the time of writing is below the rate at which money could be borrowed.

Looking now at the area of liquidity, what is generally understood by this is whether you can meet your commitments as they fall due. In general the major area for concern is the short term, which is often taken to be a year. This fits with the definition used for current assets and current liabilities, so we have a convenient measure simply by looking at the balance sheet. For example, Leek Hotels has current assets of £6 119 000 and current liabilities of £15 880 000. This means that if it was required to pay off its debts during the year it would not get enough money in during the next year to do so. This is, of course, a slightly simplistic analysis as the amounts receivable in a hotel business may include a lot of cash and because of this an excess of current liabilities over current assets may be sustainable. In other words, a problem that arises with this apparently simple measure is that current can mean due tomorrow or in twelve months or even more. Another problem is the question of what is the correct liquidity level for the business. If, for example, there is a lot of cash sitting around in the bank that is hardly an efficient use of resources. In the case of Leek Hotels there is only £303 000 held in this form. There is also the question of whether £5 481 000 tied up in debtors is excessive on the sales. However, if we compare it to last year where the debtors were £4 946 000 on sales of nearly £21 million, the position has improved.

Other problems with interpreting the information may arise if we try to compare different businesses; for example, an airline will have different needs from a catering business or a tour operator. Even within the same industrial sector the needs will differ; for example, a restaurateur will have different needs from a hospitality operation such as Formula 1 as the former does not necessarily have as high an investment in fixed assets. On the other hand, as the latter operation does not provide food there would be no requirement for what could be a substantial investment in a wine cellar.

Financial risk – summary

- Financial risk involves long-term and short-term solvency.
- Requirements and norms differ widely from industry to industry.

Case study 11.1 below illustrates these points.

Once again the general conclusion to be drawn is that on its own the analysis of the financial statements is only a small part of the story and that that analysis needs to be put into a wider context of knowledge of the industry and the environment. The maxim that a little knowledge is a dangerous thing applies equally to business analysis as it does elsewhere. With that firmly in mind we can now move on to look at some of the techniques that can be used to analyse the financial information.

TECHNIQUES OF ANALYSIS

There are many techniques used in financial analysis varying from simple techniques such as studying the financial statements (in a manner similar to the exercise we have just done) and forming a rough opinion of what is happening to sophisticated statistical techniques. It should be pointed out that this rough analysis based on 'eyeballing' the accounts is vital as it forms the base on which the more sophisticated techniques can be built. If, for example, we fail to notice that a business has made a loss for the past few years the application of the most sophisticated techniques will not help as we have failed to grasp an essential point.

We shall limit ourselves to an examination of some of the simpler techniques. The choice of technique is once again a function of what you are trying to do and the purpose of your analysis. For example, managers and auditors may be interested in establishing any variations from past norms and explaining these and, where necessary, taking appropriate action. However, for a shareholder in a large company such an analysis, even if it were possible, would be inappropriate as no action could be taken and the level of detail is too specific.

Comparison of financial statements over time

With limited data a simple comparison of the rate and direction of change over time can be very useful. This can be done both in terms of absolute amount and in percentage terms. In fact both are normally required in order to reach any meaningful conclusions. For example, a 50% change on £1000 is less significant than a 50% change on £50 000. However, if you only have £1000 to start with a change of £500 may well be significant. Thus it is not only the absolute figure but also the amount relative to other figures that is important.

CASE STUDY 11.1

British Airways plc Annual Report and Accounts 1993

The following extract from the financial statements shows the balance sheets:

£million	Group 1993	1992	Company 1993	1992
FIXED ASSETS				
Tangible assets				
Fleet	3,537	2,829	3,511	2,804
Property	464	420	456	415
Equipment	229	223	214	206
	4,230	3,472	4,181	3,425
Investments				
Subsidiary undertakings			668	136
Associated undertakings	448	7	11	5
Trade investments	98	86	22	20
	546	93	701	161
CURRENT ASSETS				
Stocks	40	34	38	31
Debtors	1,009	920	1,015	889
Short-term loans and deposits	495	706	439	650
Cash at bank and in hand	33	27	23	23
	1,577	1,687	1,515	1,593
CREDITORS:				
amounts falling due within one year	(1,851)	(1,706)	(1,846)	(1,717)
NET CURRENT LIABILITIES	(274)	(19)	(331)	(124)
TOTAL ASSETS LESS CURRENT LIABILITIES	4,502	3,546	4,551	3,462
CREDITORS:				
amounts falling due after more than one year	(2,899)	(1,888)	(3,203)	(2,183)
PROVISIONS FOR LIABILITIES AND CHARGES	(69)	(54)	(69)	(54)
	1,534	1,604	1,279	1,225
CAPITAL AND RESERVES				
Called up share capital	185	182	185	182
Reserves				
Share premium account	30	10	30	10
Revaluation reserve	45	60	40	54
Profit and loss account	954	1,032	1,024	979
	1,214	1,284	1,279	1,225
CONVERTIBLE CAPITAL BONDS 2005	320	320		
	1,534	1,604	1,279	1,225

Hogg Robinson plc Annual Accounts 1992

The following extract from the financial statements shows the balance sheets:

	Notes	Group 1992 £'000	Group 1991 £'000	Company 1992 £'000	Company 1991 £'000
Fixed Assets					
Tangible assets	11	**25,501**	22,941	**270**	302
Investments	12	**838**	695	**5,208**	5,208
		26,339	23,636	**5,478**	5,510
Current Assets					
Debtors	13	**56,387**	53,442	**32,773**	27,621
Cash at bank and deposits		**67,278**	56,126	**50,556**	45,043
		123,665	109,568	**83,329**	72,664
Creditors: amounts falling due within one year	14	**(92,445)**	(79,572)	**(38,070)**	(27,776)
Net Current Assets		**31,220**	29,996	**45,259**	44,888
Total Assets less Current Liabilities		**57,559**	53,632	**50,737**	50,398
Creditors: amounts falling due after more than one year	14	**(11,764)**	(7,825)	**(729)**	(353)
Provisions for liabilities and charges	15	**(893)**	(1,121)	**(116)**	(31)
Net Assets	16	**44,902**	44,686	**49,892**	50,014
Capital and Reserves					
Called up share capital	17	**6,899**	6,899	**6,899**	6,899
Share premium account	18	**32,871**	32,871	**32,871**	32,871
Exchange reserve	19	**418**	289	**–**	–
Unrealised reserve – goodwill	19	**(15,240)**	(11,158)	**–**	–
Revaluation reserve	19	**27**	27	**–**	–
Profit and loss account	19	**19,927**	15,758	**10,122**	10,244
Shareholders' Funds		**44,902**	44,686	**49,892**	50,014

Forte plc Annual Accounts 1994

The following extract from the financial statements shows the balance sheets:

	Group		Company	
	1994 £million	1993 £million	1994 £million	1993 £million
Fixed assets				
Tangible assets	3,353	3,967	–	–
Investments	229	212	3,699	3,780
Total fixed assets	3,582	4,719	3,699	3,780
Current assets				
Stocks	45	61	–	–
Debtors	187	230	130	366
Amount receivable from disposal of a subsidiary undertaking	155	–	–	–
Short term deposits and cash	36	51	–	–
Total current assets	423	342	130	366
Creditors due within one year				
Bank and other borrowings	248	534	211	438
Other creditors	351	422	100	112
Total current liabilities	599	956	311	550
Net current liabilities	(176)	(614)	(181)	(184)
Total assets less current liabilities	3,406	3,565	3,518	3,596
Creditors due after one year				
Bank and other borrowings	987	794	899	685
Other creditors	17	14	403	375
Total net assets	2,402	2,757	2,216	2,536
Equity				
Share capital	216	205	216	205
Share premium	120	131	120	131
Revaluation reserve	1,553	1,781	1,539	2,099
Profit and loss reserve	427	520	341	101
Shareholders' investment	2,316	2,637	2,216	2,536
Minority interest	86	120	–	–
Total equity	2,402	2,757	2,216	2,536
Net borrowings as a % of total equity				
As at 31 January	50%	46%		
After receipt of proceeds from disposal of a subsidiary undertaking	43%	46%		

Commentary

If you compare the balance sheets of two companies in the same industry you will inevitably find differences. For example, when comparing those of British Airways plc with those of Hogg Robinson plc you will see that British Airways has a greater proportion of its money invested in fixed assets and that, by comparison, Hogg Robinson is a fairly cash rich company.

If you then compare different industries, for example Hogg Robinson with Forte plc, you will note that the fixed assets are higher in Forte as one would expect from a group that owns a large number of hotels.

The period of time chosen is also worth considering. Too short a time period will not be very meaningful. This was the case with Leek Hotels Ltd where we can say that the profit had increased but have no idea about whether that is part of a trend or whether it is because last year was a particularly bad year. Conversely, too long a period may bring its own problems. For example, the nature of the business or the environment may have altered drastically. Finally, it must be borne in mind that there may be other changes which have affected the figures. For example, the business may have decided to depreciate its vehicles over three years instead of four with consequent distortions in profit trends. While keeping these warnings in mind, let us now look at how we could do the comparisons.

Trend analysis

This technique is normally used for time periods in excess of two to three years in order to make the results easier to understand and interpret. It involves choosing a base year and then plotting the trend in sales or profits or whatever from there on.

Key concept

Trend analysis

In trend analysis the choice of the base year is vital. If the base year chosen is not typical the resultant analysis will at best be extremely difficult and at worst misleading.

EXAMPLE 11.1

Leek Hotels Ltd – further information

Leek Hotels Ltd profit and loss summary

	19X7	19X6	19X5	19X4	19X3
	£000	£000	£000	£000	£000
Sales	29 603	28 734	31 236	26 558	20 921
Cost of sales	11 697	11 526	12 919	11 513	9 287
Gross profit	17 906	17 208	18 317	15 045	11 634
Administration costs	16 650	14 690	11 391	9 824	8 030
Operating profit	1 256	2 518	6 926	5 221	3 604
Other operating income	667	618	374	627	271
	1 923	3 136	7 300	5 848	3 875
Interest payable	1 549	1 188	1 552	813	704
Pre-tax profit	374	1 948	5 748	5 035	3 171
Taxation	164	662	721	755	662
Profit after tax	210	1 286	5 027	4 280	2 509
Dividends	2 004	1 987	1 943	1 615	827
Retained profit	–1 794	–701	3 084	2 665	1 682

If we take the sales figure it is clear from a casual examination of the figures that it rises in 19X3 and 19X4 to a peak in 19X5. There is then a drop in 19X6 and a rise in 19X7. If we plotted that on a graph it would look like Figure 11.1.

As you can see the information shown on the graph is fairly limited; it merely reflects what we have already found. To make any sensible comment we need to see how these sales are behaving in relation to something else. This could be in relation to another item in the profit

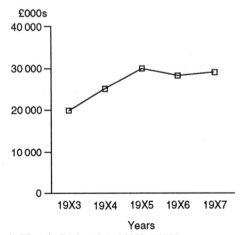

Figure 11.1 Leek Hotels Ltd: sales 19X3–19X7.

and loss account such as costs or in relation to the sales in a comparable company. To do the latter comparison, however, we first have to find some common means of expression as the companies being compared are unlikely to be exactly the same size. One way of doing this is to use index numbers to express the figures we are looking at and the way in which they change from year to year.

Index number trends

As with other forms of trend analysis this technique is normally used for time periods in excess of two to three years. It is intended to make the results easier to understand and interpret. It does this by choosing a base year, setting that base year to 100 and expressing all other years in terms of that base year.

If, for example, we used 19X3 as the base year and set that at 100 we would be able to calculate the sales trend as follows:

$$\frac{19X4 \text{ Sales}}{19X3 \text{ Sales}} \times 100 = \frac{26\,558}{20\,921} \times 100 = 127$$

For 19X5 the calculation would be:

$$\frac{19X5 \text{ Sales}}{19X3 \text{ Sales}} \times 100 = \frac{31\,236}{20\,921} \times 100 = 149$$

Using the same formula we can find the index for each of the other years and we can then look at the trend. In this case the figures are: 19X3, 100; 19X4, 127; 19X5, 149; 19X6, 137; 19X7, 141.

We could do the same for the cost of sales and the profit figures and then these could be analysed. In the case of sales we can see that the sales peaked in 19X5 and then declined in 19X6, and although they picked up in 19X7 they did not reach the same level as 19X5. This can be seen more easily in Figure 11.2 which shows the sales in the left-

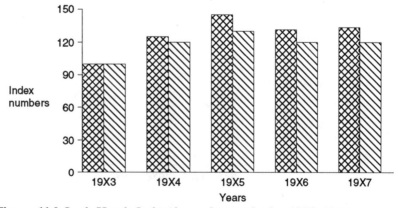

Figure. 11.2 Leek Hotels Ltd: sales and cost of sales 19X3–19X7.

hand blocks and the cost of sales in the right-hand blocks for each year.

This graph is much more informative than that in Figure 11.1 because it relates sales to cost of sales. In addition the use of index numbers (see the vertical axis) allows us to compare this company with another irrespective of size. The graph in this case shows that both sales and cost of sales peak in 19X5. While this tells us that the cost of sales seem to be controlled – they are rising at a lower rate than the sales – however, it does not explain the losses in 19X6 and 19X7. This information may in fact be found elsewhere in the full published accounts.

Percentage changes

Another technique often used in trend analysis is to identify the percentage change from year to year and then examine the trends in this. For example, if we look at the sales we find that the change from 19X3 to 19X4 was 27%, whilst that from 19X4 to 19X5 was 17%. These figures are calculated using the following formula:

$$\frac{\text{This year's sales}}{\text{Last year's sales}} \times 100 = \frac{26\,558}{20\,921} \times 100 = 127 \text{ or } 27\% \text{ up}$$

Once again it should be pointed out that these trends are of most use if they are compared with other trends, either in the business itself or in the industry. You should also bear in mind that these percentage increases are often illusory as they merely reflect the increase that would be expected as a result of the rate of inflation in the particular period and the particular country concerned.

Common size statements

A technique which can be used to turn the large numbers we often encounter in accounts into more digestible information is 'common size' statements. This technique, as the name implies, deals with the problem of comparisons of different size companies. It involves expressing the items in the balance sheet, for example, as percentages of the balance sheet total. Once again this is best illustrated by looking at Leek Hotels Ltd, the balance sheets of which are reproduced below. We can derive certain information and questions from just looking at the balance sheets but it is not easy to identify exactly what is happening. For example, we can see a steady increase in fixed assets and in current assets. However, without looking at the notes to the accounts all we can do at this stage is to highlight some questions for further investigation.

EXAMPLE 11.1

Leek Hotels Ltd – further information

Leek Hotels Ltd summary balance sheets

	19X7	**19X6**	**19X5**	**19X4**	**19X3**
Fixed assets	£000	£000	£000	£000	£000
Tangible assets	101 000	98 998	87 475	73 425	58 606
Investments	4 454	4 350	4 293	4 327	81
	105 454	103 348	91 768	77 752	58 687
Current assets					
Stocks	286	315	352	335	297
Debtors	8 049	7 863	6 896	5 481	4 946
Cash at bank and in hand	128	116	169	303	734
	8 463	8 294	7 417	6 119	5 977
Creditors: amounts falling due in one year	16 756	18 415	15 918	15 880	12 168
Net current liabilities	–8 293	–10 121	–8 501	–9 761	–6 191
Total assets less current liabilities	97 161	93 227	83 267	67 991	52 496
Creditors: amounts falling due after one year	25 033	18 862	9 795	5 149	10 391
	72 128	74 365	73 472	62 842	42 105
Capital and reserves	£000	£000	£000	£000	£000
Share capital	23 204	23 323	23 506	23 514	12 627
Share premium	8 949	9 202	8 864	8 856	5 647
Revaluation reserve	34 695	34 695	33 211	25 504	21 528
Profit and loss account	5 248	7 113	7 859	4 936	2 271
Other reserves	32	32	32	32	32
	72 128	74 365	73 472	62 842	42 105

The problem when looking at standard balance sheets is that the figures often disguise what is really happening. If, however, we convert the statements to some common measure the underlying trends become clearer. We could take the share capital for 19X3, for example, and express it as a percentage of the balance sheet total. If we do this we find that it is 30% in that year as compared to 37% in 19X4. To calculate this we simply divided the share capital figure by the balance sheet total and then multiplied the result by 100. Thus for 19X5 we would have:

$$\frac{\text{Share capital}}{\text{Total}} \times 100 = \frac{23\,506}{73\,472} \times 100 = 32\%$$

Following this for all items in the balance sheets produces the common size statements shown below.

Leek Hotels Ltd common size balance

	19X7	19X6	19X5	19X4	19X3
Fixed assets	%	%	%	%	%
Tangible assets	140	133	119	117	139
Investments	6	6	6	7	0
	146	139	125	124	139
Current assets					
Stocks	0	0	0	1	1
Debtors	11	11	9	9	12
Cash at bank and in hand	0	0	0	0	2
	12	11	10	10	14
Creditors: amounts falling due in one year	23	25	22	25	29
Net current liabilities	–11	–14	–12	–16	–15
Total assets less current liabilities	135	125	11	108	125
Creditors: amounts falling due after one year	35	25	13	8	25
	100	100	100	100	100
Capital and reserves	%	%	%	%	%
Share capital	32	31	32	37	30
Share premium	12	12	12	14	14
Revaluation reserve	48	47	45	41	51
Profit and loss account	7	10	11	8	5
Other reserves	0	0	0	0	0
	100	100	100	100	100

You will note that the statements above have been produced in round numbers and as such there are some inconsistencies due to rounding. These do not, however, affect their usefulness for analysis. One of the things that we can see from an analysis of these statements is that there has been a slight increase in the proportion invested in fixed assets and a fairly marked increase in borrowing for periods in excess of a year. It should be pointed out that with this technique the choice of the base year is just as important as it was with trend analysis. For example, any analysis of Leek Hotels Ltd that uses 19X4 as a base year would produce different results. For example, using 19X4 as a base year would lead to the conclusion that there has been a dramatic increase in fixed asset investment, i.e. from 124 to 146. Similarly the long-term borrowing would show an even more dramatic increase from 8% to 35% of the balance sheet total.

The technique of common size statements can be applied just as easily to the profit and loss account as to the balance sheet. In the case of the profit and loss account it is normal to express all items as a percentage of sales as illustrated below:

Leek Hotels Ltd common size profit and loss account

	19X7	19X6	19X5	19X4	19X3
	%	%	%	%	%
Sales	100	100	100	100	100
Cost of sales	40	40	41	43	44
Gross profit	60	60	59	57	56
Administration costs	56	51	36	37	38
Operating profit	4	9	22	20	17
Other operating income	2	2	1	2	1
	6	11	23	22	19
Inerest payable	5	4	5	3	3
Pre-tax profit	1	7	18	19	15
Taxation	1	2	2	3	3
Profit after tax	1	4	16	16	12
Dividends	7	7	6	6	4
Retained profit	−6	−2	10	10	8

Apart from the rounding errors which result from working in whole numbers, the statement above is fairly self explanatory. An item that is worth highlighting is that the increase in the administration costs in 19X6 and 19X7 has squeezed the operating profit down to only 4% return on sales in 19X7 which is a year when the interest charges are 5% of sales. This illustrates the risk of high gearing which we referred to in Chapter 8. It also raises questions about what is included in the administration costs that have caused such a dramatic rise.

Common size statements and the other techniques we have examined so far have largely ignored the relationship between the balance sheet and the profit and loss account. The effect of this is that we have not been able to extract everything we could from the information available. For example, we know from the common size balance sheets that long-term borrowing has increased dramatically from 19X6 to 19X7 yet the interest payable as a percentage of sales has not shown such a dramatic rise. Other techniques of analysis are available which look at the relationship between items in the balance sheet and items in the profit and loss account. The most common of these techniques is known as ratio analysis and this is explored more fully below.

RATIO ANALYSIS

Although ratio analysis is seen in virtually every accounting textbook most students, whilst having little difficulty in calculating ratios, find extreme difficulty in understanding what they mean once they have been calculated. Because of this we shall not deal extensively with all the possible ratios that can be calculated but instead we shall try to concentrate on the relationships we are trying to express through the ratios we calculate. This approach will increase your understanding of the reasons for calculating these ratios and will therefore enable you to interpret the results from a sound basis of understanding. We shall discuss some ratios which express relationships between items in balance sheets, and then those based upon items in the profit and loss account. We shall then examine ratios which combine information from these two statements. Finally we shall consider how the cash flow statement and the information contained in that statement fits with the rest of our analysis.

Before doing that, we need to understand exactly what a ratio is. This is defined in the following Key concept.

Key concept

Ratios

A ratio (R) is quantity A divided by quantity B:

$$R = A/B$$

In essence a ratio is merely a shorthand notation of the relationship between two or more things. It is the relationship that it is expressing that must be understood. Without that understanding the ratio, no matter how precisely calculated or sophisticated, is meaningless.

Apart from understanding the relationship underpinning the ratio we also need to examine ratios in a wider context. For example, if we want to work out how many police we need to police a rugby match we could work on the basis of one policeman to a number of spectators. If we found that we needed two hundred police for a crowd of forty thousand spectators the ratio would be one to two hundred or 1:200.

Obviously this ratio is meaningless on its own as it does not tell us whether we are using the right number of police. To decide that we would need to establish whether problems of violence existed at rugby matches or, if not, whether we could achieve the same result with fewer police. The former problem would require additional information whilst the latter could perhaps be judged, in part at least, by looking at what other rugby clubs do and what ratio of police to spectators they use. This simple example serves to illustrate the fact that the ratio on its own cannot tell us very much; it needs to be looked at in the context of other information and experience.

Ratios based on the balance sheet

As we have already said, the important point to bear in mind is what the ratio is attempting to illustrate. For example, we could look at the balance sheet of Leek Hotels Ltd and calculate the ratio of tangible fixed assets to other fixed assets but this would be of little use unless we knew what the relationship meant and what we expected. Calculation of ratios is not an end in itself as many are meaningless. There are some relationships, however, that do mean something. For example, earlier in this chapter we discussed the need to find out about liquidity and financial risk. We said that financial risk was related to the amount of debt finance compared with equity finance. If we wanted to express this as a ratio, using Leek Hotels Ltd for example, we could take the loans in 19X3 and compare them to the equity in that year. The figure for loans for that year was £10 391 000 and the equity figure was £42 105 000. The ratio could be calculated by dividing the equity figure by the loans figure as follows:

$$\frac{£42\ 105\ 000}{£10\ 391\ 000} = 4.1 \text{ times or } 4.1{:}1$$

This tells us that for every £1 of loan finance there is £4.1 of equity finance or that there is 4.1 times more equity than debt. If we compare that to 19X7 we find that the ratio in that year is:

$$\frac{£72\ 128\ 000}{£25\ 033\ 000} = 2.9 \text{ times or } 2.9{:}1$$

If we had calculated this ratio for all years we would find it goes up dramatically in 19X4 and then falls each year from then on indicating an increasing reliance on debt capital rather than equity. This is something we could have established by looking at the common size statements. We still do not know whether this is good or bad or why it is going up and down. To answer those questions we need to look at the environment, industry norms and what else is happening in the particular business we are analysing.

To illustrate the latter point we can look in more detail at the balance sheets for the two years in question. We find that, on the face of it, the ratio we have just calculated would suggest that the business is more reliant on debt in 19X7 than it was in 19X3. This greater reliance is partly offset by a lesser reliance on short-term borrowing which was 29% of the balance sheet total in 19X3 and has dropped to 23% in 19X7. This illustrates that the ratio we calculated only tells us part of the story as we need to look at Leek Hotels Ltd's total borrowing.

One way to overcome this problem is to calculate more than one ratio to establish the relationship between debt and equity. We could, for example, also calculate the ratio of total debt to equity or the ratio of the total debt less cash balances to equity. All these ratios attempt to give some indication of the financial risk involved.

Other balance sheet ratios that are commonly used relate to the relationship between current assets and current liabilities and to the relationship between current monetary assets, such as debtors and cash, and current liabilities. These relationships are used to express what is happening in relation to what is often referred to as 'short-term liquidity'. They are calculated by dividing, for example, the current assets figure by the current liabilities figure. Once again, on its own, the result of this calculation does not necessarily tell us much. We need to look at trends and take into account the nature of the business. For example, we would expect a tour operator to be in a different position regarding cash, debtors and creditors than a hotel group. We also need to take into account the size of the business in our interpretation of the results.

We can calculate the liquidity ratios of Leek Hotels Ltd for the five years and see if the trend in these gives us any idea of what is happening. The first liquidity ratio is the current ratio. This is defined as:

$$\text{Current ratio:} \quad \frac{\text{Current assets}}{\text{Current liabilities}}$$

$$\text{19X3:} \quad \frac{\text{£5 977 000}}{\text{£12 168 000}} = 0.5 \text{ times or } 0.5{:}1$$

The ratio for the other years is as follows:

19X4, 0.4:1; 19X5, 0.46:1; 19X6, 0.45:1; 19X7, 0.5:1

These show that the ratio is hovering around the figure of 0.5 to 1, but what does this mean? To answer that we need to think about the relationship being expressed, i.e. the relationship between those assets that will be turned into cash in the short term and the amounts we potentially have to pay out in the short term. If the ratio is less than one to one it means that if all our debts were called in there may be problems paying them. However, this does not take account of the timing of the receipts and payments and the nature of the business. However, at a general level we can say that if the ratio is going down it means that we have less cover and therefore there is more risk. If we find that the risk is increasing we may then wish to use a more sensitive measure to try to establish what is causing the increase in risk. One such measure simply excludes the stock from the current assets and compares the remaining current assets to the current liabilities. The reasoning behind the exclusion of stock is that it will first have to be sold and then the debtors will have to pay before we can use the cash to pay our creditors. In the case of the hospitality and tourism industries, because stock is generally fairly insignificant, this ratio is not likely to tell us any more than the current ratio.

The ratio, i.e. the ratio of current assets, excluding stock, to current liabilities, is often referred to as the 'acid test' or 'quick ratio' and is defined as:

$$\text{Quick ratio:} \quad \frac{\text{Current assets} - \text{Stock}}{\text{Current liabilities}}$$

Calculating this ratio for 19X3 we obtain:

$$19\text{X3:} \quad \frac{£5\ 977\ 000 - £297\ 000}{£12\ 168\ 000} = 0.47 \text{ times or } 0.47\text{:}1$$

The fact that the ratio is less than one to one tells us that we could not pay our current debts if we were called upon to do so. Or, to put it another way, the ratio tells us that we have 47p to pay each £1 of current liabilities. The question is: does this matter? Leek Hotels Ltd has after all stayed in business well after 19X3.

The interpretation of the information obtained from calculating this ratio, as with all other ratios, only makes sense if it is judged by comparison to a set of industry norms. Even this is not as straightforward as it sounds as there are often different norms within an industry depending on the size and relative power of the firms in that sector. There is also the point that any norm based on a number of firms will actually be the average not the best and so care has to be exercised when looking at these norms and applying them to a particular firm. This all seems to imply that comparison with norms may not be meaningful in any case. This is certainly true if it is done without adequate attention to what constitutes the norm that the results are being compared to.

The question of the usefulness or otherwise of an industry norm does not apply in the case of Leek Hotels Ltd as we do not have that information.

Having looked at some of the balance sheet ratios for measuring financial risk it is worth remembering that because the balance sheet represents the position at a point in time the ratios we calculate may not be typical of the position throughout the year. Because of this we would be better using the cash flow statement when attempting to judge the liquidity position of a firm. However, before we look at the cash flow statement let us turn our attention to the profit and loss account.

Ratios based on the profit and loss account

Most ratios that relate solely to the profit and loss account are really expressions of costs as a percentage of sales, for example the gross profit or net profit expressed as a percentage of sales. These relation-ships are also made apparent with common size statements, which we have already examined, therefore we shall not discuss them further here. There are some other ratios based on the figures in the profit and loss account that are required to meet the needs of the users which we identified earlier which are not related to sales. These are the interest cover and dividend cover. Both these ratios express the relationship between the profit available and the item in question. We shall start with interest cover. This can be expressed as:

$$\text{Interest cover} = \frac{\text{Profit available before interest charge}}{\text{Interest charge}}$$

$$19X3: \frac{£3\,875\,000}{£704\,000} = 5.5 \text{ times}$$

The trend can also be calculated:

19X4, 7.2; 19X5 4.9; 19X6, 4.3; 19X7, 2.6 times

We can see a decline in this ratio from 19X4 on. Clearly the fewer times interest is covered by profits the more at risk that interest is from the lender's point of view. From the point of view of the shareholders the lower the cover the more likely it is that all the profits will be absorbed by interest charges, especially if they rise. This then leaves no profits available for the payment of dividends.

We shall now consider the ratio for dividend cover as this will give the shareholders an indication of how safe their dividends are. The ratio for dividend cover is given below.

$$\text{Dividend cover} = \frac{\text{Profit after taxation}}{\text{dividends}}$$

$$19X3: \frac{£2\,509000}{£827\,000} = 3 \text{ times}$$

The trend can also be calculated:

19X4, 2.6; 19X5 2.6; 19X6, 0.6; 19X7, 0.1 times

We can see a decline in this ratio from 19X3 on. Clearly the fewer times dividends are covered by profits the more at risk they are from the shareholders' point of view. You may wonder why Leek Hotels Ltd continues to pay dividends when it has no profits to cover them. This may be because the management has made a decision to maintain the level of dividends in a bid to boost shareholder confidence. Conversely it could be that most of the the share capital is in the form of cumulative preference shares on which dividends accrue irrespective of profits. This information could be found in the notes to the accounts and it is in fact the case here.

We shall now move on to examine some of the relationships between the profit and loss account and the balance sheet.

Profit and loss and balance sheet relationships

In many areas the balance sheet and the profit and loss account are directly related such that a movement in one will have a consequential effect on the other. For example, if we have an increase in sales we would expect our debtors to go up, we would probably have to buy more goods to sell so our creditors may rise, and in all probability our level of stocks would also have to rise to cope with the increased demand. In the case of Leek Hotels Ltd the sales have risen as have the debtors. At this stage we are not sure whether the increase in debtors is solely due to the increase in sales or whether it is in part caused by the debtors taking longer to pay up. The use of a ratio that compares sales and debtors would provide answers to questions such as this.

When calculating ratios that relate balance sheet items to profit and loss account items we have to bear in mind that if prices are changing the relationship can be distorted. This is because the balance sheet represents prices at one point in time, whereas the profit and loss account represents the results of operations for a period. This can be shown diagrammatically as:

T_0 Profit and loss account T_1

Opening balance sheet   Closing balance sheet

Thus the opening stock figure or debtors figure would be expressed in start-of-year prices, the profit and loss figures in average prices and the closing figures in end-of-year prices. Added to this problem of a changing price level is the fact that the volume will also change. For example, as sales increase so we need to hold more units of stock to provide the same service. Thus we have two problems, i.e. changes in prices and changes in volumes. One way to compensate for this is to use the average of the opening and closing balance sheet figures and compare that average figure for stocks, debtors, etc., to the figure from the profit and loss account which is already expressed in average prices. Thus to calculate the relationship between sales for 19X7 and the debtors we would take the debtors at 19X6 and at 19X7 and take the average of the two figures. This would give us a better approximation of the true level of debtors required to sustain that volume of sales.

The relationship thus calculated can be expressed either as the turnover of the balance sheet figure, e.g. debtors turnover, or as the number of days debtors take to repay. We shall use the latter for the purposes of illustration as experience shows that this is more readily understood.

To calculate this ratio the formula we require is:

$$\text{Debtor collection} = \frac{\text{Average debtors}}{\text{Sales}} = \times 365$$

Thus for 19X7 for Leek Hotels Ltd the debtor collection period is:

$$\frac{1/2(8049 + 7863)}{29\,603} \times 365 = 98 \text{ days}$$

Once again we cannot comment on whether this is good or bad without some reference point and some more information. For example, if the sales mix had changed and Leek Hotels Ltd had moved into the business and conference markets this may mean that it takes longer to collect money.

A number of other ratios of this type can be calculated, e.g. the period taken to pay creditors using cost of sales and purchases respectively. However, as this is an introductory text we shall not deal with these other ratios in depth. Instead we would encourage the reader to identify the relationships which will aid their understanding and derive their own ratios. If having done that readers are interested in looking at some of the more commonly used ratios they should make reference to one of the texts suggested at the end of this chapter.

The cash flow statement

We have talked about the use of balance sheet based ratios such as the current ratio and the quick ratio as measures of liquidity. The problem with these ratios is that they are based upon a static position statement and they can be manipulated by changing the timing of stock purchases etc. round the year end for example. A better guide to the liquidity position can be found in the cash flow statement which tells us what money is coming in, where it is coming from, and how it is being spent. The cash flow statement for Leek Hotels Ltd for 19X7 is reproduced below. (**Note**: You should not try to reconcile this to the main statements as without the notes to the accounts you do not have sufficient information to do so successfully.)

Cash flow statement of Leek Hotels Ltd for 19X7

	£000	£000
Net cash inflow from operating activities		2458
Returns on investments and servicing of finance		
Interest paid	2 195	
Dividends paid	1 980	
Net cash flow from returns on investment		(4175)

Taxation

Corporation tax paid	660	
Net cash outflow from taxation		(660)

Investing activities

Payment to acquire tangible fixed assets	7 370	
Receipts from sales of fixed assets	(2 777)	
Payment to acquire intangible assets	113	
Net cash outflow from investing activity		(4706)
Net cash outflow before financing		(7083)

Financing

Repayment of bank loans	(8 204)	
Receipt of sale and leaseback	479	
Receipts of debenture issue	13 628	
Net cash inflow from financing		5903
Decrease in cash or cash equivalents		(1180)

The cash flow statement tells us that there is a net cash inflow from operating activities of £2 458 000 which would appear to be healthy until we look at the remainder of the cash flow statement where we find that our dividend and interest payments are far in excess of what was earned from operations. This means that we must be financing these payments either by selling assets, increased borrowing or by running down our cash reserves. An analysis of the rest of the statement shows that it is in fact a combination of increased borrowing and running down of cash reserves or, to be more precise, an increase in short-term borrowing that is being used. This is clearly a situation that cannot continue for very long as in the long term we have to be able to service our capital from the cash received from operations.

Before leaving the subject of financial analysis and in particular ratio analysis it is worthwhile reminding ourselves of some of the points made in this chapter about putting the analysis into context and also reiterating the limitations of this sort of analysis.

SUMMARY OF MAJOR ISSUES

There is no point in using sophisticated techniques for analysis without an understanding of the following.

- The wider context, i.e. the economic, social and political pressures, the type of industry and where the industry as a whole is going.
- The organization's environment, i.e. the type of organization we are dealing with: is it a charity? does it have an American parent company? what business is it in? How are these factors affecting the information that is being presented and the way in which that information is presented, and how should they affect our analysis?

- The organization and its structure, i.e. what sort of organization are we dealing with, how big is the organization, is it a partnership, sole proprietorship or company and how does that affect the information provided, its presentation and our analysis?
- Who is the analysis for? As we have seen, different users have different needs in terms of analysis and, even when these needs appear to overlap, it is often the case that the emphasis is different from group to group.
- Any analysis will only be as good as the base data. In this case we are dealing with analysis based upon historic cost accounts which assume prices do not change when in practice this is not the case. Even if we overcome that problem, there is the question of how up to date or out of date the information is. There are also issues of comparability because of different accounting policies being adopted, because of the effects of organizational size on the norms, and the question of what norms actually mean.

Finally, we need to be clear on purpose of the analysis. Are we providing the base for a decision about the future actions of a user of accounting information and, if so, what alternatives in terms of decisions is that user facing? Having identified in our case that Leek Hotels Ltd seems to have some problems we now need to identify what, if any, action can be taken to solve some of those problems. In general, the role of the outside user is probably limited to that of problem identification as in most cases there is little that the outside user can do in terms of problem-solving. This is a task that should be carried out by the management of the company.

In order for management to be able to carry out this task, as we have already suggested, they will need more detailed information and often they will also require different forms of information. For example, the fact that the costs are rising does not help as they need to know which costs are actually rising. They also need to know whether the problem is due to the fact that at a lower level of sales they are losing economies of scale. Then they need to know the level of sales and costs they would expect in 19X8 and thereafter so that they can take appropriate actions to improve the performance of their business. Whether such forecasts can be made from a base of historic cost information is questionable. However, before leaving the area of financial analysis it is important that we summarize some of the key features and limitations of financial statement analysis.

Key features

- Financial analysis has to be looked at in the wider context of the industry, the environment, etc.
- Financial analysis has to be targeted to meet the needs of the user of the analysis.

- Financial analysis is only as good as the base information that is being analysed.
- Financial analysis involves both inter-temporal and inter-firm comparisons and this imposes limitations.

The key features outlined above point to some limitations that have to be borne in mind when discussing financial analysis. These can be usefully summarized under three headings as follows.

Key limitations

Information problems

- The base information is often out of date, i.e. timeliness of information leads to problems of interpretation.
- Historic cost information may not be the most appropriate information for the decision for which the analysis is being undertaken.
- Information in published accounts is generally summarized information and detailed information may be needed.
- Analysis of accounting information only identifies symptoms not causes and thus is of limited use.

Comparison problems – inter-temporal

- Effects of price changes make comparisons difficult unless adjustments are made.
- Impacts of changes in technology on the price of assets, the likely return and the future markets.
- Impacts of a changing environment on the results reflected in the accounting information.
- Potential effects of changes in accounting policies on the reported results.
- Problems associated with establishing a normal base year to compare other years with.

Comparison problems – inter-firm

- Selection of industry norms and the usefulness of norms based on averages.
- Different firms having different financial and business risk profiles and the impact of this on analysis.
- Different firms using different accounting policies.
- Impacts of the size of the business and its comparators on risk, structure and returns.
- Impacts of different environments on results, e.g. different countries, home-based versus multinational firms.

Thus there are a number of issues that you need to bear in mind when carrying out your analysis. They should not, however, be used as a reason not to attempt the analysis but should be an integral part of your thinking when interpreting and reporting the results of your analysis.

FURTHER READING

A full explanation of the techniques of financial analysis can be found in B. Lev (1974) *Financial Statement Analysis – a New Approach*, Prentice Hall.

REVIEW QUESTIONS

1. Identify the main user groups and their common needs in terms of financial analysis.
2. How do the needs of long-term lenders differ from those of equity investors?
3. What factors do we need to take into account in order to put our analysis in context?
4. What sources of information outside the business are available to you and how would you use this information in your analysis?
5. What information would you derive from reading the chairman's statement?
6. What other parts of the annual report would you use in your analysis?
7. Explain briefly what the difference is between financial risk and business or commercial risk.
8. How would you measure financial risk in the short and long term?
9. What are the limitations of financial analysis that are inherent in the accounting data being used?

PROBLEMS FOR DISCUSSION AND ANALYSIS

Given below are the summarized accounts of Happy Inns for the past five years. These form the basis for the questions which follow.

Summarized profit and loss accounts of Happy Inns

	19X7	19X6	19X5	19X4	19X3
	£000	£000	£000	£000	£000
Sales	88 800	86 200	94 000	79 700	62 800
Cost of sales	39 960	37 928	38 540	32 677	25 120
Gross profit	48 840	48 272	55 460	47 023	37 680
Administration costs	34 200	30 800	32 900	27 895	21 980
Operating profit	14 640	17 472	22 560	19 128	15 700

Other operating income	1 930	1 820	1 650	1 672	700
	16 570	19 292	24 210	20 800	16 400
Interest payable	5 728	3 432	4 712	2 439	2 112
Pre-tax profit	10 842	15 860	19 498	18 361	14 288
Taxation	3 253	4 758	5 849	5 508	4 286
Profit after tax	7 589	11 102	13 649	12 853	10 002
Dividends	6 010	5 950	5 950	4 850	2 467
Retained profit	1 579	5 152	7 699	8 003	7 535

Summarized balance sheet for Happy Inns

	19X7	19X6	19X5	19X4	19X3
Fixed assets	£000	£000	£000	£000	£000
Land and buildings	344 176	297 124	266 345	221 146	178 124
Equipment and fittings	70 494	60 857	54 553	45 295	36 483
	414 670	357 981	320 898	266 441	214 607
Current assets					
Stocks	858	945	1 054	987	897
Debtors	25 490	22 030	19 011	16 742	14 986
Cash at bank and in hand	197	313	325	789	2 138
	26 545	23 288	20 390	18 518	18 021
Creditors: amounts falling due in one year	59 879	51 982	46 342	46 983	37 682
Net current liabilities	–33 334	–28 694	–25 952	–28 465	–19 661
Total assets less current liabilities	381 336	329 287	294 946	237 976	194 946
Creditors: amounts falling due after one year	98 675	54 663	28 759	16 475	31 301
	282 661	274 624	266 187	221 501	163 645
Capital and reserves	£000	£000	£000	£000	£000
Share capital	70 542	70 542	70 542	70 542	37 634
Share premium	24 634	24 634	24 634	24 634	16 457
Revaluation reserve	119 589	113 131	109 846	72 859	64 091
Profit and loss account	63 757	62 178	57 026	49 327	41 324
Other reserves	4 139	4 139	4 139	4 139	4 139
	282 661	274 624	266 187	221 501	163 645

1. From a review of the information above identify the areas which you would concentrate on in your analysis of the position of Happy Inns.
2. Produce common size profit and loss accounts for the five years and analyse these statements with particular reference to the profitability of Happy Inns.
3. Calculate the trends in the sales and cost of sales and comment on the information disclosed by your analysis.

4. Using whatever form of analysis you consider appropriate comment on the financial risk profile of Happy Inns for the five years under review.

5. Based on your analysis write a brief report for the bank advising them on whether to continue to provide finance for Happy Inns.

6. Apart from the information arising from your analysis what other information would you advise the bank to consider when making their decision.

7. Discuss how your analysis would have been altered if you were carrying out the analysis on behalf of a prospective shareholder.

Internal users and internal information 12

INTRODUCTION

The theme we have followed in the book so far has been to examine the needs of users of financial information. In Chapter 1 we identified the various users of information. More recently in Chapter 11 we discussed the information needs of external users, the sources of information available to them, and the ways in which they could use the financial information available to them. That information was derived from the annual accounts of the enterprises being analysed.

As we illustrated, in Chapters 5 to 11 the underlying information for the annual accounts is contained within the organization's accounting system. This accounting system may be very simple, as would be the case with a hot-dog stand for example, or extremely sophisticated as is the case with that of British Airways or Forte. The level of sophistication will not only depend upon the size of the business but also its complexity. For example, a travel organization that operates solely as a travel agent will need a less sophisticated system than one such as that of Thomas Cook where part of the business is concerned with providing package holidays, part is an agent for other holiday companies and part is a foreign exchange and partial banking service. Looking at this from another angle we could say that the accounting system will depend upon the decisions that have to be made and the needs of those people making the decisions, i.e. the users of the accounting information.

We have dealt with the main external users and their needs in Chapter 11. In that chapter we also identified management as one of the main users of accounting information. We stated that management would need more detailed information than that normally contained in the financial accounts. We also indicated that their information requirements would be for more detailed and more up-to-date information. In fact in many cases they need information of a different type. All of this information which management may need could of course also be useful to other users, i.e. those that are external to the organization; however, they do not necessarily get it. This may be because they do not have the power to demand access to the information or because it is too detailed for their purposes, or because public disclosure of the information would be commercially sensitive. For example, if as a shareholder you were trying to forecast next year's profits for a package holiday company an essential piece of information would be the price at which the organization planned to sell its holidays. However, in a competitive industry such as this the disclosure of that information would mean that competitors could also access that information and adjust their marketing and pricing policies accordingly.

At the other end of the spectrum there are organizations that are too small to warrant the building of a sophisticated accounting system to provide regular information for management and, in these cases, external users would not be able to access the information simply because it does not exist. This trade-off between costs and benefits from the collection and provision of accounting information is very important and should be borne in mind as you work through the remainder of this book where the focus is on the needs of internal users, i.e. management.

We will examine the needs of management in terms of the information they may require in order to make choices between alternative opportunities, to plan activities and to ensure that the plans are carried out. It is this future orientation that is important as it is one major distinguishing factor between much internal accounting information and that which is reported externally. That is not to say that all management accounting – or internally oriented – information relates to the future. Indeed in most cases it is as important for management to know what the actual costs and revenues associated with a particular product or service are as well as what they expected them to be.

MANAGEMENT'S INFORMATION NEEDS

As a starting point we will examine the situation of an existing business where management has already decided on the course of action to follow. In this situation management will be interested in the outcomes of those past decisions. They can obtain certain information from the annual accounts, but often this will be insufficient for this purpose. One reason why this may be the case is that the annual accounts often contain summarized and simplified information. This is almost certainly the case in anything other than the smallest of enterprises. For example, the fact that the accounts for a hotel show a loss does not enable management to identify what is causing the loss. It may be that the food and beverage side is making a large loss that is swallowing up the profits on rooms. All the summarized information will do is to alert management to the fact that there is a loss or that profit is lower than anticipated, but it is unlikely to be sufficiently detailed to enable management to identify the cause of this variation. For management purposes, there is almost invariably a need for more detailed information. They need more detailed information about the results of their past decisions and actions than that contained in the annual accounts.

As the name implies, annual accounts are only drawn up once a year. This is another reason why they are unlikely to be sufficient to meet the needs of managers who need more regular and up-to-date information. The fact that annual accounts are only produced at the year end and then are subject to audit in the case of most organizations of any size means that even if they do enable managers to establish why the results have varied from those anticipated it may well be too late to take appropriate action. For example, if an enterprise has an accounting year end in June its audited accounts will not be available until some time after the end of August. Therefore even if the accounts do show an area where corrective action is required this action will be delayed. The delays involved in the production and audit of the published accounting information vary from about three to four months for quoted companies to periods in excess of ten months for smaller enterprises and although management would have access to the preliminary results much earlier than they are published there may still be considerable delays.

In addition to needing more timely information management will also need more regular information than an annual report on progress. They will need regular, up to the minute reports on what is happening in each major division of the organization if they are to take action when and where appropriate.

Thus we have established some needs of management that are not satisfied by the production of annual accounts. These are summarized in following Key concept.

Key concept

Management information needs

- Management generally needs more detailed information.
- They need up-to-date information.
- They need more frequent information.
- They need information suited to the decision they are required to take.

The reason that management is likely to require information more frequently is so that they can monitor the results of their actions and decisions and fine tune the business as and when required. This does not mean that none of the needs of managers are met by the financial information system on which the annual accounts are based. For example, although the annual accounts of a hotel group will only show one figure for debtors, the accounting records will contain much more information about the individual debts making up that debtors figure. This will include information about the customer, when the sales took place and the customer's past payment record. This detailed information allows management to collect the money more quickly and to chase the slow payers. By doing this management will be able to ensure that the business does not face more problems because of poor cash flow than are absolutely necessary. We shall explore the question of cash flow management in more detail in Chapter 17 as part of our discussion on the management of working capital.

There are, of course, other examples of information contained within the accounting system that if presented and used in different ways from that required for drawing up annual accounts meets management needs better. For example, the basic information required for a cost plus approach to pricing is available from the accounting system. This approach to pricing is covered in some detail in Chapter 14 where you will see that for the pricing decision management may use basic information about costs in different ways. For example, to make a decision about whether to continue to operate in a particular market sector they will require forward looking information in the form of forecasts. They may, for example, wish to know the point at which the revenue is going to be equal to the cost, i.e. the breakeven point, and how likely it is that such a point will be reached. Whilst the latter question of the likelihood of sales reaching the level to provide a breakeven position is a question for the sales and marketing department, the question of what the costs are at different volume levels is one that accountants will be called upon to answer.

A full discussion of the way in which costs behave and how to establish the breakeven position is contained in Chapter 13. An understanding of those principles is vital if appropriate decisions are to be made by management no matter which industry one is looking at. For example, Sir Freddy Laker of Laker Airways argued that in the airline industry you needed to know a breakeven position that would cover costs, a breakeven position that would cover costs plus the interest charges incurred in buying planes and a third position at which you were profitable. In that case these breakeven positions could be expressed in terms of seat occupancy. Unfortunately as it turned out this was not the only information necessary to run a successful airline and Laker Airways subsequently went bust.

It is important to understand that the base information used to produce the annual accounts is the same information which is used as the source for many different reports which are provided to meet the specific needs of management. It should also be borne in mind that, as with the other users referred to in Chapter 11, for management purposes financial information is only one of a number of sources of information needed in order to make decisions about the future direction and actions of the business. It is not our intention to deal with these other sources of information as they are outside the scope of this text but they could include marketing information, employment legislation, etc. We will continue our discussion of management's information needs within the relatively narrow confines of financial information.

The discussion to date has suggested that management needs more frequent and more detailed information, and that information may be required in a different format from that contained in the annual accounts. More explicitly we can view management information needs at a general level in terms of their needs for information to plan future activities and control present and future activities. In terms of planning future activities four stages of the process can be identified. These are the process of setting objectives, making strategic decisions, making operating decisions and monitoring the results and taking corrective action. Setting of objectives and the processes involved in strategic decision-making are extensively covered in the literature on corporate strategy and we shall therefore not be dealing with this within this text. However, it is appropriate at this level to look in some detail at the information managers require to enable them to make operating decisions. This is done in Chapter 15 and we then move on to look at how management monitors the results of its decisions, the information required and the techniques available. This forms the basis of the discussion in Chapter 16.

As we have said, most if not all of this information may also be useful to other users than managers. However, some of this information is commercially sensitive and achievement of the enterprise's goal may be dependent upon their plans being kept secret from their competitors. Thus not all external users will be able to demand access to this information and the question of whether they have access will depend not only on who they are but also upon their importance to the enterprise. We will now consider what these external users' needs may be, who they are, and the factors, such as relative power, competition and confidentiality, that determine their access or lack of access to internal information.

EXTERNAL USERS' INFORMATION NEEDS

One external user group which can demand access to internal accounting information is the taxation authorities. The nature of the information they require will vary but will normally be either more detailed breakdowns of particular expense headings or details of the timing of purchases and sale of fixed assets. The reason for this is that the taxation system is based upon a different set of rules for arriving at the taxable profit from that used to arrive at the accounting profit. The taxation authorities which will include both the Inland Revenue and the Customs and Excise who deal with value added tax (VAT) have a statutory right of access to information.

Another external user which often is in a sufficiently powerful position to demand and obtain further information is the enterprise's bankers. The information they demand will of course depend on the circumstances. For example, if the enterprise is doing well the information demanded will be quite different from that which would be required if the enterprise had problems. We will discuss at a general level some of the additional information they may require and why this is required before going on to examine what determines whether or not this information is available to these external users.

In general, the information demanded by an enterprise's bankers can be divided into two categories: that required for routine monitoring and that required to arrive at judgements about the future needs of the enterprise. The former category would include regular management accounts such as monthly profit statements, an analysis of debts in terms of how old they are known as an aged debtors analysis, and other up-to-date information such as the amount owed by the enterprise, i.e. the monthly creditors balances. All of this information is required to monitor the health of their customer's business on a more regular basis than would be possible if they had to rely on the information provided by annual accounts which as we have already said is likely to be a few months out of date when it is produced.

Bankers also require other information to make judgements about the future needs and prospects of the enterprise in order to ascertain whether to lend money, when it is likely to be repaid and the risk involved. The information on future prospects is normally required in the form of projected cash flow statements and profit and loss accounts, but would also include information about other loans the enterprise may have and their due dates for repayment. The financial information is of course only part of the information that the banker may require, this could also include future plans, projected occupancy levels, analysis of competitors, etc.

As we have already indicated there are circumstances where, like other external users such as shareholders and competitors, the banker cannot get access to this additional information. We will examine those circumstances in our discussion of the impact of organizational size and structure on the information produced for management purposes which is, of course, one factor which determines what these external users have access to.

IMPACTS OF ORGANIZATIONAL SIZE

We have discussed the needs of management in terms of information to make decisions about the future, to plan future actions and to control the business on a day-to-day basis. It should be clear that the more complex and sophisticated the business, the more likely it is that they will require additional information. For example, the local cafe owner may be able to carry all the information needed in his or her head to enable the business to be run effectively on a day-to-day basis. This is because the business is sufficiently small and the proprietor, who is of course in this situation also the manager, is directly involved in the running of the business and is on the spot to take whatever action is necessary.

On the other hand, in a large and complex business there is a need for a more formalized system for a number of reasons. Firstly the amount of information required, for example, in a multi-product service organization, e.g. Thomas Cook, is such that it is unlikely that the management would be able to carry in their heads all the detail necessary to effectively run the business. Another important point to bear in mind with larger businesses is that it is probably the case that the larger the business the further the senior managers will be removed from the day-to-day operations. This will not only change their information needs to requiring information of a more strategic type but will also impose a requirement for additional information to control the activities and actions of those below them.

Thus the size of the organization will influence the information needs of its managers and the way in which these needs are met, i.e. the need for more formal systems as the size of the business increases. We have also suggested that the nature of the business has an effect on the information needs, thus a multi-product business will require more sophisticated information systems than a single product business. Consider, for example, the different information required to run a restaurant where the only product is food as against that required to run a hotel. In the latter case not only do you need information about the food operation, but information is also required on bed occupancy rates, the bar profits, etc.

We should also remember that more up-to-date information is not in itself better *per se* as it also needs to be relevant to the use to which it is to be put. A fuller discussion of what constitutes relevant information in relation to costs and benefits and how these relate to short-term decisions is contained in Chapter 18. The issue of obtaining relevant information at a reasonable cost is part of the explanation of why in the case of many small businesses there is little in the way of formal management information. In many of these cases the information if it exists at all is held in the owner manager's head in a form that is not readily accessible to others. In these situations bankers are often able to exercise considerable influence as a major provider of finance. However, at the end of the day no matter how much pressure is exerted they cannot access information that does not exist. They therefore have to rely on the annual accounts and any other information that is available.

We have shown that the information available is influenced not only by the needs of managers but also by the size and complexity of the organization's products. Equally the service sector or part of the sector in which the business operates may have a major impact upon the information requirements. For example, the needs of a manager of a tourist attraction such as EuroDisney may be very different from those of the manager of a tour operator or a travel agency. Similarly the needs of the manager of a hotel group could be quite different from those of an airline manager.

There are of course many other factors which will have an influence on what information is required and what is produced. Rather than pursuing the effects of different organizations in different industries or even within the same industry sector we will consider a more general influence upon the information needs of managers, i.e. the structure of the organization.

IMPACTS OF ORGANIZATIONAL STRUCTURE

It is clear from looking at a few well known examples that different organizations have different structures and these structures mean that their information needs may also differ. If we consider the case of the hospitality industry. It is obvious that an international hotel group such as Sheraton is going to need different information about its operations than a domestic hotel group if for no other reason than the effect of different currencies. In general, an organization that has a multi-national operation will have different information requirements than one whose operations are solely in the domestic market.

Similarly many hotels are organized round functions as profit centres, where the profits related to those functions are identified separately. This implies that both the cost records and the takings from sales have to be identified and recorded by function. It may well be the case in such organizations that management is rewarded on the basis of schemes such as profit sharing, or by comparing profits achieved against predetermined targets. In such circumstances the information system would have to be designed to meet the structural requirements of the organization.

We could of course find many more examples of different organizational structures apart from those referred to above as the organizational structure will depend on and to some extent be determined by the market and the competitive environment as well as more mundane factors such as geography and the location of its outlets. To do so would be extremely time consuming and outside the requirement of this text. We can, however, say that in general terms that the more decentralized an organization is the more complex the information system will be.

SUMMARY

In this chapter we have looked at the information needs of internal users. We have suggested that management's information needs cover a wide range of information which will vary from the detailed information needs of the manager of the housekeeping function within a hotel to the strategic needs of the general manager of that hotel. This analysis can of course be applied to other organizations where there are multiple layers of management ranging from those involved in the day-to-day running right up to the board of directors. We have also indicated that the size and complexity of the organization as well as its structure will affect the information requirements of those within the organization and the relative availability of this information to those external users who may have the power to access such information. However, the common thread that runs through all management information needs is that they need detailed, up-to-date information for the purposes of planning, decision-making and control of the organization and it is to a more detailed examination of these areas that we will turn in the following chapters.

REVIEW QUESTIONS

1. What are the main reasons why management would require additional information to the annual accounts?
2. One of the major improvements bankers wish to see in respect of financial information is an improvement in the timeliness of information. Explain what this means and why it is important to bankers and how this might differ for managers.
3. What is likely to be the major impact of organizational size on the information needs of managers?
4. What useful management information is available from the accounting system from which the annual accounts are produced?
5. What additional information would managers require in order to make a decision about whether to open a new outlet or provide a different service?

PROBLEMS FOR DISCUSSION AND ANALYSIS

1. In each of the situations outlined below identify what you believe your information needs would be.

Situation 1
You are the manager of a local branch of a national chain of fast-food restaurants. The vast majority of the buying is done centrally through organizations with nationwide distribution networks. Thus these costs like the prices charged to the customers are fixed. You are in charge of the day-to-day management, the staff mix and the hiring and firing of staff as well as setting pay rates in accordance with local conditions. Your annual remuneration is fixed.

Situation 2

The situation is the same as above except that in addition to your annual salary you receive a bonus of £1 for each £100 profit made above that expected.

Situation 3

As in situation 2 above except that you are able to vary the selling prices within a specified range to match the prices with local conditions.

Situation 4

You have been so successful as a manager that the company has promoted you to the position of regional manager in charge of 20 fast-food outlets all of whose managers work under the conditions outlined in situation 3 above.

2. You have just been appointed as the managing director of a travel organization primarily involved in bespoke package holidays but with a certain amount of business which is carried out on a commission basis such as sales of flights, insurance and other sundry services. The business has a head office staff consisting of yourself and two other directors who also own some of the shares in the business. It has a number of high street offices. Each of the offices has a manager in charge who looks after the day-to-day running of that office including the level of staffing and the negotiation of staff wages. Advertising, the negotiation and buying of the services that go into the packages you offer is carried out by one of the directors whilst the other director looks after the billing of clients, collection of monies due, payments for wages and all other bills. The overall profitability of the organization has fallen drastically in the last year and you have decided to investigate the situation.

Required:

Identify what information you would need and what level of detail would be required in order to start your investigation.

Cost behaviour and cost/volume/profit analysis

13

INTRODUCTION

For managers to be able to choose between alternative opportunities, they need information regarding future costs and revenues. In order to use this information effectively managers also need to understand how costs are determined and the way in which costs and revenues behave at varying levels of activity.

In this chapter we will begin by examining cost behaviour and the ways in which costs are predicted. We then consider the application of this information to decision-making using the technique of cost/volume/profit analysis (CVP analysis). This technique examines the interrelationships between cost, volume and profits at differing activity levels. We will also critically appraise the traditional methods and models that are used and the underlying assumptions. Finally in this chapter we consider types of cost structures.

ELEMENTS OF COSTS

To understand now costs behave it is important to examine the elements of costs. Costs are traditionally categorized into three elements: materials, manpower and expenses. The relative proportions of these three elements will vary depending upon the industrial sector and between different types of business within a particular industry sector. Materials are the physical goods used up in the provision of service or in producing goods for sale. They may constitute a large part of the value of a product, as in the retail trade as compared with the cost profile of accommodation in hotels, where material costs tend to be less significant. Manpower is the labour effort that is employed in producing the product or service. The significance of this cost in terms of the total cost of a product of service will depend upon the labour intensity required to produce the service or product. Expenses are perhaps the most diverse of the three elements because the term expenses itself covers a multitude of costs associated with running the business. Expenses typically include costs such as rent, rates, insurance and the cost of maintenance and support staff that are not directly employed in providing a service or producing a product. Invariably in firms the majority of costs categorized as expenses cannot be directly linked to a particular product or service. These costs are classified as indirect costs or overheads. These cost classifications will be considered in more detail in the following section.

CLASSIFICATION OF COSTS

Direct and indirect costs

One of the main classifications employed in accounting is the notion that costs can either be direct or indirect. The Key concept 13 below defines these two terms.

> ### *Key concept*
> *Direct and indirect costs*
>
> A direct cost is one that is traceable, and thus attributable, to a product or service. Indirect costs (also known as overhead costs) are those costs that cannot be easily and conveniently traced and identified with a particular product.

Often it will be necessary to allocate and apportion indirect costs to products and services. For example, finished goods stocks will invariably be valued by businesses at their full cost; full cost includes both direct and indirect costs. However, the process of allocating and apportioning indirect costs to products and services is often problematic and inevitably inaccuracies can occur. The salary of a general manager of a leisure complex, for example, would need to be allocated and apportioned to all the different services provided by the leisure complex if the full cost of these different services were to be established. This could only be achieved by carefully observing and recording the time that the general manager directly spends on each service. The implementation and operation of a system to carry out this function is likely to be too costly and as a compromise the salary may be apportioned on the basis of the turnover of each service. Turnover in this case is considered a reasonable surrogate basis for allocation of this cost – it may not be accurate but it may be good enough for the purposes required!

Fixed and variable costs

Costs can also be classified according to their behaviour, i.e. the way they behave or change in a given situation. Some costs are essentially fixed in nature, for example the standing charge for the domestic telephone service. Others vary with usage or activity, for example the cost of each telephone call made. These are known as variable costs. This classification is critical in planning and decision-making where it provides information of how costs will behave in different circumstances. For example, a restaurant's food costs will increase the more meals it sells; however, no matter how busy or otherwise the restaurant is, it will still have to pay the rent on the property from which it is operating.

Food and beverage costs and labour are traditionally considered to be variable costs, although one could argue that labour is not totally variable.

Key concept

Variable costs

Variable costs are those costs that change in a direct relationship to a change in output or activity.

Costs that are typically classified as fixed costs are: rent, rates, salaries of administrators and standard charges such as the standard charge for telephones. Fixed costs of this type will normally be classified as indirect costs or overhead costs (the two terms being synonymous).

Key concept

Fixed costs

Fixed costs are those costs that do not vary with fluctuations in the level of activity.

It is important to recognize that although we refer to them as fixed costs because we assume the cost will remain unchanged during the reporting period, e.g. accounting year, they do not stay fixed forever. Fixed costs are likely to vary in the longer term. Typically, each year a firm may face a rent review on its rented properties which may result in an increase in rental charges. It must also be recognized that it is likely in the longer term that as output rises beyond a certain level fixed costs rise. These assumptions clearly limit the precise accuracy of our analysis and the legitimacy of these assumptions will be discussed later in this chapter.

LINEAR COST FUNCTIONS

A basic notion of science is the idea that one thing will depend on another. It is likely that in your study of economics you have come across the application of this concept. For example, economists when considering the relationship between the total spending of a nation on all consumption goods (C) in one year and the total income (Y) of all persons in the nation in one year use the expression:

$$C = f(Y)$$

This expression states that consumption is a function of the level of income. That is, the level of consumption in one year will be dependent upon the level of income.

Similarly in accounting this basic notion is also applied in order to understand the functional relationships between cost and activity levels.

There are two important variables involved in the construction of cost functions. They are detailed below. (We will use the example of the cost of travelling to illustrate the nature of these variables and their interrelationship.)

- the **dependent** variable (y) is the cost to be predicted, that is the total cost for an activity, for example the cost of petrol for a journey;
- the **independent** variable (x) is the level of activity, for example the amount of miles to be travelled on the journey.

The dependent variable is expressed as a function of the independent variable:

$$y = f (x)$$

In our example, like the functional relationship of consumption and income described above, this relationship can be expressed as follows:

The total cost of petrol for a journey is a function of (or dependent upon) the number of miles travelled.

In this relationship we have assumed that there is only one independent variable i.e. The number of miles travelled. However, in this example, and often this is the case in general, there is more than one independent variable. In the case of the cost of petrol for a journey the consumption of petrol and thus cost will also be dependent upon, for example, the speed that the vehicle travels.

The relationship between the dependent and independent variable is illustrated in Figure 13.1 where the vertical axis is the dependent variable measuring total cost of petrol, and the horizontal axis is the independent variable measuring the activity, as in our earlier example, the miles travelled.

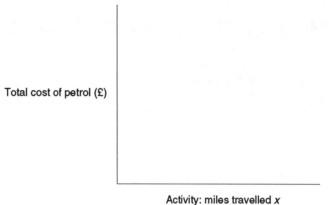

Activity: miles travelled x

Figure 13.1

The cost for the number of miles travelled can be plotted onto the graph to produce a cost function. The function may be linear or non-linear. Traditionally accountants assume cost functions to be linear, which is not necessarily a realistic assumption as often costs behave in a non-linear fashion.

Key concept

Linear cost functions

Mathematically we can express the linear cost function as follows:

$$Y = a + bx$$

where:

- Y is the total cost to be predicted;
- a is the constant, that is the element of cost that remains unchanged whatever the activity level. In accounting terminology this is known as the fixed cost, for example road tax payable on a car;
- b is the cost that will be the same for each unit of activity, and thus as the activity varies so will the cost; this cost is known as the variable cost, for example the cost of petrol;
- x as before, is the level of activity measured in units of output.

Figure 13.2 illustrates a linear cost function of the telephone bill, which was referred to earlier, plotted on a graph. Point a represents the fixed costs, which remain the same for any level of activity – in our example the standing charge. The line $b(x)$ illustrates the variable cost b, the cost per call, rising in proportion to increases in activity (x), the number of calls made.

Continuing the example of telephone charges, we can determine the total cost of the use of the telephone using the above expression if we

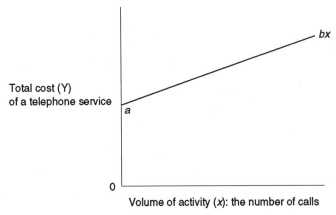

Figure 13.2 Total cost function.

know the cost of the standing charge, the cost per call and the amount of calls to be made:

- standing charge (a) = £14;
- cost per call (b) = 4p (£0.04);
- the number of calls to be made (x) = 1500;
- the total cost of the bill:

$$Y = £14 + £0.04 \ (1500) = £74$$

If the number of calls increased to 1800 the total cost of the bill will be:

$$Y = £14 + £0.04 \ (1800) = £86$$

To help you to understand this expression and its usefulness you should examine a recent telephone bill for your household and calculate the total cost of the bill if the number of calls made increased by, say, 50%. This exercise may also result in you spending less time on the telephone!

The choice of the independent variable

Often, as previously mentioned, there will be more than one independent variable that will affect the total cost of an activity. The speed that the vehicle travels as well as the miles travelled was cited as a variable that can affect the amount of petrol consumed and thus the total cost of petrol for a journey. However, very often it is too complex to take account of all independent variables that affect total costs. Because of this, the independent variable that is chosen when there are more than one should be the most influential variable in relation to the movement of costs. In the case of the cost of petrol for a journey it is likely, in general, that the most influential variable would be the miles travelled rather than, for example, speed.

In some cases the selection of the most influential variable will be obvious; however, in other cases it may not be so obvious. In such cases past costs should be examined at different activity levels to establish which of the independent variables are most influential. In the example of the cost of petrol, the consumption of petrol could be measured for a journey of, say, five miles at differing levels of speed. A decision, based on the evidence of this journey and judgement, will then have to be made as to whether the miles travelled or the speed at which the vehicle travels is the most influential variable in the cost of petrol for a journey.

Figure 13.3 illustrates the movement of variable costs over activity levels. In this illustration you will see that the intercept of costs and activity is zero. This is because variable costs relate directly to activity levels; thus if activity is zero the variable costs will be zero and as activity increases so the variable cost function (i.e. the total variable costs) increases. This can be compared to Figure 13.2 where the fixed costs were also included in the illustration.

In reality it is unlikely that costs that are traditionally classified as variable will behave strictly in a linear fashion. The variable cost function tends therefore to be curvilinear. The following examples illustrate some of the reasons why variable costs are not strictly linear.

- In the case of food purchased, at certain levels of activity restaurateurs are likely to benefit from bulk discounts.
- The price of resources, in general, will rise as scarcity rises due to demand. For tour operators this may occur in respect of the price of villas at a particular popular resort.
- Economies of scale can be achieved where the level of activity increases. For instance, contract caterers can make greater profits if they are catering for more clients on one site; this will result in the distribution/transport costs per unit decreasing.

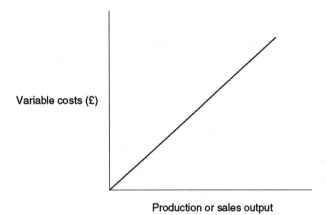

Figure 13.3 Variable cost function.

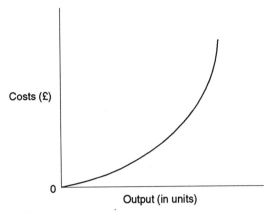

Figure 13.4 Curvilinear cost function.

Figure 13.4 shows a curvilinear cost function illustrating the rise in costs due to scarcity of a resource.

Figure 13.5 shows the graphical representation of fixed costs. In the graph the vertical axis represents fixed costs and the horizontal axis is the activity level measured in units. The line XY is the plotted fixed cost function, which illustrates that the cost will be the same for any level of activity. This graph can be compared to the graph in Figure 13.2 where point *a* represented the fixed cost; note in the earlier illustration, for the sake of clarity, the fixed cost function was not extended for all activity levels.

However, the concept of fixed costs being constant over all levels of activity is not realistic. In reality a fixed cost will only be fixed over a limited range of output. For example, in the case of a telephone, the standing charge will be fixed if only one phone is rented; if an extension is required the standing charge increases. Similarly, a bakery has a

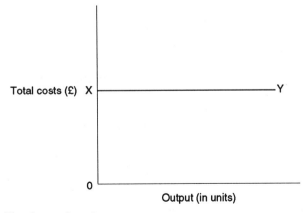

Figure 13.5 Fixed cost function.

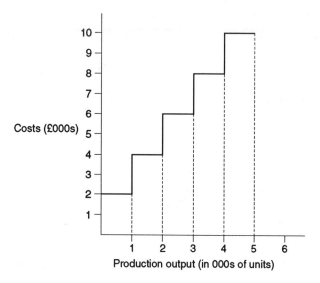

Figure 13.6 Stepped cost function.

limited capacity: if production were to exceed that capacity another facility would be required, and thus the costs would also increase. Therefore these type of costs tend to behave in a stepped fashion. Figure 13.6 illustrates a stepped cost function in the case of a bakery as output increases. The rent of one commercial baking machine is £2000 which has a capacity in output terms of 1000 loaves; another machine will therefore be required for output levels exceeding 100 000 loaves, the total rent increasing to £4000 (assuming the rental and the capacity is the same). This cost will remain at £4000 up to 2000 loaves when another machine will be required and costs will increase in the same fashion, and so on.

The relevant range of activity

In predicting future cost behaviour, we assume that the intention is to operate in the relevant range of activity, this relevant range being activity levels that we have experienced before. We can therefore be reasonably confident about the pattern of cost behaviour. This confidence is important to managers as the information regarding the way in which costs behave will be the basis for future decision-making. If the costs do not behave as predicted this could lead to decisions being taken that may jeopardize the organization's future.

Outside the relevant range we cannot be confident that the relationship between the variables would hold. Figure 13.7 shows a cost function in the relevant range of activity and other cost functions outside this range which are not of a similar pattern.

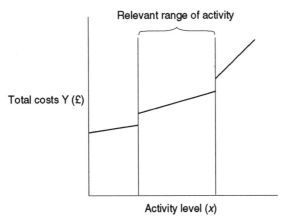

Figure 13.7 Relevant range of activity.

Therefore if an organization is intending to operate at an activity level not experienced before, it must be extremely cautious in the prediction of future costs, relying more on forecasting methods than predicting costs based on past behaviour. The examination of forecasting methods is outside the scope of this text and you can find references to the methods in advanced management accounting texts.

Conventionally, for convenience, graphical representations of the relations between cost and volume do show cost functions that are the same for all levels of activity, i.e. the same pattern of costs are shown inside and outside the relevant range of activity. This is the case in all the graphical representations showing cost functions illustrated before Figure 13.7 in this chapter.

Cost behaviour – assumptions and limitations

As we have already mentioned decision-makers conventionally employ cost functions that are linear for use in making operating decisions. This is based on a number of assumptions and although we have discussed most of the main assumptions, for clarity they are summarized below.

- All cost can be divided into either fixed or variable.

- Fixed costs remain constant over the relevant range of activity.
- Variable costs vary with activity but are constant per unit of output.
- Efficiency and productivity remain constant over all activity levels.
- Cost behaviour can sufficiently be explained by one independent variable.

From our earlier analysis it will be recognized that these assumptions are a little simplistic and tend to be approximations of reality. Therefore the question arises: are the cost functions used by managers justified? The answer to this question is often difficult to establish with much confidence. It comes down to whether the extra cost of establishing the more sophisticated non-linear functions will be justified by the more accurate forecast of costs they produce. Although the cost and benefits of an information system, as previously mentioned, are difficult to establish, it is theoretically a sound concept and therefore should be borne in mind when deciding in practice what models to employ. It is also the case that the relatively recent developments in information technology have tended to reduce the cost of developing and using these more sophisticated models.

Arnold and Hope (1990) argue that the use of a linear cost function '... is not unreasonable as statistical studies have presented evidence which suggests that within specified output limits (the relevant range of activity), organizations do have cost functions which are approximately linear.' Figure 13.8 shows how a curvilinear cost function approximates to a linear function within the relevant range of activity.

COST ESTIMATION

> ### Key concept
>
> *Cost estimation defined*
>
> Cost estimation relates to methods that are used to measure past (historical) costs at varying activity levels. These costs will then be employed as the basis to predict future costs that will then be used in decision-making.

There are many methods of cost estimation. Detailed knowledge of each of these methods is not necessary at this stage of your studies. However, it is important that you appreciate the basic principles and limitations of cost estimation. For a detailed examination of the methods see Drury (1992).

The methods of cost estimation that can be used range from those that tend to be extremely simple to others that are mathematically complex. The essential point is to choose the estimation technique that

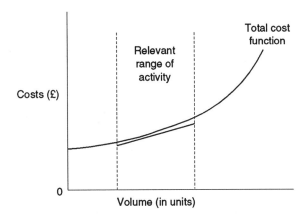

Figure 13.8

generates the greatest benefits in relation to the costs of deriving the information. This to a great extent will depend upon the size of the organization. The smaller the organization the less likely that a sophisticated method will be employed, as the costs will be relatively high as compared to the benefits that will be generated from the use of such a method.

Cost estimates will be based on historical cost accounting data, i.e. on the costs related to past service and sales activity. One of the simplest methods is the account classification method. This method involves simply observing how costs behave in a previous period from past accounting data and classifying these costs into fixed and variable. The method relies on much subjective judgement and thus it is limited in its ability to accurately predict the future behaviour of costs.

A more sophisticated method of cost estimation is regression analysis. The linear regression model involves making a number of observations from past cost behaviour, statistically analysing the data to produce a line of best fit. Figure 13.9 shows graphically a number of points that have been determined from past cost behaviour at varying levels of activity, and a line of best fit is established using regression analysis. A clear pattern of behaviour, i.e. where the points are closely clustered together over the ranges of activity, indicates a high correlation between cost and output (activity), whilst a widely dispersed arrangement of points indicates, a low correlation. In the example illustrated in Figure 13.9 there is a fairly clear pattern of behaviour and thus we can conclude that there is a relatively high correlation between cost and output.

There are more sophisticated statistical techniques using regression analysis for estimating cost. These include multiple, which takes account of more than one independent variable, and curvilinear regression.

The use of past data to determine future costs and the way in which they behave does have its problems. The following briefly summarizes some of them.

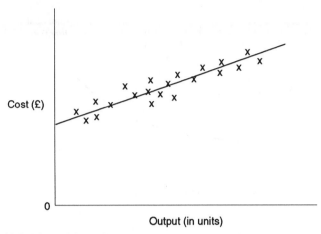

Figure 13.9 Line of best fit.

- **Relevant range of activity**. As previously mentioned, little confidence can be placed in cost estimates beyond the range of activity from which the data has been derived. It is therefore dangerous to extrapolate cost trends well beyond the levels of output previously experienced.
- **The number of observations**. It is important in statistical analysis to derive many observations of output and cost levels to be able to make accurate predictions about future behaviour. The greater the number of observations the more likely the accuracy of the estimate and, it follows, the prediction.
- **Changes in prices**. Past costs may not reflect current price levels and they will bias the estimates downwards. There is thus a need to adjust these prices to current levels.
- **Changes in technology**. Only observations made under current production procedures should be included in the analysis. Costs of work practices using, for example, machinery that is obsolete are irrelevant to future decisions.
- **Incorporating past inefficiencies**. If operations were performed in an inefficient manner in the past and cost estimates are derived from this past period, they will incorporate inefficiencies.

COST/VOLUME/PROFIT ANALYSIS

Organizations are constantly faced with decisions relating to the products and services they sell such as the following.

- Should we change our selling price? If so, what would be the effect on profit?
- What would be the effect on net profit of a 20% drop in sales?

- If sales were to start declining, at what level of sales would we no longer make a profit?
- What level of sales is required to achieve our target profit figure?
- Should we spend more money on advertising?

These questions are particularly pertinent in the hospitality and tourism industries where concepts such as occupancy levels, seats sold, etc., are vital to the effective conduct of a successful business.

Key concept

Cost/volume/profit (CVP) analysis

CVP analysis is a tool used by organizations to help them make decisions by examining the interrelationship between cost, volume and profits.

The cost data used in CVP analysis will, in the main, be derived from the prediction of future costs discussed earlier in this chapter.

Sales revenue

It is normally assumed in CVP analysis that sales revenue, like costs, behaves in a linear fashion over varying output levels. That is, the sales price per unit sold will be the same for all levels of output. Figure 13.10 illustrates a sales revenue function; the vertical axis represents the total sales revenue and the horizontal axis is the sales output. It can be seen that the sales revenue function increases in direct proportion to sales output. This is because the selling price is the same for every unit sold.

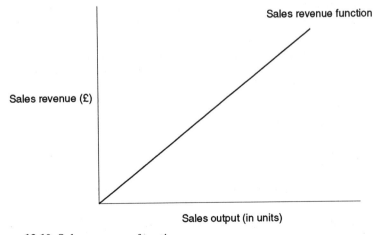

Figure 13.10 Sales revenue function.

The assumption that the selling price will remain constant for all levels of sales is rather unrealistic. For example, often you will find discounts being offered to parties in respect of entrance fees to stately homes and package holidays.

CVP analysis: the equation

The CVP relationship can be expressed as an equation:

$$\text{Profit} = \text{Total sales revenue} - \text{Total costs}$$

where:

$$\text{Total costs} = \text{Variable costs} + \text{Fixed costs}$$

This equation describes the relationship of profit, revenue and costs and you should find it familiar from your studies of the profit and loss account earlier in this book. However, it does not explicitly deal with the volume: a more detailed equation is required.

$$\text{Profit} = S(x) - (VC(x) + FC)$$

where:

S = Selling price per unit;
VC = Variable cost per unit;
FC = Fixed costs;
x = Volume of sales in units.

This expression can be rearranged as follows. This time we will also abbreviate expected profit to P:

$$S(x) = VC(x) + FC + P$$

This is the basic CVP equation. It is a linear equation and can be manipulated to provide the answers to various questions. The nature of this equation is very similar to the cost functions considered earlier. You will notice that only one independent variable is being accounted for in the equation, that is the activity measured in units. Also the fixed and variable costs are expressed in a similar way and added together to equate to total cost. The only additional variables are sales price and profit, profit being the difference between sales revenue and total costs.

To illustrate the application of CVP analysis in decision making we will consider Example 13.1 below.

EXAMPLE 13.1

Big & Busy Restaurant Ltd

The following revenues and costs have been estimated for the forth-coming year:

- Selling price per unit (meal) = £12;
- Variable costs per unit (meal) = £4;
- Fixed costs = £160 000.

The management of the restaurant want to know the following.

1. How many meals are required to be sold to break even (that is to make neither a profit or loss)?
2. How many meals must be sold to make a profit of £6000?
3. If an advertising campaign were launched at a cost £10 000 and sales output could be to increased from 40 000 to 42 000 meals per annum, would this be a worthwhile policy to pursue?
4. What should be the selling price per meal to achieve a profit of £24 000 on sales, if turnover were expected to be only 16 000 meals?

The solution to Example 13.1 is set out below.

1. The number of units to break even:

$$S(x) = VC(x) + FC + P$$

Note that at breakeven point profit will be zero, therefore we drop the element P (profit) from the original equation. The new equation that shows breakeven point is:

$$S(x) = VC(x) + FC$$

Using the data given we have the following equation:

$$12x = 4x + 160\,000$$
$$8x = 160\,000$$

Therefore $\qquad x = 20\,000$ units.

Proof:

		£
Sales (£12 × 20 000 units)		240 000
Less costs:	£	
Variable cost (£4 × 20 000 units)	80 000	
Fixed costs	160 000	240 000
Profit		0

2. The amount of units that have to be sold to make a profit of £6000:

Since $S(x) = VC(x) + FC + P$, using the data given we have the following equation:

$$12(x) = 4(x) + 160\,000 + 6000$$

Therefore $\quad x = 20\,750$ units

3. Advertising cost £10 000; sales to increase from 40 000 to 42 000 meals per annum:

Using the original equation:

$$P = S(x) - (VC(x) + FC)$$

The profit for 40 000 units is therefore:

$$Profit = 12(40\,000) - (4(40\,000) + 160\,000)$$
Therefore profit = £160 000

Advertising costs will increase fixed costs by £10 000 and the profit will be:

$$Profit = 12(42\,000) - (4(42\,000) + 170\,000)$$
Therefore profit = £166 000

Presumably the firm will go ahead with the campaign as it generates greater profits.

4. The selling price to make a profit of £24 000 on sales of 16 000 meals:

$$S(x) = VC(x) + FC + P$$
$$S(16\,000) = 4(16\,000) + 160\,000 + 24\,000$$
Therefore S = £15.50

The breakeven chart

A useful method of illustrating the relationships between cost, volume and profits is through the medium of what is commonly referred to as a breakeven chart. The relationship between these variables is plotted on a graph. The cost functions and the sales revenue function, which in previous illustrations have been shown separately, are now included together in the breakeven chart.

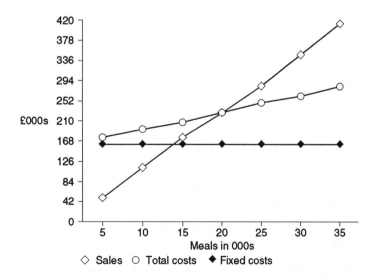

Figure 13.11 Big & Busy Restaurant Ltd: breakeven chart.

Figure 13.11 shows the breakeven chart for Big & Busy Restaurant Ltd, using the data given earlier.

You will notice that in the construction of this particular chart the variable costs are plotted above the fixed costs resulting in a total cost function that rises from the intercept at £160 000 and increases at the rate of £4 per meal. There is another way of constructing the total cost function in breakeven charts which will be illustrated later. The main advantage of the chart to management is that from the chart the break-even point and the areas of loss and profit can clearly and quickly be identified. This enables management to quickly establish the effect of varying scenarios relating to output levels that they may wish to consider. For example, the profit at an output level of 22 000 meals can easily be read from the chart without any calculation required in the solving of an equation.

The contribution margin method

The contribution margin is equal to the sales price per unit less variable cost per unit. It is also common to find the contribution margin described as the contribution per unit. Using the data from Big & Busy Restaurant Ltd the contribution margin is:

	£
Sales price per unit	12
Less: Variable cost per unit	4
Contribution margin	8

Figure 13.12 is another version of the breakeven chart, once again using the data relating to the case study Big & Busy Restaurant Ltd.

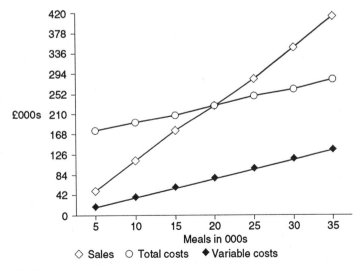

Figure 13.12 Big & Busy Restaurant Ltd: contribution margin.

The total cost function is constructed by first plotting the variable costs then the fixed costs. By constructing the total cost function in this way we can identify the contribution margin, that is the difference between the sales and variable cost functions as shown on the chart. The interesting point to notice is that each meal sold will make a contribution of £8. The contribution initially reduces the loss incurred by fixed costs by £8 per unit. When fixed costs have been covered by the contribution generated by sales at the output level of 20 000 units (i.e. at the breakeven point) every unit sold thereafter contributes £8 to profits. For example, at the origin (i.e. nil sales) a loss is made of £160 000 which is the sum of the fixed costs. When 1000 units are sold they contribute £8000 thereby reducing the loss to £152 000. As sales output increases the loss will be reduced by £8000 per 1000 units to the breakeven point where the fixed costs are now totally covered. After the breakeven point each unit sold increases profit by £8 per unit (or £8000 per 1000 units); thus if 21 000 units are sold a profit of £8000 would be made.

The contribution margin is an important concept and is used widely to aid managers in making decisions. Using the contribution margin approach we can answer the problems posed earlier such as the determination of the breakeven point for Big & Busy Restaurant Ltd:

$$S(x) = VC(x) + FC + P$$

Rearranging this expression in terms of contribution margin, where:

$$S(x) - VC(x) = \text{Contribution margin } C(x)$$

we have:

$$C(x) = FC + P$$

and for the breakeven point:

$$C(x) = FC$$

and it follows that:

$$x = FC/C$$

Using the data from Big & Busy Restaurant Ltd:

$$x = 160\,000/8 = 20\,000 \text{ units}$$

Profit/volume chart

Another very useful presentation is the profit/volume chart. This is particularly useful in that it highlights very effectively the loss-making and profit-making levels of activity.

Figure 13.13 shows the profit/volume chart for Big & Busy Restaurant Ltd. From this you can see that it is only the contribution margin line that is plotted as described above onto a graph where the

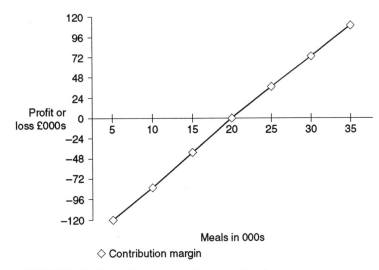

Figure 13.13 Big & Busy Restaurant Ltd: profit/volume chart.

vertical axis shows profit and loss against turnover on the horizontal axis measured from zero. This has the effect of clearly showing how long it will take (in term of sales units) to achieve breakeven point and exactly when the business will start turning a profit.

CVP analysis: assumptions and limitations

- The CVP model is based on assumptions that fixed costs are constant and that variable costs vary in direct proportion to sales, i.e. are linear, and also that they are affected by one independent variable and that there are no economies of scale.
- CVP also assumes that costs can be broken down into their fixed and variable elements with some degree of accuracy.
- The analysis assumes that the sales function is also linear, which means that the selling price will not vary as output changes. Empirical evidence suggests that this is unlikely for the majority of goods and services. A more realistic sales function would be represented by a curvilinear pattern.
- CVP analysis described in this chapter assumes that the firm operates only one product or department. When multi-products or departments are considered CVP analysis becomes very complex. New assumptions have to be made about the interdependency of two products or departments and how you should allocate shared costs to departments.
- If one or more of the resources available to a firm are scarce there will be a constraint on the potential total sales output (e.g. seats on a plane, bedrooms in a hotel). These are finite resources upon which the business depends for its income.

Margin of safety

The margin of safety is a crude measure of risk. It can be expressed in two forms depending on the individual situation, they are:

Margin of safety = Planned unit sales − Breakeven unit sales

or:

Margin of safety = Actual unit sales − Breakeven unit sales

It is often expressed as a percentage calculated as follows:

$$\text{Margin of safety \%} = \frac{\text{Planned unit sales} - \text{Breakeven unit sales}}{\text{Planned unit sales}}$$

or:

$$\text{Margin of safety \%} = \frac{\text{Actual unit sales} - \text{Breakeven unit sales}}{\text{Actual unit sales}}$$

Let us calculate the margin of safety for Big & Busy Restaurant Ltd.

If we assume that the budgeted sales were 42 000 meals or units then the margin of safety is 22 000 units (42 000 − 20 000) or 52.3% If the actual sales for the year were only 30 000 meals the actual margin of safety would be 10 000 units (30 000 − 20 000) and the percentage reduced to 33.3% The margin of safety shows the extent to which the business is cushioned against reductions in turnover.

COST STRUCTURES

The specific cost structure of a business has a major impact on its profitability. It is often called **operating leverage** and relates to the proportion of fixed and variable costs within the business and the way in which a firm's profits will respond to changes in activity or sales levels. Firms may have relatively high fixed costs and low variable costs, or relatively high variable costs and low fixed costs. Those firms with high fixed costs tend to be more vulnerable to decreases in turnover and conversely earn greater profits from an increase in sales compared to those firms with high variable costs. This means that the profits fluctuate much more widely in a high fixed costs firm. In firms with a lower proportion of fixed costs and higher variable costs the profit fluctuation is less for a given change in sales.

The following details some examples of varying cost structures and the effect on profits when activity fluctuates:

	Company A	Company B
	£	£
Sales	20 000	20 000
Variable costs	5 000	12 000
Fixed costs	12 000	5 000
Total costs	17 000	17 000
Net profit	3 000	3 000

Sales increase by 10%:

	Company A	Company B
	£	£
Sales	22 000	22 000
Variable costs	5 500	13 200
Fixed costs	12 000	5 000
Total costs	17 500	18 200
Net profit	4 500	3 800
% increase in profits	50%	26%

Sales decrease by 10%:

	Company A	Company B
	£	£
Sales	18 000	18 000
Variable costs	4 500	10 800
Fixed costs	12 000	5 000
Total costs	16 500	15 800
Net profit	1 500	2 200
% decrease in profits	50%	26%

Company A fixed costs as a proportion of total costs are much higher than those of Company B. This results in a wider fluctuation of profits for Company A (50% compared with 26% for Company B) when there is a change in activity.

For a fuller discussion of the impact of cost structures on profitability in the hospitality industry see Harris and Hazzard (1987: Chapter 12).

SUMMARY

In this chapter we examined the nature of fixed and variable costs and the way in which these costs behave over activity levels. We explained the way in which these costs are measured for use in predicting future costs. In practice, important decisions will be made by organizations based on the understanding of cost behaviour and the ability to predict costs accurately. However, it was stressed that often rather simplistic assumptions were made in deriving this information. Whilst the adoption of these assumptions limits the accuracy of the information, invariably we can derive reasonable approximations of the real world by using methods that may not be considered wholly realistic. CVP was examined which is an extremely useful technique in the decision-making process of organizations. Finally, the nature of cost structures was considered which also examines the relationship between fixed and variable costs from another perspective.

REFERENCES

Arnold, J. and Hope, A. (1990) *Accounting for Management Decisions*, 2nd edn, Prentice-Hall.
Drury, C. (1992) *Management and Cost Accounting*, 3rd edn, Chapman & Hall, London.
Harris, P. and Hazzard, P. (1987) *Managerial Accounting in the Hotel and Catering Industry*, Stanley Thornes, Leckhampton

FURTHER READING

Chapter 4 in Neale, A. and Haslam, C. (1994) *Economics in a Business Context*, 2nd edn, Chapman & Hall, London examines curvilinear cost functions from an economics perspective.

REVIEW QUESTIONS

1. It is often assumed that in cost behaviour there is only one independent variable. Explain the nature of independent variables and why this assumption is made.
2. Explain what is meant by the relevant range of activity and its significance to CVP analysis.
3. Variable and fixed costs are traditionally assumed to be linear. Describe why this assumption is unrealistic.
4. What are the problems associated with CVP analysis in a multi-product firm?
5. What is the margin of safety? What does it tell about the business and when would it be particularly important to monitor.

PROBLEMS FOR DISCUSSION AND ANALYSIS

1. In the table below fill in the blank spaces:

Sales	Variable costs	Fixed costs	Total costs	Profit	Contribution
£	£	£	£	£	£
1000	700		1000		
1500		300		500	
	500		800	1200	
2000		300		200	

2. Seagul Airlines is a small family-run charter company that operates a shuttle service from Southampton Airport to Guernsey and Jersey. They operate two small aircraft and provide four return journeys per day. The following information is available:

- maximum number of passengers per flight 120;
- tickets cost £140 return.

Costs calculated on the basis of an average load factor of 75%.

- Fixed costs per flight:
  Staff costs   £1000
  Airport charges   £2200
  Insurance – aircraft £ 800
  Fuel   £4500

- Variable costs per return flight:
  Other variable costs   £20

Required:
(a) Calculate: (i) the breakeven point;
              (ii) the maximum profit given a load factor of 75%.
(b) The company owning Southampton Airport is proposing to increase airport charges by 10%. What would the impact of such a change be on (i) and (ii) in (a) above?

3. Saddlecombe House in Berkshire is an attractive stately home dating back to the thirteenth century. It has substantial extensions dated during the seventeenth century and earlier and 250 acres of grounds including beautiful landscaped gardens designed by Capability Brown. Only the house is open to the public between April and September each year. On average there are 15 000 visitors who pay £2.00 entrance fee. The trustees who manage the estate feel that the gardens would attract many more visitors if they were open to the public and that by including the gardens in the attraction the entrance fee could be increased to £2.75.

The costs involved in opening the garden would be £15 000 for extra staff.
(a) Based on the information given and that the house as it is operated at the moment breaks even, with fixed costs equalling 80% of total costs. What are the variable costs?
(b) How many extra visitors will be required to make opening the gardens worthwhile?
(c) The trustees have recently seen more research that implies visitors to stately homes are price sensitive and they fear that entrance fees can only be increased to £2.50. How many visitors are needed to break even if entrance fees were only £2.50?

Pricing and price determination 14

INTRODUCTION

In the last chapter we examined cost/volume/profit analysis and the relationship between costs, volume and profit. A critical factor in this analysis is the selling price and in this chapter we are going to consider how selling prices are ascertained. A number of approaches will be described and the advantages and disadvantages of each will be considered. By necessity this will require us to turn our sights outside the organization and consider the market in which we operate and, of course, the customer.

Why is price so important? Without exception, commercial organizations aim to make profit; without long-term profitability an organization cannot survive. Organizations must also ensure that cash inflows exceed cash outflows if they are to remain solvent. Cash – and indeed profit – are generated by sales, therefore the pricing decision which sets selling prices is critical to business success. Managers have to decide what price to fix for the goods and services they provide for their customers. In setting prices managers need to balance the demands of the marketplace with the characteristics of the product or service of the firm. Prices have to be set that will yield sufficient sales to cover costs.

If the price is set too high the consequences can be disastrous. In a highly competitive market a price that is too high will result in low volumes which may not cover fixed costs. Equally, it can be dangerous to set the price too low because this could lead to pressures on costs and operating standards and perhaps safety. Setting the 'right' price is a particular problem in the tour operating business. Prices in this business are often fixed prior to brochures being printed and well in advance of selling the holidays. Companies have to strike a balance between the benefits of getting their brochure out first and the risks of setting prices too high and being priced out by competitors several days later. In an attempt to reduce this problem in this highly competitive market companies are now operating small brochure runs initially, so they can adjust their prices if necessary thereby taking account of competition.

Companies in setting prices will normally take account of the market. Often companies will have a price imposed on them by market forces. In the most competitive markets the majority of firms are 'price takers'; only a few market leaders will actually be able to influence the price to any great extent.

WHAT IS PRICE?

Price can be described as the amount a consumer is prepared to pay for goods or services. The term 'amount' implies it is an amount of money. This is not, however, the full story. Buttle (1986) argues that: 'Price is the summation of all sacrifices made by a consumer in order to experience the benefits of a product.' Here sacrifices include not just money but also time and energy.

> ### *Key concept*
>
> *Definition of price*
>
> Price is the total amount of sacrifice a consumer is prepared to make to acquire a good or service. This sacrifice could be either money, energy or any other valuable commodity, such as time.

For example, if there are two sandwich shops and one offers better quality and more variety and is cheaper than the other but is farther away, a consumer will normally take into consideration not just the money they will have to pay for the sandwich but also the time and effort required in acquiring the sandwich. Consumers will often sacrifice value for convenience. Therefore the price to the consumer is not merely the monetary sacrifice they have to make. Sacrifices other than money are categorized as qualitative factors in the pricing decision. Although, it is possible to give some monetary value to these factors (primarily using economic techniques such as cost-benefit analysis) it is invariably too complex. Therefore whilst these factors are in the main not quantified they are influential in terms of consumer behaviour, and therefore in setting prices firms must bear these factors in mind.

THE IMPORTANCE OF PRICING

Pricing is one of the most critical decisions managers have to make. Price is vitally important for many reasons.

- The price is normally the most influential factor in the consumer's decision to purchase. This is particularly the case where there is little product differentiation.
- Pricing is normally the only active revenue creating decision made within a business. All other decisions tend to focus on costs.
- The price setting decision is critical because it is often very difficult to change. For instance, in the travel industry where prices are published in brochures, a new edition of the brochure may be required in order to change the prices.
- Many new product failures can be attributed to misjudged pricing decisions.
- In price sensitive markets a small change in price can have a dramatic effect on demand.
- Price directly affects sales volume and sales revenue. It is important to remember the impact this has on the financial position of a company, particularly when you remember that businesses with high fixed costs such as hotels have very little room to manoeuvre on costs. Price will directly affect profitability and consequently dividends paid to shareholders.
- Service industries, particularly tourist attractions, are market driven with great volatility of demand. If a company misjudges its pricing decision it can have disastrous consequences.

FACTORS AFFECTING PRICE

There are many factors that affect the pricing decision. These are either controlled from within the organization, i.e. internal factors, or they are outside the control of the organization and are therefore classified as external factors.

Internal factors include costs and the cost structure of the organization, the design of the product or service, organizational objectives in relation to marketing and pricing, the nature of the company, how it is organized and the resources at its disposal. There is evidence that in practice cost-based pricing methods are the most popular methods of price setting (Mills, 1988). Later in this chapter we will be focusing on cost-based pricing methods and in particular those methods used in the hospitality industry.

External factors include the elasticity of demand for the product or service, the nature of the industry, its structure and competitiveness. Environmental factors can also be an important influence in determining the pricing policy. It is these external factors that constrain the firm pricing products and services without any reference to the nature of the market in which goods and services are sold.

The structure of the tour operators market in the UK is an interesting example of a market that is controlled by a small number of operators who collectively have a large share of the market. According to an ICC Keynote Report Market Sector Review (1991) the percentage share of the market for tour operators during the early 1990s was as follows:

	%
Thomson Travel Group	33.2
International Leisure Group	13.8
BA/Redwing	5.7
Airtours	4.9
Cosmos	1.5
Other operators	40.9

International Leisure Group ceased trading in March 1991 which no doubt has had a significant impact on the market.

In a market such as that of tour operators inevitably a single company will be unable to set a price in isolation from other companies without it being detrimental to their profits and/or their market share. For example, a price that is set too high by one company may result in other companies setting lower prices and capturing a higher proportion of the market. The international nature of the travel industry and the impact of such events as the Gulf War means that making pricing decisions in isolation from these external factors could have an extremely adverse effect on a company's ability to survive and be profitable.

ELASTICITY OF DEMAND

Economists lay claim to a model which determines the price and the level of output that will maximize profits. The model is based on how responsive demand is to changing prices which is conventionally referred to as the 'price elasticity of demand'. Whilst it may be argued that the model is theoretically sound from an economic perspective, observations in the real world make it clear that it is too simplistic. For example, sociological factors are ignored which may conflict with the assumed objective of profit maximization. That being said the model does clearly show the relationship between price and output which in the majority of cases will be an important factor, albeit one of many, in a firm's price setting process. It is therefore appropriate for us to examine this model in some detail.

The term 'elasticity' is used in economics to describe the relationship between a proportionate change in one variable and a proportionate change in another related variable. In the context of pricing, the related variables are price and demand. The price elasticity of demand therefore measures the relationship between a change in price and a change in demand for a product or service.

Key concept

Price elasticity of demand

The term price elasticity of demand describes the sensitivity of quantity demanded for a product or service to changes in the price. The measure is based on the following formula:

$$\frac{\text{Percentage change in quantity demanded}}{\text{Percentage change in price}}$$

Price elasticity of demand is expressed as a number and can be **elastic**. This is where the numerical value of the measure is less than or equal to one but greater than zero. In these circumstances demand tends to be responsive to price changes and it follows that a relatively small change in price will have a more substantial effect on quantity demanded. Where price elasticity of demand is **inelastic** the numerical value of the measure will be greater than or equal to one. This means a change in price will have a relatively small effect on quantity demanded.

Figures 14.1 and 14.2 shows the typical demand curves derived from plotting the quantity demanded against price in the two situations of elastic and inelastic demand. From these figures it can be seen that by decreasing the price from P_1 to P_2 increases the quantity demanded more when demand is elastic *vis-à-vis* inelastic.

If we understand elasticity and can measure the elasticity of demand for a particular product or service, in theory we should be able to forecast the quantity demanded at any given price.

One of the main factors affecting elasticity of demand is the availability of substitutes. There are very few, if any, true substitutes for potatoes, for example. Therefore, no matter what the price of

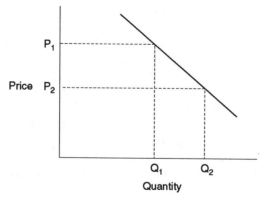

Figure 14.1 An elastic demand function.

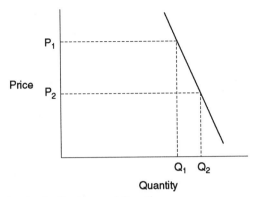

Figure 14.2 An inelastic demand function.

potatoes, consumers will tend to still purchase about the same amount each week. The demand for potatoes tends therefore to be price inelastic. There are many different makes of medium-priced family cars, and one is probably a reasonable substitute for another. The demand for such cars is likely therefore to be elastic. If the price of one make of car was to increase, many consumers are likely to buy another make instead. There is only one supersonic passenger aircraft operating, Concorde; flying on a Boeing 747 is unlikely to be a good substitute, therefore the demand for flights on Concorde is likely to be price inelastic. Certain hotels and restaurants in major cities are unique, for example the Savoy in London or the Hard Rock Cafe in New York. There will be no alternatives and thus the price of services from these establishments will also tend to be price inelastic.

Assuming a firm can identify the shape of the demand curve for a product or service, to maximize profits it needs to establish which combination of price and quantity is the most profitable. To do this, economists introduce costs into the model. Profits are maximized where the difference between total costs and total revenues are at their greatest and it follows the optimum selling price is at the output where this occurs. Figure 14.3 shows the total cost and revenue functions for a product and indicates the quantity at which profits are maximized.

In Figure 14.3 it can be seen that the profit-maximizing position is where the difference between the total cost and revenues function is at its greatest; in quantity terms this is at output level Q_x.

It should be noted that in Figure 14.3 both the cost and revenue functions are curvilinear. This means that the price and cost per unit are not constant over output levels; that is, the cost of resources will vary depending upon quantity consumed and prices vary depending upon the amount sold. Whilst prices and costs are likely to reflect something like this pattern in reality it is unlikely that firms will be able to determine these functions with any accuracy. This is in fact one of the main reason why accountants assume linear cost and revenue functions; that is, variable costs are constant per unit of output, fixed

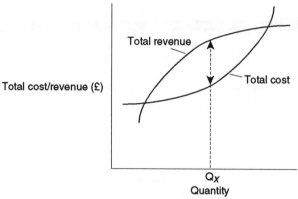

Figure 14.3 Total cost and revenue functions.

costs do not vary over output levels and lastly prices are constant at all levels of output. The rationale for adopting linear functions with regard to cost and revenue functions was explained in detail in Chapter 13.

The economist's model that embodies total revenues and costs is conventionally extended to marginal analysis. In this analysis the marginal cost is the cost of one extra sale and the marginal revenue the revenue from one extra sale. The optimum output level, i.e. for profit-maximizing, is where marginal cost equals marginal revenue. Figure 14.4 plots the marginal cost and revenue functions and the point at which they are equal, i.e. the profit-maximizing output level denoted as Q_x on the graph.

It should be noted that Figure 14.3 deals with total costs and revenues and profit is maximized where the difference between total revenues and total cost is at its greatest. This point Q_x in the graph is the same as the point at which marginal cost equals marginal revenues, also denoted as point Q_x in Figure 14.4.

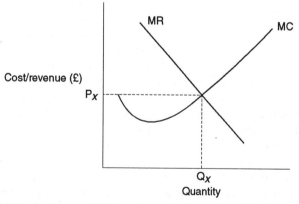

Figure 14.4 Marginal cost (MC) and marginal revenue (MR) functions.

In this analysis it is assumed that marginal costs begin by declining then rise as output continues to increase. The rationale for this behaviour in costs is that it is assumed that the initial decline in marginal costs is the result of economies of scale as output increases. This is then followed by the increase in costs due to the rising prices of scarce resources as demand increases for those resources. Marginal revenue in this analysis is assumed to decline as output increases. The rationale for this downward sloping marginal revenue function is that the firm can only increase sales by reducing the price.

It can be seen from Figure 14.4 that marginal cost equals marginal revenue at output level Q_x and this is where profits are maximized. If output was fixed to the left of Q_x, whilst marginal revenues exceed marginal costs it can be seen that more profits, albeit at smaller margins, could be made by moving towards Q_x. In contrast a firm would not, assuming its objective is profit-maximizing, want to move to the right of Q_x because at any output past Q_x marginal costs exceed marginal revenues; that is, a loss would be made.

A word of caution: the cost and revenue functions described here are only examples. Some products and services may have very different functions depending upon the nature and market for the product or service.

The economist's model of consumer behaviour upon which demand theory is based implies that consumers are perfectly informed about the price characteristics of services or products on offer, and are constantly changing their expenditure patterns in response to price changes in order to maximize their utility or satisfaction. However, in reality, this is not the case. In today's markets the range of services and products on offer makes it unlikely that a consumer would have the knowledge or inclination to acquire information necessary to make decisions in this way. Also price is not the only variable influencing consumer demand. Factors such as quality, design, reliability and prestige have strong influence on consumer choice. It is important to recognize that price is not the only variable and firms must understand consumer perceptions and tailor their products and services to meet consumer expectations which are influenced through sociological, legal and environmental factors.

The above explanations of the problems associated with the economist's model are some of the main reasons why firms do not behave as predicted in the model. This helps to explain why a majority of firms use a cost basis for setting prices. We will therefore now examine cost information produced by accounting systems and see how it is used to support 'cost-based' pricing methods.

TRADITIONAL COST-BASED METHODS OF PRICING

Cost-plus pricing

This is perhaps the most simple of all pricing techniques and is widely used. A percentage applied to costs is added to established cost figures to ascertain the price. It can be expressed mathematically as follows:

$$P = C + f(C)$$

Where:

P = price
C = costs
f = % mark-up.

For example, if cost (C) was £1.20 and the percentage mark-up was 50%, the price would be:

$$P = £1.20 + (50\% \times 1.20) = £1.80$$

The percentage mark-up will depend upon what this proportion of the formula needs to cover in terms of costs not included specifically within 'costs' in the formula and the profit margin. The percentage mark-up will normally be based on past experience or on industry/ trade norms.

The major problem with this method is deciding which cost figure to use. Should it be total costs, variable costs or direct costs, or perhaps some other cost basis?

Harris and Hazzard (1992) use a very clear and simple diagram to highlight some of the variations of cost-plus pricing available, as shown in Figure 14.5. There are three main variations:

- full cost pricing;
- direct costs pricing;
- gross margin pricing.

The basic method of cost-plus pricing is called 'full' or 'total' cost pricing. It requires the identification of the total costs of a product or service, to which is added a mark-up to provide a profit. If we refer back to the equation above:

$$P = C + f(C)$$

in this case:

P = price (as before);
C = total costs of product or service;
f = percentage net profit.

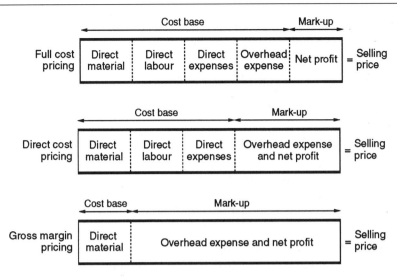

Figure 14.5 Traditional cost-plus pricing variations. *Source*: Harris and Haz-zard (1992).

In this slightly amended equation C is now defined as 'total costs' rather than simply 'costs' and includes both direct and indirect costs. The indirect costs (overheads) would have been allocated and absorbed into the product cost but the process of allocation and absorption can be fairly arbitrary. It follows that the accuracy of the accumulation of costs associated with particular products may be quite questionable. With a mark-up percentage being based on these inaccurate figures it is clear that this can lead to a magnification of the inaccuracy.

It is also likely that the indirect costs include fixed overheads that will be incurred whether or not the product or service in question is sold. From a decision-making perspective these costs would be classified as unavoidable and therefore irrelevant in the pricing decision. The principles relating to relevant costs will be considered in more detail in Chapter 18.

Direct cost pricing (see Figure 14.5) as the name implies only takes account of the direct costs of the product or service. The percentage mark-up in this case is designed to cover an allowance for indirect costs, that is, the overheads associated with operations and to provide for net profit. The definition of C in the equation is then amended as follows:

$$P = C + f(C)$$

in this case:

        P = price (as before);
        C = direct costs of product or service;
        f = percentage to cover profit and overhead expense.

Finally, gross margin pricing can be used when data on direct labour costs is not available or is not reliable. Here only the direct materials are included in terms of cost, for example for a restaurant food costs only. The mark-up added now has to provide sufficient margin to cover labour, overheads and profit. The definition of C is amended as follows:

$$P = C + f(C)$$

in this case:

      P = price (as before);
      C = direct material cost;
      f = percentage net profit and all expenses.

The main criticism cited against cost-plus methods is that they tend not to take account of the market, in particular the price elasticity of demand, the level and nature of competition and the organization's marketing strategy. However, there is some evidence from research (Skinner, 1970; Pearce, 1956) that cost-plus methods are used as the first step in determining selling prices. In these cases, after determining a price through cost-plus methods, market considerations would then be taken into account and if necessary an amendment would then be made to the price. There is also a tendency to increase the mark-up in order to generate more profit. However, this also leads to increasing the selling price which could reduce demand and thereby result in the opposite objective to that intended, that is to decrease total profits.

The information for use when applying cost-plus methods will normally be available from the accounting system. The actual process of determining price tends to be mechanical and not too overtly complex. Cost-plus methods are also seen to be advantageous because they provide sales targets, which if met, guarantee profit.

Through Example (14.1) we can demonstrate how cost-plus pricing can be adapted for use by package tour operators for setting prices. Although substantially based on actual costs, this method includes estimations for the load component and takes into account the expected actual number of passengers per flight and the rate of exchange, both of which are outside the control of the tour operator and can vary substantially.

EXAMPLE 14.1

Pricing for tour operators

Basic cost information is as follows. **Fixed costs** are:

- chartered plane, 30 return flights to Palma, seating capacity 150 cost £9000 per flight;

- transfers – coaches to transport holidaymakers from airport to hotel, cost 20 000 Spanish pesetas per coach per round trip, coach capacity 50 passengers.

Both of the above are considered fixed costs because the operator must pay the full price regardless of the number of passengers. **Variable costs** are:

- hotel costs 20 000 Spanish pesetas per person.

The contract with the hotel states that the tour operator will only pay for the number of rooms actually used.

The rate of exchange is 200 pesetas to the pound.

The final selling price per person is calculated as follows:

	£
Fixed costs:	
Flights: 30 × £9000	270 000
Transfers: $\dfrac{30 \times 3 \text{ coaches} \times 20\,000 \text{ ptas}}{200 \text{ (rate of exchange)}}$	9 000
Total	279 000
Total fixed cost to be shared between passengers:	
150 seats × 30 round trips = 4500 trips	£
Fixed cost per person: 279 000 ÷ 4500 (rounded up)	62.00
Hotel cost per person: 20 000 ptas ÷ 200 (rate of exchange)	100.00
Net price	162.00
Plus mark-up to cover agency commission, admin. costs, marketing and bank charges:	
Mark-up: anything up to 30%	48.60
Final selling price	210.60

FACTOR PRICING

Factor pricing is a variation on cost-plus pricing. Instead of a percentage, a simple factor is applied to the costs to ascertain the selling price. The term 'factor' means a number greater than 1. The factor could be as high as 30 for items such as tea and coffee and as low as 2 for a slice of buttered toast. In restaurants it is normal to apply different factors to different items to take account of price discrimination and competition. There is much written about optimizing menu profitability through pricing (for example, see Merrick and Jones (1988) or Miller (1987) for a full coverage of menu analysis and engineering).

Factor pricing has all the same advantages and disadvantages of cost-plus pricing. Like cost-plus methods it is easy to understand. However, it is based on historic cost data, and can lead to a tendency to increase prices to achieve greater profit margins which at the same time could result in a reduction of total profits. Factor pricing does attempt to take account of the elasticity of demand, albeit very subjectively.

BREAKEVEN PRICING

Breakeven pricing applies the principle from cost/volume/profit (CVP) analysis discussed in detail in Chapter 13 to calculate a price that will enable the firm to break even. Any price above the price to break even will thus result in a profit, assuming demand remains the same.

Example 14.2 shows the computation necessary to establish a price that enables the firm to break even.

EXAMPLE 14.2

Calculation of breakeven price

Variable costs: £27
Fixed costs: £18 000
Estimated demand: 600 units.

What is the selling price to break even?

Using the CVP equation from Chapter 13:

$$S(x) = VC(x) + FC$$

Where:

S = selling price;
x = number of units;
VC = variable cost;
FC = fixed cost.

$$S(600) = £27(600) + 318\,000$$
$$S = \frac{£16\,200 + £18\,000}{600}$$
$$S = £57$$

Proof:

	£	£
Sales (£57 × 600)		34 200
Variable costs (£27 × 600)	16 200	
Fixed costs	18 000	34 200

The £57 represents the selling price where no profits or losses are made, that is the breakeven point. The price at breakeven point therefore acts as a reference point. The concept of CVP is flexible and can be employed to help in the pricing decision.

PROFIT-ORIENTED METHODS OF PRICING

Covering costs is essential to make profits, but it is important to know whether the level of profit is adequate. Investors expect a return to reward them for putting their money at risk, and this return in the form of profit must be sufficient to compensate for the risks of investing. It is impossible to judge the adequacy of profit without linking it to the capital investment. The relationship between profit and investment is expressed through a measure referred to as the rate of return. Pricing methods that consider the rate of return overcome the main weakness of the cost-oriented methods by focusing on profit and taking account of the investment necessary to generate that profit.

Profit-oriented methods of setting prices have been widely used throughout the hotel industry for setting room rates. The American Hotel and Motel Association formalized a method called the 'Hubbard formula' which basically follows these principles. The Hubbard formula takes into account operating costs of the rooms (which are generally fixed), plus profit from other departments such as food and beverage and banqueting. It is designed to set prices that will yield a specified return on capital invested. The calculation also has to take account of occupancy levels. The Hubbard formula is demonstrated in Example 14.3 below.

EXAMPLE 14.3

Hubbard formula for setting room rates

	£	£
Rooms department operating costs		
Payroll	156 000	
Other departmental expenses	30 000	186 000
Unallocated costs		
Utilities	46 000	
Administration	145 000	
Repairs and maintainance	90 000	281 000
Return on capital employed		
Capital employed	1 680 000	
12% return required	1 680 000 × 0.12	201 600
Taxation		
Taxation		67 200
Fixed charges		
Interest and depreciation		24 500
		760 300
Deduct any profits from other departments		
Food and beverage	34 000	
Telephones	5 000	−39 000
Total amount to be realized from room sales to cover costs and the required return on capital employed		721 300

Calculation to establish average daily room rate £

Amount realized from room sales A **721 300**

Rooms available for sales 80
No. available annually ($\times 365$) 29 200
Reduce to reflect average occupancy (65%)
No. of rooms nights to be occupied B 18 980
Average room rate $A \div B$ **38.00**

One of the major criticisms of the rate of return pricing method is that it is introspective, concentrating on profit generation whilst ignoring the customer and the marketplace. The method is also still fundamentally cost based; essentially it takes account of costs associated with the product or service, plus an amount to represent the desired return on capital. The criticisms of cost-based methods are generally applicable to this method, for example the problems associated with allocating overhead costs.

COMPETITOR-ORIENTED METHODS OF PRICING

The most popular of competitor-oriented methods is often referred to as 'follow-the-leader'. This approach to pricing is particularly common in the hotel industry and among 'sun, sea, sand' tour operators. An organization will set a price based on what their nearest competitor is charging. Independent hotels by necessity have to operate this kind of pricing system when they are geographically close to and therefore compete with a hotel which is part of a chain or large group.

Increased publicity has made the general public more aware of the competitive nature of the package holiday business. Tour operators now face such fierce competition – usually based on price – that they cannot afford to have prices too far out of line from their main competitors. This leads to a high degree of price following resulting in firms revising their prices in the light of competitors' prices. In circumstances where price following occurs companies must concentrate on cost control, and must recognize that individual cost structures and investment programmes are not reflected in the price.

MARKET-ORIENTED PRICING

Market-oriented pricing (MOP) is suitable for pricing new products or services, especially those marketed through several distribution channels. It is particularly useful for setting rack rates (room tariffs) for new or redeveloped hotel operations. MOP has the benefit of combining demand, cost and competitor considerations into the pricing decision whilst still monitoring the impact on profitability. The method requires first that target markets be identified and the firm's competitive position assessed. Prices can then be set according to the firm's position in that market. Each different segment of the market will have prices set according to the demands of that sector and the ability of the hotel to meet those demands that require a particular mix of quality and services. This will involve a detailed review of the sales mix, in other words an analysis of sales according to the source of booking and type of customer (for example, direct to customer, via travel agent or tour operator). This analysis will reveal the average realizable room rate (after commissions) which can then be used to calculate revenue.

This method, in the main, promotes realistic sales and profit targets which are fully integrated into the overall company objectives, and provides a holistic method of pricing.

Other market oriented methods

- **Prestige pricing**. This approach to pricing acknowledges the link between price and quality. With some services, e.g. theatres and restaurants, the higher the price the higher the perceived prestige value. So for a limited number of service organizations there is an increase in demand associated with an increase in price. Obviously it is essential to ensure that the experience of customers matches their expectations.
- **Loss leader pricing**. This method can be used where one service or product generates sales in another. Here a company can price at a small margin or at a loss to attract customers who then purchase other far more profitable services or products resulting in an overall profit. For example, beer prices in a pub may be lowered for lunch-time customers with the intention to promote food which has much larger margins, and which it is perceived will increase overall profits.
- **Psychological pricing**. This approach to pricing recognizes that customers have a predetermined price range within which they are happy to purchase goods or services, and sets prices within this range.

SUMMARY

In this chapter we began by examining the importance of pricing and, from a general perspective, considered the factors that will be influential in the pricing decision. These factors were divided into internal and external factors. The significance of this classification is the extent to which a firm can control the factors involved in the pricing decision. Internal factors tend to be controllable; for example, they are cost-related factors, a proportion of which will normally be within the control of the firm. In contrast, external factors include factors that are generally outside the control of the firm such as the nature of the market and competition.

The economist's approach to pricing was examined. Whilst the approach can be described as theoretically sound it is very questionable whether it explains pricing behaviour in practice. However, it does gives us some important insights into elements of the pricing decision. This analysis was followed by an examination of cost-based methods of pricing. Evidence was cited that suggests that 'full' cost pricing is the most popular method of pricing in both service and manufacturing industries.

Finally, target-oriented, competitor-oriented and market-oriented methods of pricing were examined. These methods tend to be very popular in the hospitality and tourism industry.

REFERENCES

Buttle, F. (1986) *Hotel and Food Service Marketing. A Managerial Approach*, Cassell, London.

Harris, P. and Hazzard, P. (1992) *Managerial Accounting in the Hospitality Industry*, Stanley Thornes, Leckhampton.

ICC Keynote Market Sector Review (1991) *Travel Agents and Overseas Tour Operators*, ICC.

Merrick, P. and Jones, P. (1988) *Management of Catering Operations*, Cassell, London.

Miller, J.E. (1987) *Menu Pricing and Strategy*, Van Nostrand Reinhold.

Mills, R.W. (1988) Pricing decisions in the UK manufacturing and service companies. *Management Accountant*, November, pp.38–9.

Pearce, I.F. (1956) A study in price policy. *Economica*, May, pp.114–27.

Skinner, R.C. (1970) The determination of selling prices. *Journal of Industrial Economics*, July, pp.201–17.

FURTHER READING

Cooper, C., Fletcher, J., Gilbert, D. and Wanhill, S. (1992) *Tourism Principles and Practice*, Pitman, London.

Drury, C. (1988) *Management and Cost Accounting*, 2nd edn, Van Nostrand Reinhold.

Jones P. (ed.) (1989) *Management in Service Industries*, Pitman, London.

Jones, P. and Pizam, A. (eds) (1993) *The International Hospitality Industry. Organisational and Operational Issues*, Pitman, London.

Jones, P. and Lockwood, A. (1989) *The Management of Hotel Operations*, Cassell, London.

Kotas, R. (1986) *Management Accounting for Hotels and Restaurants*, 2nd edn, Surrey University Press.

Neale, A. and Haslam, C. (1989) *Economics in a Business Context*, Chapman & Hall, London.

Quest, M. (ed.) (1990) *Horwarth Book of Tourism*, Macmillan, London.

REVIEW QUESTIONS

1. Name as many internal and external factors that are influential in the pricing decision as you can.
2. 'The economist's approach to pricing is too difficult to apply in practice.' Discuss
3. Why do those who argue that price setting should be related to the market also state that costs are irrelevant?
4. What are the major criticisms of cost-plus pricing models?
5. How would you determine the mark-up when using cost-plus pricing methods?
6. What is meant by the term market-oriented pricing?
7. What is the difference between a price setter and a price follower?

PROBLEMS FOR DISCUSSION AND ANALYSIS

1. The board of a small hotel chain comprising six medium-sized hotels in Scotland and the Lake District are considering what pricing strategy should be adopted for next season. Although nine months away, broad figures must be included in brochures being prepared in two weeks' time. The marketing manager is advocating a market-oriented pricing strategy; however, the group financial accountant is advocating full-cost pricing.

   What are the issues surrounding the establishment of price and which of the methods advocated, if any, is the best in the circumstances?

2. World Cup (South African) Rugby Tours Ltd are developing a package holiday for the avid rugby fan. Designed to coincide with the rugby world cup, the all inclusive package includes;

   - return flight to Johannesburg;
   - transfers from airport to hotel only;
   - hotel accommodation for ten days half-board;
   - tickets to eight games, including the semi-final and final of the Rugby World Cup;
   - book of vouchers for use at attractions in the locality.

   The basic cost information is as follows:

   Fixed costs:

   - chartered planes three return flights, seating capacity 180, cost £12 000;

- coaches to transfer holidaymakers from airport to hotel and back: cost 1200 South African rand per coach per round trip, coach capacity 30 passengers.

Variable costs:

- Johannesburg Hotel: cost 1800 South African rand per person (the contract with the hotel states that the tour operator will only pay for the number of rooms actually used);
- tickets to games: total cost 480 rand (pack of tickets are returnable up to two days before the first match);
- voucher book: 30 rand per book.

Required:
Calculate the final selling price for the tour assuming that the operator requires a mark-up of 35% and expects the load factor to be 85%. You can assume that the exchange rate will be 6 rand to £1.

3. Cornwall Crown Excelsior Hotel has to set its prices for the coming season. You have collected financial data on costs etc. and have been asked to present a proposal for average room rate based on the use of the Hubbard formula. The senior management team will use this along with market information to determine next season's prices. Your report should include any cautions and advice regarding the recommended price and the way it was calculated. The hotel has 120 bedrooms, function room and conference facilities; it is open 365 days of the year and over the last three years has experienced average occupancy of 65%.

   The company has capital employed of £2 500 000 and directors aim to achieve 10% return after tax. Taxation is currently 25%.

   The information you have managed to collect is as follows:

Rooms Department expenses:

	£
Payroll	480 000
Other departmental expenses	96 000

Unallocated expenses:	
Utilities	50 000
Administration and general expenses	34 000
Marketing	25 000
Maintenance and repairs	45 000

Interest and depreciation	60 000

Profits are expected from three other operating departments, namely Food and Beverage £45 900, Banqueting and Conference £15 000, and Income from Shop Franchises £10 000.

Budgeting – planning $\boxed{15}$

INTRODUCTION

In this chapter we are concerned with making operational decisions within a planning framework.

Key concept

Operating decisions defined

Operating decisions are decisions that focus on the efficient use of the resources available to the firm in the short term.

Operating decisions within the planning and control process are translated into short-term plans which are referred to, conventionally, as budgets. Budgets are simply plans of action expressed in money terms. The process involves the aggregation of operating decisions into a plan for the organization or parts of the organization. Such plans compel management to look ahead and coordinate their activities. For example, from this aggregation process the required level of manpower needed to support all departmental activities can be identified over the planning period. Without forward plans that coordinate operational activities the business may drift along meeting undesirable situations such as a shortfall in experienced staff in critical operational areas that could have been anticipated and avoided.

The budget also acts as a basis for judging performance, through the comparison between actual and budgeted figures. This comparison can help to highlight strengths and weaknesses within the organization. This particular feature of budgeting is central to the process of monitoring and control.

It is important that budgets should be communicated to personnel in an organization so that they are aware of the planned (budgeted) targets. This will enable personnel to act in accordance with the plan.

Key concept

Budgets defined

A budget is simply a plan expressed in monetary terms. These financial plans are normally prepared for a set period of time, showing the planned income to be generated and the expected expenditure to be incurred. They will also show the capital investment required to support the planned activity.

The degree of sophistication and detail given to these budgets will depend inevitably on the size of the organization and the needs of internal users within it. Different types of organization will require different types of budgets to enable them to function effectively. The budget must match the organization's situation; factors such as technology, the environment and the structure of the organization will have an impact on the accounting systems and will affect the type of budget to be employed in the organization. For example, the information content and design of a small fast-food outlet budget will be very different from that of a large airline catering company – the latter is essentially a manufacturing organization. The budget for the small fast-food outlet will mainly focus on the level of expected consumer sales and the necessary purchases of goods to satisfy those sales. In contrast, a manufacturing organization's budget will tend not only to focus on the level of demand but also on the resource requirements and the production function to meet this demand. However, there will be some similarities between the budgets of different types of organizations. For illustrative purposes, in this chapter we will tend to concentrate on a medium-sized hotel operation, and where appropriate use examples from other service sector organizations.

We will begin by examining the purpose of budgets and the processes involved in their preparation, followed by a detailed example of budget preparation.

THE PURPOSES OF BUDGETS

A number of purposes may be cited for the employment of budgets – are given these are given below. Although, as was stressed earlier, budgets – and thus the purpose of budgets – will depend on the type of organization, those given here will in general terms be common to most.

- **To compel planning.** The introduction of budgets within an organization forces management to look ahead and set short-term targets. By looking to the future management are then in a good position to anticipate potential problems. For example, the identification of shortages of cash resources at particular times in the budget period will give management the opportunity to ensure that provisions are made to supplement this shortage, e.g. to negotiate an overdraft facility with the bank.

- **To coordinate the different functions within an organization.** The preparation of budgets will tend to increase the coordination between different departments and units within an organization as it is essential that the individual plans of managers are integrated. Managers are therefore forced to consider the relationships between various departments. For example, the food and beverage department of a hotel needs to consider expected occupancy in the rooms department to determine their own purchasing budget.

- **To communicate.** A budget will often be a useful means by which top management can formally communicate their objectives and strategies for the forthcoming budget period. This function will be reinforced, normally periodically, through a control mechanism that reviews actual performance and compares it with the budget during the budget period.

- **To provide a basis for responsibility accounting.** Individual managers are identified with their budget centres and are made responsible for achieving the stated budget targets. These targets may be in terms of expenditure, income and other physical output measures that are considered to be within the manager's control. In the context of budgets, responsibility accounting represents an important feature of the delegation of responsibility to individuals within an organization.

- **To provide a basis for a control mechanism.** The budget may be used as a basis for comparing actual performance with a plan, and the identification of any deviation from that plan. The identification of such deviations gives management the opportunity to take corrective action so that any deviations from the plan do not persist in the future. When budgets are used in the context of a control mechanism the term budgetary control is normally used. We will examine this particular aspect of budgets in the next chapter.

- **To authorize expenditure.** The budget may act as a formal authorization of future expenditure from top management to those individuals who are responsible for it. The fact that an item of expenditure, for example, is contained in the budget that has been approved by the top management of the organization implies that the particular expenditure has been approved and no further approval will normally be required. Thus delegated authority is facilitated through the budgetary process.

- **To motivate employees to improve performance.** The budget may be used as a target to motivate employees to reach certain levels of attainment. For example, one department may in a budget period achieve sales to the value of £30 000; management may in the next period set a target of, say, £40 000, believing, rightly or wrongly, that this new target will motivate the staff to reach higher levels of attainment than in the previous period.

It is also the case that budgets may mean different things to different people within an organization. For example, whilst a budget may be introduced by management with the aim of monitoring costs, managers may perceive the main purpose of the budget as a device to monitor their performance. Budgets can therefore lead to much misunderstanding, frustration and friction within an organization. We will look at the motivational role of budgets and discuss some of the dysfunctional aspects in the next chapter.

THE BUDGET PROCESS

Key concept

The budget process defined

The term 'the budget process' refers to the sequence of operations necessary to produce a budget within the context of a particular organization. The sequence of operations will depend upon the type of organization and its perceived requirements for planning and control.

It should be stressed that essentially budgeting is a political process involving managers who are likely to have different goals and aspirations involved in bargaining and negotiation. The resulting plans and resource allocations are a product of that process of barter.

Identifying organizational objectives

The first stage of the process involves identifying some clear objectives for the organization as a whole. If the budget is an operational plan it may seem obvious but senior management must determine what the operations of the business will be, or, in other words, what the organization is trying to achieve. It might be that the organization is a prestigious luxury hotel group the objectives of which are to provide high-price, high-quality service, concentrating on a relatively small number of clients but at high profit margins. At the other end of the scale, the organization may be a low budget hotel group aiming to maximize sales and keep costs to a minimum with tighter profit margins. It is important to identify what an organization is trying to achieve because the resources required will have to be tailored to the organization's varying needs. Looking at our two examples, the former, a luxury hotel, will require high standard of fixtures and fittings, electronic facilities in rooms for business communications, automatic dispense bars, etc., and of course very high standards of service in the bar and restaurants not to mention 24-hour room service. This will require investment in fixed assets and will result in high labour costs. In contrast the budget hotel will provide a relatively lower level of service and far less facilities in the rooms. In this case the investment in fixed assets will be lower and the labour costs will also be much lower.

Corporate objectives provide a framework from which to produce the operational plan or budget. They result from a holistic review of the organization and its environment and specify the overall levels of activity expected in the future and the organization's policies regarding things like customer care, equal opportunities and purchasing. In setting these objectives senior management will consider the internal strengths of the organization and the external factors affecting the marketplace in which it operates in terms of competition and customers.

These objectives provide the parameters within which the managers can set their departmental budgets. Therefore it is very important that objectives are clearly communicated in terms of operational targets. These targets must be practical and must be expressed in financial terms that all managers can understand. Many problems in budgeting result from managers misunderstanding or manipulating targets.

Setting budgets to achieve objectives

Once the objectives of the organization have been agreed and specified in the form of targets, departmental or divisional managers can construct their budgets. They will apply judgement and experience to determine what resources will be needed to achieve the stated objectives. They will construct detailed operational plans in financial terms often using prepared formats and schedules (frequently referred to as pro formas) to submit their figures. Managers will need to consider carefully how they use scarce resources. These are resources which are limited in the medium term, e.g. seating capacity in a restaurant, as effective use of these resources is vital to the organization. It is at this stage that the process of negotiation becomes important. Managers will need to justify their submissions to their immediate superiors and they must show that the resources they are requesting through the budget process are really necessary. It is this aspect of the budget process that is highly political.

Impact of individual aspirations and the process of negotiation

There is some debate about the extent to which managers who are responsible for spending and income generating departments should be involved in the preparation of their own budgets. It is normally the case, however, that the managers of these responsibility centres will have some influence over the content of the budget, though the extent of their influence will vary from organization to organization and will depend upon the overall management style. Some organizations' top management may adopt a regime of imposing rules on subordinates without any discussion. In other less hierarchical organizations managers may be encouraged to make their own decisions and participate in the budget process.

However, if a manager is solely responsible for the preparation of the budget it is likely that the budget will reflect a bias in favour of the manager. This bias may not be in the best interests of the organization as a whole. For example, it is likely that a manager who is responsible for the sales of a particular product range will set a sales target within the budget that can be easily attained. The attaining of such targets will invariably be looked upon favourably by the manager's superiors.

The manager of a responsibility centre, however, will undoubtedly have a greater degree of knowledge and understanding of the operation of his or her own centre than any other personnel within the organization, and this knowledge is important in the formulation of budgets. Thus there is a strong case for at least some involvement by the manager of a responsibility centre in the preparation of the centre's budget.

Typically in the budgeting process of an organization, the individual budgets for each responsibility centre will be the subject of negotiations before approval and adoption. The parties to this negotiation stage will normally include the manager of the responsibility centre, the preparer of the budget (if that is not the manager) and the manager's superior. The accountant who is responsible for budgets within the organization will, normally, act as an intermediary in this negotiation process. Often in large organizations the negotiation process will be in a number of stages as the budget moves up the management hierarchy for approval.

At each stage of the negotiation process, bargains will be struck between the managers responsible for the budget and their immediate superiors. The negotiations between managers in the hierarchy of an organization in effect, therefore, represent a bargaining process where the individual goals of managers are formulated for a forthcoming budget period.

At board of directors level the final fine-tuning of the respective budgets will take place. This process involves ensuring all the budgets are consistent with each other: for example, that combined unit budgets for a particular region are achieving the correct market growth and overall return on capital employed. When all the individual budgets have been finalized and approved at this level they are summarized into what is commonly referred to as a master budget. The master budget will normally take the form of a budgeted balance sheet and profit and loss account for the budget period. Thus the master budget represents the overall plan for an organization. It clearly sets out the targets for the organization in an easily understandable form and can be compared with the actual balance sheet and profit and loss account.

After the final approval at board level the budgets will be passed down the organization to the responsibility managers. It will be these managers who will be delegated the task of carrying out the plans contained within each individual budget.

The process that has been described above is often called the 'bottom up' approach to budgeting, which is used widely throughout many organizations to produce the original budgets. There are, however, still some companies where senior executives and management simply impose budgets on individuals without any consultation. In the next chapter the behavioural aspects of budgeting are discussed together with the benefits and drawbacks of different approaches to budgetary planning and control.

THE BUDGET PERIOD

At this point of our analysis it is appropriate to consider the budget period. The budget period normally employed by organizations is one year. The reason for this would appear to relate to the periodic reporting requirements for published accounts regulated by the law. Public companies, for example, are required by law, with some few exceptions, to publish accounts annually. Mainly for control purposes the budget for the year will be broken down into shorter periods – quarterly, monthly or weekly. The extent to which the budget is broken down to these shorter periods will depend on the information needs of the particular organization. For example, if an organization operates in a very competitive market it is likely that management will want to monitor performance on a fairly regular basis to ensure the organization is maintaining its competitive position as reflected in planned revenues, costs and output.

Kosturakis and Eyster (1979), in an article on operational budgeting in small hotel companies, recommend that hotel companies operate a continuous budgeting system preferably preparing budgets on a 12-month basis and updating each quarter for the subsequent 12-month period. These types of budgets are conventionally referred to as rolling budgets. Rolling budgets, it is argued, facilitate more accurate forecasting because they are more timely and reflect changing conditions. The timescale for rolling budgets (or any budgetary feedback system) will be dependant on the business environment in which the company operates. In a highly volatile market with changing customer demands and high levels of competition, fast feedback on performance will be critical in order to attain business advantage. In the tour operating and travel agency business budgets are reviewed very frequently, particularly in relation to sales and gross margin.

Key concept

Rolling budget

A rolling budget is one that is regularly reviewed and updated, maintaining a perpetual 12-month forecast. They provide a more flexible planning tool in a business where levels of activity or key costs can change rapidly.

TYPES OF BUDGET

Budgets are often categorized into two main types: capital budgets and operational (revenue) budgets. Operational budgets are concerned with the everyday operations of the business. They include all the forecast expenses and revenues that the firm expects to incur over the forthcoming budget period. Capital budgets, on the other hand, are concerned with assets and liabilities. In the main this type of budget is concerned with the acquisition of the fixed assets needed to support the operational plans. Both kinds of budget combine to form the master budget.

PREPARATION OF THE MASTER BUDGET

The master budget is extremely useful to management as it should clearly set out the objectives and the targets for the forthcoming budget period. It also provides a basis for coordinating the individual functional budgets.

Key concept

The role of the master budget

The master budget will normally consist of the budgeted profit and loss account and balance sheet and the cash forecast, representing a summary of the individual functional budgets of the organization as a whole.

Within the context of a medium to large-size hospitality organization functional budgets that make up the master budget will normally consist of departmental budgets. It is important to recognize that some departments will be merely cost centres, preparing budgets only for expenditure, whereas other departments will be profit centres planning for both revenue and expenditure.

For small organizations, it will often be the case, that the projected profit and loss account, balance sheet and cash budget will be sufficient for the organization's management requirements. The information contained in these three budgeted statements can provide management with a reasonable base to analyse the forthcoming period. In particular, a number of ratios and indicators can be derived from these statements such as those relating to profitability, liquidity and financing. The use of these ratios and indicators were discussed in Chapter 10.

In Example 15.1 which follows a budgeted profit and loss account, balance sheet and cash forecast are constructed from given information for a small family-owned hotel business. This will be followed by a commentary concerning the usefulness of these statements to management.

EXAMPLE 15.1

DeSilva Ltd

DeSilva Ltd is a small family-owned hotel business, preparing to start its second year of trading. As is usual at this time of the year the proprietor is preparing the budget for the forthcoming six months' trading.

The balance sheet at the end of the first year of trading is shown in Figure 15.1.

The share capital is held by John DeSilva, who is the major shareholder and proprietor of the hotel; his three brothers have also invested in the company but are not operationally involved.

The company has adopted a policy of depreciating fixed assets in the year of acquisition on the following basis:

Fixtures and fittings	20%	straight line basis
Vehicles	20%	reducing balance basis

The company plans to buy a vehicle for the business. John plans to do this in April and expects to spend £17 300.

We will start by producing a cash budget. To construct this we need to know details of the inflows and outflows of cash, in particular the amounts and the timing of these flows. Let us begin with the inflows.

Example 15.1

DeSilva Ltd – further information

The total sales for the first six months are expected to be as follows:

January	£18 000
February	£19 000
March	£22 300

April	£22 000
May	£25 000
June	£26 500

However, we have to remember that there are two types of sales, that is cash sales where the money is received straight away, and credit sales where the money is received at some future date.

The company's policy is to give one month's credit to business customers only. The credit sales for the next six months are expected to be as follows:

January	£5000
February	£4000
March	£4000
April	£5000
May	£5000
June	£5000

Balance sheet of DeSilva Ltd as at 31 December 19X1

Fixed assets	Cost	Depn	NBV
	£	£	£
Premises (leasehold)	108 000	0	108 000
Office equipment	22 500	4 500	18 000
	130 500	4 500	126 000
Current assets			
Stock	8 000		
Debtors	6 000	14 000	
Current liabilities			
Creditors	5 300		
Overdraft	14 500	19 800	(5 800)
Total net assets			120 200
			£
Financed by			
Owners' equity			90 000
Retained profit			30 200
			120 200

Figure 15.1

It is now possible to identify the amount and the month in which cash will be received. Each month, therefore, receipts will be made up of cash sales for the month plus the credit sales from the previous month. Any monies outstanding from customers at the end of the month are classified as debtors. The debtors balance at the end of December, which is also the debtors owing at the beginning of January, is shown in the balance sheet in Figure 15.1. The amount shown is £6000. This amount, therefore, with one month's credit, will be received in January.

Cash sales for January will amount to £13 000, which is calculated by taking the credit sale figure for January of £5000 from the total sales figure of £18 000. If you repeat this calculation you can ascertain the cash sales figure for each month.

Figure 15.2 shows the actual monthly sales divided between cash and credit sales, followed by an analysis of the monthly cash receipts from cash and credit sales over the six-month period.

Month:	Jan. £	Feb. £	Mar. £	April £	May £	Jun. £	Total £
(a) Sales	18 000	19 000	22 300	22 500	25 000	26 500	133 300
Cash	5 000	4 000	4 000	5 000	5 000	5 000	28 000
Credit	13 000	15 000	18 300	17 500	20 000	21 500	105 300
(b) Cash receipts:							
Cash sales	13 000	15 000	18 300	17 500	20 000	21 500	
Credit sales	6 000	5 000	4 000	4 000	5 000	5 000	
Totals	19 000	20 000	22 300	21 500	25 000	26 500	

Figure 15.2 Desilva Ltd: (a) monthly actual sales; (b) monthly cash receipts from cash and credit sales.

We now turn our attention to the amounts that we expect to spend each month. In the context of the cash budget expenditure is catgorized as cash outflows. Typically these outflows of cash for a small hotel business will relate to paying suppliers for purchases of food and consumables, paying wages to employees and paying for expenses such as gas and electric. We also need to budget for purchases of capital equipment. In the case of DeSilva, it is anticipated that a car will be purchased part way through the year.

The exact timing and value of these various payments has to forecasted. We will begin by looking at purchases – or more accurately payments to suppliers for purchases.

EXAMPLE 15.1

DeSilva Ltd – further information

The purchases of supplies for the next six months are anticipated to be:

January	£6100
February	£6550
March	£7930
April	£8100
May	£9250
June	£9640

These goods will be purchased on credit and the credit period given is one month.

Wages are anticipated to be £4400 per month and general expenses to be £2500 per month. Both wages and expenses will be paid in the same month as they are incurred.

We now have all the necessary information to prepare the cash budget for DeSilva Ltd as shown in Figure 15.3.

From this cash budget it can be seen that each month there is a balance bought forward. The January balance of £(14 500) represents the bank overdraft at the end of December as shown as shown in the Balance sheet in Figure 15.1. The brought forward amounts for all the other months relate to the cash balance at the end of the previous month; therefore the cash balance of £(7700) at the end of January becomes the brought forward balance for February.

It can also be seen from the cash budget that the inflows and out-flows of cash are recorded in the budget statement when the cash is actually received or paid. There are a few important points to re-member when constructing a cash budget, as follows.

DeSilva Ltd: cash budget

Month:	Jan. £	Feb. £	Mar. £	April £	May £	Jun. £
Balance b/f	(14 500)	(7 700)	(700)	8 150	(2 480)	7 520
Sales receipts	19 000	20 000	22 300	21 500	25 000	26 500
Total receipts	19 000	20 000	22 300	21 500	25 000	26 000
Payments:						
Creditors	5 300	6 100	6 550	7 930	8 100	9 250
Wages	4 400	4 400	4 400	4 400	4 400	4 400
Overheads	2 500	2 500	2 500	2 500	2 500	2 500
Capital expenditure				17 300		
Total payments	12 200	13 000	13 450	32 130	15 000	16 150
Balance c/f	(7 700)	(700)	8 150	(2 480)	7 520	17 870

Figure 15.3

- The dates of receipt and payment of cash, not the dates of sale or purchase, are relevant; thus allowance has been made for any credit period given or received.
- Provisions should be excluded as they do not affect cash flows; for example, depreciation on fixed assets is excluded as the cash flow associated with the acquisition of fixed assets occurs when the asset is paid for. Thus in the case of DeSilva the relevant cash outflow relates to the £17 300, which was paid out for a new vehicle when it was purchased. The depreciation charge is irrelevant for the purposes of constructing a cash budget and therefore should be ignored.
- Any inflows of capital and outflows such as drawings, payment of tax and dividends must also be included. In the example, of DeSilva there are no such transactions.
- The format of the cash budget is very similar to the worksheets which were introduced in Chapter 5. In the case of cash budgets the horizontal headings should relate to the discrete time period chosen for the budget. Thus in this example, the requirement is monthly for six months to the end of the period. The company alternatively could have chosen, for example, weeks; in such a case there would be a column for each week of the six-month period. The time dimension will depend upon the requirements of the managers of the organization.

This example clearly demonstrates the value of cash budgets as a useful management tool. You can observe a trend that the company is moving systematically away from being overdrawn. However, due to the purchase of the vehicle there is a sudden reduction in cash, and a move back into the red or overdraft. It is important for the managers to be able to anticipate such 'blips' and make arrangements for financing them with the bank manager.

We can now proceed to look at the forecast profit and loss account and the balance sheet for DeSilva Ltd.

The forecast profit and loss account (Figure 15.4) has simply, for convenience, been constructed in a summary form rather than through the use of a worksheet. Unlike the cash budget, the profit and loss account is constructed applying the concept of accruals accounting (i.e. matching revenues with costs associated with those revenues) rather than cash flow accounting. Thus, in our example, the cost of goods sold is the cost of purchases actually associated with sales rather than the cash paid to suppliers for food and consumables.

The depreciation charge for the six months is calculated as follows.

- Fixtures and fittings at 20% straight line equates to an annual charge of £4500, which for six months is £2250.
- The vehicle is depreciated in the year of acquisition. For simplicity we have ignored the fact that it was purchased part way through the year. The depreciation policy for vehicles is 20% reducing balance,

DeSilva Ltd: forecast profit and loss account

	£	£
Sales		133 300
Cost of sales		46 655
Gross profit		**86 645**
Less expenses:		
Wages	26 400	
Overheads	15 000	
Depreciation: Fixtures and fittings	4 500	
Vehicles	3 460	
		49 360
Net profit for the year		**37 285**
Retained profit b/f		30 200
Retained profit c/f		67 485

Figure 15.4

which equates to an annual charge of £17 300 × 20% = £3460, which results in a charge for the first six months of £1730.

- The retained profit brought forward derives from December's balance sheet, which was shown in Figure 15.1.

The forecast balance sheet (Figure 15.5) like the forecast profit and loss account, has been constructed without the use of a worksheet. The following is a brief explanation as to how the value of some of the assets and liabilities have been derived.

- The stock figure of £8915 simply represents a management estimate of future demand.
- Debtors of £5000 is the credit sales receipts outstanding for June, the last month of the period. This amount is expected to be paid in July.
- The sum of £9640 for creditors represents the outstanding balances with our suppliers and relates to our purchases in June.
- The bank overdraft is derived from the cash budget and is the balance at the end of the six months.

The use of worksheets as previously described in earlier chapters in the construction of the profit and loss account and the balance sheet illustrated the interrelationships between these statements. Although worksheets were not used in this example the interrelationships between these statements should still be apparent.

From a brief analysis of these three budgeted statements for DeSilva Ltd, their usefulness should be apparent to you in the context of planning, for example in anticipating overdraft requirements and making arrangements with the bank. Banks would look more favourably on an

DeSilva Ltd: forecast balance sheet

Fixed assets	Cost	Depn	NBV
	£	£	£
Premises	108 000	0	108 000
Fixtures and fittings	22 500	9 000	13 500
Vehicles	17 300	3 460	13 840
	147 800	12 460	135 340
Current asset			
Stock		8 915	
Debtors		5 000	
Cash		17 870	
		31 785	
Current liabilities			
Creditors	9 640		
Overdraft	0	9 640	22 145
			157 485
			£
Financed by			
Owners' equity			90 000
Profit and loss account			67 485
			157 485

Figure 15.5

application for an overdraft after having some insight into the future profitability of the company reflected through the profit and loss account and the general stability of the company reflected through the balance sheet. This situation can be contrasted to the negative attitude of the bank when an application for funding is made after a firm has gone into debt without any prior communication with the bank.

We shall now examine by means of Example 15.2 a slightly more complex situation where sales are derived from six departments. The previous year's results are used to help us prepare the budgeted profit and loss account.

EXAMPLE 15.2

Happy Holiday Group

Happy Holidays Group is a medium-sized hotel group offering good quality accommodation, mainly targeted at the tourist market. The following information is available for one of the group's hotels in

Southend and from this data we will construct a detailed forecast trading account.

Total room nights available for budget period: 4800
Forecasted occupancy rate: 50%
Forecasted average room rate: £40.00

Based on these figures and previous years' results, other departmental sales are expected to be as follows:

Department	Expected sales £
Food	30 000
Beverage	10 500
Leisure	300
Telephone	9 000
Other	4 200

Figures from previous years have also been used to forecast expected primary costs as a percentage of sales. These are

Department	Cost of sales %	Payroll %	Other expenses %
Rooms	0	15	5
Food	34	35	11
Beverage	36	24	1
Leisure	0	309	43
Telephone	24	8	4
Other	26	0.2	15

There are also some general expenses and other charges that cannot be directly identified to any of the three departments of the hotel. They are:

	£
Administration and general expenses	11 600
Repairs and maintenance	2 800
Insurance	3 160
Rates	4 500
Depreciation	6 000
Interest charges	8 400

From this relatively small amount of information we can produce a budgeted profit and loss account for the Happy Holiday Southend

Happy Holidays Southend hotel: Departmental profit and loss account

Departments	Net sales £	Cost of sales £	Payroll £	Other expenditure £	Dept. profit £
Rooms	96 000	0	14 400	4 800	76 800
Food	30 000	10 200	10 500	3 300	6 000
Beverage	10 500	3 780	2 520	105	4 095
Leisure	300	0	927	129	(756)
Telephone	9 000	2 160	720	360	5 760
Other	4 200	1 092	8	630	2 470
	150 000	17 232	29 075	9 324	94 369

		£	
Less general expenses			
Admin. and general expenses		11 600	
Repairs and maintainance		2 800	(14 400)
Gross operating profit			79 969
Less fixed charges	£		
Insurance	3 160		
Rates	4 500		
Depreciation	6 000		(13 660)
Operating profit before interest charges			66 309
Less interest charges			(8 400)
Net operating profit			57 909

Figure 15.6

hotel as in Figure 15.6. This is laid out to show the departmental results and then the combined total of all departments' revenues and expenses.

The layout of this profit and loss account will be very useful for internal management purposes. It will convey to departmental managers exactly what profit they are expected to contribute to the hotel and the level of costs that are estimated will be spent generating the budgeted sales. Ideally, this should have a motivational effect on these managers. The process of setting individual department budgets should also enhance the communications between those responsible for the departmental budgets as there is a need coordinate plans. For example, the level of service in respect of beverages is likely to be a function of the number of occupants of rooms as is the estimate of the number of budgeted meals. The following paragraphs detail how the figures for the budget were calculated.

The sales figure for the Rooms Department can be calculated by first determining the expected room occupancy as follows: Total rooms available (4800) × Occupancy (50%) = Number of rooms sold (2400). Now we merely multiply the number of rooms sold by the expected average room rate to give us the sales for the period: 2400

$\times$ £40.00 $\times$ £96 000. The other departmental sales figures were given above.

To calculate the various expenses, the cost as a percentages of sales (as given in the case) is multiplied by the sales figure. The following examples illustrate the computation:

Rooms payroll costs:

$$£96\,000 \times 15\% = £14\,400$$

Beverage Department direct costs:

$$£10\,500 \times 36\% = £3780$$

You will notice that the Leisure Department has payroll costs of 309% of sales, thus the costs of this department exceed the revenue. This is because it is a service department operating the leisure facilities within the hotel. As such it receives no direct revenue from hotel guests using the facilities, only a little from outside membership fees.

The cost percentages of sales have been established by the management team carefully examining the resources needed to operate each department and setting targets for expenditure in the light of expected sales levels.

Lastly, the common costs that have not been directly identified to the departments are deducted to establish the overall net profit for the hotel.

FLEXIBLE BUDGETS

The budgets we have described so far are static and assume one level of output which is normally measured through sales volume. Static budgets therefore do not allow any flexibility. In reality this is often required to reflect the changing business environment. It is possible, once, the budget is established, to calculate a 'flexible budget' which will show the impact of changing situations.

Key concept

Flexible Budget

A flexible budget is a master budget that is adjusted for potential changes in volume, i.e. level of sales.

When making plans and forecasts, managers and accountants have to assess all kinds of data about the product or service they provide, the nature of the market in which they operate and the state of the economy both nationally and internationally. They must try to take account of what might happen in the future, which is rather like gazing into a crystal ball. Budgets are based on assumptions about these and many other factors.

It is likely that some assumptions, for instance an assumption about future UK interest rates and their impact on consumer spending, may turn out to be wrong, and as a result we may have set sales targets too high or perhaps too low. Flexible budgets enable us to see what impact these sorts of changes can have on profitability. It is possible and prudent to prepare a flexible budget before commencement of the budget period. This enables the preparation of preliminary plans to rectify any potential problems before they arise.

Before we can construct a flexible budget we must determine how costs are affected by changes in sales or activity levels. The way costs behave in relation to sales levels was examined in Chapter 13 of this book but we will quickly recap here some of the points relevant to cost behaviour.

Costs can be classified, according to the way they behave, as either fixed or variable. Fixed costs do not change in the short term when levels of activity increase or decrease. Some examples include insurance charges for a hotel which will not be affected by increases in occupancy or the business rate for a travel agency which is not linked to the level of business or number of customers; similarly airlines have to pay the same airport landing fees regardless of the number of passengers on board the aeroplane. It is assumed that these costs will not change during the budget period.

Variable costs do change in the short term. They are assumed to change in direct proportion to changes in sales volume. Some examples include restaurant food costs which will change directly in proportion to the number of covers. In a hotel rooms or food and beverage department, the costs of labour will be variable at the operational level due to the use of shifts and flexible working practices, but fixed at supervisory and management level.

Traditionally, different types of business have differing amounts of fixed and variable costs as proportions of their regular operating cost. Travel agents have traditionally high fixed costs, airlines too. The hotel industry is rather capital intensive so many costs here are linked to premises and therefore are not variable.

For the purposes of budgeting we need to make assumptions about which costs are variable and which are fixed. Given that we can establish this it is possible to calculate a flexible budget. By means of

Example 15.3 below the principles involved in preparing a flexible budget are illustrated.

EXAMPLE 15.3

Camelion Cafe

The proprietor of Camelion Cafe has prepared the budget shown in Figure 15.7 for the forthcoming period. Due to the recession business is not good so the budget has been a conservative one.

The local bank manager is concerned about the low profit margin and the uncertainty of the economic climate, and has asked the proprietor to prepare a flexible budget showing what impact a 10% increase or decrease in turnover would have on profits.

To prepare the flexible budget the Camelion's proprietor separates the costs into fixed and variable. Food is obviously variable and accounts for 35% of sales; wages are also variable (because the proprietor employs a lot of casual labour) amounting to 25% of sales. All other costs are fixed in the medium term.

The budget is recast separating fixed and variable costs and taking account of the impact of a 10% increase in turnover and 10% decrease in turnover. The amended budget is shown in Figure 15.8.

The layout of the budget has changed slightly, identifying variable costs namely the cost of food and wages, and fixed costs separately.

Number of covers	20 000
Average spend	£5.95

	£
Sales	119 000
Food costs	41 650
Gross profit	77 350
Less expenses:	
Wages	29 750
Management salaries	22 500
Rent and rates	14 500
Depreciation	7 500
Total expenses	74 250
Net profit	**3 100**
Net profit as a % of sales	**2.6%**

Figure 15.7 Camelion Cafe: original budget.

		Original budget	Increase 10%	Decrease 10%
Number of covers		20 000	22 000	18 000
Average spend		£5.95	£5.95	£5.95
		£	£	£
Sales		119 000	130 900	107 100
Food costs	35.0%	41 650	45 815	37 485
Wages	25.0%	29 750	32 725	26 775
Contribution		47 600	52 360	42 840
Less expenses				
Management salaries	Fixed	22 500	22 500	22 500
Rent and rates	Fixed	14 500	14 500	14 500
Depreciation	Fixed	7 500	7 500	7 500
Total expenses		44 500	44 500	44 500
Net profit		3 100	7 860	(1 660)
Net profit as a percentage of sales		2.6%	6.0%	(1.5%)

Figure 15.8 Camelion Cafe: flexible budget.

The difference between the sales revenue and the variable costs is classified as 'contribution'. The concept of contribution you will remember was introduced and discussed in an earlier chapter. All overhead costs have been assumed to be fixed.

To calculate the flexible budget showing an increase of 10% in sales the variable costs need to be multiplied by the factor 1.10. To calculate the effect of a 10% decrease in turnover variable costs need to be multiplied by 0.90.

The overall impact from an increase or decrease of 10% on contribution and profits can be seen in Figure 15.8. If turnover did decline by 10% the cafe would be making a loss. With this knowledge the proprietor is able to take evasive action, for example to seek ways of reducing costs, increase prices or simply withdraw from the business.

This simple example shows how flexible budgets can assist even small businesses plan for unseen eventualities, and demonstrates clearly the value of flexible budgets.

The increased use of information technology even in small companies has enabled managers to do far more numerical analysis of data themselves, quickly and accurately. Flexible budgets lend themselves very well to the application of spreadsheets. Once a budget has been set up on a spreadsheet it is relatively simple and very quick to carry out 'What-if' analysis to see the impact of changes in sales.

SUMMARY

We began this chapter by referring to and discussing the role of budgeting particularly within this process, making operational decisions. We defined the concepts of both operating decisions and budgets which provided a basis for reviewing the main purposes of budgets. These were described under the following headings:

- compel planning;
- coordinate the different functions;
- communicate;
- provide a basis for responsibility accounting;
- provide a basis for a control mechanism;
- authorize expenditure;
- to motivate employees to improve performance.

From the above list it is apparent that budgets are introduced and used for a variety of reasons. Whilst it may initially appear that the introduction of budgets can only be to the advantage of the organization they can, in fact, create conflict. To be effective budgets need not only to be comprehensive and detailed but also realistic and flexible.

The sequence of operations needed to effectively implement a budget planning system was described. This sequence is known as the budget process, which is substantially a political process of negotiation. We stressed the need to understand this process as it links the reasons for the implementation of the budget and the preparation of budgets. It was also stressed that the budget process and the form of budgets would be dependent upon such factors as the size and culture of an organization and the nature of technology employed by the organization, as well as many external factors such as the competitive nature of the market in which the organization operates.

The preparation of budgets was then considered. Two examples were examined both of which illustrated how the process of preparing budgets effectively coordinated the plans of the various functions within the organization, for example the sales budget and its relationship with the purchasing and stock budgets. A number of principles were stressed in the preparation of different budgets, for example in the case of cash budgets the effect of timing differences and the differences between cash and accruals accounting. We also stressed the need for flexibility, showing how flexible budgets can be used to take account of the dynamic nature of the business environment and how they can aid planning, by allowing managers to see the impact of changes in activity levels.

REFERENCES

Kosturakis, J.G. and Eyster, J.J. (1979) Operational budgeting in small hotel companies. *The Cornell HRA Quarterly*, **20** (1), 80–4.

FURTHER READING

Harris, P. (1992) *Profit Planning* (Hospitality Manager's Pocket Book), Butterworth–Heinnemann, provides a practical guide to budgeting with spreadsheets, with simple, step-by-step instructions.

REVIEW QUESTIONS

1. What is a budget?
2. What are the main reasons for an organization to introduce budgets?
3. Explain why budgets may mean different things to different people within an organization, giving reasons.
4. Explain, giving examples, the main advantages of identifying cash surpluses and deficits in a cash budget.
5. What is a master budget? Describe its role in relation to other budgets.
6. What is a flexible budget? How can it assist the planning process.

PROBLEMS FOR DISCUSSION AND ANALYSIS

1. Dinasaur Diner Limited has opened its restaurant on 1 January 1994 with £3000 cash. It serves burgers and other fast food, the speciality of the house being the giant Dinaburger 'big enough for two'. Of the capital costs already incurred £5000 is due for payment on 25 March.

    An extract of figures expected in the next six months shows:

	Sales	Purchases	Wages	Rent	Depreciation	Other expenses
	£	£	£	£	£	£
January	2000	1000	700	300	250	900
February	2000	800	700	300	250	400
March	3000	1250	900	300	250	450
April	4000	1600	1200	300	250	500
May	4500	1750	1200	300	250	550
June	5000	2000	1500	300	250	600

- Rent is paid quarterly in advance.
- Each month it is anticipated that £200 of purchases is for cash. The balance, bought on credit, is payable in arrears, i.e. the following month.
- The 'other expenses' will be paid two months in arrears.
- One tenth of the sales are expected to be credit sales collected two months after they have been made.

From the above information prepare a cash budget for the period January to June 1994 inclusive on a monthly basis. Comment on the advantages of budgeting for cash with reference to the cash budget you have prepared.

2. Pizza Palace is a relatively new takeaway restaurant in a central position of a busy market town. The owner is worried about how the business will develop, and whether the turnover will increase enough as the business gets established to generate a healthly profit. He has committed a lot of money to advertising and marketing activities as he knows these must be front loaded, i.e. that he must pay a disproportionate amount early in the business's life to get it going. His backers want to see the business in profit by the end of the sixth quarter, i.e. after 18 months of trading, otherwise they will withdraw their support.

He has prepared the following budget information based on the first quarter's trading:

Sales	£
Food costs at 35%	18 000

Other expenses are fixed: the amounts shown below are per quarter:

Wages	6 300
Management salaries	2 500
Rent and rates	6 500
Depreciation	2 650

Required:

(a) Calculate the budget for the first quarter, and state what would be the resultant annual profit or loss if nothing changed.
(b) Prepare a flexible budget showing increases in sales of 50% and 100% based on the original budget.
(c) Discuss the implications of the increases in (b) in terms of fixed and variable costs and the subsequent effect on profits.

3. The following is a summary of the profit and loss account and balance sheet for Briggs Co. Ltd.

Profit and loss account for Briggs Co. Ltd for the six months ended 31 May 19X4

	£	£
Sales		72 000
Less cost of sales:		
Opening stock	13 600	
Purchases	55 000	
	68 600	
–Closing stock	11 000	57 600
Gross profit		14 400

Less expenses			
Wages and salaries		5 800	
Administration		3 600	
			9 400
Net profit			5 000

Balance sheet for Briggs Co. Ltd as at 31 May 1994

		£	£
Fixed assets			9 000
Stock		11 000	
Debtors		9 600	
Bank		5 400	
		26 000	
Admin. expenses:			
–Outstanding	600		
Trade creditors	9 330		
	9 930		16 070
Total net assets			25 070
Financed by			£
Issued share capital			10 000
Retained profit			15 070
			25 070

At a meeting of the directors the following forward projections for the six months to 30 November 19X4 were agreed to:

(i) The gross profit percentage is expected to stay the same at 20% of sales. The period of credit is to be increased from one month to two months after the date of sale. As a result it is expected that sales will be increased immediately from £12 000 to £18 000 each calender month.

(ii) It is assumed that Briggs will pay for all purchases one month after purchase. The stock is to be increased to £20 000 by the end of November. Purchases each month are of an equal amount.

(iii) Wages and salaries will be £1100 per calender month payable each month.

(iv) Administration expenses will be £720 per calender month. It is expected that at the end of each month there will be one month's expenses owing.

(v) The firm is to issue 5000 ordinary shares of £1 each in September at a premium of 25p payable in full on application. The issue is expected to be a success.

(vi) Further finance is expected to be by bank overdraft. All sums received are to be paid into the bank and all payments made by cheque. No discounts will be received or allowed.

You are required to prepare a summary of the company's bank account for each of the next six months (i.e. a monthly cash budget for the six months to 30 November 1994), the profit and loss account for the six months to the end of November 1994 and balance sheet as at that date. Depreciation of fixed assets is at a rate of 10% per annum straight line. Make no allowance for interest and dividends at this stage and ignore taxation.

Budgeting – control $\boxed{16}$

INTRODUCTION

In the previous chapter we examined planning in the context of short-term budgets. The chapter focused on the process of structured negotiations and the subsequent development of individual departmental budgets and their consolidation into the master budget. This particular aspect of the process is only one part of the overall budgetary process. Budgets need to be monitored and evaluated to be useful. However, plans in the form of budgets in themselves are extremely useful. In the last chapter a number of the purposes of budgets were identified. A number of these purposes highlight the usefulness of budgets from a purely planning perspective; for example, they compel organizations to look ahead and thereby anticipate any particular problems that may arise in the future.

The type of budgets that have been described in the context of planning have tended to be static in the sense that the planning process is based upon certain assumptions and events that will occur in the forthcoming budget period. In reality the business environment tends to be dynamic, and thus events may not turn out as anticipated in the budget. It may well be that deviations from the budget are harmful to the organization; for example, the cost of providing a service may be greater than that anticipated in the budget, resulting in losses being made. It is therefore important that these actual events in a budget period are monitored against the budget plan, so that action may be taken to alleviate any undesirable situations arising.

Deviations from the budget may be due to events within the control or outside the control of the organization. An event is within the control of the organization if management can direct action to ensure such an event, assuming it is undesirable, will not occur in the future. In contrast, events outside the control of the organization cannot normally be directly influenced by management action. However, management can reassess the organization's overall strategy to deal with such extraneous events. For example, a downturn in the economy may mean that it will be necessary for the organization to reconsider its future plans. Typically, such events will result in organizations 'trimming' their operations to lower levels of activity or diversifying into other markets. The point here is that the long-term effect of undesirable situations directly or indirectly in the control of the organization may be averted if an efficient system of monitoring and control is imposed. It is vitally important therefore to develop a system of monitoring and control that will highlight deviations that will enable managers to assess their cause and impact and take appropriate corrective action.

MONITORING AND CORRECTIVE ACTION

Key concept

Monitoring and corrective action defined

Monitoring is the process of comparing actual performance with a predetermined target (plan). It provides the basis from which corrective action can be planned and taken.

The process of monitoring and then taking corrective action, if appropriate, is at the core of the control activities of any organization. The monitoring of actual performance against budget will inevitably result in the identification of differences. These differences are commonly referred to as 'variances'. It is unlikely that the actual performance will be exactly the same as the budget. The reason for this is that the operating decisions embodied in the budget will normally be determined well in advance of actual performance, and the process of forecasting cost and revenues in a dynamic economic environment is surrounded by uncertainty. Later in this chapter the process for identifying the causes of variances and how to quantify them are examined.

To effectively monitor performance, personnel in an organization who incur expenditure and generate revenues will be identified and made responsible for costs and revenues. The underlying approach adopted here is known as 'responsibility accounting'. The concept of responsibility accounting was introduced in Chapter 11 and further discussed in the context of planning in Chapter 15. This concept recognizes various decision centres throughout an organization and traces costs and revenues to the individual managers primarily responsible for making the decisions and controlling the costs and revenues of those centres. The managers' knowledge of the centre places them in a relatively advantageous position within an organization to ensure that budget targets are achieved. These responsibility centres will normally take the form of departments or divisions within the organization.

THE CONTROL SYSTEM

Within the accountant's control system, the monitoring and corrective action stages of the information system are often compared with those of the engineer, using the analogy of a central heating system – Figure 16.1 provides a relatively simple example.

In the central heating system the desired temperature is set and the comparator compares this with the actual room temperature. If there is any deviation from the set temperature action is automatically taken by the system to fuel the boiler to enable it to compensate for any temperature variance. This system, therefore, involves the process of monitoring actual output against a desired output, and when a variance is identified corrective action will automatically be taken.

Earlier, in Chapter 12, when the planning and control process was introduced very similar stages to the central heating system were identified and described. However, there are a number of interesting differences between the two systems, some of which will give us a greater insight into the limitations of the planning and control process and the problems associated with budgeting.

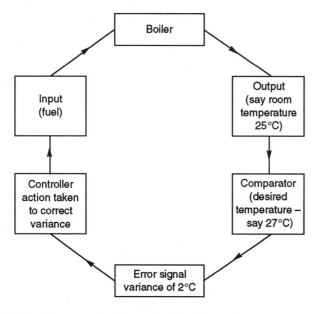

Figure 16.1 Simple example of a central heating system.

An important difference between the two systems is that the central heating model is a physical system where there are automatic responses to outputs. That is corrective action is taken to obtain the desired temperature automatically and without any reference to operatives. In contrast, the control model within the planning and control process is normally dependent upon humans. In this system the response to deviations from the budget is not automatically taken. In all accounting reporting systems time lags will be experienced, and people will have to be motivated to respond to variances and take corrective action if perceived necessary.

The extent of these time lags in reporting will depend upon the sophistication of the accounting information system. In the case of some large companies the monitoring of performance will be on a weekly basis and, with computerization helping to quicken up the reporting process, the capability of taking corrective action is relatively quick. However, in the majority of organizations control reports will normally be generated on a monthly basis. The main restrictions to implementing more timely systems will be the installation and running costs of the system. The introduction of information systems is governed by the cost and benefits of the system, that is an information system should only be installed if the benefits generated from the system exceed the cost of installing the system.

An important feature of all control systems, of course, is that any variances that are reported can only be used to guide future operations. An organization cannot remedy past mistakes.

It is only in recent years that the accounting function and its interaction with human behaviour has been brought to the forefront of accounting research and literature. It is now well recognized that the effectiveness of accounting information systems is very much dependent upon the attitudes of individuals associated with an organization.

In the context of the control systems, the process of setting targets will be influenced and affected by the behaviour of individuals. For example, sales managers may respond negatively if they are set targets that, in their opinion, they are unable to achieve. Another example is the action required to correct further undesirable variance – this will very much depend upon the reaction and motivation of the responsible manager and his or her subordinates. If a manager perceives that targets are unrealistic it is unlikely that he or she will be motivated to take corrective action to ensure they are met in the future. The accountant's control system is therefore limited in its application by the motivation of individuals in setting budgets and taking action on variances that have been identified.

We will look in more detail at some of the behavioural aspects of budgeting towards the end of this chapter. For now we will examine how variance analysis can assist in the monitoring and control process by enabling us to establish the cause of deviations and take appropriate corrective action.

VARIANCES AND VARIANCE ANALYSIS

> ### *Key concept*
>
> *Variances*
>
> Variances are deviations from budgeted costs and/or revenues. They occur when the actual performance is different to the planned or budgeted performance.

Traditionally, texts have tended to concentrate on variances that have been caused through operating problems, such as the price of food being greater than anticipated in the budget perhaps because of inefficient buying practices by buyers. A few academics, in particular Demski (1967) and Bromwich (1980), have argued that there could be other causes of variance that have tended to be overlooked in the control process. They basically identify three causes of variances.

- **Operating variances.** These variances are related to human or mechanical factors that result in the budget target not being achieved.
- **Planning variances.** These variances will occur if plans are not realistic at the time of actual performance, even if operations have been efficiently carried out. Put simply, the plans may be out of date. For example, during the planning stage food costs in a restaurant may have been set with due care, but because of rapid inflation these planned costs can be out of date and therefore do not represent realistic budget targets to compare actual and planned activities.
- **Random variances.** These are caused by divergences between actual and planned costs arising at random; that is, they occur by chance and there is no means of controlling them. For example, in the brewing process the reaction of sugar and yeast does not always produce the same level of alcohol and taste, resulting in variations of the quantity and quality of the finished product. Similarly, in the airline industry fuel requirements are affected by weather conditions. Prolonged periods of unusual weather, for example the prevailing winds on a given route, may result in the actual consumption of fuel being very different from that budgeted.

It is important to identify not only the extent of the deviation (variance) but to ascertain the cause, so that effective corrective action can be taken. When responsibility accounting is in operation it is important to recognize that variances can be both within and outside a manager's control. If variances are attached in terms of responsibility to mangers who do not have control over their cause, this will inevitably have a strong demotivating effect on those managers.

A number of the methods for the identification of variances and their causes are highly sophisticated and not appropriate to be included in this text. It is, however, appropriate to give some insights into the general nature of the causes of variances. In addition, we will examine how basic variance analysis can assist managers to take appropriate corrective action.

Key concept

Variance analysis

The systematic process of breaking down variances to find the true causes for deviation with a view to eliminating inefficiencies.

Variances can be either favourable or unfavourable. Favourable variances occur when costs are lower than planned and/or revenues higher than planned. Unfavourable or adverse variances occur when costs exceed the plan or revenues are lower than planned. This classification of variances being favourable or adverse can be linked to the effect on the net profit/income of the organization. For example, as revenues decrease we can normally expect profit to decrease which is likely to be detrimental to the organization and thus the variance is considered adverse or unfavourable.

It is also worth noting that despite this classification of variances, into favourable or adverse, it might be that a so-called favourable cost variance in the short term can lead to adverse variances or increased spending in the long term. For example, spending less on roof maintenance in a hotel in the first quarter of the budget period may result in substantial repairs being required before the end of the year. So it is very important to analyse the variances accurately to establish their true cause and effect on the organization's overall performance.

We will use Example 16.1 which gives details of Mark Ltd to demonstrate a simple analysis of variances.

EXAMPLE 16.1

Mark Ltd

Mark Ltd owns a medium-sized hotel and employs a budgetary control system. The original budget for 19X3 included food costs which were estimated at £1.85 per cover. It was anticipated that the number of covers would total 75 000 during the year. Therefore the budget for the cost of food in total cost terms would be £1.85 × 75 000 = £138 750. During the year, however, actual costs were £163 200 and the number of covers amounted to 85 000.

Traditionally, the analysis of the cost variances between actual and budget would be presented as follows:

	Actual	**Budget**	**Variance**
	£	£	£
Food costs	163 200	138 750	(24 450)

The brackets around the variance of £24 450 indicates that it is 'unfavourable' or 'adverse'; that is, actual costs exceed budget.

This cost variance analysis does not, however, give any indication of the cause of the variance. It could, for example, be due to the actual food costs per cover exceeding the planned cost, or it could be due to more covers being sold during the period than had been planned. It is therefore necessary to differentiate between variances caused by cost factors and those caused by the volume of business. It should be noted that if the volume of business is increasing, i.e. it is greater than budget, the cause of the so-called unfavourable variance is unlikely to be detrimental to the firm! Increasing volume will normally subsequently result in increased sales revenue and profit. Therefore we must be cautious when using the term unfavourable in the context of variances.

To separate these two causes of variances (cost and volume variances) it is first necessary to recalculate the costs included in the budget based on the increased volume of business in terms of sales turnover. The result of 'flexing' the cost budget to the actual level of volume is to eliminate the variance caused by sales volume. Budgets that have been adjusted in this way for volume variations are referred to as flexed budgets. In other words, the flexed budget will provide a benchmark against which to judge the actual total cost of food. As you would expect, food costs are bound to rise if we sell more meals, so the flexible budget will tell by how much we can expect them to rise based on our original plan, that is £1.85 per cover.

The actual number of covers sold have increased by 10 000 to 85 000. Therefore, based on our original expectations or food costs at £1.85 per cover, we can expect actual food costs to be 85 000 × £1.85 = £157 250.

Now we can compare the actual performance with the flexed budget figures. First, however, we will identify the variance caused by the difference in volume between the original budget and the flexed budget.

Volume variance:

	Original budget	**Flexed budget**	**Variance**
	£	£	£
Food cost	138 750	157 250	(18 500)

We can see from the above that approximately 75% of the total variance of £24 400 is due to increased business. In the classification referred to earlier this variance would be classified as a planning variance. Although the variance is shown as 'unfavourable' because the actual cost exceeds budget, it is likely that the sales revenue has increased which is likely to increase profits.

We now consider those variances caused by variations in the cost of food by comparing the flexed budget with the actual cost.

Cost variances:

	Actual	Flexed budget	Variance
	£	£	£
Food cost	163 200	157 250	(5950)

From the analysis above it can be seen that the actual cost of the food exceeded the budgeted cost by £5950 in total. In terms of per cover the actual cost was £163 200/85 000 meals = £1.92 per cover. Thus the variance per cover was £0.07 (£1.85 – £1.92). This variance of £0.07 could be due to:

1. the cost of the food purchased being more due to inefficient buying practices;
2. the cost of producing the food being more costly due to inefficiencies;
3. a general increase in the cost of food due to inflation.

In the cases of causes 1 and 2 above it is likely these would be classified as operational and probably controllable by the organization. In contrast, cause 3 would be classified as a planning variance and in this case it is likely to be seen as outside the control of the organization.

To be able to take corrective action, therefore, managers need to be able to identify the cause of the variance which can be a difficult task.

You can see by the illustration above using Example 16.1 that variance analysis is essential to ascertain what, if any, corrective action needs to be taken. Variances can be very complicated and difficult to identify in terms of cause. The key is to isolate various causal factors that result in an overall deviation or total variance. It is often the case that favourable variances can counteract and mask large unfavourable or adverse variances. For example, in the case of food cost variances, if there is a fall in food prices resulting in a saving on food costs per cover, yet the actual food cost per cover does not decrease, it is likely that there is an operational problem associated with food preparation. The necessary breakdown of operational variances to identify these causes is beyond the scope of this book but is well covered in texts such as Kotas (1986) or Jones (1993).

Cost variances can be due to deviations in the volume of sales, the cost of commodities or the use of commodities as we have seen in the previous example. Variances in revenues, in terms of hotels, can be due to changes in the planned price or occupancy levels or changes in the planned sales mix, that is a change in the mix of different services sold to that originally planned. We will now go on to calculate a sales volume variance in a hotel scenario and then look at a short example illustrating a sales volume and mix variance in a travel agency business.

EXAMPLE 16.2

Downprice Hotel Ltd

Downprice Hotel Ltd has an overall adverse sales variance of £1700 for its rooms department. The general manager asks the accommodation manager to explain the cause.

The original budget submission was as follows:

- Total bed nights available in budget period: 4000;
- Planned occupancy levels: 65% = 2600 beds;
- Expected average room rate: £19.50.

The actual results showed an increase in the occupancy rate but a decrease in the average room rate as follows:

- Actual occupancy: 70% = 2800 beds;
- Actual average room rate: £17.50.

By using variance analysis techniques the causes of the £1700 adverse sales variance can more clearly be identified.

Summarizing the information so far:

	Budget	Flexed budget	Actual
Bed nights available	2 600	2 800	2 800
Occupancy	65%	70%	70%
Average room rate	£19.50	£19.50	£17.50
Sales total	£50 700	£54 600	£49 000

The adverse variance of £1700 relates to the difference between the original budget (£50 700) and the actual (£49 000). However, when the flexed budget (£54 600) and actual (£49 000) are compared the variance is £5600 adverse. This latter analysis of the variances, using the concept of flexed budgets, eliminates the volume differences caused by varying occupancy rates.

The following analysis shows the split variances caused through volume (occupancy) and cost:

	Budget	Actual	Variance
Sales	£50 700	£49 000	£1700

Variance due to increased occupancy:

	Actual/flexed budget	Original budget	Variance	
Sales	£54 600	£50 700	£3900	Fav.

Thus occupancy variance is £3900 favourable. The reason for this is that more rooms have been occupied than originally budgeted for and it follows there is an increase in sales revenue compared to that anticipated in the orginal budget.

Variance due to lower average room rate:

	Actual	Flexed budget	Variance	
Sales	£49 000	£54 600	£5600	Adv.

The £5600 adverse variance is the result of the average room rate being less than anticipated.

The net effect of these two variances of course is £1700, the overall sales variance.

These variances can often occur if hotels get their discounting policy wrong. In Chapter 13 on pricing there is a fuller discussion about discounting prices. In this particular case it is likely that the marketing department promoted cheaper room rates to increase occupancy, but in this budget period the increase in occupancy was not sufficient to counter the lost revenue from a lower average room rate. It is only through a systematic process of variance analysis that managers are able to see the true impact of the deviation from the budget plan.

We will now move on to look at sales variances that typically occur in the travel and tour operators business. Example 16.3 illustrates the analysis of sales volume and mix variances.

EXAMPLE 16.3

Southern Travel

Southern Travel have an overall adverse variance on net income despite an increase of £5000 on the budgeted sales (Figure 16.2). The managing director needs to know the reason for this adverse variance so that the appropriate corrective action can be taken.

From Figure 16.2 it can be seen that actual total sales is £5000 greater than budgeted but the total net income is £654 less. In the language of variance terminology the £5000 sales variance is 'favourable' and the income variance of £654 is 'adverse'. It is also noticeable from an examination of the column showing the proportion of total business that the balance of sales (the sales mix) between the four different areas of business has changed from the original budget. This change

	Turnover	Proportion of total business	Commission rate	Net income
Original budget	£	%	%	£
Package holidays	50 050	77	14	7 007
Air tickets	6 500	10	7	455
Insurances	5 200	8	45	2 340
Car rental and other	3 250	5	8	260
	65 000	100		10 062
Actual performance				
Package holidays	52 000	75	14	7 350
Air tickets	11 900	17	7	833
Insurances	2 100	3	45	945
Car rental and other	3 500	5	8	280
	70 000	100		9 408
Overall variance				
(Actual – Budget)	£5 000 (F)			–£654 (A)

F = Favourable
A = Adverse

Figure 16.2 Southern Travel: budgeted and actual performance figures.

will also affect the overall income because of the differing individual profit margins, shown under the heading of 'commission rate' in the next column. For example, increasing the proportion of sales of insurances in relation to the other services without any increase in overall sales revenue will increase the overall income as the commission rate is 45% whereas the next highest rate is only 14%. However, the effect of changes in sales mix cannot be clearly identified solely from the analysis shown in Figure 16.2.

To determine the sales volume variance the original budget is flexed to reflect the total actual sales revenue, assuming that the same sales mix, and then compared with the original budget. This analysis is shown in Figure 16.3. The sales turnover for each part of the business is calculated by multiplying the percentage shown in the column 'proportion of total business' for the original budget by the actual total sales revenue of £70 000 for example in the case of package holidays 77% × £70 000 = £53 900. The net income for each part of the business is then multiplied by the original budget commission rate. In terms of the total sales volume variance turnover shows £5000 favourable variance and net income £774. In term of sales volume we can conclude that the increase in turnover by £5000 has increased profits by £774.

From the comparison of the turnover and net income shown in the flexed budget with the actual figures the variance caused through changes in the sales mix can be identified. This analysis is shown in

	Original budget		Flexed budget	
	Turnover	Net income	Turnover	Net income
	£	£	£	£
Package holidays	50 050	7 007	53 900	7 546
Air tickets	6 500	455	7 000	490
Insurances	5 200	2 340	5 600	2 520
Car rental and other	3 500	280	3 500	280
	65 000	10 062	70 000	10 836

Variance due to increase in sales volume
(Flexed budget – Original budget)   £5 000   (F)   £774 (F)

F = Favourable
A = Adverse

Figure 16.3 Southern Travel: sales volume variance.

Figure 16.4 which shows that changes in the planned sales mix have caused an adverse variance of £1428. You can observe that a higher proportion of the actual turnover has derived from less profitable business. For example, the total amount of insurance, which has the highest profit margin, is much lower than planned.

With this information available, which clearly shows that the variance was caused by the change in the sales mix, management are in the position to take corrective action that will hopefully improve the actual performance of the company in the future. For example, it may be decided to increase the marketing budget for the more profitable sectors of their overall sales portfolio. Typically with travel agents there will be changes in the commission rates from that originally

	Flexed budget		Actual performance	
	Turnover	Net income	Turnover	Net income
	£	£	£	£
Package holidays	53 900	7 546	52 500	7 350
Air tickets	7 000	490	11 900	833
Insurances	5 600	2 520	2 100	945
Car rental and other	3 500	280	3 500	280
	70 000	10 836	70 000	9 408

Variance due to change in sales mix
(Actual performance – Flexed budget)   £0   –£1 428 (A)

F = Favourable
A = Adverse

Figure 16.4 Southern Travel: sales mix variance.

budgeted. For instance, many travel agents negotiate the commission rates with the tour operators based on the level of sales they expect to make. If the travel agent sells more holidays than originally planned and exceeds predetermined targets, the tour operator will normally pay increased rates of commission. The increase in commission is not just on the sales over and above the plan, but for all sales. These increases in commission rates are called 'overrides' and can result in large favourable variances in net income.

We can see how variance analysis can help evaluate the impact of overrides.

EXAMPLE 16.4

Northern Travel

Northern Travel have exceeded their sales targets and as a result are expecting overrides to be paid by the tour operators. The managing director wishes to know exactly what impact this will have on the net income. Figure 16.5 shows the original budget and actual performance.

From Figure 16.5 it can be seen that there is an overall deviation from the budget of £1781.50, which is a favourable sales variance. The following analysis identifies the extent to which the variance is caused by sales volume increase and by the higher commission.

	Turnover	Commission	Net income rate
Original budget	£	%	%
Package holidays	45 500	10	4 550.00
Air tickets	9 750	5	487.50
Insurances	3 250	50	1 625.00
Car rental and other	6 500	8	520.00
	65 000		7 182.50
Actual performance			
Package holidays	50 400	12	6 048.00
Air tickets	10 800	5	540.00
Insurances	3 600	50	1 800.00
Car rental and other	7 200	8	576.00
	72 000		8 964.00
Variance	£7 000 (F)		£1 781.50 (F)

F = Favourable

Figure 16.5 Northern Travel: budgeted and actual performance figures.

The first stage in the analysis is to isolate the effect of the sales volume increase. As in Example 16.2 this analysis is facilitated through the use of a flexed budget. Figure 16.6 shows the flexed and original budgets.

The difference between these two budgets, £773.50 favourable variance (increased profits), is the result of the higher sales volume (measured in turnover).

If we now compare the flexed budget with the actual performance we can isolate the variance due to commission rate changes. Figure 16.7 below shows this variance.

The variance due to increased commission rates (or overrides) is £1008. A summary of the sales variances for Northern Travel is shown in Figure 16.8.

It is important to recognize the value of structured analysis of variances. Through the type of analysis illustrated above managers may be able to avoid undesirable situations in the future, whilst making the most of and promoting desirable ones. However, no matter how sophisticated the techniques used for the analysis of variances and the identification of their cause, the information derived from the analysis will be redundant if managers cannot generate appropriate action from subordinates. In the final part of this chapter we will leave the numeric calculations of variance analysis behind and concentrate on some of the behavioural aspects of budgeting. We will look at how

Flexed budget

	Turnover £	Net income £
Package holidays	50 400	5 040.00
Air tickets	10 800	540.00
Insurances	3 600	1 800.00
Car rental and other	7 200	576.00
	72 000	7 956.00

Original budget

	Turnover £	Net income £
Package holidays	45 500	4 550.00
Air tickets	9 750	487.50
Insurances	3 250	1 625.00
Car rental and other	6 500	520.00
	65 000	7 182.50

Variance £773.50 (F)

F = Favourable

Figure 16.6 Northern Travel: sales volume variance.

	Flexed budget	
	Turnover	**Net income**
	£	£
Package holidays	50 400	5 040
Air tickets	10 800	540
Insurances	3 600	1 800
Car rental and other	7 200	576
	72 000	7 956

	Actual performance	
	Turnover	**Net income**
	£	£
Package holidays	50 400	6 048
Air tickets	10 800	540
Insurances	3 600	1 800
Car rental and other	7 200	576
	72 000	8 964

Variance   £1 008   (F)

F = Favourable

Figure 16.7 Northern Travel: commission rate variance.

people and budgets interact and how budgets can succeed or fail to engender appropriate action from managers and employees.

BEHAVIOURAL ASPECTS OF BUDGETING

The following sections discuss a few of the important issues related to the influence of human behaviour in the budgetary control process.

The motivational impact of budgets

Behavioural scientists suggest that trusting an individual with responsibility for a task or goal can increase his or her motivation to accomplish it. McClelland (1961) stated that individuals with a high need for achievement work hardest in situations where they can take personal responsibility for goal accomplishment. He goes on to state

	£	
Variance due to increased sales	773.50	(F)
Variance due to overrides	1008.00	(F)
Total	1781.50	

Figure 16.8 Northern Travel: summary of variances.

that high achievers relish responsibility and derive great satisfaction from achieving demanding targets. However, if targets are set too low no challenge exists and it is argued no satisfaction can be derived. At the other end of the scale standards set too high tend to demotivate individuals because the risk of failure is too great. Hofstede (1967) recommended that top management:

> ... realize that budgets only motivate when they are tight enough to be a challenge, and that they only challenge if there is a risk that they will not be fully met. If some budgets are not met this is only a sign that the system is healthy and it does not mean somebody is at fault. If you take the habit of interpreting it in this latter way, the budgets will soon be met, but they will not motivate.

Budgetary slack

Slack can be defined as the process of overstating costs and understating revenues with a view to ensuring good performance against budget targets. In an empirical study of attitudes of 32 managers in five large organizations to building slack into their budgets, Onsi (1973) found that 80% of the managers interviewed stated that in the bargaining process of setting budgets they aimed to create slack in their budgets. The managers gave two reasons for creating slack: (a) as a result of pressure stemming from top management to attain the budget and to show yearly profit growth, and (b) as a hedge against uncertainty. Clearly, slack in budgets can lead to a loose budget and result in organizational inefficiency.

Although a considerable amount of attention is now correctly given to the influence of individuals on accounting information systems, particularly budgetary systems, there is still considerable scope for further research as well as the appreciation in practice that human behaviour can distort the effectiveness of budgeting systems.

SUMMARY

The chapter began by illustrating the importance of budgetary control in the overall planning and control process. It was explained how the budgetary review was a vital part of the monitoring and corrective action stage of the overall planning and control process. We explained that without comparing the budget with actual performance we would not be able to judge how effectively the organization was operating.

Variance analysis, which provides managers with information upon which to base the necessary corrective action, was introduced. How variances can be classified into operational, planning and random variances was discussed and illustrated through a number of examples. These examples focused on the types of variances that can be calculated. Flexible budgets were introduced and it was illustrated why they are critical in isolating the true cause and effect of variances.

Variances were classified into either favourable or adverse and it was explained that in certain circumstances, unless full investigation is carried out, favourable variances can hide or counteract adverse variances.

The chapter concluded with a brief review of the behavioural aspects of budgeting, showing that, no matter how sophisticated the accounting system, it is the way in which people and budgetary systems interact that determines their usefulness.

REFERENCES

Bromwich, M. (1980) Standard costing for planning and control, in *Topics in Management Accounting* (eds J. Arnold, B. Carsberg and R. Scapens), Philip Allen.

Demski, J.S. (1967) Analysing the effectiveness of the traditional standard costing variance model, in *Information for Decision Making*, 3rd edn (ed. A. Rappaport), Prentice Hall International.

Hofstede, G.H. (1967) *The Game of Budget Control.* Tavistock Institute.

Jones, P. (ed.) (1993) *Management of Food Service Operations*, Cassell, London.

Kotas, R. (1986) *Management Accounting for Hotels and Restaurants*, 2nd edn Surrey University Press.

McClelland, D.C. (1961) *The Achieving Society.* Reprinted in O'Dea, W.A. (1985) Budgetary control – a behavioural viewpoint. *International Journal of Hospitality Management*, **4** (4).

Onsi, M. (1973) Factor analysis of behaviour variables affecting budgetary slack, *Accounting Review*, July. Reprinted in O'Dea, W.A. (1985) Budgetary control – a behavioural viewpoint. *International Journal of Hospitality Management*, **4** (4), 179–80.

FURTHER READING

Hopwood, A.G. (1976) *Accountancy and Human Behaviour*, Prentice Hall.

REVIEW QUESTIONS

1. What are the main features of a control system?
2. What is a variance? Give examples of variances. Explain what is meant by favourable and adverse variances.
3. Variances have been classified into planning, control and random variances. Explain the differences in this classification and its usefulness.
4. How can flexible budgets assist in analysing variances?

5. Why is it important to determine the true cause and effect of variances from budget?
6. Why is it important to understand the behavioural aspects of budgeting?
7. What is budgetary slack?

PROBLEMS FOR DISCUSSION AND ANALYSIS

1. Big Country Burger House is a franchised burger outlet, operated by your friend Don that provides takeaway service only. The information system provided by the franchisor gives monthly printouts of operating figures. Don complains to you that these printouts are a waste of money, as he admits to you in the pub one night he never looks at them. Having recently graduated from a service management degree, which had an accounting module in it, you offer to have a look at them for him.

   The following day, Don sends you the report with a note saying, 'I looked at these after our chat in the pub last night and I think I'm doing really well, my profit is only down from the budget by £645. Not bad uh?! Not much need for improvement here, but if you have any suggestions let me know, mate! See you soon, Don.'

   ### Big Burger, Brighton franchise: monthly management report

	Budget	Actual
Sales units	192 000	204 500
Sales	£264 960	£271 985
Cost of sales	£86 400	£94 070
Gross operating profit	£178 560	£177 915
Variance		£645

   You decide to:
   (a) calculate a flexed budget;
   (b) prepare a statement of variances including volume and price variances;
   (c) write a brief report for Don telling him where he should start to look for operational efficiencies.

2. The Special Sunshine Holiday Company is a medium-sized independent travel agent operating from a prime site in the high street of a large town. The managing director monitors the business regularly reviewing total variances. The budget statement for this half year showing the overall variances is as follows:

   Budgeted sales   £1 000 000 Actual sales   £950 000   5% Drop

   Budgeted income   £160 225 Actual income £139 650 13% Drop

You have been asked to prepare a detailed statement of variances explaining exactly how these variances arose. You should prepare a brief explanation to support you calculations, which should include some suggestions for management action.

The budgeted sales mix and commission rates were as follows:

	Sales mix	Commission rates
	%	%
Package holidays	80.0	15
Air tickets	8.5	10
Insurances	5.0	55
Car hire and other	6.5	6

The actual sales mix was as follows:

Package holidays	82.0
Air tickets	8.5
Insurances	2.0
Car hire and other	7.5

3. An international airline monitoring key costs calculated a range of variances, of which the following is a selection. Classify the following variances as either planning, control or random. Explain for each what management action might be required, be it further investigation, direct operational changes or other.

   (a) Adverse – fuel consumption showed variance due to an extra-ordinary number of prevailing winds during winter months.
   (b) Adverse – load factor decreased on all internal flights.
   (c) Favourable – Average ticket revenues increased due to increased surcharges.
   (d) Adverse – ground staff payroll costs increased due to increase in amount of overtime.
   (e) Adverse – unallocated operating costs increased due to increase in need for airport accommodation costs.

4. Mile High Meals Ltd is a small food production unit operating close to Gatwick Airport. They supply a limited range of meals to five or six small carriers. They have information on average food costs per unit per menu type plus unit selling prices. The cost data and the actual results are detailed below:

Budget data	Cost price	Selling price	Units
	£	£	
Menu 1 (hot)	1.15	3.30	2375
Menu 2 (hot)	1.45	4.15	2375
Menu 3 (cold)	1.25	3.60	4750

Actual results

Menu 1 (hot)	1.30	3.30	1800
Menu 2 (hot)	1.50	4.15	2520
Menu 3 (cold)	1.35	3.60	3780

The overall effect is a deviation from budgeted gross profit of £3898.25 in this month. You have been asked to prepare a budgeted and actual profit and loss account and to produce a statement of variances explaining and reconciling the drop in gross profit.

The management of working capital 17

INTRODUCTION

All organizations that produce and sell goods and services will need to invest in current assets in order to support their operating activities. Although the nature of this investment will depend upon the type of goods or service produced and sold, typically it will include the investment in debtors and stocks, as well as the maintenance of a cash balance. Normally, the main source of the finance for this investment, as discussed in Chapter 8, is from short-term credit sources, for the most part trade creditors and bank overdrafts. The term used for these short-term funds in financial reports is 'creditors: amounts falling due within one year'; however, for convenience we will use the shorter term 'current liabilities'.

The term working capital refers to the difference between the current assets and current liabilities. When current assets exceed current liabilities working capital is said to be 'positive'. Negative working capital is where current liabilities exceed current assets. The term working capital is also, confusingly, used in a general sense to refer to the current assets and current liabilities. In this chapter the term 'working capital' is intended to be interpreted in the former sense.

Key concept

Definition of working capital

Working capital, measured in monetary terms, is the difference between current assets and current liabilities.

In terms of finance, when working capital is positive, additional capital other than from short-term sources will have been used to fund the investment in current assets. It follows that in such cases these funds must derive from medium- or long-term sources such as bank loans or equity. If, for example, current assets total £1600 and current liabilities sum to £800, the excess of £800 working capital must have been sourced from medium- or long-term finance. Negative working capital, in contrast, is when the current assets have been fully funded by short-term creditors and additionally a proportion of fixed assets are also being funded from these short-term sources. Therefore, if a firm's current liabilities consist of trade creditors and bank overdraft collectively summing to £2400 and the current assets total £2000, this means that short-term sources of finance are funding all the current assets and £400 of the firm's fixed assets.

The level of working capital has important implications for the liquidity of the firm. The relationship between current assets and current liabilities as a measurement of liquidity can also be expressed by means of the current ratio. The nature of the current ratio was discussed in Chapter 11 on financial statement analysis. Although liquidity has already been considered in that chapter, it was from the external user's perspective. Here we will consider liquidity in a slightly different context, that is from an internal user's perspective, i.e. management's perspective.

Management's interest in the management of one specific current asset such as debtors cannot be considered in isolation. Inevitably decisions regarding the level of the investment into one current asset will have implication for the others as well as resulting in further decisions relating to the financing of these assets. For example, decisions related to the level of debtors are likely to affect the volume of sales, the levels of stocks due to the change in the volume of sales and the levels of funding necessary to finance these changes in current assets. In addition such changes are likely to have implications for a firm's liquidity.

We begin this chapter by first examining in general terms why working capital is important and the need to manage working capital. This is followed by a look at the way in which the working capital cycle is computed and a consideration of the elements of this cycle in detail in assessing the opportunity to minimize investment whilst maintaining a sufficient level of investment to carry out day-to-day operations efficiently. At this stage we start to focus on working capital from the perspective of the tourism and hospitality industry. Reference is made to different companies in this sector. Finally, individual items of current assets relevant to the tourism and hospitality industry are then examined in respect of the control in which management should maintain. Particular emphasis is given to cash and other current assets which tend to dominate the balance sheets of a large proportion of companies the hospitality and tourism industry. A number of concepts and techniques which we will be drawing upon in this chapter have been examined before in earlier chapters, for example the economic concept of opportunity cost. In such cases reference will be made to the relevant chapter.

THE NEED TO MANAGE WORKING CAPITAL

Importance

The funding of working capital represents, for most businesses, a large commitment of finance. The investment into current assets does not, unlike fixed assets, appear to generate any direct future benefits which are easily measurable in monetary terms. However, the investment is necessary to be able to carry out day-to-day operating activities.

The cost of investing in working capital

The cost of investing in current assets is the opportunity cost. (The concept of opportunity cost is defined more fully later in Chapter 18.) In the context of working capital it is represented by the returns forgone by investing in current assets rather than some alternative investment opportunity. For example, the opportunity cost of having a large cash balance in a bank current account which pays no interest could be the interest that would have been received from investing this cash elsewhere, say in a short-term deposit account. There may, of course, be other better opportunities. When there are a number of alternative opportunities the opportunity cost is the alternative opportunity that renders the greatest return.

> ### *Key concept*
>
> *Opportunity cost – current assets*
>
> The returns forgone by investing into current assets rather than some alternative investment opportunity.

The cost of the investment in current assets is generally borne by those who supply short-term funds, for example trade creditors, and by the business itself. The investment contributed by the business is, of course, working capital. That is, the finance necessary to fund current assets over and above that sourced by short-term creditors.

Management of working capital

It is to the firm's advantage to keep this investment in working capital to a minimum but at the same time invest sufficiently into current assets to be able to carry out day-to-day trading activities efficiently. This balance between cost and the level of working capital sufficient to run the organization efficiently has to be carefully managed. If, for example, in a retailing business, stocks are kept at too low a level this may result in running out of goods which ultimately may culminate in losing custom. On the other hand, to invest too much in stocks will result in a high opportunity cost to the business due to having an unnecessary large amount of capital tied up in stocks.

Financing of working capital and types of business

It is important from a financing perspective that firms effectively manage their level of working capital. In particular, they need to ensure medium- and long-term funding sources are available, and need to make informed decisions between the different types of finance available, that is the choice between debt and equity finance and the various capital instruments within these types of finance. Sources of finance were examined in Chapter 8 and for further detail reference should be made to that chapter. Particular problems will inevitably occur when a business is subject to seasonal trading variations. In such circumstances, it is likely that the investment in current assets will reflect this seasonality and the funding will also have to mirror these trading variations. Businesses therefore need to plan and determine their working capital needs. These plans will normally be translated into annual budgets. In terms of the planning of working capital the cash budget discussed in Chapter 15 plays a significant part in the management of working capital.

Liquidity

In terms of liquidity the management of working capital is critical. Businesses must ensure there are enough liquid resources to meet any demands. For example, banks normally have the right to call in bank overdrafts at their discretion without notice. Businesses which have overdrafts ideally must ensure that they have enough liquid or near to liquid resources to call upon. In cases where there is negative working capital, which means that a proportion of short-term creditors are financing fixed assets, it may be the case that the firm is unable to obtain liquid funds quickly to pay off creditors thus creating a liquidity crisis. This is not to say that when a business has a negative working capital there is a strong possibility that it will result in insolvency or desperate funding problems. British Airways Plc accounts for the year ended 31 March 1991, for example, shows a negative working capital of £543 million. Primarily, the reason for this negative working capital is due to accruals and deferred income, in particular money paid in advance for airline tickets prior to passengers taking their journeys. This situation of receiving sales receipts before they have been earned is normal for airlines. In this case, although British Airways has a large negative working capital, it is unlikely that the company will experience any serious short-term liquidity problems as it is normal practice for firms in this business to have negative working capital. British

Airways are also, of course, a prestigious company and could presumably call upon alternative credit facilities.

External users

It is important that management are aware that external parties to the firm will also be monitoring the company's management of working capital and in particular aspects related to its liquidity. Management will therefore not only make decisions regarding working capital which they perceive are important for the effective operating of the firm itself but must also take account of external parties' perceptions of the firm's management of working capital. For example, when banks make a lending decision, they will normally closely examine an applicant's working capital and how well it is managed. Similarly, for quoted firms, analysts will closely examine the management of working capital. If analysts conclude that liquidity is weak and the management of working capital needs to be tighter this may result in the market 'marking' down the share price.

THE WORKING CAPITAL CYCLE

The working capital cycle – sometimes referred to as the 'cash cycle' or the 'operating cycle' – can be used to determine the time from any outlay in respect of an investment in current assets to the inflow of cash derived from this investment. The measure is usually in terms of days, that is the number of days it takes to transform current assets into cash, taking into account the number of days credit given by suppliers. In the hospitality and tourism industry, however, often the cycle is likely to be very short or negative. This is because firms in this industry tend to have relatively low levels of stock and are paid in cash rather than giving their customers credit. For example, the 1989 accounts of Friendly Hotels Plc show their stocks and debtors to total £3 162 000, whilst their trade creditors amounted to £3 458 000.

Key concept

The working capital cycle

The working capital cycle is the period of time from the investment into current assets to the inflow of cash derived from this investment.

Although the analysis of the working capital cycle may not be so useful or appropriate in all cases in the hospitality and tourism industry, it will be beneficial to illustrate how the cycle is determined so that we may get a better understanding of the nature of working capital and its

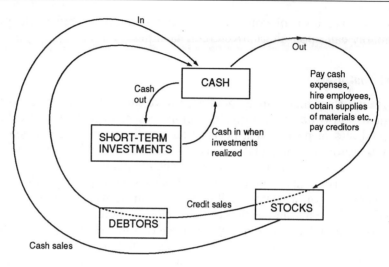

Figure 17.1 The working capital cycle.

elements. The simple diagram in Figure 17.1 illustrates the flows of cash within the working capital cycle.

The diagram shows that payments are continually made in respect of operating expenses and other costs which subsequently result in the inflow of cash through sales. The diagram also shows cash outflows and inflows in respect of short-term investments. Businesses will invariably use facilities available at their banks and other institutions to invest surplus cash balances. There are some liabilities that are only paid once or a few times each year, such as business taxation. In these circumstances, during the year cash reserves should ideally be prudently built up to pay such expenses. These reserves will often be deposited into some short-term investments until payment becomes due. The alternative is to leave such balances in an account that is not earning interest for the business! There are of course other payments which are not explicitly referred to in the diagram, such as the purchase of fixed assets and payments of VAT and the like. These payments must also be carefully managed.

By means of Example 17.1 we can show the necessary analysis to determine the working capital cycle.

EXAMPLE 17.1

Conference View Ltd

The following are figures extracted from the accounts of Conference View Ltd, a small company which owns one hotel that specializes in catering for small company conferences for the year ended 31.12.19X1. All customers are given credit payment terms.

	£
Stocks	19 200
Debtors	28 200
Creditors	12 000
Sales	146 000
Cost of goods sold	132 500

The working capital cycle in days can be calculated as follows:

1. **Stocks**   Days

   Turnover of stocks $\quad = \dfrac{\text{Stocks}}{\text{Cost of goods sold}} \times 365 \text{ days}$

   $\qquad\qquad\qquad = \dfrac{19\,200}{132\,500} \times 365 \text{ days} \qquad\qquad = \qquad 53$

2. Less: **Creditors**

   Credit taken $\qquad = \dfrac{\text{Creditors}}{\text{Cost of goods sold}} \times 365 \text{ days}$

   $\qquad\qquad\qquad = \dfrac{12\,200}{132\,500} \times 365 \text{ days} \qquad\qquad = \qquad \dfrac{33}{20}$

3. **Debtors**

   Credit given $\qquad - \dfrac{\text{Debtors}}{\text{Sales}} \times 365 \text{ days}$

   $\qquad\qquad\qquad = \dfrac{28\,000}{146\,000} \times 365 \text{ days} \qquad\qquad = \qquad \dfrac{70}{90}$

   (365 days represent the number of days in the year.)

Therefore the working capital cycle of 90 days is the approximate time-span from the purchasing of supplies and goods to receipts of cash from customers.

The individual calculations can be interpreted as follows:

1. Stock 53 days – the number of days stock of supplies held by the company.
2. Credit taken 33 days – the number of days it takes, on average, for the firm to pay suppliers, or alternatively it can be interpreted as the credit that has been 'taken' from the company's suppliers. Normally, this time period will be influenced by the contract conditions between the supplier and customer. Typically, 30 days (approximately a month) credit is given by suppliers to customers. This means that payment has to be made within this specified time period. These time periods are, however, often abused, but it is unlikely that in the majority of cases suppliers will take legal action to obtain the payment due to them. Normally, a series of reminders

and threats of legal action will be the first and normally the only step to securing payment. The number of days credit is conventionally deducted from the number of days stock in hand because it is the creditors who, it can be interpreted, are partially financing this investment into stock.

3. Debtors: credit given 70 days – the number of days the company is giving customers to pay. This period will also be influenced by the contract conditions between the company and customers.

The longer the cycle the greater the investment in working capital and vice versa. A reduction in the working capital cycle can also improve liquidity. For example, reducing the time given to customers to pay their debts, currently 70 days, will clearly reduce the cycle and thereby free the cash resources available for alternative profitable employment. However, the potential cost of reducing the credit period is that customers will go elsewhere and find suppliers who will offer relatively more attractive credit periods.

Other possible ways of decreasing the working capital cycle are:

- to increase the rate of turnover of stocks by reducing the level of stock held. Management must be careful, however, when employing such policies because of potential stockout costs which can be excessive, for example resulting in the loss of custom due to not satisfying in a timely fashion customer demand;
- to delay payments to creditors which effectively reduces the operating cycle by increasing the finance available to companies. The main problem here is the possible loss of goodwill from suppliers.

It should be apparent that whilst there are benefits to reducing levels of working capital there are clearly costs. The benefits and the costs have to be carefully balanced in deciding the level of individual current assets and creditors. A number of models have been developed that give companies a reasonable indication of optimum levels of working capital, some of which we will be examining later.

The use of the working capital cycle measure is a useful tool for management in the overall control and management of working capital. In particular, comparisons may be made historically, e.g. by comparing the current year with previous years, and by comparing the cycle with industry averages.

CASH MANAGEMENT

In the hospitality and tourism industry a significant proportion of services are cash sales in contrast to other sectors where sales tend to be through credit arrangements. For example, in the case of both restaurants and hotels the convention is that most customers pay by cash for services received. Credit is only offered in exceptional cases, though some companies will have accounts with hotels where credit terms are offered. Therefore, the efficient management of cash in this industry is very important. This involves making sure the business has enough cash – access to it – to meet bills and other expenditure, whilst ensuring any surplus cash is efficiently employed. The inherent nature of the tourist industry characterized by seasonality makes the management of cash relatively more problematic. In industries which are subject to seasonality the inflows of cash tend not to coincide with the way in which expenditure is spread over the year. Therefore at varying points in the year there will be large surpluses, and at other times large deficits, of cash in these industries.

The reasons for holding cash

John Maynard Keynes, the economist, in his most famous publication the *General Theory of Employment, Interest and Money*, published in 1936, identified three main reasons for businesses to hold cash. These are still relevant in today's context.

- **The transaction motive** – to be able to meet payments when they fall due. It should be remembered that often the inflows and outflows of cash in business operations tend not to synchronize which means that cash has to be carefully managed.
- **The precautionary motive** – cash should be kept by a business in order to meet any unexpected outgoings. The nature of business lends itself to uncertainties which may mean that expenditure cannot always be anticipated. The larger the near liquid assets which can be quickly transformed into cash, the less the amount of cash that needs to be held.
- **The speculative motive** – cash should be kept to take advantage of any unexpected beneficial investment opportunity.

The cost of holding cash

The benefits of holding cash have been identified. Inevitably, however, there is a cost to holding cash: the opportunity cost. This is the profit that is forgone by not employing the cash elsewhere, e.g. the return from investing the money in short-term investments or into less liquid assets, such as an extension to a hotel so that more rooms can be let.

The management of a business therefore has to balance the benefits of holding cash against the costs. Put in another way management has to balance the advantages of liquidity against the profitability of employing the cash in some investment opportunity.

Cash and cash equivalents

In general, the term 'cash' in this text is used in the context of receipts and payments for goods and services, and includes cash equivalents such as payments and receipts through credit cards and cheques. However, there is normally an additional opportunity cost when using cash equivalents. This cost relates to the time it takes to administratively recognize the payment or receipt. For example, for cheques paid or drawn outside the City of London area, a minimum of three working days is needed for clearance. The firm receiving the cheque has first to deposit it at its own bank. This bank will then present the cheque to the bank named on the cheque (i.e. the drawing bank). Only when the drawing bank transfers the funds to the bank at which the cheque was deposited does the firm which received the cheque technically benefit from the receipt of funds. This delay in recognizing cheques into an account creates the opportunity cost, as the cash could alternatively be employed profitably elsewhere during this delay. The following simple example illustrates the calculation of the opportunity cost in such circumstances.

EXAMPLE 17.2

Suppose a customer pays £10 000 by cheque and the cheque takes five days to clear. If bank interest payable on a bank deposit account is 10% p.a., the opportunity cost of accepting a cheque rather than cash is:

$$£10\,000 \times 5/365 \times 10\% = £13.70$$

The opportunity cost of accepting a cheque for £10 000, in this example, rather than cash is £13.70, assuming that the next best alternative is to deposit the £10 000 in a bank deposit account. There are also other direct costs that may be charged at varying rates for banking cheques and credit card transactions.

There are inevitably benefits in accepting or paying with cheques and other forms of 'cash equivalents' as compared to cash. Probably the most important benefit is security. Security, in terms of cash management, is an important issue and should therefore be an important consideration in deciding on the means of payment that is acceptable.

The frequency of banking cash – the decision

A problem for a number of businesses – and those particularly in the hospitality and tourism industry – is how often they should bank cash receipts. By means of Example 17.3 below this problem is examined and a solution is offered.

EXAMPLE 17.3

Rupert Greene owns a chain of coffee houses in the London area which are open during the day, Mondays to Saturdays, 52 weeks a year.

Takings are currently banked once a week on Friday mornings. As Rupert's business has expanded he has been incurring what he considers to be high bank overdraft charges at a rate of 11%. He has been advised by a consultant that he should bank his receipts daily, except on Saturdays. Saturday's takings could be banked on Mondays. It is anticipated that total turnover will amount to £1.95 million next year. It is estimated that the bank will charge £12 for each banking receipt.

To evaluate these two alternatives we need to examine the costs and benefits of each alternative and then to choose the alternative that minimizes costs (assuming this is the objective). We will examine the problem in stages.

1. Calculation of the overdraft rate per day: if the annual rate is 11%:

$$11/365 \text{ days} = 0.03\% \text{ per day}$$

2. Daily takings (assuming takings are evenly distributed over the working week), if annual takings are £1 950 000, amount to:

$$£1\,950\,000/312 \text{ days} = £6250 \text{ per day}$$

(NB. The number of working days in the year = 312 days (52 weeks × 6 days).)

3. The cost of holding the daily takings, £6250, for one day instead of banking it would be:

$$£6250 \times 0.03\% = £1.875 \text{ per day}$$

4. The number of days' delay incurred by only banking one day per week (Thursday evening):

Takings on	Days that receipts could be banked	Number of days' delay incurred by Friday banking
Monday	Tuesday	3
Tuesday	Wednesday	2
Wednesday	Thursday	1
Thursday	Friday	0
Friday	Monday	4
Saturday	Monday	4
		14

(It is assumed that the takings on each day could be banked at the start of the next day with the exception of Friday's and Saturday's takings which as previously mentioned will be banked on Monday morning.)

In one week, the total number of days' delay incurred by Friday banking is therefore 14. At a cost of £1.875 per day, the weekly cost of Friday banking is £26.25 (£1.875 × 14), and it follows that the annual cost of Friday only banking is £1365 (£26.25 × 52). Therefore in terms of bank overdraft charges Rupert could have saved £1365 per year, assuming that the overdraft rate remains at 11% and turnover remains constant.

5. The total incremental cost of banking on a daily basis:

£12 per visit × Additional visits.

Additional number of visits per week = 5 less 1 visit previously = 4; therefore annually the additional visits are 208 (4 × 52).

£12 × 208 visits = £2496.

6. The costs and benefits of banking daily:

	£
Benefits – less bank charges	1 365
Costs – incremental cost of visits	2 496
Loss	(1 131)

Therefore, of the two alternatives available, it is less costly to bank once a week rather than daily. This example has been used to illustrate the type of decisions related to the management of cash and some of the costs and benefits that should be accounted for in such circumstances. However, in practice, all possible options should be identified and examined, for example the effect on costs if the firm were to bank twice a week, as well as other potential additional costs such as additional insurance costs for holding varying amounts of cash.

In these types of decisions it is often the case that some costs and benefits are difficult to identify and measure. In the above case study it is likely that the incremental costs of visiting the bank would be difficult to measure. The process of banking includes the employee's time in going and returning from the bank as well as the time taken to prepare the documentation, that is counting the various denominations of currency and filling in banking forms as well as the firm's own records. It is likely that much of this process cannot be precisely measured. In practice a pragmatic approach will invariably be taken, such as only including costs that are judged to be significant, and estimating the costs based on judgement and experience.

CASH BUDGET AND CASH LEVELS

A major question to be resolved by those businesses which permanently or for long periods of time hold cash balances is: how much cash should be held in purely liquid form and how much should be invested into short-term securities? If a business has too little cash, as previously explained, it may experience liquidity difficulties; on the other hand, if a business holds too much cash it is missing opportunities to earn profits. The problem is to balance these factors.

An associated decision in deciding to invest into short-term securities is: what should the balance be between securities with different maturity dates? Normally, the longer the time it takes to mature, the greater the return.

In the hospitality and tourism industry, as previously mentioned, the majority of businesses will have substantial cash balances permanently or for relatively long periods of time. For example, Hogg Robinson, in their 1992 accounts show 'cash at bank and deposits' at £67 million (total fixed assets were only £26 million!); The Savoy Hotel in their 1991 accounts showed cash balances of £1.5 million (total fixed assets £96 million). It is therefore important for these types of businesses to spend time trying to get their cash balances at the right levels to maximize profitability whilst at the same time being sufficiently liquid.

The key to getting the balance right between profitability and liquidity is planning. Planning and cash budgets were discussed in detail in Chapter 15. Through the cash budget, businesses can identify surplus funds, the size of the funds, and when and how long they will be available. From this information informed decisions can be made whether to invest these balances in short-term securities and for how long.

Unfortunately there are no precise tools available to help in deciding the desirable level of cash at any point in time. However, one ratio that has not been discussed before might usefully assist management in this decision. This ratio is the ratio of cash balances to the level of current assets:

$$\text{Proportion of cash held} = \frac{\text{Cash balances}}{\text{Current assets}}$$

The ratio gives a rough guide to the level of cash balances a firm should hold. The use of the ratio requires judgement on the part of management in deciding what is a desirable proportion of cash held to current assets. This judgement will be influenced by past experience as well as looking to future cash commitments indicated in the cash budget. The ratio may be used historically, that is in comparison with past ratios and in comparison with industry averages.

TRADE CREDIT

The nature of trade credit

Trade credit is one of the most important sources of short-term finance and is characterized by one company extending credit to another on the purchase of goods and services. In the hospitality and tourism industry this source of finance is particularly significant. For example, The Savoy Hotel Plc accounts for 1991 show trade creditors at £13.8 million (total current assets £18.3 m); Trusthouse Forte 1991 accounts show trade creditors at £295 million (total current assets £465 million). The advantage in employing trade creditors as a source of finance is that it is free, that is there are no explicit costs. This is not the case with any other sources of finance.

Although there are no direct costs associated with employing trade creditors as a source of funding, the level must be carefully managed. The balance between short-term creditors and liquid assets or near liquid assets such as short-term investments is critical to any business. Liquidity problems for a business could result in not having enough cash to pay creditors when debts fall due. Creditors are likely to respond initially in these circumstances by not supplying the company with any future credit purchases. Ultimately non-payment could result in creditors applying for a court order to wind up the business. The management must therefore carefully monitor the level of creditors.

Interested parties from outside the business will also often be concerned about the balance of trade creditors and liquid resources and use this information in judging the business for their own purposes. For example, a bank, in making lending decisions, will closely examine a business's liquidity in terms of the business's ability to remain trading for the foreseeable future and to examine the clients capability to repay the loan and interest.

Measuring the level of trade credit

The main measure used in determining the level of trade creditors at any point in time is the creditors turnover ratio which was calculated earlier in the working capital cycle computation. The ratio computes the time taken by the business to pay suppliers (measured in days).

Key concept

Creditors turnover ratio

$$\frac{\text{Trade creditors}}{\text{Cost of goods sold}} \times 365 \text{ days}$$

Ideally, the denominator in this ratio should only include costs for goods and services bought on credit. If other unrelated costs are included this may distort the ratio. For internal management purposes, information relating to supplies purchased on credit is likely to be available and accessible. For external parties this will not always be the case. In such cases surrogate information may be used. For example, the Cost of goods/Services sold shown in the annual published accounts may not exclusively relate to supplies/services purchased using credit. Other costs may be included such as wages and salaries. In these circumstances judgement must be employed in deciding how appropriate it is to use the ratio. This will primarily depend upon the proportion of supplies/services purchased on credit in relation to the total cost. If this proportion is significant the use of the ratio in establishing historical trends may be useful if carefully employed.

In terms of management's control and monitoring of liquidity the creditors turnover ratio can be usefully employed with other liquidity ratios such as the quick ratio and the current ratio. It is important, however, to recognize that the information derived from these ratios should be used historically and comparatively in terms of industry averages. From this analysis trends may be established which will help management make informed decisions.

Cash discounts

Cash discounts are given by suppliers to encourage early payment by customers within the contractual period specified. For example, the terms of payment may be 30 days credit on receipt of services rendered; a cash discount of 1% of the invoiced price is offered if the debt is paid within 10 days. The benefit of accepting the cash discount must be balanced by the cost of not having the credit available from the supplier over the normal credit period. If the cash discount is offered and is not taken there is a benefit foregone (an opportunity cost).

EXAMPLE 17.4

The following details relate to a debt of £1000 incurred by SMJQ Ltd. The terms of trade are 2% cash discount if the invoice is paid within 10 days, the normal terms of payment being within 30 days. Assume the company currently has a bank overdraft on which interest is payable at 14% per annum. Should SMJQ Ltd accept or reject the offer of a cash discount?

1. Cost if the cash discount is accepted:

$$£980 \ (£1000 - 2\% \ \text{discount}).$$

Therefore, this option would save £20.

2. Cost if cash discount is rejected:

Payment of £1000 will be made to the supplier on the thirtieth day. However, the company would have a period of 20 days extra (30 days – 10 days) to employ the money; in this case the overdraft we can assume will be reduced by this amount for 20 days. This would save the company:

$$£980 \times 20/365 \times 14\% \ = \ £7.51$$

Therefore, by rejecting the discount the net affect of paying the supplier £1000 in 30 days and employing this money to reduce the overdraft, saving £7.51, will be £1000 – £7.51 = £992.49.

The company will, on the basis of this information, accept the cash discount because there are greater savings (£20 – £7.51 = £12.49).

TRADE DEBTORS

The efficient management of debtors is concerned with the problem of achieving an optimum level of investment in this current asset. Although it was previously mentioned that some types of businesses in the hospitality and tourism industry will mainly receive payment by cash, there are many businesses in this industry sector where it is the convention to give credit in respect of the sales of goods and services. For example, Hogg Robinson Plc showed a balance of £56.3 million in respect of debtors outstanding at their year ended 31 March 1992 (out of total current assets of £123.6 million).

The optimum level of debtors

In deciding a policy for determining the optimum level of debtors the following should be taken into consideration.

- The trade-off between:
  - extending credit so as to increase the volume of sales and profits; and
  - the opportunity cost and administrative costs of carrying increased debtors, as well as the potential increase in bad debts.
- The level of risk a business is prepared to extend to individual customers wishing to purchase goods/services on credit. This risk can be identified through an analysis of individual customers.
- The investment in debt collection management.

Debt collection policies

The overall debt collection policy of a firm should be set where the margin between the administrative costs and other costs incurred in debt collection and the benefits received from incurring these costs is at its greatest. The benefits will be the profits generated from the sales of goods and services.

It is common to find that extra spending on debt collection management will reduce bad debts and reduce the average collection period. This in turn will reduce the cost of the investment in debtors (that is, the opportunity cost of this investment). However, beyond a certain level of expenditure on debt collection management would not reduce losses or the average collection period to sufficiently justify the extra administrative cost.

Credit control – individual accounts

An important aspect of the management of trade debtors is the initial investigation of potential credit customers and the continuing control of outstanding accounts. The main points to consider in these two processes are as follows.

- References from, for example, banks regarding a potential customer's financial standing.
- Checking customers' credit rating with agencies such as Dun and Bradstreet.
- Initially adopting a conservative policy. This may include the amount of credit allowed in money terms and the period allowed for payment. If the customer consistently pays on time and generally behaves reasonably the firm may then decide to increase the level of credit.
- The annual accounts of customers, if available, may be a useful source of information to assess a customer's creditworthiness.
- Aged debtors lists should be produced periodically, detailing outstanding debts by customer, and the time these debts have been outstanding. The list should be regularly monitored and action if necessary taken in respect of breaches of the credit allowed individual customers.
- Press comments should be checked, in particular information relating to the creditworthiness of current and potential future customers.

Total credit

An important decision that management of businesses must make is the level of total credit to be maintained and whether this level should be extended. In determining whether it is profitable to extend credit, the following should be taken into consideration:

- the extra sales that a more generous credit policy would stimulate;
- the profitability of extra sales;
- the extra length of the average debt collection period;
- the required rate of return (opportunity cost) on the investment in additional debtors;
- the increase in bad debts that would normally result from an increase in the volume of sales which would follow the introduction of a more generous credit policy;
- additional administration costs in managing additional credit sales.

The average debt collection period can be measured by the debtors turnover ratio.

By means of Example 17.5 we may examine a typical decision regarding the extension of credit.

EXAMPLE 17.5

The Jarvo Company

The Jarvo Company is considering whether to adopt a more liberal credit policy as a means of increasing sales above the present monthly level of £40 000. The current average collection period is one month with no bad debts. If the credit period is lengthened, however, it is anticipated that sales will increase and some bad debts will be incurred. The following details two options:

Increase in credit period	Increase in sales above £40 000 per month	% bad debts
$\frac{1}{2}$ month	£2 000	1
1 month	£3 200	2

The price of the only product manufactured is only £1 per unit with variable cost of £0.60, which is anticipated to remain constant as production increases. Fixed costs are estimated to be £98 000 per annum.

No increase in stocks is required, even though sales increase. All investment in debtors will be financed from retained earnings; taxes can be ignored.

Total investment in net assets, excluding debtors, is fixed at £1 400 000 for all the options.

The analysis below shows the policy that will maximize reported profits:

	Current policy (1 month) £	Increase in credit period by ½ month (to 1½ months) £	Increase in credit period by 1 month (to 2 months) £
Sales per month	40 000	42 000	43 200
Sales p.a.[1]	480 000	504 000	518 400
Variable costs[2]	288 000	302 400	311 040
Contribution	192 000	201 600	207 360
Bad debts[3]	—	5 040	10 368
Net contribution	192 000	196 560	196 992
Fixed costs	96 000	96 000	96 000
Profit	96 000	100 560	100 992

Notes
1. Sales p.a. = Sales per month × 12 months.
2. Variable costs per annum = Sales p.a. × £0.60.
3. Bad debts = Sales × % of bad debts, representing what is forgone by Jarvo if debtors become bad.

The above analysis shows that the most profitable option in terms of reported profits is to increase the credit period by one month to two months – a profit of £100 992. This solution, however, ignores the additional investment required in debtors, that is the opportunity cost.

The following examines the above results in relation to the increased investment in debtors for the options and assumes that the company's return on investments (their opportunity cost) is 20%. The criteria will then be to select the option that has the highest profit after charging the opportunity cost of using to invest in debtors.

	Current policy (1 month) £	Increase in credit period by ½ month (to 1½ months) £	Increase in credit period by 1 month (to 2 months) £
Debtors[1]	40 000	63 000	86 200
Reported profits (as above)	96 000	100 560	100 992
Less: Opportunity cost (20% × Debtors)	8 000	12 600	17 280
Net profit	88 000	87 960	83 712

Note
1. Debtors = Sales per month × the number of months credit, e.g. 2 months credit = £43 200 × 2 months = £86 400.

If the opportunity cost of the investment in debtors is taken into account the preferred option is increasing the credit period allowed to $1\frac{1}{2}$ months.

STOCKS

Stocks in the hospitality and tourism industry generally are less important in the context of management control than is the case with the majority of other industrial sectors. Primarily, this is for two reasons. First, stocks in value terms are often insignificant or do not exist; for example, in the tourism industry Hogg Robinson in their 1992 accounts show no stocks in their balance sheet. Secondly, the turnover of stock in this industrial sector tends to be quick. That is, stocks will not be held for a long period of time; for example, restaurants will hold stocks of food but the nature of food means that it will be resold normally within a very short period.

It is important that customers are always satisfied and in the case of the purchase of goods and services it is imperative that these are always readily available to the customer. If they are not available it could lead to customers going elsewhere and subsequently they may not return to this source of purchase. For example, a connoisseur of real ale may go to a hostelry for one of the particular brands of ale it sells. If the hostelry is out of stock of this ale the connoisseur may go elsewhere and perhaps never return! A similar case can be made for restaurants where the availability of food is an important feature in satisfying customers. The loss of custom in these circumstances is often referred to as a stockout cost. It might therefore seem beneficial if at all times large stocks of goods are available for sale. There are, however, costs to holding stocks. The main costs associated to maintaining stocks are summarized as follows:

- the cost of goods perishing;
- deterioration in the goods;
- the cost of pilfering and the associated costs of preventing pilfering;
- the opportunity cost of the investment;
- obsolescence;
- warehousing/space costs;
- administrative costs of ordering.

The main problem of stock control is to find the optimum stock level where there is a balance between the benefits of holding stocks and the associated costs of holding the stock. This involves focusing on the frequency of replenishing stock, the size of each replenishment and the stockout consequences. Traditionally the model employed to determine this optimum level of stocks and other related decisions is the economic batch quantity (EBQ) model. Details of this model and others can be found in Samuels *et al.* (1990).

Another way of measuring how well or badly a business is managing its stock is to compare the business with the industry average. The assumption underlying this comparison is that the industry average reflects a level of holding stock that is appropriate for that industry. This is of course not necessarily the case. Although this measure may be crude if used cautiously it is useful as a benchmark. The average measures published for the industry is in terms of stock turnover. For the hotel industry the average was 15 days in comparison with some individual hotel businesses such as The Savoy whose stock turnover is six days and Friendly Hotels whose turnover is five days. This information can be the basis of investigating the reasons why these two hotel businesses hold less stock than the industry average.

SUMMARY

In this chapter we have considered the need for working capital and methods for optimizing the individual levels of current assets that are likely to be confronted by firms in the tourism and hospitality industry. In particular the concept of opportunity cost was introduced as a cost of maintaining current assets.

Cash was highlighted as a particular item within the tourism and hospitality industry that needs to be managed with care. The planning of cash requirements is critical in the management of this current asset. However, cash budgets were not illustrated in this chapter as they were shown in Chapter 15.

The management of trade creditors and debtors was examined. Some measures, in terms of ratios, were introduced to aid management control of these elements of working capital. Finally, the cost and benefits of holding stock was considered.

REFERENCES

Samuels, J., Wilkes, F.M. and Brayshaw, R.E. (1990) *Management of Company Finance*, 5th edn, Chapman & Hall, London.
This text provides a detailed analysis of the management of working capital from a general perspective.

REVIEW QUESTIONS

1. What are the main costs and benefits associated with holding stocks?
2. What does the working capital cycle measure?
3. List the reasons why it is important to manage the level of working capital.
4. What are the motives for holding cash?

5. What are the variables to be considered when considering the frequency of banking cash?
6. What are the hidden costs to late payment?
7. What are the main considerations in deciding whether to extend the credit period given to customers?

PROBLEMS FOR DISCUSSION AND ANALYSIS

1. Eatsomuch Ltd is a small chain of restaurants in South East England. It is estimated that their sales receipts for the next year will be £14 million. These receipts will be spread evenly over the following 50 working week year. The restaurant is open only five days per week: Tuesday, Wednesday, Thursday, Friday and Saturday. The pattern of receipts within each week is that the daily rate of receipts on Friday and Saturday is twice that experienced on Tuesday, Wednesday and Thursday.

   Receipts for the whole week are normally banked on Saturdays of each week but this practice is being reconsidered. It is suggested that banking should be carried out either daily or twice weekly, on Wednesday and Saturday. The incremental cost to Eatsomuch Ltd of each banking is £50. Eatsomuch Ltd always operates on a bank overdraft and the current overdraft rate for the company is 14%. This interest charge is applied on a simple daily basis.

2. Margin Plc requires advice on its debt collection policy. The current policy and two alternative options are detailed below:

	Current policy	Option 1	Option 2
Cost of debt collection p.a.	£240 000	£300 000	£400 000
Bad debts (% of sales)	3%	2%	1%
Average collection period	2 months	1.5 months	1 month

   Current sales are £4.8 million per year, and the company requires 15% return on its investments.

   Should the company discard the current policy in favour of Option 1 or 2?

3. A study of debtors of the PHJ Company Ltd has shown that it is possible to classify all debtors into certain categories with the following characteristics:

	Average collection period (days)	Bad debts %
A	15	0.5
B	20	2.5
C	30	5.0
D	40	9.5

The average profit/cost schedule for the company's range of products is as follows:

	£	£
Selling price		2.50
Less:	£	
Materials	1.00	
Wages	0.95	
Variable overheads		
Fixed overheads	0.05	2.30
Profit		0.20

The company has the opportunity of extending its sales by £1 000 000 split between categories C and D in the proportions 40:60. The company maintains an overdraft with the bank. The current rate of interest on the overdraft account is 11%.

Discuss the factors to be considered in the formulation of a policy for credit control management, and use the above data in your discussion.

Accounting for short-term decisions 18

INTRODUCTION

Within the framework of the planning process management will need to make decisions regarding future business opportunities to ensure that the organization objectives are met. A large proportion of these decisions will be of a short-term nature and will be expressed in financial terms in the organization's budget. Management will also be required to make decisions of a more immediate nature, which relate to opportunities that were not anticipated at the planning stage. To ignore profitable opportunities because they have not been specifically included in the budget would clearly be irresponsible in a dynamic business environment.

In this chapter we are restricting the analysis to decisions where there are no resource constraints. In these circumstances organizations will be free to make decisions knowing that the decision will not affect other opportunities, for example the decision to introduce a new product where the decision will not affect in any way the demand for and the ability to service other opportunities. These decisions can also be simply described as 'accept or reject' decisions. It is worth remembering that the main principles examined in this chapter are applicable also to where constraints exist.

We will also be considering in this chapter the effect that qualitative factors may play in decision-making.

The reference to the short term will be interpreted to mean decisions that will affect the firm within a period of a year, which is the convention. It will be assumed that the values of cash inflows and outflows throughout the year will be of an equivalent value. This tends to be a little naive in that clearly all individuals and firms will prefer to receive, for example, cash today rather than in 11 months' time. For reasons of clarity, however, it is convenient in our analysis to make this assumption as complexities arise when we begin to take account of the time value of money in the decision-making process. This is of course more important when considering long-term decisions which are examined in Chapter 19.

RELEVANT COSTS AND BENEFITS

Decisions relate to the future and the function of decision-making is to select courses of action for the future that satisfy the objectives of the firm. There is no opportunity to alter the past, although past experience may help us in future decisions; for example the observation of past cost behaviour may help to determine future levels of cost.

Relevant costs and benefits can therefore be defined, in general terms, as those costs and benefits that will result from making a specific future decision. A more precise definition will be established after we have examined the underlying principles of relevant costs and benefits and considered some examples illustrating the application of these principles.

The relevant costs for decision-making are different from those used in accruals accounting. This is not surprising as the principles of traditional costing (e.g. overhead absorption methods), within the framework of accruals accounting, evolved from the need to report historical events rather than determining future costs and benefits. A number of the methods adopted by accountants to account for future decisions have derived from economic theory and therefore may be familiar to you.

We will now proceed to consider the principles underlying relevant costs for decision-making and the application of these principles to specific types of decisions. The differences between the application of relevant costs and traditional costing will also be discussed in this analysis.

FUTURE AND PAST (SUNK) COSTS

Costs of a historical nature, which are normally referred to as sunk costs, are incurred as a result of past decisions and are therefore irrelevant to future decisions and should be ignored.

Key concept

Sunk costs

Sunk costs or past costs can easily be identified in that they will have been paid for or they are owed under legally binding contracts and therefore the firm is committed to paying for them in the future.

By means of Example 18.1 we may illustrate the irrelevance of sunk costs and identify the relevant future costs.

EXAMPLE 18.1

Wimbledon World of Adventures Ltd

Wimbledon World of Adventures Ltd has an obsolete 'ride' that was purchased and paid for two years ago and has been superseded by a newly acquired ride. The net book value of the old ride, as shown in the accounts of Wimbledon World of Adventures Ltd, prior to it becoming obsolete is £72 000. The alternatives now available to the company are:

- to make a number of alterations to the ride at a estimated cost of £20 000 and then sell it for £40 000, or
- to sell it for scrap, the estimated selling price being £15 000.

The net book value of £72 000 represents the original cost of purchasing the ride less the accummulated depreciation relating to the charge for depreciation over the two-year period. The original cost is the result of a past decision and was incurred two years ago and therefore it is a sunk cost and irrelevant to the future decision whether to alter the ride and sell it or to sell it for scrap. The depreciation is also based on the original cost of the ride and is thus irrelevant to this future decision. The only relevant costs and benefits are those related to the future; we can analyse these as follows:

	Alter £	Scrap £
Future benefits	40 000	15 000
Future costs	20 000	
Future income	20 000	15 000

From the analysis of relevant costs and benefits it can be seen that the company will be £5000 better off altering the ride and selling it rather than selling it for scrap.

We can therefore conclude, from this analysis of Example 18.1 that costs which are historic by nature, which are referred to as sunk costs, have no effect on future decisions and therefore are irrelevant and should be ignored in such decisions. In this study, the only relevant costs and benefits were those that relate to the future and are incurred as a result of the decision.

DIFFERENTIAL (INCREMENTAL) COSTS

Another important principle in the determination of relevant costs and benefits is that only differential (incremental) costs and benefits are relevant to future decisions.

> *Key concept*
>
> *Differential costs defined*
>
> Differential (incremental) costs are the differences in costs and benefits between alternative opportunities available to the organization. It follows that when a number of opportunities are being considered costs and benefits that are common to these alternative opportunities will be irrelevant to the decision.

The application of this principle underlying differential costing will be illustrated by considering Example 18.2 concerning an opportunity for a hotel which has spare capacity to accept a 'special order'.

EXAMPLE 18.2

Haslemere Hotel

John and Jackie Parmiter own and manage the Haslemere Hotel. The hotel's capacity is 12 000 rooms per year. However, they anticipate only 9000 rooms will be taken up during the forthcoming year. A travel agency offers to take 2000 of the rooms for the year at an average price of £25 per room. The acceptance of this 'special order' will not affect regular bookings. John and Jackie are reluctant to accept the offer because £25 is below the average unit cost per room of £30 and well below the 'normal' price of £40 per room.

The following details show the predicted income in total and per unit, in a traditional costing format, if the order were not accepted.

		Total £		Per unit £
Sales (9000 rooms)		360 000		40
Less:	£		£	
Variable costs	180 000		20	
Fixed costs	90 000	270 000	10	30
Net profit		90 000		10

Jackie and John review these costings and come to the conclusion that the variable costs will be incurred if the 'special order' is accepted at the same rate per unit. However, it is anticipated that the fixed costs of £90 000 which relate to the general running expenses of the hotel will remain the same in total.

Using the differential costing approach we can compare the total income for the year if the offer is accepted or rejected:

	Accept £	Reject £	Differential costs and revenue £
Sales	410 000	360 000	50 000
Less costs:			
Variable costs	220 000	180 000	40 000
Fixed costs	90 000	90 000	–
Net profit	100 000	90 000	10 000

Notes: Accept 'sales' = 9000 rooms at £40 each (£360 000) plus 2000 rooms at £25 (£50 000); total £360 000.

From the differential analysis it can be seen that Jackie and John will be £10 000 better off if the special order is accepted. Also it can be observed that the fixed costs in this case study are irrelevant in the decision analysis. That is, they are the same whether or not the order is accepted. Therefore, the analysis of data could have been simplified by only considering the differential costs and revenues related to the special order. If the differential analysis of costs and revenues results in a profit, from a purely quantitative perspective the order should be accepted.

Through the comparison of the costs and benefits associated with the opportunities available to the firm we are able to identify differential costs and benefits. It is these costs and benefits that are relevant to decisions between competing opportunities.

AVOIDABLE AND UNAVOIDABLE COSTS

An alternative way of determining whether a cost is relevant or irrelevant in decisions (such as the accept/reject decision of a special order illustrated above) instead of using differential analysis is by asking the question: Will a cost be avoided if the company did not proceed with the special order? If the answer is positive the cost is relevant and should be included. For example, consider this question with regard to the variable costs for the special order above: Will the cost be avoided if the company does not proceed with the order? The answer is yes: the cost is relevant to the decision as it will only be incurred if the order is accepted. Alternatively, a cost is described as unavoidable if the cost will be incurred whether or not the decision is to accept or reject, i.e. the cost is irrelevant to the decision.

OPPORTUNITY COST

> ### Key concept
> *Opportunity cost*
>
> The opportunity cost of a resource is normally defined as the maximum benefit which could be obtained from that resource if it were used for some alternative purpose. If a firm uses a resource for alternative A rather than B, it is the potential benefits that are forgone by not using the resource for alternative B that constitute the opportunity cost. Therefore, the potential forgone benefits, the opportunity cost, are relevant costs in the decision to accept alternative A.

The economist's concept of opportunity cost has been adopted by accountants for decision-making purposes. This concept relates to the cost of using resources for alternative opportunities and is illustrated in Example 18.3.

EXAMPLE 18.3

The management of a hotel is currently considering opening a kiosk within the hotel selling confectionery. The kiosk would be managed by the hotel. It is anticipated that the kiosk would earn £6500 net profit a year. A local firm has also offered to take over the concession and run the kiosk and pay the hotel £4500. This £4500 is the opportunity cost to the management of opening and running the kiosk. That is, the hotel will be £2000 (£6500 – 4500) better off by running the kiosk themselves. The £4500 can also be described as what the firm forgoes by operating the kiosk themselves.

REPLACEMENT COSTS

In cases where a resource was originally purchased for some purpose other than an opportunity currently under consideration, the relevant cost of using that resource is its replacement cost. This cost has come about as a direct result of the decision to use the resource for a purpose not originally intended and the need to replace the resource. Example 18.4 will help you to understand the application of this principle.

EXAMPLE 18.4

Hick Bats Ltd has been approached by a customer who would like a special job done. The job would require the use of 500 kilograms of

Material A. Material A is used by Hicks Bats for a variety of purposes. Currently the company holds 1000 kilograms in stock which was purchased one month ago for £6 per kilogram. Since then the price per kilogram has increased to £8. If 500 kilograms were used on this special job it would need to be replaced to meet the production demand from other jobs.

The relevant cost of using Material A on this special job is the replacement cost (500 kilograms × £8) £4000. This is because the material will need to be replaced and as result of its use the replacement will cost £4000. That is, the cost of £4000 will have arisen as a direct result of accepting the special order and therefore is relevant to the decision. It should be noted that the original cost of £6 per kilogram is irrelevant to the decision as it relates to a past decision and has already been incurred (i.e. is a sunk cost).

THE MEANING OF RELEVANCE

Earlier in this chapter relevant costs and benefits were defined, in general terms, as those costs and benefits that will result from a specific decision. We are now in the position to derive a more precise definition.

Key concept

Relevant costs and benefits

Relevant costs and benefits are those that relate to the future, and are additional costs and revenues that will be incurred or result from a decision. Costs that are relevant to a decision may also be:

- the cost of replacing a resource used for an opportunity that was originally purchased for some other purpose;
- the opportunity cost of using a resource that could be used for some alternative purpose.

There are also costs and revenues that are incurred or generated by an organization that will not be relevant to a decision, that is cost and revenues that will not be affected by a decision. It is also important to be able to identify these costs and benefits so that we may eliminate them from our analysis.

FIXED AND VARIABLE COSTS AND THE CONTRIBUTION APPROACH TO DECISION-MAKING

The concept of contribution was introduced in Chapter 13 on cost volume/profit analysis. The contribution is the difference between sales revenue and variable costs. We reintroduce the concept here in the context of relevant costs and decision-making.

It is normally assumed that costs will behave in a linear fashion. That is, fixed costs are constant over all volumes and variable costs will vary in direct proportion to volume.

Therefore in a number of situations in decision-making fixed costs will be irrelevant to decisions as they will remain the same whether or not the decision is accepted or rejected, i.e. they are unavoidable. Therefore, when there are no scarce resources in the making of a decision and the sales revenue exceeds the relevant variable costs an accept decision will be made. This decision rule is applicable to a number of the types of decisions.

A word of caution: there will be some situations in considering future opportunities when costs will not necessarily behave in a linear fashion, so that variations in unit variable costs or in fixed cost levels might occur. For example, the cost of new equipment specifically purchased for a future contract would be classified as a fixed cost, but it is a relevant cost to the contract as it is avoidable. When fixed costs are directly attributable to opportunities they will be relevant to the accept/reject decision. However, unless you are given a clear indication to the contrary, you should always assume that costs do behave in a linear fashion. It should be noted that this assumption was also adopted in Chapter 13 on cost/volume/profit analysis.

The contribution approach can be applied to a number of types of decisions that management must take in the course of efficiently running a business. The following sections illustrate the concept.

The range of products offered

The management of an organization will be confronted with a number of opportunities each year and will have to decide which opportunities should be embodied within their plans. In Example 18.5 below the products are assumed to be independent of each other.

EXAMPLE 18.5

Wimbledon World of Adventures Ltd

Wimbledon World of Adventures Ltd has three specialist catering products which are sold in separate facilities at different parts of the leisure complex:

- A – Ice Cream Parlour;
- B – Burger Bar;
- C – Self-Catering Restaurant.

The following is a draft summary of the profit and losses of these products for the forthcoming year:

	Total £	A £	B £	C £
Sales revenue	200 000	30 000	20 000	150 000
Variable costs	136 000	21 400	13 200	101 400
Fixed costs	44 000	3 400	7 400	33 200
Total costs	180 000	24 800	20 600	134 600
Profit/loss	20 000	5 200	(600)	15 400

The fixed costs of £44 000 represent overhead costs which have been apportioned to the products and will remain the same whether or not all or some of the products are sold during the year.

Due to the loss shown by the Burger Bar (Product B) the management propose to eliminate the facility from its range.

The firm would be making a profit of £20 000 if all three products were sold. However, if only A and C were sold, as the management suggest, the profit would be reduced to:

	Total £	A £	C £
Sales	180 000	30 000	150 000
Variable costs	122 800	21 400	101 400
Contribution	57 200	8 600	48 600
Fixed costs	44 000		
Profit	13 200		

This reduction in profit is because Product B makes a contribution of £6 800 (£20 000 – £13 200) and the fixed costs remain the same at £44 000 whether or not A, B or C are sold.

From this example we can derive a simple rule: if a product makes a positive contribution it is worthy of consideration for acceptance within the firm's programme. The fixed costs, in this example, have been apportioned to products. Normally, these fixed costs will be unavoidable and thus not relevant as in the example above. Overhead costs will only be relevant if they are incremental in nature.

Closing an unprofitable department/division

Organizations, in a dynamic business environment, will inevitably need at times to appraise the economic viability of their departments and divisions. Although the decision whether or not to close or keep open a department/division is a very different decision to those involving the determination of the range of products to be sold described above, the same underlying principles of relevance should be adopted.

Invariably, in practice, there are a number of costs that are allocated to departments which are outside their control and relate to overheads that are incurred by the firm as a whole. A typical example is head office expenses, which relate to the administrative costs of running the business. These types of costs are irrelevant as they are unavoidable.

The rule to be applied in such decisions is if a department makes a positive contribution, i.e. revenue exceeds variable costs, the department should remain open, and vice versa. However, when there are fixed costs that are directly attributable to a department, and therefore are avoidable, the rule can be amended and expressed as: if the revenue generated by a department exceeds the costs directly attributable to that the department, it should remain open, and vice versa.

EXAMPLE 18.6

The following are the costs and revenues of three departments, summarized in a traditional costing format:

Department:	A	B	C	Total
	£000	£000	£000	£000
Revenue	80	40	60	180
Department costs	24	15	46	85
Apportioned costs	20	10	20	50
Total costs	44	25	66	135
Profit/loss	36	15	(6)	45

The apportioned costs of £50 000 in total are unavoidable and relate to head office overhead costs. From the way in which the data is presented above it may well be argued that Department C should be closed down as it makes a loss of £6000. Currently, the total profit of the three departments is £45 000. However, if Department C was closed the profit would be reduced to.

	Total	A	B
	£000	£000	£000
Revenue	120	80	40
Department costs	39	24	15
Departmental profit	81	56	25
Apportioned cost	50		
Profit	31		

The reduction in profit to the firm as a whole of £14 000 is due to closing Department C which in fact makes a departmental profit of £14 000 (£60 000 – £46 000) which contributes to the head office overhead costs and the firm's overall profit. Thus Department C should remain open.

Unfortunately in practice a number of organizations still persist in ignoring the principles of relevant costs and benefits in making future decisions. This can only distort decision-making and result in organizations taking wrong courses of action.

Make or buy decisions

Key concept

Make or buy decisions defined

A make or buy decision involves the problem of an organization choosing between making a product or carrying out a service using its own resources, and paying another external organization to make a product or carry out a service for them.

An example of a make or buy decision is the decision whether an organization should design and develop their own new computer system or hire an external software house to do the work. The 'make' option should give the management of the organization more direct control over the work. However, it will often be the case that an external contractor will have more specialist skills and expertise in doing the work. Like the majority of the types of decisions considered in this chapter, the make or buy decision should not be exclusively made on the basis of cost alone. Factors other than the costs and benefits of a decision, which are normally referred to as 'qualitative factors', will be considered in more depth at the end of the this chapter.

By means of Example 18.7 we may examine the decision whether to make or buy when an organization has spare capacity. In this situation we assume the organization is not working at full capacity and thus has enough resources available to make a product/component, if it so wishes, without affecting the production of other products.

EXAMPLE 18.7

Burns Hotels Plc are currently assessing whether to carry on managing their own cleaning which includes the hiring and supervising of staff or contracting out the work. Smarten Up Plc, the cheapest of all the outside contractors bidding for the contract, have priced the contract at

£123 400 per year. The current costs per year of cleaning the hotels are:

	£
Labour	76 000
Supervision	23 000
Materials	21 000
Overhead charge	38 000
Total cost	158 000

It would initially appear that it is more economical for Burns Hotels to contract out their cleaning; the total cost of cleaning is £34 600 (£158 000 – £123 400) more for the firm to manage itself rather contracting out. However, it is important that in such decisions management should closely examine their costs before any decision is made ensuring that only relevant costs are included in the computation.

When the costs are investigated in the above example it comes to light that labour, supervisors and material costs are all incremental costs. However the overhead charge is a general charge based on labour cost – the charge being 50% on labour (£76 000 × 50% = £38 000). These overhead costs include personnel costs and other management and administrative costs which are considered to be unavoidable. That is, they are costs that would be incurred whether or not the work is contracted out. Therefore the cost is irrelevant to the decision.

Ignoring these overhead costs the cost of cleaning in-house which is to be compared with the contractor's charge is £120 000. Therefore, the company will be £3400 better off keeping the contract in-house.

In such decisions there will normally be another consideration that is relevant. Often by contracting out, that is 'buying', spare capacity will be made available. For example, in the example of Burns Hotels Plc there may be additional floor space available within the hotel when the contract is administered by an outside contractor. This may be the result, for example, of storage space for materials and equipment not now being required. It may also be the case that this spare floor capacity has some value to the company; for example, it may decide to let the space to an outside party which would generate additional income. This additional income should then be included as a relevant cost to the option of maintaining the contract inside the company, as this revenue will forgone if the cleaning is carried out by the hotel staff, i.e. is an opportunity cost.

As previously mentioned, in these types of decisions there will inevitably be other qualitative factors that should be taken into account. Specifically in Example 18.7 it may well be that the organization is apprehensive about the quality of the work of the outside contractor. This factor may lead to the company favouring keeping responsibility for cleaning within the company.

QUALITATIVE FACTORS

In our analysis of decision-making all the decisions made were based on financial criteria. Often, however, qualitative factors will be of great influence in such decisions. Indeed, on some occasions it may be the case that purely on quantitative (financial) criteria an opportunity may be rejected but for other reasons, primarily of a qualitative nature, the opportunity is accepted.

Qualitative factors can be described as factors which are not capable of being quantified in terms of costs and income. They may stem from either non-financial objectives or factors which might be quantifiable in money terms but which have not been so quantified because there is insufficient information to make a reliable estimate.

The nature of qualitative factors in decision-making will inevitably vary with the circumstances related to the opportunities under consideration. The following sections provide some examples of qualitative factors that may influence decisions.

Customers

Decisions as to the inclusion or exclusion of services and products from the range offered, the quality of the service or product and after-sales service will invariably affect the demand for the service or product and customer loyalty. For example, the exclusion of one service from a range, because in financial terms it may be uneconomic to provide and sell, could affect the demand for other services. Services and products sold by firms can often be interdependent and this interdependency should be taken into account in the decision-making process.

Employees

Any decisions involving the closure of parts of a firm, relocation and changes in work procedures will require the acceptance of employees. Bad labour relations caused by decisions that involve such changes could lead to inefficiencies and losses.

Competitors

In a competitive market decisions by one firm to enhance their competitive advantage may result in competitors responding in a similar way to maintain the status quo. For example, the decision to reduce selling prices in order to raise demand will not be successful if all competitors take similar counter-action.

Another example is when a firm decides to continue selling an unprofitable product or offering a service because otherwise they would be leaving the market for competitors to enjoy which may eventually affect the demand for other products offered by the firm.

Legal constraints

An opportunity may occasionally be rejected because of doubts regarding pending legislation. The decision to open a hotel, for example, may be influenced by pending legislation regarding safety precautions that will incur additional costs in physically implementing. The cost of these precautions may be complex to estimate.

Suppliers

A firm may rely heavily on a good relationship with a particular supplier for the prompt delivery of supplies. Some decisions may affect a supplier and the relationship must be considered in any decision.

SUMMARY

In this chapter we have considered decisions that organizations are required to make regarding future opportunities where there are no constraints in respect of resources. In the context of all the types of decisions considered it is clear that the application of traditional costing methods will not result in organizations satisfying the assumed objective of maximizing future cash flows. It was illustrated that the maximization of cash flows will only be satisfied when the principles of relevant costs are applied to such decisions. The costs and benefits that are relevant were described and are summarized below:

- future costs and benefits;
- differential and incremental costs and benefits;
- avoidable costs;
- replacement cost;
- opportunity costs.

The main limitation to the analysis described in this chapter is that it tends to ignore qualitative factors. In practice many of these decisions will be made based on qualitative criteria and these factors were discussed in the context of decision-making.

FURTHER READING

An excellent analysis of decision-making can be found in Chapters 9 and 10 of *Accounting for Management Decisions* by J. Arnold and T. Hope (Prentice–Hall International, 1990).

REVIEW QUESTIONS

1. Discuss the reasons why accruals accounting methods are not appropriate to future decision-making.
2. In the context of decision-making explain the meaning of:
   (i)   sunk costs;
   (ii) differential costs;
   (iii) avoidable and unavoidable costs;
   (iv) opportunity cost.
3. Depreciation is an important concept in the determination of profit. Discuss why it is classified as an irrelevant cost in decision-making.
4. In the majority of cases fixed costs will be irrelevant in decision-making, but on some occasions they may be relevant. Describe the circumstances when fixed costs are relevant to future decisions.
5. Qualitative factors are often influential in the decision-making process. Describe the nature of qualitative factors and give three examples that may influence a decision to make a component rather than buy it from another firm.

PROBLEMS FOR DISCUSSION AND ANALYSIS

1. Paradise Tours Ltd are currently examining their packaged holiday programme for the forthcoming year. One of their more popular products is the catered villa holidays in Albania. Last year they sold 1000 of these holidays at £750 each. The variable cost per holiday was £500 and the fixed costs in total were £100 000. Of this £100 000 fixed costs, £60 000 was a charge apportioned to the product which was associated with the costs of running the company. It is anticipated that these costs will not change and the volume will be the same.

   An alternative plan has been suggested. Currently the holidays are labour intensive. If they were changed to being self-catering holidays, variable costs would be reduced to £300 each; however, fixed costs, would increase to £350 000. The head office element of the charge would remain the same. Whilst selling prices would be reduced by 10% the number of holidays sold would increase by 5%.

   Required:
   (a) Assuming the same holiday programme as last year what would be the contribution per holiday and the total profit or loss based on the relevant data available?
   (b) Calculate the contribution per holiday and the overall total profit or loss for the alternative holiday.
   (c) Advise the company which option should be taken up for the forthcoming year. Comment on the risk associated with these

variables and suggest ways in which risk can be considered in a fairly basic way in formulating a decision.

2. Country Parks Safari plc has approach an animal feed firm, Healthy Farm Foods Ltd, to supply them with a special animal feed in bulk over the forthcoming year. Country Parks Safari plc are prepared to pay £8000 for the contract over the period. The following cost estimates and other relevant details have been made available to the management of Healthy Farms Foods Ltd:

Materials:

  (i) The company will have to mix two materials, 'lush' and 'hash' to make the mix.
 (ii) The company has sufficient 'lush' in stock for the mix. This cost £2000 a few months back. However, 'lush' is only made to special order. Although it would now cost £3000 to buy, as there is little demand for the material and the company have no foreseeable use for the material its resale value is only £1000.
(iii) 'Hash' was purchased a month ago and cost £750. It was intended to be used on another mix. To purchase the replacement material would now cost £1000.

Labour and supervision:

  (i) Quality control supervisors will be expected to spend 100 hours checking the mix. They are salaried at £400 per week, for a 35-hour week. The existing supervisors will be able to cope with the supervision of this special mix so no new supervisors will be employed.
 (ii) The firm uses casual labour for mixing. This is paid at £4 per hour. The casual labour would have to work 1000 hours on this contract during the coming year. However, the supply of casual labour is not completely elastic and it seems that 400 hours of these hours would be worked as overtime. Overtime is estimated to be payable at time and a half.

Capital

The special feed will be made over the next year using a mixer which cost £5000 five years ago. When purchased it had an estimated life of ten years and is being depreciated over this period using the straight line method. The machine has no other use nor a scrap value.

Overhead:

General overheads for the firm will be unchanged whatever products are produced. These are apportioned to all products at 100% of direct labour cost (excluding quality control supervisors' salaries, but including overtime premium).

Required:
(a) Prepare statements:
  (i) using conventional cost accounting to match revenue with costs; and
  (ii) which clearly state whether the company should accept the order.
(b) Explain the reasons for the differences between the two statements above.

Clearly state any assumptions you wish to make concerning the data.

Investment decisions $\boxed{19}$

INTRODUCTION

In this chapter we shall examine some of the methods of investment appraisal available to managers to assist them in making investment decisions. The main difference between investment decisions and short-term decisions is that the benefits, in the case of investment decisions, will accrue over a longer period, usually well over one year, and often much longer. This difference in the time dimension has important implications in terms of the value of money, and the value of money over time will be an important feature in the evaluation of the different methods of investment appraisal available to managers.

Investment decisions by their nature tend to be strategic. This means that resources are committed for a long period of time and these decisions determine the long-term policies of the firm that are necessary to meet its objectives. However, the nature and size of the investment opportunity may vary considerably; for example, the investment could range from the construction and development of a new hotel to the acquisition of a new computer for recording and accounting for reservations.

The methods of investment appraisal we will be considering are designed primarily to satisfy one objective, that is to maximize the profits of the firm. The maximizing of profits can also be translated into the maximizing of the value of shareholders' wealth. The shareholders are the owners of the firm and the management of the firm are accountable to these owners. The link between the investment decision and the finance necessary to fund the investment is that the return from an investment must adequately satisfy those providing the finance. Therefore the criteria that is to be applied in terms of accepting or rejecting individual investment opportunities will reflect the demands of those who finance the firm. The sources of finance are discussed in Chapter 8.

Risk will play an important part in determining the return demanded by those funding the business. The higher the risk the greater the returns that will be demanded by the providers of funds. Differing investment opportunities have different risk profiles. Consider the following investment opportunity available to a UK-based company: opening a new hotel in Kampala the capital of Uganda, or opening a similar hotel in Torquay, Devon. The investment in Uganda, for this company, with all its economic and political uncertainties, is likely to be much riskier than the investment in Torquay. It follows that if the overseas investment were to be attractive to the company the returns must at least reflect the additional risk of this opportunity. The main factors that will affect risk are the structure of the market and industry, changes in technology and tastes, and exposure to macroeconomic variables.

It should, however, be recognized that there are criteria that a firm may adopt in determining whether to invest other than maximizing profits. It may be that a firm's objective at a particular point in time is, for example, to maximize market share, which may be in conflict with the maximization of profits. It is likely that in such cases the methods of investment appraisal that we will be considering would then be inappropriate.

In this chapter we will be examining and evaluating four methods of investment appraisal they are:

- the accounting rate of return (ARR) method;
- the payback method;
- discounted cash flow (DCF) methods, namely:
  - the net present value (NPV) method; and
  - the internal rate of return (IRR) method.

ACCOUNTING RATE OF RETURN

A long-term investment project may be assessed by calculating its estimated accounting rate of return and comparing it with a pre-determined target ARR set by management which will presumably reflect their objectives in terms of a satisfactory return. The ARR is sometimes also referred to as return on investment (ROI). In principle these two measures are the same.

Unfortunately – and confusingly – there are several different definitions of ARR. These differences relate to whether average or total profits and average or initial investment are utilized in the calculation. One of the most popular definitions is:

$$\text{ARR} = \frac{\text{Estimated average profits}}{\text{Estimated average investment}} \times 100\%$$

Other definitions include:

$$\text{ARR} = \frac{\text{Estimated total profits}}{\text{Estimated initial investment}} \times 100\%$$

and:

$$\text{ARR} = \frac{\text{Estimated average profits}}{\text{Estimated initial investment}} \times 100\%$$

There are various arguments in favour of each of the above definitions which need not concern us here. The most important point is that the method adopted should be used consistently, thereby ensuring that like is compared to like.

The profit figure in this measure is the accounting profit based on accruals accounting principals. It is normally taken as after depreciation but before taxation. Taxation is ignored as the variation in taxes over time, which may be outside the control of the firm, can distort the measure from one period to another. This would be problematic for appraising investment projects as there would not be any consistent basis upon which to compare investments.

The use of the ARR method of appraisal involves estimating the ARR on the proposed project and comparing it with a target ARR. If the estimated rate of the proposed project exceeds the target rate the project should be undertaken. Conversely, if the estimated return is less than the target the proposed project should be rejected.

Key concept

Accounting rate of return decision rule

Compare the estimated ARR of a proposed project with the target ARR. If the estimate exceeds the target, accept the project; if it is lower, reject the project.

EXAMPLE 19.1

Hilditch Leisure Parks Ltd are currently appraising an investment opportunity to introduce a new 'ride'. The company uses the accounting rate of return for assessing these types of projects. The target ARR for the company is 20%. The following details relate to the proposed investment opportunity:

- Investment – cost of the equipment: £80 000.
- Estimated life of equipment: 4 years.
- Estimated profit from the investment before depreciation.

	£
Year 1	20 000
Year 2	25 000
Year 3	35 000
Year 4	25 000

If the equipment were to be depreciated on a straight line basis and it had a nil residual value, the annual depreciation charge will be

£80 000/4 years = £20 000 per year. The annual profits after depreciation, the mid-year net book value of the equipment for each year, and the ARR for each of the years would be as follows:

Year	Profit after depreciation £	Mid-year book value £	ARR in the year %
1	0	70 000	0
2	5 000	50 000	10
3	15 000	30 000	50
4	5 000	10 000	50

The mid-year net book value in the above table is the mid-point between the beginning of each year and the end of each year. For example, the value of the equipment at the beginning of year 1 was £80 000 and at the end £60 000 (after deduction of depreciation of £20 000); the mid-year net book value is therefore £70 000.

From this table it can be seen that the ARR, from a yearly perspective, is low in the early years of the project. This is partly because of low profits in year 1, but in the main it is due to the net book value of the equipment being much higher in the early years. The relatively higher net book value of the equipment in the earlier years is a characteristic of the straight line depreciation method in comparison with the reducing balance method of depreciation as previously discussed in Chapter 7 on fixed assets and depreciation.

The project does not achieve the target ARR of 20% in its first two years, but exceeds it in years 3 and 4. This begs the question whether the investment should go ahead.

When the ARR from a project varies from year to year, it makes sense to take an overall view, as was implied earlier when definitions of the method were being discussed. Using the most common definition cited earlier, that is:

$$\text{ARR} = \frac{\text{Estimated average profits}}{\text{Estimated average investment}} \times 100$$

where:

$$\text{Estimated average profits} = \frac{\text{Total profits}}{\text{Number of years}} = \frac{£25\,000}{4}$$

$$= £6250$$

Estimated average investment over the 4-year period = £80 000 + £0/2 = £40 000

the average investment being the average value of the asset at the beginning of its life, £80 000, and at the end of its life, in this case £0. So:

$$ARR = £6250/£40\,000 \times 100 = 15.63\%$$

As the estimated ARR is less than 20%, the target rate, this investment opportunity should be rejected.

Although ARR adopts accounting measures which can be manipulated more easily than, say, simple inflows and outflows of cash, the measure is consistent with the way in which organizations report in their annual accounts. That is, both ARR and financial accounting information reported in the annual accounts are based on accruals accounting. Therefore, if the ARR of a project is estimated, some reasonable assessment may be made as to the effect of a proposed project on future reported profits.

The main criticism of the ARR is that it does not take account of the timing of profits generated from the investment. The model therefore assumes that the profits earned in the first year, for example, are equivalent in terms of value as profits earned in later years. That is, ignoring inflation, £1 today is assumed to be the same, for example, as £1 in 10 years' time. Intuition will lead us quickly to the conclusion that this is not so! This assumption therefore ignores the concept of the time value of money. The theme of the time value of money will be considered in more detail later in this chapter when considering the methods based on discounted cash flow.

THE PAYBACK METHOD

> ### Key concept
>
> *Definition of payback*
>
> Payback is normally defined as the period, usually expressed in years, which it takes the cash inflows from an investment project to equal the cash outflows.

It should be noted that in the above definition of payback the term cash flow is used rather than accounting profit. Therefore this method is not based on accruals accounting concepts and thus does not, for example, take account of depreciation.

Example 19.2 illustrates the use of the payback method where there are two investment opportunities available to a firm which are mutually exclusive, that is where only one opportunity can be accepted.

EXAMPLE 19.2

Project	A	B
	£	£
Cost of investment	50 000	50 000
Cash inflows		
Year 1	10 000	40 000
Year 2	15 000	30 000
Year 3	20 000	10 000
Year 4	25 000	5 000
Year 5	60 000	5 000

To help identify the payback period it is useful to calculate the accumulated cash flows of the individual projects:

Year	Project A cash flows		Project B cash flows	
	yearly	accumulated	yearly	accumulated
	£	£	£	£
0	(50 000)	(50 000)	(50 000)	(50 000)
1	10 000	(40 000)	40 000	(10 000)
2	15 000	(25 000)	30 000	20 000
3	20 000	(5 000)	10 000	30 000
4	25 000	20 000	5 000	35 000
5	60 000	80 000	5 000	40 000

Following the definition of payback in the Key concept above, Project 'A' will pay back the investment after the third year. By the end of year 3, it has paid back £45 000 (£10 000 + £15 000 + £20 000) and the other £5000, as can be seen in the above table showing accumulated cash flows, will be paid back during year 4. When the actual payback occurs during a year it is the convention to express this point in time as a fraction of a year or in months. For example, in the case of Project 'A', in the fourth year £25 000 is received, but only £5000 is necessary to add to previous years' cash inflows to pay back the original investment; this £5000 can then be expressed as a fraction of the total for that year – £5000/£25 000, i.e. one fifth of the year, or in months £5000/£25 000 × 12 months = 2.4 months.

In contrast, Project 'B' pays back the investment in 1 year and 4 months. This project would therefore normally be preferred under the payback criteria.

It should be noted that in calculating the fraction of the year or the month in which payback takes place, as in the example above, it has been assumed that the cash flows are received evenly throughout the year. Due to the inevitable uncertainty involved in long-term investment appraisal this is a reasonable assumption. It would normally be very difficult and problematic to precisely estimate the spread of cash flows within years.

When examining, two mutually exclusive projects, as in the case of Projects 'A' and 'B', the usual decision rule is to accept the project with the shortest payback, assuming the payback period satisfies some preconceived target. However, when only one investment opportunity is being examined the payback of that opportunity will be compared with a target payback. This concept of a target payback could be employed in the case of Projects 'A' and 'B' above, assuming that these two projects are not mutually exclusive, that is to say we could, if we so wished, accept both investment opportunities. For example, if our payback target was three years, Project 'B' would be accepted because it pays back after 1 year and 4 months though Project 'A' would still be rejected because its payback of 3 years and 2.4 months is greater than the target.

Much of the perceived risk associated with investment projects is related to uncertainty due to the timespan in which benefits in terms of cash flows are received. The longer the time period for receipt of cash the greater the risk. Therefore the payback method, by differentiating projects in terms of the period to pay back the investment, measures this type of risk. Thus in terms of Example 19.1 Project 'B' could be seen as less risky than Project 'A' because the payback period is shorter.

The method is relatively simple to understand and to calculate. Not surprisingly, the method is often used as a first screening method in the appraisal of investment opportunities before any other of the more sophisticated methods are employed. Thus, in this context, the first question to ask in assessing an investment proposal is: How long will it take to pay back its cost? The organization may, for example, have a policy that only projects that pay back within three years will be appraised using other more rigorous methods of appraisal.

There are two important criticisms of the payback method. The first, which is fundamental, relates to the fact that cash flows after the payback period are ignored. So, it could be the case that, whilst a project produces a large net cash flow (i.e. where cash inflows significantly exceed outflows), they are generated in the later part of the project and may be ignored as this is after the payback period. For example, in the case of Projects 'A' and 'B' in Example 19.2 above, Project 'B' was preferred because of having a shorter payback period, but overall Project 'A' generates more cash inflows totalling £130 000 as compared to only £90 000 in the case of Project 'B'. However, Project 'A's cash inflows were mainly earned after the payback.

The second criticism of the payback method relates to the method not taking account of the time value of money as with the ARR method. This criticism is not entirely valid as the method can be adapted to take account of the timing of cash inflows.

DISCOUNTED CASH FLOW

To recap briefly: the ARR method of investment appraisal ignores the timing of cash flows and the time value of money. Payback considers the time it takes to recover the original investment cost, but ignores total cash flows over a project's life.

Discounted cash flow, or DCF for short, is an investment appraisal technique which takes into account both the time value of money and also total profitability over a project's life. It is therefore often argued, with much credence, that DCF is superior to both ARR and payback as a method of investment appraisal.

From the term 'discounted cash flow' two important characteristics can be identified about the method.

- The timing of cash flows is taken into account by a process of discounting. The effect of discounting is to give a bigger value per £1 for cash flows that occur in earlier years. For example, £1 earned after one year will be worth more than £1 earned after two years, which in turn will be worth more than £1 earned after 10 years. The process of discounting involves selecting a discount rate that reflects an individual's or an organization's time value of money.
- Cash flows are accounted for in the appraisal rather than the costs and revenues used in accruals accounting. The reason for this is that in accounting for cash flows, receipts and payments are recognized when they actually occur. This is not the case for the majority of costs and revenues when employing accruals accounting. For example, the cost of an investment will be accrued over the life of the investment employing a system of depreciation. In contrast, the whole of the cost of the investment, when accounting for cash flows, would be recognized when the payment is made. This was illustrated in Chapter 10 on cash flow statements. In accounting for the time value of money it is appropriate only to recognize the cash inflows and outflows when they actually occur.

Key concept

The time value of money

The term 'time value of money' means that, ignoring inflation or deflation, a given sum of money will have a different value depending upon when it occurs in time.

The process of discounting

Discounting is compounding in reverse. By means of Example 19.3 we may explain the relationship between discounting and compounding.

EXAMPLE 19.3

Suppose that a company invests £10 000 to earn a return of 10% (compound interest). The value of the investment with the interest will accumulate as follows:

After 1 year: £10 000 × (1.10)   = £11 000
After 2 years: £10 000 × (1.10)^2 = £12 100
After 3 years: £10 000 × (1.10)^3 = £13 310 and so on.

This is compounding. The formula for the future value of an investment, including accumulated interest earned after n time periods, is:

$$FV = PV(1 + r)^n$$

where: FV = the future value of the investment with interest;
          PV = the initial or present value of the investment;
          r = the compound rate of return (reflecting the time value of money) per time period;
          n = the number of time periods normally measured in years.

Discounting converts future values to present values and is the reverse of compounding. For example, if a company expects to earn a (compound) rate of return of 10% on its investments, how much would it need to invest now (the present value of the future sum) to have an investment of:

£11 000 after 1 year? or
£12 100 after 2 years? or
£13 310 after 3 years?

The answer is £10 000 in each case, and we calculate it by discounting, as follows:

After 1 year: $11\,000 \times \dfrac{1}{1.10}$ = £10 000

After 2 years: $12\,100 \times \dfrac{1}{1.10^2}$ = £10 000

After 3 years: $13\,310 \times \dfrac{1}{1.10^3}$ = £10 000

The discounting formula to calculate the present value of a future sum of money at the end of n time periods is:

$$PV = FV \frac{1}{(1 + r)^n}$$

It should be noted that when discounting cash flows to their present values, instead of multiplying by $(1 + r)$ as in the case of compounding, we divide by $(1 + r)$.

Key concept

The definition of present value

Present value can be defined as the cash equivalent now of a sum of money receivable or payable at the stated future date, discounted at a specified rate of return.

Discounting can be applied to both money receivable and also to money payable at a future date. And so by discounting all payments and receipts from a capital investment to a present value, they can be compared on a common basis at a value which takes account of when the various cash flows will take place.

By means of Example 19.4 we may illustrate the use of discounted cash flow method in investment appraisal.

EXAMPLE 19.4

Harvey Ltd is investigating an investment opportunity which will generate £40 000 after two years and another £30 000 after three years. The company's target rate of return is 12%. The present value of these cash inflows is:

Year	Cash flow £	Discount factor 12%	Present value £
2	40 000	$\dfrac{1}{(1.12)^2}$	31 880
3	30 000	$\dfrac{1}{(1.12)^3}$	21 360
		Total PV	53 240

The present value of the total future inflows of cash discounted at 12% is £53 240. This means that if Harvey Ltd can invest now to earn a return of 12% on its investments, it would have to invest £53 240 now to earn £40 000 in two years' time plus £30 000 in three years' time.

In the application of DCF to investment decisions only future cash flows are relevant. Therefore, the principles detailed in Chapter 18 relating to decision-making in the short term are also applicable to long-term investment decisions. Thus, for example, past costs are not relevant because they are sunk, whilst opportunity costs are relevant.

In relation to the payback method of investment appraisal, as examined earlier, the yearly cash flows can be discounted. Therefore, by discounting the cash flows the payback method would then take account of the time value of money. When discounting is applied to the payback method the term 'discounted payback' is commonly used.

We will now consider the two main methods of using DCF to appraise investment opportunities, namely the net present value (NPV) method and the internal rate of return (IRR) method.

THE NET PRESENT VALUE METHOD

Net present value (NPV) is the value obtained by discounting all cash outflows and inflows of an investment opportunity by a chosen rate of return. It was said earlier that the rate of return was directly associated with an individual's or, in the context of business, a firm's time value of money which will reflect shareholders' opportunity cost. The opportunity cost in this context is the rate of return shareholders and other providers of capital forgo by investing in the firm. In the context of a business this opportunity cost is commonly referred to as the 'cost of capital'.

The present value of cash inflows minus the present value of the cash outflows is the NPV. Therefore if the NPV:

- is positive, it means that the cash inflows from the investment will yield a return in excess of the cost of capital, and therefore the investment project should be undertaken. In this situation it can be seen that the business can pay its providers of capital the necessary returns and still have cash to employ in the business;
- is negative, it means that the cash inflows from the investment will yield a return less than that required to satisfy the providers of capital and therefore the opportunity should be rejected;
- is exactly zero, it means that the investment has generated exactly the required returns to satisfy the providers of capital, without any surplus to employ in the business.

The discount factor that was calculated using the formula $1/(1 + r)^n$ can be more conveniently determined by simply using discount tables. The discount tables for the present value of £1, for differing values of r and n are given in Appendix A at the end of this book.

By means of Example 19.5 we may illustrate the use of the NPV method using the present value tables.

EXAMPLE 19.5

Benaud Ltd is considering a capital investment where the estimated cash flows are:

Year		Cash flow
		£
0	(i.e. now)	(100 000)
1		60 000
2		80 000
3		40 000
4		30 000

The company's cost of capital is 15%.

What is the NPV of the proposed project, and should the project be undertaken?

The solution is presented below.

Year	Cash flow	Discount factor	Present value
	£	at 15%	£
0	(100 000)	1.000	(100 000)
1	60 000	0.870	52 200
2	80 000	0.756	60 480
3	40 000	0.658	26 320
4	30 000	0.572	17 160
			56 160

The present value of cash inflows exceeds the present value of cash outflows by £56 160, which means that the project produces a DCF yield in excess of 15%. The project should therefore be undertaken. In using DCF methods for investment appraisal there are some important conventions to note regarding the timing of cash flows.

- A cash flow at the beginning of an investment project, described in the example above as 'now', is assumed to occur in year 0. The present value of £1 now, in year 0, is $1/(1 + r)^n = 1/(1 + r)^0 = £1$, regardless of the value of r. Therefore, as in the example above, the discount factor to use for cash flows arising in year 0 is 1.0.
- A cash inflow or outflow that occurs during the course of a year rather than at the year end is assumed to happen at the end of the year. For example, £2000 received half way through the year is assumed to be received at the end of that year. This convention is adopted because of the complexity of discounting sums throughout time periods. Given the uncertainty relating to the future, it is considered that, whilst the calculation does not result in an absolutely precise present value, it is a reasonable approximation of reality.

Annuities

Where there are constant cash flows arising at annual intervals for a number of years (known as annuities) time can be saved by using the annuity tables in Appendix B. By means of Example 19.5 we may illustrate the use of annuity tables as well as some of the other aspects that are pertinent to decision-making using DCF techniques.

EXAMPLE 19.6

Galaxy Leisure Ltd currently owns some land and is considering whether to develop this land into a golf range. The company has already received a feasibility study from a firm of surveyors which suggests that the land would be suitable for such a development. The surveyor's report cost Galaxy Leisure £20 000. The land cost Galaxy £450 000, fifteen years ago. However, the surveyor's report estimates that they could sell the land for residential development for £1 million.

A total cost of £1 200 000 will be incurred within the first year in the development of the range; for evaluation purposes you can assume all the outflows of cash associated with this development will be incurred on the first day of year 1. The marketing team of Galaxy Leisure forecast the project will generate net cash inflows of £300 000 for a period of 10 years. At the end of the 10 years it is anticipated there will be no material residual value in respect of the plant and equipment related to the range. However, it is anticipated that the company would still be able to sell the land for residential development after the 10 years for £1 million.

It can be assumed that the annual cash inflows are received on the last day of each year.

To support this investment it is estimated that the company will need to invest in working capital. £20 000 will be spent at the beginning of the first year rising to £30 000 in the second year and remaining at that level until the end of the project when it will be recovered.

The company's cost of capital is 10%. Ignore taxation.

Should the company accept this opportunity?

The solution is presented below.

The NPV is calculated as follows:

Years	Equipment	Working capital	Contribution	Net cash flow	Discount rate	Present value
	£	£	£	£	£	£
0	(1 200 000)	(20 000)		(1 220 000)	1.000	(1 220 000)
1		(10 000)		(10 000)	0.909	(9 090)
10			300 000	300 000	6.145	1 843 500
10	1 000 000	30 000		1 030 000	0.386	397 580
					NPV =	1 011 990

The following notes provide a brief commentary on the calculations above.

1. The NPV of this investment opportunity has now to be compared with any other opportunities available to the company. From the information we have at our disposal there is just one other opportunity, that is to sell the land now for £1 million to developers for the building of residential properties. The golf range project yields, however, £11 990 more. Therefore, in purely monetary terms, the company should go ahead with the golf range development.
2. The cost of the surveyor's feasibility study is a sunk cost and therefore is irrelevant to this decision.
3. The original cost of the land is also a sunk cost and is therefore irrelevant. It is the opportunity cost of using the land for some alternative purpose which is relevant to this decision which we have taken account of in making the decision and which is referred to in 1 above.
4. The cash inflow will not change over the 10-year period and therefore we can use the annuity tables in determining the present value of these cash flows. The annuity discount factor can be obtained from the annuity table in the appendix – where n is 10 years and r is 10%, the factor is 6.145. This discount factor is simply the sum of the individual factors for each of the 10 years where r is 10% from the present value tables. By multiplying the annual contribution of £300 000 per annum by this factor we obtain the present value of this annuity.
5. The investment in working capital is a relevant cost because the company will forgo the possibility of being able to invest this money elsewhere for the life of the project. The amount invested in working capital is £20 000 at the beginning of the project, rising to £30 000 at the end of year 2, that is £10 000 additional investment. The full £30 000 is recoverable at the end of the project's life.

Perpetuities

A perpetuity is an annuity which is expected to last indefinitely, for example undated government stocks where a fixed rate of interest is received annually but where the capital is unlikely to be repaid. Often perpetuities are used to approximate perceived long timespans, for example for calculating the present value of anticipated returns on an investment that will be held for the foreseeable future. Another more concrete example is the revenue generated from the toll on the Dartford tunnel and bridge which will continue for the foreseeable future.

The present value of any perpetuity is given by the annual receipt or payment divided by the relevant discount rate. For example, the PV of £1 per annum in perpetuity at a discount rate of 10% would be £1/0.10 = £10. Similarly, the present value of £1 per annum in perpetuity at a discount rate of:

15% would be : $\dfrac{£1}{0.15}$ = £6.67

20% would be : $\dfrac{£1}{0.20}$ = £5

To apply the present value of £1 per annum in perpetuity to an investment evaluation we simply multiply the total cash outflow or inflow by the sum of the present value of £1 per annum in perpetuity. So, if it is anticipated that the revenue from the tolls at the Dartford tunnel and bridge are to generate inflows of cash of, say, £10 million pounds per annum for the foreseeable future, at a discount rate of 15% the present value of these streams of cash flows would be:

$$\dfrac{£1}{0.15} \times £10 \text{ million} = £66.7 \text{ million}$$

THE INTERNAL RATE OF RETURN METHOD

The internal rate of return (IRR) is the second investment appraisal method based on discounted cash flow techniques. Whilst a number of the principles applicable to IRR are similar to the NPV method there is a notable difference in the final outcome and the decision criteria. In the application of the IRR method it is necessary to calculate the exact DCF rate of return which an investment opportunity is expected to achieve, that is the rate of return at which the NPV is equal to zero and compare this with a target rate which should be the project's cost of capital. If the expected rate of return exceeds the target rate of return, the project should be undertaken. Conversely, if the expected rate of return is less than the target, the opportunity should be rejected.

Without a computer or a programmed calculator, the calculation of the internal rate of return is made by a 'trial and error technique' called interpolation.

The first step is to calculate two present values, both as close as possible to zero. The closer to zero the more accurate will be the end result. Ideally, in applying these two rates the result should be one NPV being positive and the other negative. It is then necessary to use interpolation to establish the rate where the NPV is zero. By means of Example 19.7 we illustrate the process.

EXAMPLE 19.7

A company is investigating an opportunity to buy a machine for £80 000 now which, it is anticipated, will save £20 000 per annum for five years. It is also anticipated that the machine will have a resale value of £10 000 at the end of the five years.

We begin by selecting a trial rate, say 9% (note that in this calculation we can use both the PV tables and the annuity tables):

Year	Cash flow £	PV factor at 9%	Present value £
0	(80 000)	1.0	(80 000)
1–5	20 000	3.890	77 800
5	10 000	0.650	6 500
		NPV	4 300

£4300 is fairly close to zero considering the amounts we are computing. We can therefore use 9% as one of the two rates necessary for the calculation of the IRR. In addition the NPV is positive which means that the real rate of return, where NPV is zero, is higher than 9%. We could now try, say, 12%:

Year	Cash flow £	PV factor at 12%	Present value £
0	(80 000)	1.0	(80 000)
1–5	20 000	3.605	72 100
5	10 000	0.567	5 670
		NPV	(2 230)

This NPV is also fairly close to zero and negative. The real rate of return is therefore greater than 9% (NPV = +4300) but less than 12% (NPV = –2230).

The interpolation method assumes that the NPV rises in a linear fashion between the two NPVs. The formula to apply is:

$$\text{Rate of return} = A + \left(\frac{P}{P+N} \times (B-A)\right)$$

where:
A = the (lower) rate of return with positive NPV;
B = the (higher) rate of return with a negative NPV;
P = the amount of the positive NPV;
N = the amount of the negative NPV.

Now applying this formula to the data calculated for the project we can calculate the IRR:

$$IRR = 9\% + \left(\frac{4300}{4300 + 2230} \times (12-9)\right)\%$$

$$= 9\% + 1.98\%$$
$$= 10.98\%, \text{ say } 11\%$$

If the cost of capital was 10% we would accept the project because its IRR is greater; if, on the other hand, the cost of capital was 15% we would not accept this project.

The concept of accounting for the time value of money through using the cost of capital as a discount rate is appealing from a number of perspectives. There are, however, problems in determining the correct discount rate. The cost of capital for an individual project should take account of the risk associated with the project. It is often difficult to precisely measure the risk for individual projects. A detailed discussion of the ways in which the cost of capital can be determined and the particular problems involved can be found in a number of financial management texts including Lumby (1991).

By means of Example 19.8 we may examine an investment opportunity and employ all four investment appraisal methods in determining an outcome.

EXAMPLE 19.8

Holefoods Ltd

Holefoods Ltd, an expanding catering firm, is considering tendering for a local authority contract to supply school meals. If they decide to tender and are successful, this will be their first contract in the public sector. The contract is for a period of five years.

The company has spent £2500 on a feasibility study related to this contract. From this study they have obtained the following estimates of costs, revenues and volumes.

- The initial cost of the investment for the necessary cooking equipment will be £30 000. This sum will be payable at the beginning of the contract.
- Selling price of meals: £1.00 per meal for the first three years, then £1.20 for years 4 and 5.
- Cost of meals: £0.60 per meal for the first three years, then £0.70 for years 4 and 5.
- Rent of premises are estimated to be £2000 per year.
- Forecast of the number of meals to be sold:

Year	No. of meals
1	30 000
2	32 000
3	32 000
4	33 000
5	33 000

- Transport costs: £2000 per year.
- The company uses straight line depreciation.

- The company's cost of capital is 14%.
- The company expects a payback within four years and its target accounting rate of return is 25%.

Calculate: The NPV, IRR, payback period (undiscounted and discounted) and the ARR.

The solution is presented in following paragraphs.

NPV

The £2500 spent on the feasibility study is considered to be irrelevant to the decision as it is a sunk cost.

Net present value:

Years	0	1	2	3	4	5
	£	£	£	£	£	£
Cost of equipment	(30 000)					
Sales		30 000	32 000	32 000	39 600	39 600
Cost of meals		(18 000)	(19 200)	(19 200)	(23 100)	(23 100)
Transport costs		(2 000)	(2 000)	(2 000)	(2 000)	(2 000)
Rent		(2 000)	(2 000)	(2 000)	(2 000)	(2 000)
Net cash flow	(30 000)	8 000	8 800	8 800	12 500	12 500
Cost of capital (14%)	1.00	0.877	0.769	0.675	0.592	0.519
Present value	(30 000)	7 016	6 767	5 940	7 400	6 487

Total NPV = + £3610 (i.e. −£30 000 + £7016 + £6767 + £5940 + £7400 + £6487)

Therefore under the NPV decision rule accept the proposed project.

IRR

At 14% the NPV was positive £3610 therefore the IRR, where the NPV is zero, must be greater than 14%; let us try 20% (note we only need to discount the cash flows):

	£	£	£	£	£	£
Cash flow	(30 000)	8 000	8 800	8 800	12 500	12 500
Cost of capital (20%)	1.00	0.833	0.694	0.578	0.482	0.402
Present value	(30 000)	6 644	6 107	5 086	6 025	5 025

Total NPV = −£1113 (i.e. −£30 000 + £6644 + £6 017 + £5086 + £6025 + £5025)

Using interpolation:

$$\text{IRR} = 14\% + \left(\frac{£3610}{£3610 + £1113} \times (20-14)\% \right) = 18.59\%$$

The IRR of the project exceeds the cost of capital therefore the project will be accepted.

Payback: undiscounted

Year	Cash flows	Cumulative cash flows
	£	£
0	(30 000)	(30 000)
1	8 000	(22 000)
2	8 800	(13 200)
3	8 800	(4 400)
4	12 500	8 100
5	12 500	20 600

Therefore the project pays back in the third year, more precisely £4400/£12 500 × 12 months = 3 years 4.2 months (assuming the cash flows arise evenly throughout the year). As this period is less than four years, the target payback period, we would accept the project.

Payback: discounted

Using the discounted cash flow figures in the NPV calculation above based on a 14% cost of capital, the payback profile is as follows:

Year	Cash flows	Cumulative cash flows
	£	£
0	(30 000)	(30 000)
1	7 016	(22 984)
2	6 767	(16 217)
3	5 940	(10 277)
4	7 400	(2 877)
5	6 487	3 610

Therefore the project pays back after the fourth year, more precisely £2877/£6487 × 12 months = 4 years and 6.7 months. As this is more than the target payback period of four years we would reject the project.

Accounting rate of return

Depreciation based on the straight line depreciation convention:

$$\frac{£30\ 000}{5\ \text{years}} = £6000 \text{ per annum}$$

So £6000 p.a. needs to be deducted from the undiscounted cash flows per annum. This is £30 000 (£6000 × 5 years) over the total life of the project. The sum of the undiscounted cash inflows from the project are £20 600, and the average annual returns are £20 600/5 years = £4120. The average investment is (£30 000 + 0)/2 = £15 000. So:

$$\text{ARR} = \frac{£4\,120}{£15\,000} \times 100 = 27.5\%$$

The ARR of 27.5% is greater than the target of 25%. Therefore the project is acceptable under this criterion.

THE METHODS COMPARED

It was stated earlier that the accounting rate of return (ARR) and the payback methods of investment appraisal each suffer from serious disadvantages. The first ignores the timing of cash flows whilst the latter does not take account of all the relevant cash flows after the payback period. Both the DCF methods which we have examined take account of the timing of cash flows and all the relevant cash flows.

By discounting relevant cash flows by the cost of capital and only accepting opportunities that exceed this return, both DCF methods ensure that shareholders' wealth is maximized. Research suggests that of these two DCF methods of investment appraisal the IRR method is favoured in practice. The main explanation given for this preference is that managers appear to prefer to talk in relative percentages rather than absolute sums of money. However, although in the majority of situations both the NPV and IRR methods of appraisal will give the same decision, there are occasions, namely when considering mutually exclusive projects, where the two methods are incompatible. In these circumstances the NPV should be used. A full discussion of why the NPV method is preferred can be found in Lumby (1991).

The main problem associated with the DCF methods is establishing the correct discount rate, referred to as the firm's cost of capital. It is not appropriate here to enter into a discussion surrounding the problems as they are too complex for such an introductory text. It is enough to recognize there are problems.

In many situations long-term opportunities will either be accepted or rejected based purely on financial criteria through the employment of one or more of the methods that we have examined in this chapter. However, it will also be the case that qualitative factors, that is factors that cannot be explicitly quantified in money terms, will be influential and sometimes overriding in a situation. Examples of qualitative factors were given in Chapter 8 on accounting for short-term decisions. Although, this chapter has focused on long-term decisions, the nature of the qualitative factors are likely to be similar. For example, decisions that in monetary terms seem profitable may be rejected because it is considered they will have a negative effect on labour relations.

SUMMARY

In this chapter we have examined the four main methods of financial investment appraisal – accounting rate of return, payback, net present value and the internal rate of return. For each of the methods we looked at the use of the methods within a business decision-making environment. The attributes of all the methods were considered. It was argued that all the methods have some use within the decision-making process and this explains why a number of companies employ all four.

   The concept of the time value of money was discussed and the process of discounting was examined within the context of long-term decision-making. Although, discounted cash flow methods are more theoretically rigorous there are problems in determining the cost of capital, i.e. the discount rate.

REFERENCES

Lumby, S. (1991) *Investment Appraisal and Financing Decisions*, 4th edn, Chapman & Hall, London.

FURTHER READING

An interesting analysis of the use of investment appraisal methods is published by the Chartered Institute of Management Accountants in their Occasional Paper Series, titled *Capital Budgeting for the 1990s* by Richard Pike and Mitchell Wolfe.

REVIEW QUESTIONS

1. Explain the main differences between DCF methods of investment appraisal and ARR.
2. Discuss the main attributes of the ARR and payback methods.
3. What is meant by discounting cash flow? Why is it necessary to discount cash flows?
4. In the employment of DCF investment appraisal methods explain why cash flows are used rather than accounting profits.
5. What is the effect on the value of the firm and shareholders' wealth if an investment opportunity with a NPV of £5000 is accepted?

PROBLEMS FOR DISCUSSION AND ANALYSIS

1. The management of Boon and Border Plc are in the process of examining the company's investment opportunities. There are six opportunities and the following details provide the relevant information regarding them.

    Project A would cost £29 000 now, and would generate the following cash flows:

Year	£
1	8 000
2	12 000
3	10 000
4	6 000

    The equipment included in the cost of the investment could be resold for £5000 at the start of year 5.

    Project B would involve a current outlay of £44 000 on capital equipment and £20 000 on working capital. The profits from the project would be as follows:

Years	Sales £	Variable costs £	Contribution £	Fixed cost £	Profit £
1	75 000	50 000	25 000	10 000	15 000
2	90 000	60 000	30 000	10 000	20 000
3	42 000	28 000	14 000	8 000	6 000

    Fixed costs include an annual charge of £4000 for depreciation; all the other fixed costs are avoidable. At the end of the year 3 the working capital investment would be recovered and the equipment would be sold for £5000.

    Project C would involve a current outlay of £50 000 on equipment and £15 000 on working capital. The investment in working capital would be increased to £21 000 at the end of the first year. Annual cash profits would be £18 000 per annum for five years, at the end of which the investment in working capital would be recovered.

    Project D would involve an outlay of £20 000 now and a further outlay of £20 000 after one year. Cash profits thereafter would be as follows:

Year	£
2	15 000
3	12 000
4	8 000 p.a.

    Project E is a long-term project involving an immediate outlay of £32 000 and annual cash profits of £4500 p.a. in perpetuity.

Project F is another long-term project involving an immediate outlay of £20 000 and annual cash profits as follows:

Year	£
1–5	5 000
6–10	4 000
11 in perpetuity	3 000

The company discounts all projects of 10 years' duration or less at a cost of capital of 12%, and all longer projects at a cost of 15%.

Required:
(a) Calculate the NPV of each project, and determine which should be undertaken by the company.
(b) Calculate the IRR of projects A, C and E.
(c) Calculate the discounted and non-discounted payback periods of project A.
(d) Calculate the accounting rate of return for Project A.

2. The Waugh Travel Company Ltd is thinking of buying, at a cost of £22 000, some new computers that will be networked and will be expected to save £5000 per year. The computers' estimated useful lives are 10 years, and they will have a zero disposal value.

You are required to calculate:
(a) the internal rate of return;
(b) the net present value if the cost of capital is 16%;
(c) the payback period;
(d) the accounting rate of return based on initial investment and on average investment.

3. Dr Oliver has £1000 which he will decide to invest if he can be reasonably confident that this investment will earn at least 10% p.a. He is considering three projects, each of which would cost £1000 to begin.

(a) Project A would earn £1090 at the end of the first year.
(b) Project B would earn £1250 at the end of the second year.
(c) Project C would earn £700 at the end of the first year, and another £700 at the end of the second year.

Advise Dr Oliver.

Appendix A: Discount Tables

Present value of £1

Periods Interest rates (%)

(n)	1	2	3	4	5	6	7	8	9	10	11	12	13	14	15
1	0.9901	0.9804	0.9709	0.9615	0.9524	0.9434	0.9346	0.9259	0.9174	0.9091	0.9009	0.8929	0.8850	0.8772	0.8696
2	0.9803	0.9612	0.9426	0.9246	0.9070	0.8900	0.8734	0.8573	0.8417	0.8264	0.8116	0.7972	0.7831	0.7695	0.7561
3	0.9706	0.9423	0.9151	0.8890	0.8638	0.8396	0.8163	0.7938	0.7722	0.7513	0.7312	0.7118	0.6931	0.6750	0.6575
4	0.9610	0.9238	0.8885	0.8548	0.8227	0.7921	0.7629	0.7350	0.7084	0.6830	0.6587	0.6355	0.6133	0.5921	0.5718
5	0.9515	0.9057	0.8626	0.8219	0.7835	0.7473	0.7130	0.6806	0.6499	0.6209	0.5935	0.5674	0.5428	0.5194	0.4972
6	0.9420	0.8880	0.8375	0.7903	0.7462	0.7050	0.6663	0.6302	0.5963	0.5645	0.5346	0.5066	0.4803	0.4556	0.4323
7	0.9327	0.8706	0.8131	0.7599	0.7107	0.6651	0.6227	0.5835	0.5470	0.5132	0.4817	0.4523	0.4251	0.3996	0.3759
8	0.9235	0.8535	0.7894	0.7307	0.6768	0.6274	0.5820	0.5403	0.5019	0.4665	0.4339	0.4039	0.3762	0.3506	0.3269
9	0.9143	0.8368	0.7664	0.7026	0.6446	0.5919	0.5439	0.5002	0.4604	0.4241	0.3909	0.3606	0.3329	0.3075	0.2843
10	0.9053	0.8203	0.7441	0.6756	0.6139	0.5584	0.5083	0.4632	0.4224	0.3855	0.3522	0.3220	0.2946	0.2697	0.2472
11	0.8963	0.8043	0.7224	0.6496	0.5847	0.5268	0.4751	0.4289	0.3875	0.3505	0.3173	0.2875	0.2607	0.2366	0.2149
12	0.8874	0.7885	0.7014	0.6246	0.5568	0.4970	0.4440	0.3971	0.3555	0.3186	0.2858	0.2567	0.2307	0.2076	0.1869
13	0.8787	0.7730	0.6810	0.6006	0.5303	0.4688	0.4150	0.3677	0.3262	0.2897	0.2575	0.2292	0.2042	0.1821	0.1625
14	0.8700	0.7579	0.6611	0.5775	0.5051	0.4423	0.3878	0.3405	0.2992	0.2633	0.2320	0.2046	0.1807	0.1597	0.1413
15	0.8613	0.7430	0.6419	0.5553	0.4810	0.4173	0.3624	0.3152	0.2745	0.2394	0.2090	0.1827	0.1599	0.1401	0.1229
16	0.8528	0.7284	0.6232	0.5339	0.4581	0.3936	0.3387	0.2919	0.2519	0.2176	0.1883	0.1631	0.1415	0.1229	0.1069
17	0.8444	0.7142	0.6050	0.5134	0.4363	0.3714	0.3166	0.2703	0.2311	0.1978	0.1696	0.1456	0.1252	0.1078	0.0929
18	0.8360	0.7002	0.5874	0.4936	0.4155	0.3503	0.2959	0.2502	0.2120	0.1799	0.1528	0.1300	0.1108	0.0946	0.0808
19	0.8277	0.6864	0.5703	0.4746	0.3957	0.3305	0.2765	0.2317	0.1945	0.1635	0.1377	0.1161	0.0981	0.0829	0.0703
20	0.8195	0.6730	0.5537	0.4564	0.3769	0.3118	0.2584	0.2145	0.1784	0.1486	0.1240	0.1037	0.0868	0.0728	0.0611
25	0.7795	0.6095	0.4776	0.3751	0.2953	0.2330	0.1842	0.1460	0.1160	0.0923	0.0736	0.0588	0.0471	0.0378	0.0304
30	0.7419	0.5521	0.4120	0.3083	0.2314	0.1741	0.1314	0.0994	0.0754	0.0573	0.0437	0.0334	0.0256	0.0196	0.0151
35	0.7059	0.5000	0.3554	0.2534	0.1813	0.1301	0.0937	0.0676	0.0490	0.0356	0.0259	0.0189	0.0139	0.0102	0.0075
40	0.6717	0.4529	0.3066	0.2083	0.1420	0.0972	0.0668	0.0460	0.0318	0.0221	0.0154	0.0107	0.0075	0.0053	0.0037
45	0.6391	0.4102	0.2644	0.2083	0.1113	0.0727	0.0476	0.0313	0.0207	0.0137	0.0091	0.0061	0.0041	0.0027	0.0019
50	0.6080	0.3715	0.2281	0.1407	0.0872	0.0543	0.0339	0.0213	0.0134	0.0085	0.0054	0.0035	0.0022	0.0014	0.0009

	16	17	18	19	20	21	22	23	24	25	26	27	28	29	30
1	0.8621	0.8547	0.8475	0.8403	0.8333	0.8264	0.8197	0.8130	0.8065	0.8000	0.7937	0.7874	0.7812	0.7752	0.7692
2	0.7432	0.7305	0.7182	0.7062	0.6944	0.6830	0.6719	0.6610	0.6504	0.6400	0.6299	0.6200	0.6104	0.6009	0.5917
3	0.6407	0.6244	0.6086	0.4934	0.5787	0.5645	0.5507	0.5374	0.5245	0.5120	0.4999	0.4882	0.4768	0.4658	0.4552
4	0.5523	0.5337	0.5158	0.4987	0.4823	0.4665	0.4514	0.4369	0.4230	0.4096	0.3968	0.3844	0.3725	0.3611	0.3501
5	0.4761	0.4561	0.4371	0.4190	0.4019	0.3855	0.3700	0.3552	0.3411	0.3277	0.3149	0.3027	0.2910	0.2799	0.2693
6	0.4104	0.3898	0.3704	0.3521	0.3349	0.3186	0.3033	0.2888	0.2751	0.2621	0.2499	0.2383	0.2274	0.2170	0.2072
7	0.3538	0.3332	0.3139	0.2959	0.2791	0.2633	0.2486	0.2348	0.2218	0.2097	0.1983	0.1877	0.1776	0.1682	0.1594
8	0.3050	0.2848	0.2660	0.2487	0.2326	0.2176	0.2038	0.1909	0.1789	0.1678	0.1574	0.1478	0.1388	0.1304	0.1226
9	0.2630	0.2434	0.2255	0.2090	0.1938	0.1799	0.1670	0.1552	0.1443	0.1342	0.1249	0.1164	0.1084	0.1011	0.0943
10	0.2267	0.2080	0.1911	0.1756	0.1615	0.1486	0.1369	0.1262	0.1164	0.1074	0.0992	0.0916	0.0847	0.0784	0.0725
11	0.1954	0.1778	0.1619	0.1476	0.1346	0.1228	0.1122	0.1026	0.0938	0.0859	0.0787	0.0721	0.0662	0.0607	0.0558
12	0.1685	0.1520	0.1372	0.1240	0.1122	0.1015	0.0920	0.0834	0.0757	0.0687	0.0625	0.0568	0.0517	0.0471	0.0429
13	0.1452	0.1299	0.1163	0.1042	0.0935	0.0839	0.0754	0.0678	0.0610	0.0550	0.0496	0.0447	0.0404	0.0365	0.0330
14	0.1252	0.1110	0.0985	0.0876	0.0779	0.0693	0.0618	0.0551	0.0492	0.0440	0.0393	0.0352	0.0316	0.0283	0.0254
15	0.1079	0.0949	0.0835	0.0736	0.0649	0.0573	0.0507	0.0448	0.0397	0.0352	0.0312	0.0277	0.0247	0.0219	0.0195
16	0.0930	0.0811	0.0708	0.0618	0.0541	0.0474	0.0415	0.0364	0.0320	0.0281	0.0248	0.0218	0.0193	0.0170	0.0150
17	0.0802	0.0693	0.0600	0.0520	0.0451	0.0391	0.0340	0.0296	0.0258	0.0225	0.0197	0.0172	0.0150	0.0132	0.0116
18	0.0691	0.0592	0.0508	0.0437	0.0376	0.0323	0.0279	0.0241	0.0208	0.0180	0.0156	0.0135	0.0118	0.0102	0.0089
19	0.0596	0.0506	0.0431	0.0367	0.0313	0.0267	0.0229	0.0196	0.0168	0.0144	0.0124	0.0107	0.0092	0.0079	0.0068
20	0.0514	0.0433	0.0365	0.0308	0.0261	0.0221	0.0187	0.0159	0.0135	0.0115	0.0098	0.0084	0.0072	0.0061	0.0053
25	0.0245	0.0197	0.0160	0.0129	0.0105	0.0085	0.0069	0.0057	0.0046	0.0038	0.0031	0.0025	0.0021	0.0017	0.0014
30	0.0116	0.0090	0.0070	0.0054	0.0042	0.0033	0.0026	0.0020	0.0016	0.0012	0.0010	0.0008	0.0006	0.0005	0.0004
35	0.0055	0.0041	0.0030	0.0023	0.0017	0.0013	0.0009	0.0007	0.0005	0.0004	0.0003	0.0002	0.0002	0.0001	0.0001
40	0.0026	0.0019	0.0013	0.0010	0.0007	0.0005	0.0004	0.0003	0.0002	0.0001	0.0001	0.0001	0.0001	0.0000	0.0000
45	0.0013	0.0009	0.0006	0.0004	0.0003	0.0002	0.0001	0.0001	00001	0.0000	0.0000	0.0000	0.0000	0.0000	0.0000
50	0.0006	0.0004	0.0003	0.0002	0.0001	0.0001	0.0000	0.0000	0.0000	0.0000	0.0000	0.0000	0.0000	0.0000	0.0000

Appendix B: Annuity tables

Present value of an annuity (£1 received annually for *n* years)

Periods Interest rates (%)

(n)	1	2	3	4	5	6	7	8	9	10	11	12	13	14	15
1	0.9901	0.9804	0.9709	0.9615	0.9524	0.9434	0.9346	0.9259	0.9174	0.9091	0.9009	0.8929	0.8850	0.8772	0.8696
2	1.9704	1.9416	1.9135	1.8861	1.8594	1.8334	1.8080	1.7833	1.7591	1.7355	1.7125	1.6901	1.6681	1.6467	1.6257
3	2.9410	2.8839	2.8286	2.7751	2.7232	2.6730	2.6243	2.5771	2.5313	2.4869	2.4437	2.4018	2.3612	2.3216	2.2832
4	3.9020	3.8077	3.7171	3.6299	3.5460	3.4651	3.3872	3.3121	3.2397	3.1699	3.1024	3.0373	2.9745	2.9137	2.8550
5	4.8534	4.7135	4.5797	4.4518	4.3295	4.2124	4.1002	3.9927	3.8897	3.7908	3.6959	3.6048	3.5172	3.4331	3.3522
6	5.7955	5.6014	5.4172	5.2421	5.0757	4.9173	4.7665	4.6229	4.4859	4.3553	4.2305	4.1114	3.9975	3.8887	3.7845
7	6.7282	6.4720	6.2303	6.0021	5.7864	5.5824	5.3893	5.2064	5.0330	4.8684	4.7122	4.5638	4.4226	4.2883	4.1604
8	7.6517	7.3255	7.0197	6.7327	6.4632	6.2098	5.9713	5.7466	5.5348	5.3349	5.1461	4.9676	4.7988	4.6389	4.4873
9	8.5660	8.1622	7.7861	7.4353	7.1078	6.8017	6.5152	6.2469	5.9952	5.7590	5.5370	5.3282	5.1317	4.9464	4.7716
10	9.4713	8.9826	8.5302	8.1109	7.7217	7.3601	7.0236	6.7101	6.4177	6.1446	5.8892	5.6502	5.4262	5.2161	5.0188
11	10.3676	9.7868	9.2526	8.7605	8.3064	7.8869	7.4987	7.1390	6.8052	6.4951	6.2065	5.9377	5.6869	5.4527	5.2337
12	11.2551	10.5753	9.9540	9.3851	8.8633	8.3838	7.9427	7.5361	7.1607	6.8137	6.4924	6.1944	5.9176	5.6603	5.4206
13	12.1337	11.3484	10.6350	9.9856	9.3936	8.8527	8.3577	7.9038	7.4869	7.1034	6.7499	6.4235	6.1218	5.8424	5.5831
14	13.0037	12.1062	11.2961	10.5631	9.8986	9.2950	8.7455	8.2442	7.7862	7.3667	6.9819	6.6282	6.3025	6.0021	5.7245
15	13.8651	12.8493	11.9379	11.1184	10.3797	9.7122	9.1079	8.5595	8.0607	7.6061	7.1909	6.8109	6.4624	6.1422	5.8474
16	14.7179	13.5777	12.5611	11.6523	10.8378	10.1059	9.4466	8.8514	8.3126	7.8237	7.3792	6.9740	6.6039	6.2651	5.9542
17	15.5623	14.2919	13.1661	12.1657	11.2741	10.4773	9.7632	9.1216	8.5436	8.0216	7.5488	7.1196	6.7291	6.3729	6.0472
18	16.3983	14.9920	13.7535	12.6593	11.6896	10.8276	10.0591	9.3719	8.7556	8.2014	7.7016	7.2497	6.8399	6.4674	6.1280
19	17.2260	15.6785	14.3238	13.1339	12.0853	11.1581	10.3356	9.6036	8.9501	8.3649	7.8393	7.3658	6.9380	6.5504	6.1982
20	18.0456	16.3514	14.8775	13.5903	12.4622	11.4699	10.5940	9.8181	9.1285	8.5136	7.9633	7.4694	7.0248	6.6231	6.2593
25	22.0232	19.5235	17.4131	15.6221	14.0939	12.7834	11.6536	10.6748	9.8226	9.0770	8.4217	7.8431	7.3300	6.8729	6.4641
30	25.8077	22.3965	19.6004	17.2920	15.3725	13.7648	12.4090	11.2578	10.2737	9.4269	8.6938	8.0552	7.4957	7.0027	6.5660
35	29.4086	24.9986	21.4872	18.6646	16.3742	14.4982	12.9477	11.6546	10.5668	9.6442	8.8552	8.1755	7.5856	7.0700	6.6166
40	32.8347	27.3555	23.1148	19.7928	17.1591	15.0463	13.3317	11.9246	10.7574	9.7791	8.9511	8.2438	7.6344	7.1050	6.6418
45	36.0945	29.4902	24.5187	20.7200	17.7741	15.4558	13.6055	12.1084	10.8812	9.8628	9.0079	8.2825	7.6609	7.1232	6.6543
50	39.1961	31.4236	25.7298	21.4822	18.2559	15.7619	13.8007	12.2335	10.9617	9.9148	9.0417	8.3045	7.6752	7.1327	6.6605

	16	17	18	19	20	21	22	23	24	25	26	27	28	29	30
1	0.8621	0.8547	8.8475	0.8403	0.8333	0.8264	0.8197	0.8130	0.8065	0.8000	0.7937	0.7874	0.7812	0.7752	0.7692
2	1.6052	1.5852	1.5656	1.5465	1.5278	1.5095	1.4915	1.4740	1.4568	1.4400	1.4235	1.4074	1.3916	1.3761	1.3609
3	2.2459	2.2096	2.1743	2.1399	2.1065	2.0739	2.0422	2.0114	1.9813	1.9520	1.9234	1.8956	1.8684	1.8420	1.8161
4	2.7982	2.7432	2.6901	2.6386	2.5887	2.5404	2.4936	2.4483	2.4043	2.3616	2.3202	2.2800	2.2410	2.2031	2.1662
5	3.2743	3.1993	3.1272	3.0576	2.9906	2.9260	2.8636	2.8035	2.7454	2.6893	2.6351	2.5827	2.5320	2.4830	2.4356
6	3.6847	3.5892	3.4976	3.4098	3.3255	3.2446	3.1669	3.0923	3.0205	2.9514	2.8850	2.8210	2.7594	2.7000	2.6427
7	4.0386	3.9224	3.8115	3.7057	3.6046	3.5079	3.4155	3.3270	3.2423	3.1611	3.0833	3.0087	2.9370	2.8682	2.8021
8	4.3436	4.2072	4.0776	3.9544	3.8372	3.7256	3.6193	3.5179	3.4212	3.3289	3.2407	3.1564	3.0758	2.9986	2.9247
9	4.6065	4.4506	4.3030	4.1633	4.0310	3.9054	3.7863	3.6731	3.5655	3.4631	3.3657	3.2728	3.1842	3.0997	3.0190
10	4.8332	4.6586	4.4941	4.3389	4.1925	4.0541	3.9232	3.7993	3.6819	3.5705	3.4648	3.3644	3.2689	3.1781	3.0915
11	5.0286	4.8364	4.6560	4.4865	4.3271	4.1769	4.0354	3.9018	3.7757	3.6564	3.5435	3.4365	3.3351	3.2388	3.1473
12	5.1971	4.9884	4.7932	4.6105	4.4392	4.2784	4.1274	3.9852	3.8514	3.7251	3.6059	3.4933	3.3868	3.2859	3.1903
13	5.3423	5.1183	4.9095	4.7147	4.5327	4.3624	4.2028	4.0530	3.9124	3.7801	3.6555	3.5381	3.4272	3.3224	3.2233
14	5.4675	5.2293	5.0081	4.8023	4.6106	4.4317	4.2646	4.1082	3.9616	3.8241	3.6949	3.5733	3.4587	3.3507	3.2487
15	5.5755	5.3242	5.0916	4.8759	4.6755	4.4890	4.3152	4.1530	4.0013	3.8593	3.7261	3.6010	3.4834	3.3726	3.2682
16	5.6685	5.4053	5.1624	4.9377	4.7296	4.5364	4.3567	4.1894	4.0333	3.8874	3.7509	3.6228	3.5026	3.3896	3.2832
17	5.7487	5.4746	5.2223	4.9897	4.7746	4.5755	4.3908	4.2190	4.0591	3.9099	3.7705	3.6400	3.5177	3.4028	3.2948
18	5.8178	5.5339	5.2732	5.0333	4.8122	4.6079	4.4187	4.2431	4.0799	3.9279	3.7861	3.6536	3.5294	3.4130	3.3037
19	5.8775	5.5845	5.3162	5.0700	4.8435	4.6346	4.4415	4.2627	4.0967	3.9424	3.7985	3.6642	3.5386	3.4210	3.3105
20	5.9288	5.6278	5.3527	5.1009	4.8696	4.6567	4.4603	4.2786	4.1103	3.9539	3.8083	3.6726	3.5458	3.4271	3.3158
25	6.0971	5.7662	5.4669	5.1951	4.9476	4.7213	4.5139	4.3232	4.1474	3.9849	3.8342	3.6943	3.5640	3.4423	3.3286
30	6.1772	5.8294	5.5168	5.2347	4.9789	4.7463	4.5338	4.3391	4.1601	3.9950	3.8424	3.7009	3.5693	3.4466	3.3321
35	6.2153	5.8582	5.5386	5.2512	4.9915	4.7559	4.5411	4.3447	4.1644	3.9984	3.8450	3.7028	3.5708	3.4478	3.3330
40	6.2335	5.8713	5.5482	5.2582	4.9966	4.7596	4.5439	4.3467	4.1659	3.9995	3.8458	3.7034	3.5712	3.4481	3.3332
45	6.2421	5.8773	5.5523	5.2611	4.9986	4.7610	4.5449	4.3474	4.1664	3.9998	3.8460	3.7036	3.5714	3.4482	3.3333
50	6.2463	5.8801	5.5541	5.2623	4.9995	4.7616	4.5452	4.3477	4.1666	3.9999	3.8461	3.7037	3.5714	3.4483	3.333

Index